Sikkim
Ethnicity and Political Dynamics
A Triadic Perspective

Sikkim

Ethnicity and Political Dynamics

A Triadic Perspective

Suresh K. Gurung

KUNAL BOOKS

New Delhi-110002, India

KUNAL BOOKS
4648/21, 1st Floor, Ansari Road,
Daryaganj, New Delhi-110002.
Phones: 011-23275069, 9811043697
E-mail: *kunalbooks@gmail.com*
Website: *www.kunalbooks.com*

Sikkim: Ethnicity and Political Dynamics
A Triadic Perspective

First Published 2011
Second Reprint 2018
Third Reprint 2022
Fourth Reprint 2025

ISBN: 978-93-80752-11-2

Published in India by **Prem Singh Bisht for Kunal Books** and printed at Trident Enterprises, Noida, U.P.

PREFACE

Way back in early 1970s as a student of Jorthang Primary School (now a Senior Secondary) I remember the way we used to line up on both sides of the main road to greet the last Chogyal of Sikkim, P.T. Namgyal. Then I hardly had any idea that Sikkim was undergoing political turmoil which would change the face of Sikkim forever. The reminiscence of my school days proved to be so strong that some thirty five years down the line Sikkim became a passion for me and a subject of further academic enquiry.

Sikkim had been a monarchical state before its merger with India in 1975. During the 333 years of monarchical rule Sikkim had been exposed to number of invasions and influences at the hands of neighbouring countries which are distinctly reflected in the composition and way of life of the people, including the nature of politico-administrative structure and governance so designed to suit the convenience of the kingdom.

After the merger, a new political arrangement hitherto unknown in Sikkim was established. The principles of democracy, rule of law and the rights of the people, etc. were introduced as a basis of governance in a society which was predominantly traditional. Apparently contradiction began owing to presence of primordial belief system and emerging modernity. Politics never happens in vacuum. The contradiction became politically viable when political and non-political organizations emerged and used the issue for their respective political and socio-cultural advantages giving space for ethnic politics. Two important arguments run through out the book. The first argument is that any study of ethnic politics in Sikkim must involve historical perspective. The second argument emphasizes on the involvement of the entire political process, including state policies, for such a perspective facilitates inclusion of non-state political actors in the analysis.

In course of writing this book I met many people from different walks of life and without their support and cooperation this book certainly could not have seen the light of the day. I have the pleasure of particularly expressing my heartfelt gratitude to my teacher, Sir Dyutis Chakrabarti, Reader in the Department of Political Science, University of North Bengal, with whom I spent years discussing the subject. I am also deeply indebted to Dr. H.P.Chhetri, for his unflinching support and providing relevant information.

I should also put on record the names of various personalities, including political leaders, office bearers of various socio-welfare organizations, government officials and private individual for their much needed support and cooperation in the process of collection of primary information and for valuable suggestions. A few of them deserve special mention: Late Lhendup Dorji Khangsarpa (Ex. Chief Minister), Shri N.B.Bhandari (Ex. Chief Minister), Shri C.D.Rai, Late K.C.Pradhan, Shri B.B.Gurung, Shri R.C.Poudyal, Shri Rasaily, Shri Bharat Basnet, Shri Birbal Limboo (Tamling), T. T. Bhutia, Shri Narboo Pintso Bhutia, Shri Meghraj Gurung, Shri N.T. Lepcha, Shri P.K.Pradhan, Mrs. D.K.Bhandari, and many others. Shri Bhaskar Basnet, Shri R.K.Shrestha and Mrs. Anna Balikci Denzongpa deserve special thanks for providing me file-full of rare documents, magazines and materials of pre-merger era and old issues of Bulletin of Tibetology respectively.

I must not also forget to mention here the cooperation extended by the staff and authorities of the Sikkim Archives, the Community Library, the Institute of Tibetology, the Record Section of the Home Department, Department of Law, Directorate of Economics, Statistics, Monitoring and Evaluation (earlier Bureau of Economics and Statistics), the Information and Public Relations office, Department of Industry, Department of Tourism, Assembly Secretariat, Land Revenue Department in Sikkim. Special thanks is also due for the staff and officials of the Central Library, NBU, Centre for Himalayan Studies, NBU, Deshbandhu District Library of Darjeeling and National Library, Calcutta. I am also deeply indebted to Shri Premji of Kunal Books, New Delhi, for wishing to publish this book in the first instance itself.

Finally, I owe a lot to my parents, my wife Subhadra and our loving daughter Stuttee for supporting me ungrudgingly right from the beginning of the work and making this endeavour a successful one.

Suresh K. Gurung
Gangtok, Sikkim

CONTENTS

INTRODUCTION

BACKGROUND

Ever since the appearance of the term' Ethnicity' in English language in 1950, the concept of ethnicity has not been only the subject of diverse interpretations but also lacked universally acknowledged definition. An early meaning of the term refers to either a racial or cultural group or even a minority in an 'exotic' cultural form. There is also a reference of inclusion of 'others' i.e. different from one's own group, and 'migrant people' within the ambit of the term.

Glazer and. Moynihan (1975) consider any group of distinct culture and origin, including the majority, as an ethnic group. While studying the question of cultural-racial identity and mobilization process in the USA, they"View ethnicity as a distinct category of social process, social differentiation, articulation and social mobilization. From this viewpoint cultural-racial identity or ethnic identity may be looked upon as a universal social phenomenon like the 'class'. 0.De.Vos and L.R. Ross (1975) also subscribe to this viewpoint. Similarly, Clifford Geertz (1971) observes that the primordial ties continue to influence public action notwithstanding the establishment of a modern secular state. This is so because competing loyalties within a modern state i.e., class, party, business, union, professional loyalties etc., are considered feeble as compared to primordial loyalties. l'oclay, ethnicity is conceived as a social phenomenon embracing anything and everything of individual belonging to a particular cultural community, whether minority or majority, host or immigrant. Therefcire, all cultural-linguistic movements which emphasize common history, territory and aspirations may be considered as ethnic movements.

One of the most comprehensive accounts of ethnicity and ethnic political mobilization is represented by the effort of J. Hutchinson and A.D. Smith (1996). Hutchinson and Smith offer a workable definition, analytical framework and different manifestations of ethnic politics along with valuable excerpts from the books of various'authors. They, in their work, have attempted to classify reSearches on ethnic movements into two categories: instrumentalist argument and primordialist viewpoint or simply prirnordialism. Hutchinson and Smith's classification helps one to deal with the vast literature on the theme of ethnic political mobilization.

Primordialism, as various researchers suggest, however, is not something which is fixed; it is rather changing, revising, negotiating as per the circumstances, demands and interests. Jack Eller and Reed Coughlan (1993) argue that primordialism is a bankrupt concept so far as analysis and description of ethnicity is concerned. They continue, if primordialism is widened, as most writers do, to refer emotion, it would only mean unnecessary and unfortunate burden in ethnic analysis because 'emotion' cannot be primordial but, at best, it is sociogenesis. The counterpoint is that Eller and Coughlan have failed to understand that `.ittachinents' or 'ties' to objects necessarily postulates belief(lere emotion or affect) about those objects followed by cognizance in order to become objects of attachments (Grosby: 1994). Another recent but radical primordial argument is found in P.Van Dan Berghe (1995) who believes that social groups are bonded together due to mechanisms of 'Nepotism' (of favour) and 'Inclusive fitness' (fit for inclusion in a biological social group).

The Instrumentalist version, which is comparatively richer in terms of publications, on the other, consider ethnicity as social, political and cultural resource used by various groups and ethnic mobilization process as'a means for gaining political and economic goal. The arguments of D.1_, Harowitz (1985) and LA.Despres (1975) belong to such variety. While, Despres views ethnic mobilization as a convenient tool for asserting or reasserting monopoly, over resources; Harowitz links it with keeping of group's ethnic honor compared to others (i.e. of backward & forward). Similarly, for Brass (1991) conflict among elites for resources is a major cause behind ethnic mobilization* According to Barth (1969) it is the existence of 'set of prescriptions' (do- s) and 'proscriptions' (don'ts) imposed by rulers to maintain control over a given society which fuels ethnic mobilization. Apart from these, Michael Hechter (1975) and. B.Anderson (1991) consider ethnic differences, mobilization and national movements as inevitable corollaries of a particular type of economic development and domination in the age of capitalism. Hechter's analysis of the Celtic fringe of Great Britain indicates that modern .capitalist market system has historically evolved a social-division of labour. As a result of this social spatial division of labour, different types of cultures have gradually emerged in different regions including the Celtic Welsh. Cultural identities and cultural conflicts are thus related to a particular type of division of labour and economic domination.

An interesting argument is found in Walker Connor (1994) who equates ethnic-cultural mobilization with growth of nationalism. For him, ethnic development is almost like national development. Hence, Connor prefers to use the term ethno-nationalism instead of just ethnicity to address cultural-territorial issues. He emphasizes that the source of ethno-national loyalty cannot be explained in terms of either rationality or tangible interest. It is essentially affective and this sentiment is inherent in present societies. He Valong with A.D.Smith (1971), shares the view that nationalism is a special type of consciousness, different from patriotism.

The cultural-territorial mobilizations and efforts to conceptualize them are not new in indi;.1. However, owing to the nature of mobilizations and factors influencing variation, scholars have taken refuge to different terminological creations among which the terms like 'Nation' or 'Ethnicity' or 'Regionalism' are most commonly used. For instance, M.R.Barnett (1976) prefers to use 'Cultural Nationalism' to explain the Dravidic Movement in Tamilnadu. For her, cultural markers are the sole objective factor which determines the existence and non-existence of a nationality. Atnalendu Guha (1980) in the context of Assam describes such cultural-territorial movements as 'Little-Nationalism. The term little-nationalism owes its origin to the sociological innovations like. little community and great community. Little nationalism is like sub-nationalism which operates within the framework of great-nationalism. This is an attempt at demonstrating a dual identity or divided loyalty; one for linguistic cultural community and another for the nation-state. From this sense little nationalism may be viewed as a component or a reflection of the greater nationalism i.e. loyalty to the nation-state. The two, however, may come into conflict under certain circumstances.

Few other scholars have tried to understand the problem from the point of view of ethnicity. Urmila Phadnis (1989) and R.A.Schermenhon (1978) belong to this variety.. A combined argument of both the instrumentalism and primordiality is presented by M.Weiner (1978). To him cultural nationalism is the result of conflict between the migrants and the natives over the resources. Weiner argues that cultural-nationalism or nativism in Assam, which attempts to legitimize the claim of the 'Bhumiputras' and exclusion of the migrants, essentially is an ethnic movement which demands resource distribution on the basis of cultural identity. P.R. Brass (1991) relates such cultural-mobilization with the elite conflict in a plural society.

Another way of describing such cultural-territorial mobilization in. India is 'regionalism'. Regional movement indicates search for an intermediate control system for the purposes of resource sharing and control over local or intermediate level of administration. IqbaiNarain and A.Majeed.(1984) and Sajal Basil (1992) identify such movements as regionalism alongside the pre,senee of certain socio-economic. reasons. This viewpoint emphasizes territorial identity rather than the cultural one. S.K. Chaube (1973) treats ethnic problem in the north-eastern states of India as a manifestation of clashes between the modern values (nation-state) and primordial loyalties (i.e. loyalties towards clan, tribes, caste, race, language, tradition etc.) and emphasizes that any attetript to understanding the problem and finding reconciliation thereof must be based on the historical perspective. Authors like Susana B.C. Devalle (1992) and. Dipankar Gupta (1997) are examples of consideration of such movements as a consequence of a historical context. Gupta argues that ascriptive collective identities (cultural markers) in themselves are not always sufficient for ethnic mobilization but it undergoes context dependent transformation and mutation. Gupta points out that the Sikhs identity has developed in relation to its opposition, i.e., Hindu identity. But the former has also developed in relation to its perception of a government which discriminated the Sikhs. Such perception about the governmental context legitimizes mobilization on the basis of Sikh cultural identity. Gupta advocates for inclusion of the state or state policies as a variable, but actually the entire political process should be considered as a significant factor, for such a perspective facilitates the inclusion of non-state political actors in the analysis. While emphasizing the historical context in which a particular identity i.e., the Jharkhandi identity, has gradually evolved, Devalle equates development of ethnic identity with development of a discourse.

Paul R. Brass (1991), in his later work, argues that conditions for identity formation among various groups or emergence of self-conscious communities in a particular situation and place can be linked with the alliance strategy and policies that the groups dominating the state structure follow in relation to ethnic or cultural groups. In other words, he portrays the State in three different forms: a) State as a resource over which groups engage in struggle for greater share of it b) State as a distributor of resources which is nearly always done differentially or unequally., c) State, particularly in developing societies, acts as a promoter ofnew values and threat to locally dominant landed and religious elites. Thus, gaining control over the State becomes elite's first priority and one who is successful must either suppress the rival elites or establish collaborative alliances with other elites to maintain dominance. When elites in conflict lack bureaucratic apparatus to compete effectively, they resort to use symbolic resources in the struggle. And when elites in conflict belong to different cultural, linguistic, or religious groups, they use these ascriptive differences as a means for mobilization. Thus, for Brass, ethnic conflict or mobilization arises when elites in conflict manipulate ethnic symbols for exercising control over state power or when the state dominated by particular elite pursues policies or affirmative actions favouring its own group or groups as against the other, it may precipitate a sense of discrimination or deprivation among those who are denied benefits. Thus, nature of elites controlling the state apparatus and the policy strategies it chooses to pursue becomes a potential source of ethnic. politics.

An important analysis of ethnic mobilization for political purpose is found in the writings of Kanchan Chandra (2004). According to her, the success of ethnic parties is a natural by-product of the process by which ethnic identities become politically salient. The political entrepreneurs who float ethnic parties in ethnically divided societies find a ready-made clientele waiting to be laid. In the context of Sikkim, it may be safely said that ethnic political parties have seldom succeeded in capturing political power in the post merger period but since public sector is the major provider of resources (jobs and services) under which patronage democracy generally prosper, the analysis may be especially helpful in understanding reasons for ineffectiveness of the opposition parties in the. state.

A researcher may encounter several problems when it comes to publication on Sikkim. The historical accounts of the pre-Bhutia regime are almost non-existent and have been reduced to mere oral or folk stories. Some materials of the 17th century Sikkim still present difficulty in determining what is empirically viable aid and what is mythical. In other words, there is a dearth of secular publications on the 17th century political history of Sikkim, in general, and on ethnic politics and/or race relations and the way such ethnic relations'influence politics, in particular, though the actual political process represent frequent attempts at mobilizing people around the issues like Sikkimese — non-Sikkimese relations, rights of the minority Lepcha-Bhutia communities etc. Though such issues are present in the process of mass mobilization yet such ethnicised political issues are seldom properly attended. However, insightful discussions are available in historical and sociological accounts.

Risley's "Gazetteer of Sikh im" (1928/1993) is one of the earliest publications on the history and population of Sikkim. Apart from the discussion on the nature of governance under various rulers of Namgyal dynasty, it provides interesting reading on the purpose ofthe British involvement in Sikkim and adoption of ways and means, particularly racial and religious, to maintain its political control over the affairs of Sikkim and maximize economic benefits. Talking about the modus operandi of the British officials, Risley writes, "here (Sikkim) also religion will play a leading part. In Sikkim, as in India, Hinduism will assuredly cast out Buddhism, and the praying-wheel of the Lama will give place to the sacrificial implement of the Brahman. Thus, race and religion, the prime movers of the Asiatic world, will settle the Sikkim difficulty for us, in their own way. We have only to look on and see that the operation of these causes is not artificially hindered by the interference of Tibet and Nepal." Similar accounts on the history and population of Sikkim can also be found in the writings and travelogues of many British officers among which J.D.Hooker (1854/1969), J.W.Edgar (1874/2005), Richard Temple (1875), Colman Macaulay (1885/1977/2005), J.C.White (1909/1999) are interesting for reading.

Apart from C.J. Morris's "Living with the Lepchas: A book about the Sikkim Himalayas" (1938), Geoffrey Gorer's "The Lepchas of Sikkim" (1938/1996) represent some of the pioneering works on the Lepcha community of Sikkim. Gorer believes that the confinement of the Lepchas in the Dzongu reserve area had far reaching consequences on the religious, educational and economic backwardness of the community. A.R. Forming's 'Lepcha: My Vanishing Tribe' (1987) is an inside view about the Lepchas: 'fracing the cultural history of the Lepchas, the author provides **Valuable** information about the Christian and Buddhist influence that were brought to bear on the tribe, and how the Lepcha habitat, "Mayal Lyang", fell into the hands of immigrants from other areas. K.P.Tamsang's 'The Unknown and Untold Reality about the Lepchas' (1983) highlights the perversion appearing in the cultural history of the Lepchas at the hands of both foreign and Indian writers. R.K. Sprigg, also called `Lepcha Saheb' is perhaps the only living Englishman today who possesses an excellent knowledge on the Lepcha language, literature and history. His recent publication "Shedding Some Light on the History, Language and Literature of the Lepehas" (2005) provides some of the rarest information with documentary evidences about the history and life of the Lepcha community during the early nineteenth century.

The existence of multiple ethnic groups in. Sikkim is as old as the Namgyal dynasty of Sikkim but mobilization of these ethnic categories for political purposes began only during the late 1940's. First hand information regarding arousal of ethnic consciousness and political manipulation of it at the party or organizational level can be found in Basnet's work, "Sikkim-A Short Political History" (1974). Basnet writes that with the emergence of the Sikkim National Party in 1948 the use of ethnic symbols such as race, culture, religion etc. for political purposes also began.

Another oft-quoted article on Sikkim is "A Plural Society in Sikkim: A Study of the Interrelations of Lepchas, Bhotias and Nepalis" by Chie Nakane (1966). On the basis of her field work carried out during February and March, 1955, in the vicinity of three monastarial hamlets of Gangtok namely Pabyuk, Phodong and Phensung, she provides an interesting views on the belief, way of life and inter-community relationship among the three communities of Sikkim, though the observation derived from a particular area, i.e. Pabyuk village, still poses difficulty in accepting the same as that of the whole of Sikkim. I.ler observation on the Nepalis gives an impression that either she was blatantly oblivious to the then prevailing socio-political structure of Sikkim or she was trying to avoid them intentionally. At the outset it must be emphasized that not all of the castes and communities which now constitute Nepal is 'vere immigrants or coolies or farm labourers. Furthermore, Nakane also seems to be unaware of the fact that the Limboos or Tsongs, Mangers etc. were living in Sikkim lona before the establishment of the Naingyal dynasty in Sikkim.

B.S. Das (1983), who served as the Chief Executive Officer in Sikkim from 1973-74, argues that the ethnic melting pot situation was due to Sikkim's territorial contiguity with three international borders (Tibet, Nepal and Bhutan) and as well as competition prevailing among the major groups over economic and political resources of the. State. He also explains that the changing political scenario in. Tibet and Chogyai's invariable demand for independent status for Sikkim hastened the process for merger. Rao's (1978) observation is also of the same kind. On the other hand N. Sengupta (1985) and host of other writers consider ethnic divide in Sikkim as a consequence of the differential treatment meted out to the subjects at the hands of the ruling elite. Apart from this the book also explains as to how disillusion prevail among the elites after the merger and in a parliamentary democratic set up.

Dana Ray's 'Smash and Grab: A nfiexation of Sikkim' (1984) and Rustomji's 'Sikkim — A Himalayan 'fragedy. (1987) are somewhat written as a biographical account of the last Chogyal, P.T.Naingyal. Both were personal friends of the Chogyal and, thus, both of them spoke against the merger though, owing to their profession, Datta Ray advances the concept of class conflict between the Lepcha Kazis and the Royal family/Bhutia Kazis, while Rustomji rely on bureaucratic maneuver of the Indian civil servants in order to explain the issue of merger.

An aspect of culture and history of Sikkim can be found in the writings of George Kotturan (1983), S.K.Jha & Mishra (1984), and P.K.Bhattaccharya (1984). While Kottui•an highlights on the political, administrative and economic set-up of the people of

Sikkim, Jha & Mishra focuses on the evolution of various organs of the government in the light of the changing institutional framework from a protectorate to a full-fledged State of India. Bhattacharya's book, though is a study of coinage of Sikkim, highlights the contribution of the Newars' in the economic development of Sikkim in earlier days.

'Politics of Sikkim- A Sociological Study' by A.C.Sinha (1975) is a sociological investigation into the world of political elite in Sikkim. The book has three segments — the first segment deals with the political evolutions, presence of various social forces s,v ith specialized interests and pursuits, The Second segment analyses perception of the elites in Sikkim in the context of socio-economic and political parameters. His findings suggest that religious elite (i.e. the Lamas) was not only politically salient but also in many ways responsible for propagation of communal feeling in the society. The third segment deals with the dilemma regarding adaptation and re-structuring of the power hierarchy in a new democratic atmosphere in post- 1947 era and institutional accomplishment.

T.I3.Subba's 'Dynamics Of A Hill Society' (1989) is another sociological study on the Nepalis of Sikkim and Darjeeling hills. It attempts to understand caste-class relationships in view of the growing occupational mobility and effects of modernization among the Nepalis. In his 'Politics of Culture' (1999) Subba attempts to unravel the genesis of Kirata politics in Sikkim and Nepal, particularly the identity consciousness emerging among the three Kirata tribes namely Limboos (Tsongs), Kharnbus (Rais) and Yakhas (Dewans). He shares his view with Michael Foucault (1980) and considers Kirata consciousness for identity as "insurrection of subjugated knowledge". He believes that political transformation in both Sikkim and Nepal has been crucial behind the surge of Kirata identity though due to prevalence of overlapping identities and regional variations within the larger Kirata groups, he is uncertain about the future of the Kirata politics. Another ethnographic detail on ·n,Lricais castes and communities of Sikkim is found in K.S. Singh's (Ed.) work 'Sikkim'

(1993). It is the first eve•-ethnographic survey by the Anthropological Survey. of India under the project entitled, "People of. India". [his comprehensive work offers detail information on the biological, religio-linguistic and cultural profile of all the three ethnic cotnmunities of Sikkim, including other sub-cultural groups within the larger Nepali community. Sikkim Study Series, volume HI *Sz.* V, also provides interesting discussions on the linguistic and cultural profile of various communities of Sikkim and government's interest in the protection and promotion of the languages and cultures of these communities.

The role of ethnicity in determining political outcome in Sikkim cannot be denied. An analytical presentation at interplay between ethnic forecs and political alignment during the 1979 election is found in Urmila Phadnis's 'Ethnic dimension of Sikkimese Politics-The 1979 election' (1980). The author has highlighted on the significant implication of emerging elite and their ethnic backgrounds in the process of readjusting power. relations. In similar vein, S.K.Chaube (1987) provides valuable discussion on the effect of various ethnic and social forces in the post-1947 political development in Sikkim and concludes that factional politics has overshadowed ethnic alignment in new democratic setup. He suggests that though politics has gained st:Ibility, political parties have not

Since the beginning of institutionalized politics of the 17th century to till present time, maintenance of ethnic equilibrium has been the primary political goal upon which rested the success and failure of the rulers/leaders/political elite in Sikkim. The question of power and privilege has given way to the issues of equal rights (economic, social and political) and of opportunity which, to a large extent, depended upon the ingenuity of political leaders to maintain ethnic balance without harming or causing to harm the interests of other ethnic communities and endangering prospect for development of the State. A discussion of this variation is found in Dhamala's article "Ethnicity and Development in Sikkim'. On the basis of various social indices she contends that the leadership pattern has changed in Sikkim with the emergence of young, secular and educated politicians, though ethnic representation continue to be a thorny problem. In yet another article, 'Struggle for Identity Maintenance: The. Bhutias of Sikkim' (1999) she maintains that the transformation in the status of the Bhutias from a socially and politically dominant group before 1975 to that of a subordinate in the post-merger period has created an identity crisis among the Bhutias which is manifested in the formation of various soc io-po I itical organization.

J.N.tiazi's 'Inside Sikkim — Against the Tide (1993) is a journalisticiton the political development of Sikkim, particularly during the 14yrs rules of the Chief Minister Mr. N.B.Bhandari. The book is an attempt to highlight the political conditions of Sikkim during the period and exposes the hollowness of the democratic system. This book is resourceful in terms of perception of the ethnic Bhutias on various issues of socio-political importance. Pahalman Subba's "Who. Ruined Sikkim" (1998) also belongs to the same category.

Although the demand for merger. of Sikkim and Darjeeling is not new, the re-emergence of the demand in recent past has acquired lot of attention among the authors. Fred Pinn's 'The Road of Destiny-Darjeeling Letters - 1839'(1986) is one such historical account on the transfer of Darjeeling by the Chogyal of Sikkim Taking clue from Pirm's work, S.B.Wangyal, (2002) explains the extent of insincerity on the part of Major Lloyd. He argues that the Deed of Darjeeling Grant was neither binding nor was it signed on 25 February, 1835.

Though the issue of merger of Sikkim and: Darjeeling is not the subject of the book, he however, believes that the social peculiarities together with elements of proximity of the people of Darjeeling and Sikkim arc such that a good number of people believe, and even fear, that the two areas will one day amalgamate to form a bigger and a more viable state. Relevant documents regarding Darjeeling and Sikkim can be found in R.Moktan's, 'Sikkim: Darjeeling - Compendium of Documents' (2004):

Among the edited books containing articles on Sikkim, mentioned must be made of 'The Himalaya: Aspects of Change (1981) edited by F.S.Hall, '1'he Himalayas: Profiles of Modernization and Adaptation' (1985) edited by S.K.Chaube, 'Eastern Himalayas: Environment and Economy (1986) edited by R.L.Sarkar and M.P.Lama, fhe Himalayan Heritage' (1987) edited by M.K.Raha, 'Religion and Society in the Himalayas (1991) edited by T.B.Subba & Karubaki Data, `Sikkim- Society, Polity, Economy &..Environment' (1994) edited by M.P.Lama, provide introspective views and valuable information about Sikkim and its people.

All these publications on society and politics of the State of Sikkim constitute a valuable information-store on which the present work relies heavily to understand the process of evolution of emergence of cultural-territorial or ethnic politics in Sikkim. However, the present work is different from previous publications. in the sense that the present study addresses the issue of interrelations between political process and emergence of cultural-ethnic politics directly.

The Problem:

A steady growth in cultural-territorial identity and mobiliiation based on it has been seen in different parts of the world since the late 20th century. Such cultural-territorial movements have been described or conceptualized with reference to different terms such as ethnicity, tribalism, cultural-nationalism, internal colonialism, regionalism etc. The lack of unanimity among scholars may be due to the nature of mobilization itself as well as divergent disciplinary background of scholars. However, among various factors, a great deal of primacy is assigned to economic reasons and the issue of cultural identity. Sometimes, the theme of elite manipulation of economic and cultural issues is emphasized and sometimes discussions on such cultural-territorial movements expose multiple dimensions of such mobilizations which are generally conceptual ind as ethnic mobilizations. The above dimensions of cultural-territorial identity and mobilization included changing nature of cultural identity, structure of identity, political economic foundations ranging from relative deprivation to internal colonialism of such movements, symbols and pattern of mobilization etc. Very often researchers also focus on integrative disintegnitive role of such movements.

India, being a multi-racial and multi-linguistic country, is also not altogether untouched by the problem of cultural-territorial identity and movements In fact such identity related issues and mobilizations have been a part and parcel of Indian politics since the beginning of the 20th century. The demand for linguistic states iifter the independence also constituted a significant part of Indian politics. However, after the 1980s there has been a phenomenal growth in the number of occurrences of such movements and very often demands for political autonomy and secession have been advanced as an integral part of the movement. Attempts have been made to conceptualize this cultural-territorial mobilization of a culturally self-defined community in India in various ways among which ethnicity, cultural-nationalism, regionalism, elite manipulation, incompatibility between modernity and primordial loyalties are considered significant. Sometimes the historical context and development of a typical cultural discourse have been also highlighted as factors contributing towards the emergence of such cultural-territorial movements.

The cultural assertion as well as redistribution of resources; conflicts over cultural identity as well as over resources, is not free of power distribution. Assertion as well as promotion of a particular cultural identity needs the support of authority without which cultural protection is not conceivable. Similarly, redistribution of resources in modern times requires changes in the legal system, policies and decisions by the political authority. Hence it is impossible to separate culture and resource distribution from the concept of power and domination.

Another basic paradox underlying ethnic-cultural mobilization is that it intends to accommodate the old notion of community space and community rights with modern detnocratic values like equality and individual rights. Political parties and organizations which raise the issue of community rights actually also deny those same rights to other communities. Often such denials arc legitimized in the name of territorial claim of indigenous people. Indigenousness is not substantiated with reference to history but is done with the aid of interpretations / reinterpretation of history by. the majority or those who are in power. It is also to be noted that the whole idea of individual rights guaranteel by the constitution or legal system is paid scant attention in the face of assertion of community rights. Such denials (rights) cannot be completed through the process of social or economic reconstruction but they evolve through political mobilization, bargaining and finally decisions.

The substitution of individual rights by community rights is done through a particular type of political articulation and political mobilization. Therefore, political organizations play a critical role in moderating as well as aggravating ethnic-cultui·al consciousness and demands.

Sikkim, which was a tiny Himalayan kingdom tucked between China and. India till its merger with the latter in 1975, is at present one of the smallest states of North East India Sikkimese society consists of multiple cultural-racial groups like Nepalis, Lepchas, Bhutias etc. of which Nepalis constitute the majority. Together with them, there exist some smaller groups like Sherpas, Tsongs (Limboos) etc. who are identified as Nepalis in. Sikkim.

Sikkim, like other parts of India, has been invaded by attempts at cultural-territorial mobilization or popularly known as ethnic mobilization since the introduction of parliamentary democracy after the merger with India. Before the merger, the ruling Naingy1.11 dynasty belonging to a minority Bhutia racial community was ruling over subjects belonging to different racial-cultural communities; and this helped the Bhutia community to acquire a predominant position though members of other communities also occupied important positions in the monarchical administration. Cultural-territorial mobilizations or ethnic mobilizations were not altogether unknown under the monarchical form of government in Sikkim. Incidents of Lepcha or Nepali, including the Tsongs (Limboos), protests against the Bhutia dominations did occur, but such mobilizations though had community orientation were not cultural or ethnic mobilizations in the inodern sense; they were primarily directed against the state or its agents. Attempts at cultural-ethnic mobilization became discernible with the emergence of political parties during the second half of the 20th century. There were political parties like Sikkim National Party, formed in April, 1948, which articulated interests of a particular community. Such community interests, however, were never presented as the interest of any particular community. Rather such community interests were aggregated and'presented as the general interests of Sikkim. Even when the general subjects of whom Nepalis constituted the majority, protested against the discriminatory and oppressive rule of the Bhutia king and elites, the protest movement was not known as the movement by the Nepalis. Rather it was the grievances surfaced in the form of movement for introduction of democracy in Sikkim.

After the merger Parliamentary democracy and notions of equality, individual freedom, and modern legal system have been introduced. It was hoped that the cultural differences and ethnic politics would be gradually triarginalized with slow permeation of notions of individual rights and equality. But, contrary to the general expec'tations, cultural or ethnic consciousness and the political actions based on cultural or ethnic identity have become more frequent. New political parties and organizations have been formed with community oriented claims and demands, and are competing with each other for the ethnic space. A cursory look at the manifestoes of various political parties since 1977 generally reflect attempts at mobilization of ethnic categories by raising community oriented issues either in isolation (i.e. emphasizing a particular community interests) or in conglomerate form (i.e. common issues concerning more than one group). By raising community oriented issues political, parties have facilitated the process of articulation or aggregation as well as legitimization of demands of various cultural categories.

Apparently, cultural and /or ethnic mobilizations process in Sikkim cannot be regarded as an expected development. As mentioned earlier that Sikkim does not have a long history of conflict among different communities though some communities were discriminated against. There are evidences showing cultural exchanges and inter-community marriages among the members of the three major communities in the past though it was not as common as in the present day.

The Bhutias and Lepchas are Buddhists while Nepalis are predominantly Hindus (certain sections of the Nepalis, particularly Tamangs, Gurungs and Shakyas are Buddhists). But there is no histoiy of perpetual religious conflict or a history of ethnic violence and social conflict among the groups apart from the resentment expressed sporadically against the rulers and their agents. In other svords, history does not appear to be a strong basis for emergence of ethnic or cultural politics in Sikkim. Yet cultural-ethnic politics did not only emerge, it is sustained and proliferated further in. Sikkim in recent past.

The growth in easte/community consciousness among different groups and sub-groups has led to mushrooming of several caste/ community organizations with claims and demands of their own. The Lepcha organizations like Rangjyong Mutanchi Rang-Ong Shej UM (Sikkim Lepcha Youth Association) demands for fifty percent reservation in the State Assembly, education and public employment, legal protection of their land, separate delimitation etc. The Bhutia dominated organizations like Survival Sikkimese and Sikkim Bhutia Lepcha Apex Committee emphasize for restoration of rights and privileges of the community which they had been enjoying before the merger. On the other hand, the Nepali organization like Gorkha Apex Committee has demanded for equal treatment at par with the Lepchas and Bhutias, and extension of 'creamy layer' concept to exclude members of royal fainily and Kazis from the tribal list. Thus, when political mobilization takes place, appeals to these caste/ community organizations naturally take place and the community centered demands and grievances are also represented in the political arena.

An interesting 'spill-over effect' of such proliferation of cultural-racial-ethnic mobilization by major communities like Nepalis, Bhutias and Lepchas, is that certain smaller communities which were considered as sub-groups of larger communities have also started to assert their distinct language, culture and identity. For instance, the Tsongs (Litnboos) are acknowledged as a Nepali tribe in adjacent district of Darjeeling, but in Sikkim the Tsongs now claim to be a separate community with their own language and culture, distinct from the Nepali community. Contrarily, the Bhutias in recent times have demanded for exclusion of Sherpas from the Bhutia fold though the Sherpas for generations are acknowledged as Bhutias. All these deVelopments are indicative of a sharp increase in community consciousness and community identity in which redefinition of ethnic boundary ofthe community and community's name is also underway.

Thus, the matter of determination of ethnic boundary is still flexible and in a dyadic stage in Sikkim. The prevalence of different layei·s of identities and their political uses poses difficulty in carrying out an enquiry into identity categorization because what is a sub-category from one perspective is regarded as an ethnic category from another. This attempt at creating political-civil identity on the basis of ethnic-cultural affiliation has been a major issue in Sikkimese politics, though the trend towards politicization of ethnicity is universal.

Another aspect of ethnic cultural politics in Sikkim is that community oriented demands or attempts at community oriented political mobilization is common but ethnic parties, however, are not electorally successful. Besides, ethnic organizations with very aggressive community oriented approach also have so far failed to capture popular imagination. For example, the Nepalis have so far not raised any serious demand for abolition of Bhutia-Lepcha reserved seats in the State Assembly except for reorganization on the basis of population. Similarly, aggressive Bhutia organizations like Survival Sikkimese or Sikkim Bhutia Lepeha Apex Committee also could not become electorally or politically very. effective. Thus, ethnic politics is there because. demands and issues are raised and even manipulated by non-ethnic parties, but aggressive ethnic mobilization is not effective.

The process of political development in. Sikkim, therefore, presents a problem of understanding. Sikkimese society, conspicuous by the absence of a long history of ethnic or religious conflict, has increasingly become subject to assertive cultural or ethnic mobilization despite the introduction of parliamentary democracy and individual oriented legal system after its merger with. India. Community and ethnic assertiveness of recent years is demonstrated by rediscovery of hitherto neglected ethnic names and boundaries. Political parties and organizations also are actively participating in this process, though these organizations defend individual rights and modern political institutions as well. Such attempts at combining traditional community identity and modern legal-political institutions themselves demand special attention.

Political parties in a democratic setup are expected to represent public interest rather than segmented or exclusive interest though due to ideological differences polarization of opinion is possible. From the structural-functional viewpoint, various social organizations or interest groups are expected to articulate interests and issues whereas political parties are involved in interest aggregation. But in case of India, or Sikkim, such clear divisions of spheres of activities are non-existence.

Thus, by articulating and aggregating demands and aspirations of a group of people, political parties and organizations mobilize people in support of the issue or demand, and generate consciousness regarding the demands. Thus, through political parties and organizations, aspirations and demands of cultural-linguistic groups are expressed and legitimized.

Similarly, it is generally acknowledged that norms of politics are not fixed. In an ethnically divided society or societies, political parties often rely on social bonds, community sentiments, and symbols in order to garner popular support. In this way the relationship between the political parties and socialie.thnic organizations is established for mutual benefit - political parties use community or ethnic category as vote bank while ethnic groups use political parties to legitimize group interest and influence the decision making process.

the political institution I ike State may also precipitate formation of identities among various categories through equalizing policies like "affirmative actions" or "protective discriminations". In fact, in a country like India certain equalizing policies seem inevitable and the State may do so, according to Brass (1991), for variety of reasons such as (a) the State may be controlled by .a class or ethnic group or some combination of classes and / or ethnic groups, whose members the State chooses to favour; or (b) the dominant group may seek support among cettakicategories in the population and may adopt an 'equalitarian' policy for that purpose; or (c) the State may choose a particular equalitarian strategy for its own administrative convenience. Both post-industrial and contemporary developing societies represent these features but mere formulation of equalizing policies may not precipitate organization or mobilization among, all relevant categories. On the contrary, it is the selection of particular leadership, elites and organizations within the ethnic group by the government or state as instruments or channels of distribution of government patronage. The leadership or the elites often initiate policies, slogans, or particular patterns of mobilization which aggravate ethnic cleavages. The selection criteria itself is based on the criteria of reliability and high level of political loyalty (Rothschild: 1981). In such a case, not only the government I state tends to work or shape policies on the advice of such selected leaders or elites, but, sometimes a particular leadership within a group may even gain control over an entire area of government policy and the institutions associated with it and use them as means for consolidating the leadership of their own community. The domination of a particular group/groups in state affairs may result in disproportionate distribution or sharing of state resources causing resentment among others who have been denied benefits. Thus, due to its own political compulsions and composite elements, the state is unlikely to be a harbinger of distributive justice. Its policies may benefit some groups and communities but it may as well be a potential threat to others. It is this perceived threat or denial which . strengthens community consciousness in both categories (the favoured group consider it a right and resist any policy diversifying benefits to others while the group which is denied mobilizes its own forces to win concession from the government) and ultimately manifest in the form of organizations articulating community interests.

Thus ethnic-politics in general and growth of ethnicity-oriented political mobilization in Sikkim in particular, throw up a number of interrelated theoretical problems which create uncertainties in the process of understanding. In this connection, the basic problem that a student of political science confronts is related to the behaviour of the state and other democratic political organizations which are expected to promote democratic structure and values in lieu of traditional community orientation. But in Sikkim, the state machinery and political organizations have been seen doing the contrary, though cultural-territorial mobilization intends to limit the scope of democratic, legal-constitutional rights of individual. Then there is the paradox of growth of cultural-territorial mobilization though electorally aggressive cultural mobilization has not been very beneficial in Sikkim. Besides, the question of assertion of identity by smaller communities also needs to be addressed.

Methodology:

Political mobilization based on social and cultural and territorial identity has been primarily conceptualized with reference to the idea of ethnicity, which is the derivative of the original Greek vvord "Ethnikos" meaning 'living together'. It is identified formerly with the elements of culture and race and even refers to minority groups or 'groups in an exotic primitive culture'. During the 1970s Glazer and Moynihan (1970) further elaborated the'concept to include any group of distinct culture or origin, including the majority, as an ethnic group. And a recent analysis oldie concept includes both objective and subjective ingredients besides the interplay of historical forces. For instance, Hutchinson and Smith (1996) draw attention towards certain features which they consider important in an any ethnic group such as (a) A common name of the community; (b) An idea or a myth of common origin; (c) Shared memories ofa common past, events, heroes etc.; (d) One or more elements of common culture including language, customs, religion etc.; (e) Idea of a common homeland; and (f) A sense of solidarity, at least among a substantial section of the group.

The above mentioned features of ethnicity indicate that it is essentially a group identity in which group boundary is created and group solidarity is maintained by involving essentiality and pertnancnce of certain selective cultural elements and historical events, real or mythical. Existence of such a group identity is not unnatural in societies, ancient or modern, but, the problem arises when such identity is presented as the sole ingredient around which political articulation, mobilization and decisions should occur. The modern idea of politics, particularly development of ideas and institutions during the post-French revolutionary days, has empl- LisiAld the values of equal ity, individual freedom, secularization etc. and the ideas of legal equality, representative government, adult suffrage etc. Division of society on cultural lines and political decision on cultural basis become incompatible with such a concept of politics. Thus, ethnic cultural political mobilization, in a sense, creates problem for the concept of modern politics which is based on either individual or class, and not cultural communities. It creates a dichotomy between the concept of politics and actual behaviour of people engaged in it The research problem which arises from this dichotomy concerns how it does happen and why does it happen?

The present work focuses on the general question, of why, how and under what circumstances ethnic-cultural identity and consciousness become instruments of political action. The study further attempts at, in a specific sense, an examination of the relationship between political institutions, organizations in the one hand and ethnic politics on the other. To examine such questions, the present work attempts an analysis of the issue of growrh of ethnic politics in Sikkim. For such an analysis, generally either the primordialist or the instrumentalist perspective is employed. Hut the present study avoids either of these two perspectives as they emphasize on one single element: either the cultural factor or economic interest of a group.

It tends to make the work primarily mono-causal. Rather the perspective of 'triadic' analysis is more acceptable as it examines the political or governmental context in which an ethnic mobilization occurs. Similarly, the present work is based on contextual analysis of ethnic politics, i.e., it attempts at an examination of Sikkim's ethnic politics by situating it in the socio-economic and political context which has nurtured It At the same time, historical and analytical methods has been used to examine the process of development of ethnic politics in Sikkim and to analyze the relationship among various elements/factors; generalizations have been formulated partly on the basis of the norms of case-study method as observations are based on the findings about the specific case of Sikkim.

the findings are based on both secondary and primary sources of information and through interviews of important political activists and members of ethnic organizations though structured interviews have not been emphasized. Observations have been drawn on the basis of analysis of information in the context of actual socio-economic and political situation.

As has been stated above, a very little work focusing on ethnic pc)litics on. Sikkim has been carried out so far. Therefore, the present attempt would be a significant contribution in the field of ethnic politics. More importantly the ethnic issue is one of the burning questions of recent time and has been a major concern for both the government and the scholars alike. There is alt ElfgellCy to understand ethnic moveinents or ethnicity oriented politics particularly the causes behind such issues. The present Work, in its own little 'vay expects to contribute in this process of understanding though it doc,s not claim to provide a comprehensive theory of ethnicity.

FOOTNOTES AND REFERENCES

1. Brass, Pau' R. 1991. Ethnicity and Nationalism Theory & Comparison, New Delhi: Sage Publication.
2. Rothschild, Joseph. 1981. Ethno-Politics: A Conceptual Analysis, New York: Columbia University Press.
3. Glazer and Moynihan (Ed.). 1975. Ethnic Theory and Practice, Cambridge: Howard University Press.
4. De Vos, George & Ross, R. (Ed.). 1975. Ethnic Identity - -Cultural Communities and Change. Polo Alto: Mayfield Publishing Co.
5. Geertz, Clifford. (self Ed.) 1971: The Integrative Revolution in 'Old Societies and. New States', New York: Free Press.
6. Hutchinson, J & Smith, A.D (Ed.). 1996. Ethnicity, Oxford, OUP.
7. Caughan, R. & Eller, J. 1993. The Poverty of Primordialism: The Demystification of Ethnic Attachments, Ethnic and Racial Studies, 16:2.
8. Grosby, Steven. 1994. The Verdict of History: The Inexpugnable Tie of Primordiality A response to Eller and Coughan, Ethnic and Racial Studies, 17:2.
9. Berghe, P. Van Den 1995: Does Race Matter? Nations and. Nationalism, 1:3.
10. W. Horowitz, DJ.. 1975. "Ethnic Identity" in Glazer and. Moynihan (Ed.), Ethnic Theory and. Practice, Cambridge: Howard University Press.
11. Despres, LA. 1975: Ethnicity and Resource Competition in Plural Societies.
12. Barth, F. 1969. Ethnic Groups and Boundaries, Boston: Little Brown and Co.
13. Hechter, M. 1975. Internal Colonialism, Berkeley: University of California Press,
14. Anderson, B. 1991. Imagined. Communities Reflection on the Origin and Spread of Nationalism, London: Verso.
15. Connor, Walker. 1994. Ethno-Nationalism — The. Quest for Understanding, Princeton University Press.

16. Smith, A.D. 1971 *7'heories* of London:Duckworth.
17. Barnett, M. R. 1976., *The. Politics of Cultural Nationalism in. South Asia,* Princeton.
18. Guha, A. 1980. *Little Nationalism Turns Chauvinist,* Vol. 15, No 41 & 42, Special Number, October, Economic & Political Weekly.
19. Phadnis, Urmila. 1990. *Ethnicity and Nation Building in South Asia,* New Delhi: Sage. Publications.
20. Schermenhon, R.A. 1978. *Ethnic. Plurality in India,*
21. Weiner, M. 1978. *Sons of the Soil,* New Delhi: OUP.
22. Narian, I & Majeed, A. 1984. *Regionalism — Development Tension in India,* Delhi: Cosmos Publications.
23. Basu, Sajal. 1992. *Regional Move.ments*
24. Chaube, S.K. 1973. *Hill. Politics in North East India,* Hyderabad: Orient Longman.
25. Devalle, Susana. 1992. *Discourses of Ethnicity— Culture and Protest in Jharkhand,* New Delhi: Sage Publication&
26. Gupta, Dipankar. 1997. *The Context of Ethnicity,* New Delhi: OUP.
27. Chandra, Kanchan. 2004: *Why Ethnic Parties Succeed,* London: Cambridge University Press.
28. Risley, 11.H. 1993. *The Gazetteer of Sikhint,* Delhi: 1.,ow Price Publications.
29. Hooker, J.D. 1874/2005_ *Himalayan Journals, New* Delhi: Today and Tomorrow.
30. Edgar, J. W. 1874/2005. *Sikkim and the Tibetcm Frontier,* New Delhi: Pilgrim Publishing House.
31. Temple, Richard. 1998. *Two Diaries of Travel in Sikkin: in 1875 —An Introducation,* New Delhi Anmol Publication.
32. Macaulay, Colman. 1885/1977/2005/. *Report of a Alission to Sikkim and the Tibetan Frontier,* 1984, Gangtok: Rachna Books and Publications.
33. White, J.C. 1909/1999. *Twenty-One Years on the North-East Frontier, 1887-1908,* Delhi: Low Price Publication.

34. Morris, C.J. 1938. *Living with: the Lepchas: .,4 Book about the Sikkim HiMalayas,* LondOn: Heinarnan.

35. Gorer; Cieoffrey.1996. *The Lepchasof Sikkim,.* New Delhi, Cyan Publishing House.

36. Fonning, A.R. 1987. *Lepcha My Vanishing lithe* Kalimpong: Chy'tt Pandi. Farm.

37. Tamsangt K.P. 1983. *The· linknoWn and 1.,'"itold Reality about the .Lepchas,* Kalimpong: Mani Printing Press:

38. Sprigg, R.K: 2005. *Shedding Some Light on the Ili.s•tory,. Language and Litennure of the LepchaS,* Kalimpong.: Indigenous Lepcha Tribal AssoCiation.

39. Basnct, 1974 *Sikkim: A Short Political History,* NeW Delhi: S.Chand and Co.

40. Nakano; Chic. 1966. *'A Plural S·ciety in. Sikkim; A Study o the Interrelations of Lepchas,i Bhuticis and ;Nlepalis' in* Purer. Haimendort (Ed.) Caste:and. Kin in Nepal, India and Ceylon·; New Delhi: Sterling Publishers Pvt.

41. Das, B.S. 1983. *Sikkim Saga,* Vikash PublicatiOns, New Delhi: Vikash Publication.

42. Rao, P.R. 1978: *Sikkim The Story of its Integration with Indiet,* New Delhi: Cosmo Publications.

43. Sengupta, N. 1985. *State Government and Polities in Sikkim,* New Delhi: Sterling Publientions,

44. Dattn-Ray. S: K. 1984. *Smash and Grab: Annexation of Sikkini,* New Delhi: Vikash PubliCations.:

45. Rustornii, N.K. 1987. *Sikkim it Himalayan Tragedy*; Ahmedabad: Allied Publication's.

46. Koffman, George. :1983. *The Himalayan Gateway.:: History and Cultrire of Sikkim,* New Delhi: Sterling Publications:

47. Jha, S.K.: 84: MiShra. 1984. *Sikkim :.• Government and Politics,* New Delhi': ESS' Publication's.

48. Bhattacharva, P.K. 1984.. *Aspect of Cultural Histoly of Sikkim* New Delhi: Bagchi and Co.

49. Sinha, A.C. 1975. *Politics of Sikkim Sociological Study:* Harayana: Thomson Press.

50. Subba, T:13. 1989. *Dynamies of a Hill SOciety,* New Delhi: j Mittal Publications:

51. Subba, T: B. 1999. *PaliticS of Cu!hire,* Madras Orient Longman.

52. Foticault; Michael: 1980.*poli·er/Knowlecl.0.: Selected interWew and OtherWritings,:1972-77,* New York: Random Hank.

53. Singh K.S. (Ed.). 1993. *People of India* — Anthropological Surv'ey of India, Caletitta: Seagull Books.

54. Sikkim Study Series, 2004,:Volume III & V 1l::IPR, Government of Sikkirri; Gangtok.

55. phadnis, Ilrmila: 1980.*fi.,"thnic Dimension in Sikkimese PoliticS The 1979 Election,* Asian Survey, 20(12); Pp. 1236752.

56. Chattbe. S. K. 1987. *"Ethnicity and Politics in Sri im":* in. M.K.Raha (Ed.) The Hin-Ntlayan Heritage, New Delhi: Gyan Publishing House.

57. Dharnala, R.. *"DhPiicity. and Development in* Occasional Paper, Center Of Himalayan. Studies, University of North Bengal; Dadeeling.:

58. Dhamala; R. *"Emerging PatteM of Political Leadership in Sikkim"* Occasional Paper, Center for Hirrialayan Studies, liniversity of North Bengal, Darjeeling.:

59: Dhatnala, 1C1999. *"Struggle. for Identity Maintenance- The BhutiaS of Sikkim* Occasional Paper, Center tbr. Ifitrialayan Studies; University:of North Bengal; Dadeeling.

60. Kazi *hiSide Sikkiin —Against the Ticle,* Gart2tok: Hill Media Publications..:...

61. Subba; Pahalmati. 1998. *Who Ruined Sikkim?* Varanasi: S.A. Printers,

62. Bali, Yogendra: 2003:. *Paivan.Chamling.— Daring To. Be Different,* New Delhi: 1PR, Government of Sikkim in association: with Har Anand: Publication:

63. Pinn,i Fred. 1986. *The Road of Destiny Darjeeling :Letters. 1839,..Calcutta:* OUP.:

64. Wangyal S.B. 2002. *Sikkim and Darjeeling Division. and Deception,* Jaigatin: KMT Press.

65. Moktan, R. 2004. *Sikkim — Darjeeling: Compendiunz o Documents,* Kalinipong: Published by R. Moktan.

66. Hall, F.S. (Ed.) 1981: *The Himalayan Aspects of (...'hancre,* Ness Delhi Oxford University Press.

67. Chaube, S.K. (Ed,). 1985: *The Himalayas: Profiles. o Modernization and Adaptation,* New Delhi Sterling Publication.

68 Lama, M.P. & Sarkar, RA— 1986. *Eastern Himalayas: Environment and Economy,* Delhi: Anna Ram mid Sons Publications.

69. Raha, M.K. (Ed.). 1987: *7'he Himalayan Heritage,* Delhi: Gyan Publishing House.

70. Subba, T.B. & Dutta, Karubaki (Ed). 1991. *Religion and Socie..ty in the Himalayas,*

71. ama, M.P. 1994. *Sikkim Society, Polity, Economy Environment,* New Delhi: Indus Publications.

72. Glazer and Moynihan. 1970.*Beyond the. Melting Pot,* Massachusetts: M1'1' Press.

73. Hutchinson and Smith (Ed.). 1996. *Ethnic ity,* Oxford: Oxford 1.41 versity Press.

2

State of Sikkim: A Profile

On the basis of geographical elements and pattern of human habitation, the Great Himalaya may be divided into three major realms: a) VVestern Himalayas, b) Central Himalayas, and c) Eastern Himalayas. These realms possess certain measures of geographical homogeneity, including certain common physical and cultural traits. Sikkim is located in the western-most part of the Eastern Himalayan realms within the great and the inner Himalayan regions, From above, Sikkim looks like a gigantic amphitheatre hewn by perpetually snow-clad mountains. The tangled series of snowcapped interlacing ridges, rising range above. range even to the foot of the wall of high peaks and passes, Sikkim is aptly called an 'abode of the snows'.

· Sikkim lies between 27°5' and 2890' North latitudes, and between 88° 4' and 88'58' East longitudes. it has a total area of 2,818 square miles or 7,096 square kilometers. The physical shape is somewhat rectangular about 113 kilometers long and 64 kilometers wide. It is squeezed between Nepal on the West and Bhutan in the East. On its South lies the famous bill station of Darjeeling district and People's Republic of China on its North.

The present truncated shape of Sikkim is due to the pressures and conquests by its powerful neighbours in the past. Once the territory of Sikkim was extended as far as Limbuan (presently the eastern part of Nepal) in the West, Chumbi Valley (now in China) in the North, parts of. Western Bhutan in the East and whole of

Dadeeling district, including Siliguri in the plains, as far as Titaliya on the Bihar-Bengal border in the South.

Sikkim is a land of mountain ridges and passes. In the eastern border of Sikkim and Tibet, the Chola range contains two most important passes of Nathu-la 'the pass of the listening ear (15, 512 ft) and Jelap-la 'the lovely, plain pass' (13,354 ft) which had served as trade routes between Sikkim and. Tibet in the past. The Singalila range on the 'W'estern frontier forms a line of separation between Sikkim and. Nepal. The important pass of Chiabhanjang `the hollow where one peep over' (10,320 ft) and Kangehenjunga `the auspicious forehead peak' (28,156ft.), the third highest peak in the world, lie in this range. The Teesta along with its tributaries is an important river of the State. It rises from Cholamo Lake and flows through the heart of the State embracing numerous mountain streams in its fold. The Great Rangeet, a tributary of the 'ceesta, is another important river which rises from Kabru glaciers meets Teesta near Melli in Darjeeling district.

Apart from rivers natural springs provide alternative source of svater. Some of these springs are hot like the one at Ralong at an elevation of about 3,100 ft on the west bank of river Rangeet. Other hot spring sites are Phut Sacha on the east side of Rangeet near the Rinchingpong monastery, Ytnrithang on the east bank of river Lachung, and Mornay below the glacier of Kinchinjho. In terms of geology, Sikkim lies in the mild tremor zone but, unlike. Assam and Bihar, Sikkim has not experienced anything like disastrous earthquakes. However, landslides and mudslides are the recurring features owing to the composition of the soil (micacious), steep slopes, unplanned construction and poor drainage facilities.

Sikkim experiences, even for its small size, a climate suitable for both pineapple and apple. Her northern frontiers remain perennially snowcapped discouraging human habitation. The settlement is found between 5000 ft. to 14000 ft. Sher lies directly on the path of the South —West monsoon and receives abundant rainfall varying between 150 inches in the lower Teesta valley to 40 to 50 inches in Lachung, Valley. In short, almost all parts of

Sikkim receive rainwater during:the monsoon. About 43 per cent area is covered with lush green: of various types.' Several varieties of bambods; ferns cherry,' laurel, oak, Chestnut, firs, pines; maples,: magnolia, champs, katoos are found at an altitude between 3000ft to 7000 ft: Rhododendrons of about 36 varieties are found between 6000 ft: to 8000: ft. Ambng 5000 floral plants, abOut 500 species of orchids, 30 species of Primulas. and 424 speeies of Medicinal plants are foUnd in. Sikkim. Similarly, a wide variety of wild animals. as. Panda, Otter, Clotided Leopard,: Snow Leopard, Thar,. Ghoral, Musk Deer, Black Bear, Hyena,: Jackal; Civet Cat, and Himalayan We4asel roam about freely ambng the thicket of the jungle. Apart from this about 500 Varieties of birds and 600 Species Of butterflies are also found in Sikkim.

A brief political histolyof Sikkim:

It has been rather A common, practice among the scholars to begin political history of Sikkim with the establishment of the Namgyal dynasty.: though a rudimentary political system existed much earlier Despite lack of doeumentary evidences, whieh are: to have been dOstrOyed by the' Tibetan lamas when they migrated to . Sikkim, the information available from various Lepcha and TsOng (Limboo) oral.. traditions' indicate existence of:tribal chiefs. And a iniique institution resembling rudithentary Monarchy. The king Wias selected threugh an open conmetition held from time to time. According to:the. Lepcha legend the successor to the throne was required to posseSs expertise in the fields' of religion', admini Stratiorr, Military tactics etc. The king Was expected: to be polite, humble and a sociable person Who would. remain bachelor and would possess no property.. SuCh a platonic king was known As 'Pant!' by the Lepchas. The spiritual leader, called Athing or Bongthing, Was another important person in the Lepcha society. After: the cicath of a Panit, the Athing used to look after the affairS of administration till a new Pauli was selected: The matter of selection would often take several years:

N detail documentary and Chronological history of the Lepeha And Tsong (Limboo) tulet's is not aVailable.:HoweVer, Lepcha legends describe Pohartak Panu as the first important Lepcha ruler of the Mayel country, now called. Sikkiml. He is believed to be the contemporary of Chandragupta of the Gupta dynasty. There is no record of his immediate successor but sometime during I 230- 1316 A.D. Turvey Panu, another Lepcha king, ruled. Sikkim with his capital near Kurseong, now a town in. Darjeeling district. According to Dahal, he had Tsongs (Limboos) and Mangars among his courtiers[2]. It is believed that he was killed in a military expedition possibly by the Kirats of the eastern Nepal. He was succeeded by Tubb Athak but very little is known about him too. The last among the Lepcha rulers was perhaps Gaeboo Achok Panu of. Damsang in Kaliinpong region. According to Dahal, he was the son of the slain Lepcha Prime Minister, Tshongzod Bolek, of Sikkim. Gaeboo too was assassinated treacherously at Daling fort at the age of 36 in 1856 A.D. Contrarily, Tarnsang believes that. Lepchas of Damsang belonged to the independent principality of Kalimpong whose ruler Gaeboo Achok was murdered by the Bhutanese in 1780 in connivance with the Sikkim Raja, and then Kalimpong was annexed to Bhutan[3].. In another version, he was described as the son of Kya-bo-Rab, a Bhutia ruler of Damsang and Daling, and was killed by the Bhutanese General Ari Sethi near Ambiokh[4]. Fanning also expressed doubt about the identity of Gaeboo Achok. He contests that lie "could never have been a Lepcha. At the most, he was a half-breed, cultured, moulded and fashioned in the style of rulers themselves"[5]. Despite claims and counter-claims, one thing comes out quite clearly that this part of the territory was ruled by the Lepchas and Limboos, now a constituent of the Nepalis. These rulers wei.e more like democratic chiefs than territorial sovereigns.

Much before the 16th century the Tibetans began migrating towards the northern tracts of Sikkim in search of land and pasturef". Generally it is believed that the Tibetan migration began as a result of the defeat of the Red Hat Sect (ibllowers of Nyingma-pa) at the hands of the Yellow Hat Sect (follovvers of Geluk-pa) in Tibet in a religious strife. According to the legend a Tibetan prince, Guru Tashe, was foretold to proceed to Demozong, the Bhutia name for Sikkim. His eldest son jo-Khye-Burnsa (the superior of the ten thousand horses) married Gurtimo, the daughter of the Sakya hierarch and settled in Chumbi, then a part of Sikkim. As legends have it, being childless the couple was advised to propitiate blessing from the Lepcha spiritual head 'fhekong Tek. Khye-Burnsa met the Lepcha spiritual head and solicited blessing for sons?: Klaye Burnsa was also said to have concluded a 'Blood-brotherhood' pact with the Lepchas. It is also said that 'rhekong Tek, the Lepcha Athing, prophesized that the descendents of Khye-Bumsa would become lords of Sikkim while his own people would become their raiyats[8]. The statement perhaps is a modern innovation seeking legitimation of Tibetan occupation of Sikkim. The second son of Khye-Bumsa, Mi-tpon Rab, had four sons, the youngest of whom was Guru Tashe. His eldest son was Jawa Apha. Ja.wa Apha's son was Guru Tenzing who fathered Phuntsog Namgyal, the first Tibetan Gyalpo (king in Tibetan language) of' Sikkim. Phuntsog Namgyal was consecrated in 1642 at Yoksum by the three Tibetan lamas of Red Hat Sect namely Lhatsum Nainkha Jigmed, Sempah Chhembo and Rigdzin Kunzangpo[9]. Mulfard, however, believes that the consecration of Phuntsog Namgyal took place in 1646[1°].

The transition of political power, however, did seem peaceful. According to Dahal, Geyzing (the place of victory) got its name as a result of the armed struggle between the combined forces of the Limboos and Lepchas on the one hand and the Bhutias on the other". Mullard also writes that despite establishing himself as the dominant power in Sikkim, Phuntsog Namgyal suffered a rebel, possibly in 1649, instigated by the Lepchas of Yug-bsam (Yuksum) and Limboos (referred to as local traders)[12]. The rebellion was subdued followed by an agreement of some form which, however, was not favourable to the Lepchas. The agreement seemed to ha.ve introduced the Tibetan system of land economy marked by social difference between the land owners (Dpon) and Lepcha tenants/ servants (G.yog)I[3] though it is still premature to say anything conclusively.

The consecration of Phuntsog Namgyai could be perceived as extension of the Tibetan anthority in the affairs of Sikkirn. After haying established:the political dominatidn, it did:net take.ritueh time to have monastic influence: to penetrate and Mark its presence among the pagan Lepehas and.,Tsengs (LiMboos): Centuries old Lepcha pOlity based on non4lereditary kingship was replaced with a:theocratic and hereditary monarchical systerri. The Dalai Lama was looked uponas the ultiMate source of authority both in temporal and spiritual matters concerning Sikkirri.. The Tibetan interest was Served as far as Possible while the indigenOtis Lepchas remained in utter negligence "mostly confined to thp northern belt Of Sikkim in an area called Dzongu" and foreedto live '..`a life in indolence and negligence contributing little against the aggressive exploitation by the Bhutias of the riches in land and forest."[14]

Phuntsog.NanigYal extended the boundary of Sikkim as far as:a:nimbi valley in the North: Tagcingla (Bhutan) in the east, 110 ia (Bihar) in the soilth and Devagaon (Bangladesh) and Singalila range in the west. By : considering Bhutias (father), Lepchas (Mother) and ISongs (sons)' as Members of the same family,. he improve-0 ethnic relation with other communities. Mangars were allowed to keep their fiefdom at a payment of annual taxes while:the Tsongs could use their title of 'Subbe For administrative efficieney, he divided the territory. into twelve Dzongs or districts such as Lassu,'.Dallern,. Yangthang,: Sang, Libing, Mailing, Sim ik, Parido M etc[15] and Dzongpons (governors or administrator of forts) were appointed from among the Lepchas. There is no recorded evidence suggesting appointment of Tsongsi (Limboos) Mangars as Dzongpons. His royal council was composed of twelve ministers mostly drawn from the Bhutias. Fie died in 1670.

His son Tensung Namgyal shifted the Capital from Yoksitin to Rabdantse and reduced the nturiber of councilors from 12 to 8.: According to the legend: Sikkim inherited its present name from his thirdwife Who was the daughter *of* a Tsong chief Yo-YO Hang: of Rabdentse. Basnet, however, claims that it was the Leptha chief with win-nil:the marriage of the daughter of the Tsong chief YO:

Yo Hang of Rabclentse was solemnized. When the bride entered her husband's house, she exclaimed in her own tongue "Su Him" (the new house) which was later corrupted into Sukhim and then to. Sikkim.[16] But, according to Dr. Waddell 'Sikkim' was a parbatiya (Nepali) name given by the conquering •orkhas.[17]

Sikkim suffered first territorial loss during the reign of Chador Namgyal at the hands of the Bhutanese in 1700. The Sixth Dalai. Lama, however, persuaded Dev Raja of Bhutan to withdraw from R.abclentse. By this time the practice of finding Tibetan brides for the Gyalpos (Kings)/ of Sikkim had been established, But the circumstances under which Gyurmed Nanagyal married a Tibetan refugee girl created unhappiness among the Lepchas and Tsongs which took the form of a revolt. The Gyalpo fled to Tibet. In 'Sikkim-A concise Chronicle' published by the Sikkim Durbar 1962, the event has been explained in terms of invasion of Prithivi Narayan Shah over Sikkim which, however;. nor seemed to be correct. The Gyalpo (king) was issueless but a nun was found pregnant and the lamas concocted a story that in his death bed the Chogyal had acknowledged the child of his own. The boy born from this nun succeeded the throne after the intervention of the Tibetan authority. The boy being minor, the authority in Tibet also appointed a Tibetan regent by the name of Rabden Sarpa to take care of the administration until the heir apparent, Phuntsog Naingyal II, attained adulthood.

In the political history of Sikkim Rabden Sarpa is notable for two specific reasons. Firstly, he introduced a crude system of taxation on land and trade, called Zulung, and, secondly, he earned enmity with the Mangars. The offended Mangar chief is believed to have entered into a secret conspiracy with Dev Raja of Bhutan against the Gyalpo. Bhutan invaded Sikkim in 1770 and occupied certain areas on the east of river Teesta, i.e. Kalirnpong subdivision of present day. Darjeeling district, and remained so till 1864 when the British finally took over this portion of Iand from Bhutan.

During the reign of the Sixth Gyalpo, Tenzing Namgyal, Prithivi Narayan Shah, the ruler of a small principality of Gorkha in western. Nepal, was consolidating Nepal into a strong and unified nation and had already extended his territory as far as river Stitlez. Since 1775 the Gorkha soldiers invaded Sikkim with varying success. In 1788-89 the Gorkha General, Jahar Singh, invaded Sikkim from the western border and occupied Rabdentse. In 1791 war broke out between Nepal and Tibet, in the course of which the Gorkhas established themselves firmly in Sikkim, especially in the southern and western parts of the river Teesta.[18] In 1792 Sino-Nepal treaty was signed. The Sikkimese Gyalpo, Tsugphud Narngyal, being a minor and a fugitive, failed to protect the interest of the Kingdom. The land mass which lied on the south of river Teesta and Perniongchi area went in favour of Nepal which remained occupied till 1815, while Tibet got the Chumbi The Chola-Jelap range became the northern and eastern boundaries of Sikkim.

The British Connection

With the ascendancy of British in Bengal in the wake of the battle of Plassey. in 1757, a new political power with a modern administrative, economic and military organization appeared in the southern frontiers of Sikkim in the 18th century. Sikkim which had close political and religious connections with its northern neighbour now was forced to face its southern neighbour with which it had little contacts. This new development completely changed the history of Sikkim during the 18th and 19th centuries. The British from the very beginning viewed Sikkim as a passage for establishing trade connection with Tibet. Apart from the lucrative Tibetan gold trade which had already begun in low magnitude between the Ncwars of Nepal and Tibetan traders with their trade terminus at Patna, the British government was as much interested in commercial transaction of English manufactured consumer goods to Tibet via Sikkim. In 1767 an opportunity to come into contact with the Newars and thereby with the Tibetans had gone unutilized due to Kinlock's half-hearted expedition. The second opportunity came to British when Cooch Bihar involved in a battle with Bhutan and the former requested. Warren Hastings for help. Sikkim, on the other hand, came in support of Bhutan. Unwilling to lose this opportunity W'arren Hastings wrote to "Cash i Lama of Sikkim about the lenient treatment towards Bhutan in exchange of a friendly mission to Tibet.[2]1 Two years later in May 1774 the mission was sent "to open a mutual and equal communication of trade" under Cieorge Bhogle but it too did not prove fruituous.[21] A similar mission in 1783 also remained unsuccessful because of sudden departure of Warren Hastings to London and non-involvement policy in the Himalayan kingdoms adopted by his successors.

In view of the deteriorating relationship with Nepal, it became imperative for the British government in India to establish amicable relationship with Sikkim. In 1815, Lord Moira, the then Governor General, persuaded the Sikkim Gyalpo (king) through Captain BaiTe Latter to fight alongside the British against the common enemy Nepal and on compliance to the British offer the Sikkim Gyalpo was promised restoration of the territory occupied previously by Nepal.[22] The defeat of Gorkha force under Arnarsingh Thapa was followed by signing of the Segauli Treaty in December 1815. The interest of Sikkim was incorporated under article VI of the.Treaty. In accordance with the promise the British signed the Treaty of Titaliya with Sikkim in 1817 and the territory lying between eastward of Mechi, and westward of river Teesta, around 4000 sq. miles, which was occupied formerly by Nepal and transferred to the British by virtue of the Treaty of Segauli, was restored to Sikkim. However, some parts of the Tarai, revenue rich Dabgong, and surrounding areas were not restored. Within two months from the date of signing of the Treaty of Titaliya, Morung was gifted to Sikkim by Lord Moira. The Treaty put a check on the expansionist ambition of the Gorkhas and, at the same time, Gyalpo's freedom was to a large extent constricted. Article VIII of the Treaty says, "Sikkim authorities would afford protection to merchants and traders from the Company's provinces and would levy no transit duties on their merchandise.[23] In 1827 tension brewed once again between Sikkim and Nepal regarding the possession of Ontoo[24], a small area on the east of river Mechi.

Besides, the dispute also involved the question of about 800 Lepcha refugees, actually the relatives and supporters of the slain Prime Minister Tsongzod Bolek, of Sikkim who had taken refuge in Ontoo, then under Nepal's occupation[25] and had been harassing Sikkim continuously: [26] In spite of the joint efforts displayed by Sikkim, Tibet and China these Lepcha refugees from Sikkim could not be brought back• to Sikkim.[27] As required by article III of the Treaty of Titaliya, the Sikkim Gyalpo was obliged to seek British mediation on the border dispute with Nepal regarding Ontoo. The Governor General Lord William Bentinck authorized two British deputies, Captain G.A.Lloyd and J.W. Grant, the commercial resident at Malda, to investigate into the matter, Who eventually negotiated lbr the grant of the old Gorkha station called Darjeeling" for the purpose of a Sanitarium'.[28]

Though the grant was effected sometime in. February 1835[29] the detail analysis of the correspondences that had taken place between the concerned parties such as the Gyalpo, Captain Lloyd and the British government at Calcutta, were suggestive of the fact that the grant of Darjeeling was neither a tree gift to the British nor was it comprised of a "spot" situated "on the northern spur or ridge of the Gurdum Kutta or Sinehel mountain[3°] as Major Lloyd and Captain Herbert had deceptively put it When Major Lloyd met the Gyalpo for the first time at a place called Ponk Samp on the eastern bank of the river Teesta on 19 Februaiy 1835 to propose for the cession of Darjeeling by "offering such equivalent either in land or in money as deem reasonable",[31] the Gyalpo handed over a written list containing grievances .[32] Though no discussion took place on that day, it was quite obvious that the cession of Darjeeling depended upon compliance of three simple requests namely:

a. The western boundary of Sikkim to be extended to('? Kankai river);

b That a certain Kurnmoo Pradhan (7 Kumbhey Pradhan or Runno Pradhan) and some. Kazis be seized and delivered to Sikkim;

c That Dabgong (Dev Gaon, Debgong, Dabgong, Deb-gram) in the. Tarai, might be ceded to the Gyalpo's territory.[33]

Major Lleyd, howeVer, was in constraint to comply with the requestas he: was: not authoried to negotiate anything other than :'offering such equivalent either in land. or in cash The Gyalpo after having waited for two days: since:. February .22;: summoned Major Lloyd on February 25 and told him: that "if his requests were cornplied with he from friendshi0: would give Darjeeling to the BritiSli government, but that his country Was a Very small7:[34] Interestingly, the Gyalpol had dropped two of his oaf reqiiesis this time but the extradition of Kummoo Pradhan and exchange of Dabgong were,: however, kept as they:werü, The Gyalpo's request concluded. with "alSo if from friendship Dabgong horn Amedeggee north be given to me,: then my Dewsn will deliver to Mayor. Lloyd: the grant and agreement tinder m red Se4.i of Darjeeling that he may erect houSeS there, which l have given, in charge of the said Dewan to be delivered, dated 19 Maugh, .1891, i.e. 25 February, 18357.[35] It seetias that by that tirrie the Gyalpo had ali-eady prepared a:deed and had it left with his DeWan to be given over to Major. Lloyd on Compliance to a territorial exchange Debgong fot Darjeeling). But the shrewd Major somehow managed to See the deed (written in Lepcha) froin the Dewan who acceMpanied hint in hiS return journey and had it copied and translated. The deed :so translated read:

"That:: health may bp: obtained by residing there I from Ii iendShip Make, an offering of Dadeeling to the Governor General Sahib 1891,19 Maui; (25 February, 1835)" (True Translati), G.W. A Lloyd Major.[36]-

Thp deed being vague in terms of dotharcation of the: boundaries, Majoi Lloyd, drafted a deed of his own specifying boundaries in particular and sent it to the:'Gyalpo with a:: request either to substitute the original short deed with the new draft or to make a fresh one based upon the draft sent by hitn. The draft read;

"The Governoi General having ckpressed hiS desire for the possession, of the hill`of Darjeeling on account of its cool Climate, for the purpose of enabling: the Servants of his government. suffering from sickness; to avail themselves of its advantageS, Sikkitnputtee Raja, out of friendship tbr the said Governor General hereby present Darjeeling to the East India Company, that is, all the lands south of the Great Ranjeet river, cast of the Balasun, Kahial and little Ranjeet river, and west of the Rungno and Mahanadi rivers

The Gyalpo did not seem to have made another draft. What transpired the Gyalpo, Tsugphud Namgyal, in accepting the deed drafted by Major Lloyd could not be known. In this regard Fred Finn writes that the Gyalpo had a vague idea of the topography of Sikkim, though he knew his international frontiers quite wel1.[38] Thus, the grant that defined Darjeeling was not just confined around the Observatory Hill but comprised of a large chunk of landmass stretching about 30 miles in length and about 6 to 10 miles in breadth apart from an additional stretch of land for the construction of road to make Darjeeling accessible to the plains. The deed of transfer of Darjeeling was conditional but none of the requests made by the Gyalpo was conceded. Major Lloyd was unfaithful in his dealings with the Gyalpo and for the latter it was disgraceful or against the Sikkimese tradition to take the gift back. By sending the deed too early the Gyalpo had "trapped himself in the conventions of royal etiquette".[39] Later, the Gyalpo was sent a double barreled gun, a rifle, a pair of shawls superior, a pair of shawl inferior and 20 yards of Red Broad cloth'. In 1841 the Gyalpo was made an offer of Rs. 3,000 per annum which he wanted to be paid in terms of Rs. 1000 worth of. Gold Mobur, Rs. 1000 worth of fusils with bayonets and accoutrements and the remainder in cloth and coral.° The amount was further raised to Rs. 6,000 in 1847

The transfer of Darjeeling to the British India brought with itself number of problems for Sikkim. Nepal and Bhutan accused Sikkim of selling out to the foreigners, Bhutan even attacked Sikkim in 1844. Tibet became suspicious of Sikkim's action and expressed displeasure by denying hitherto given grazing right to the Sikkimese and restricting the visit of the Gyalpo (King) to Lhasa to once in eight years.

In order to improve the relation with Lhasa, the Gyalpo (king) appointed Dunya Namgyal, better known as Pagla Dewan (mad Chief Minister), a Bhutia of strong anti-British or pro-Tibet conviction, as the Chief Minister of Sikkim. He had absolute monopoly over the Tibetan trade and was apprehensive of the presence of British in Sikkim. Moreover, runaway slaves and criminals were given refuge in Darjeeling and, on the contrary, British subjects were kidnapped and sold as slaves in Sikkim. In 1848, Dr. Hooker's plea to visit Sikkim was denied which led to the arrest of both Dr. Hooker and Dr. Campbell in November 1848 while returning from Tibet. They were released in December 1849 and escorted to Darjeeling. This incident was followed by a military expedition against Sikkim in February 1850 and reoccupation of Tarai, and suspension of annual grant of Rs. 6,000 being given in lieu of Darjeeling. On February 1, 1861, British occupied Tumlung, the capital of Sikkim, and Dewan Namgyal escaped to Tibet.

On March 28, 1861, a new treaty was signed between Ashley Eden and Sikkim Gyalpo (actually with the Crown Prince Sidkeong Namgyal) at Tumlung. As a consequence of the treaty the staunch enemy of the British, Pagla Dewan, was banished from Sikkim, free trade began between the two countries, all previous treaties were declared ultra-vires, Gyalpo was not allowed to stay in Tibet for more than three months at a stretch, a post of vakeel from Sikkim was established at Darjeeling, Gyalpo was debarred from ceding any portion of territory to any other foreign power and allowing the passage to any foreign army through Sikkim without the consent of the British government in India. In brief, the British control in both internal and external affairs of Sikkim was established. Effectively Sikkim became a protectorate of the British government in India.

Sikkim as a protectorate State:

Sidkeong Namgyal was a liberal person and managed to improve the relations with the British as far as possible. It was during his rule the annual payment of Darjeeling was raised from earlier Rs. 6,000 to Rs. 9,000 in 1868 and then to 12,000 in 1873.[41] However, the relationship once again deteriorated with the consecration of Thutob Namgyal (1874-1914) because of latter's pr-,Tibetati attitude. The Gyalpo : even'. refused to com to Darjeeling for talks without the expressed:permissionof the Tibetan government.[42] Colman Macaulay,. the Finance Secretary: Of the government of Bengal, who Was sent in 1884 to inveStigate : into the matter and to explore the possibilities of reconeiliation, particularly held Gyalpo'S anti-British attitude responsible for bitter relationship. lie recommended for sending a mission to Tibet: to patch. up the di fferenccS. AccOrdingly, a trade mission as : deeided to be sent to Tibet in 1886 but the sante was abandoned : in presence of extreine opposition' froth the. Tibetan side. Meanwhile, the Tibetans occupied ·Lingth; abota twenty milCS inside Sikkim's border.. The occupation of Lingtu by the Tibetans Was approved by the GyaIpo which further infuriated the 13ritiSli. The military expedition was inevitable and in March 1888 the Tibetans were clriVen out of Lingtu by the British: force under: General Graham and: occupied: GnatOng; The Gyalpo. nNho had tied to Chticnbi; was h•bught·to Gangtok.

J. Claude White, an engineer by profession, was appointed :: in June 1889 as the: first political officer of the protectorate State. AdministratiVe reform becathe his first prierity and aecordingly State.. Cduneil was formed comprising of eminent personalities like Chief Dewans, Kazis and Larnas of Sikkim.. He retained the post of President of the State Council by himself. The Gyalpo waS sent to Kalimpong. 'fhotigh he returned to Sikkim in1891 he Was no less than a prisoner in the hands efJ.C.White. After his attempt to sneak to 'Tibet via Nepalhad failed,. Was imprisbriOd·ohed again at Kurseong in. Darjeeling:. He . was allowed to return to Sikkim in 1896 and remained under the.: Watchful eyes of the political officer. In the meantime a treaty. Was signed at Calcutta betWeen China and British India in 1890 in which the former recognized the Status.. of Sikkim as the protectorate of British Namgyal died in 1914. He was succeeded by his second:son Sidkeong Namg,yal. 11 (Tiilku) aS:1.C.White did not want Tchoda Namgyal, the eldest son of the late Thutob Namgyal who was: studying. in Tibet, to bethe Gyalpb of Sikkim. However, S iclkeong Naingyal 1I (Tulku). met an untimely death iii:1914 and his half-brother, Tashi Namgyal, succeeded him. In his fifty-vears of rule Sikkim witnessed several radical changes in judicial and socio-economic fields. The abolition of magisterial power of the landlords, introduction of land reforms, abolition of forcedlabour, direct payment of taxes to the state, restructuring of judiciary in the model of Indian civil and criminal procedure codes were some of his landmark achievements. But it was during his rule that agitation against the arbitrary and discriminatory system also began. He died in December 1963. He was succeeded by his second son, Palden Thondup Namgyal. He assumed the title of the Chogyal (Dharma Raja) as he was believed to be a Tulku, an incarnate of a noble soul. It was during his rule that Sikkim had to witness series of political uncertainties and agitations leading to an end of the theocratic monarchical system and beginning of a popularly elected State Assembly in 1974. In 1975 Sikkim became the 22nd state of the Indian Union.

Sikkim after the merger with India:

The Himalayan kingdom of Sikkim became the 22nd State of the. Indian Union in. May, 1975 as a consequence of the unanimous decision of the Sikkim Legislative Assembly of April 10, 1975, seeking abolition of the institution of the Chogyal followed by the referendum of April 14, 1975, by the people of Sikkim to that effect. Mr. 11.13.Lat was appointed as the first Governor of Sikkim on May 16, 1975. Article 371F was incorporated in the Constitution of India which provided for a special constitutional status to the State of Sikkim. The basic tenets of the provision may be summarized as:

The 32 member Assembly of Sikkim, as elected in April 1974, would continue to act as the Legislative Assembly of the State of Sikkim for a period of four years until other provisions are made in parliament by law. -Whole of Sikkim would constitute one parliamentary constituency and would be allotted one seat in the Lok Sabha and not in the Rajya Sabha. The members of the present State Assembly would participate in the election of the member of the Lok Sabha. The Indian Parliament for the purpose of protecting the rights and interests of the different section of Sikkimese population would make provisions for the number of seats in the Legislative Assernbl·i, to be filled by candidates belonging to such sections and to delimit Assembly constituencies accordingly.

Regarding the power of the Governor of Sikkim, article 371 F (g) states "The Governor of Sikkim shall have special responsibility for peace and for equitable agreement for ensuring the social and economic advancement of different section of the population of Sikkim and in the discharge of his special responsibility under the clause, the Governor of Sikkim shall subject to such directions, as the President may, from time to time, deem fit to issue, act in his discretions"..[44]

The existing High Court of Sikkim and all courts of civil, criminal and revenue jurisdiction, and authorities and officials - judicial, executive and ministerial — to continue and to exercise respective functions subject to provisions of the constitution.

Similarly, the article provides for continuation of old Sikkimese laws even after the merger. It stated "All laws in force immediately before the appointed day in the territories comprised in the State of Sikkim or any part thereof shall continue to be in the force therein until amended/repealed by a competent .egislature or other competent authority".[45]

For the purpose of facilitating the application of any such law, as referred above, in relation to the administration of the State of Sikkim and for bringing the provision of any such law in accordance with the provision of this constitution, the President by order would make such adaptations and modifications of the law, whether by way of repeal or amendment, as may be necessary or expedient, within two years from the appointed date, i.e. within April 1977. Every such law would have effect subject to adaptations and modifications so made, and any such adaptation or modification would not be questioned in any court of law. Furthermore, the Supreme Court and any Court would not exercise jurisdiction in respect of any dispute or other matter arising out of any treaty, agreement, engagement or other similar instrument relating to Sikkim which was entered into or executed before the appointed day and to which the Government of India or any of its predecessor Government was a party. This provision would, however, not to derogate power of the President of hidia to consult the Supreme Court under article 143 of the constitution

A cursory look at the constitutional position of Sikkim will unfold certain striking features. Firstly, article 371 F is a non-obstante article which means that neither the provisions of the constitution nor an interpretation of the Supreme Court can limit the scope of the provision. Secondly, the present constitution allowed continuation of Legislative Assembly elected in 1974 even after the merger. It is interesting to note that the electoral rolls for 1974 Assembly Election were prepared keeping December 1, 1973, as the qualifying date. The voters' lists, published on February 4, 1974, enumerated 1,03,495 names as eligible (those who were 21 years and above and had Sikkim Subject Certificate) voters which was just 49.3 per cent of the total population of Sikkim in 1971. The report suggested that a sizable number of populations also did riot participate in voting. In brief above 50 per cent population of Sikkim did not participate in the 1974 Assembly election and hence it should have been dissolved and a fresh election for constituting a new Assembly should have been ordered. Thus, by continuing the Legislative Assembly elected in 1974 a covert attempt was made both to appease the supporters of mergf-m¯ and to avoid undesirable outcome had the election for constituting a new Assembly was called for Thirdly, Sikkim Legislative Assembly was to compose of not less than thirty members with the tenure of four years. It was inconsistent with the provision of article I 70 of the constitution of India. The term of the Assem bly was made five years in 1979 and the nature of seat reservation in the. Assembly too was modified in the sante year despite the limitation imposed by article 371F (o) which states that no such order (i.e. Presidential Order adapting or modifying the provisions). shall be made after the expiry of two years from the appointed day' which was April 1977. Fourthly, the Governor of Sikkim was vested with discretionary power under 'Special Responsibility' for the maintenance of peace and for ensuring equitable advancement of different section of the population. Unlike the Governors of other states, the Governor of Sikkim exercises this power as per the provision of article 371F (g). Fifthly, by continuing the old Sikkimese laws which were considered discriminatory in favour of the erstwhile ruling community, the inter-community relations continue to mark by one of apprehension and suspicion.

Politico-Administrative structures — their evolution:

The present day politico-administrative structure has evolved from a very simple system existed hundreds ofyears ago in Sikkim. 'Ihe political structure existed then was basically the reflection of a simple and carefree tribal society with tribal chief as their ruler/ king. As mentioned earlier, the Lepcha• king, called 'Palm', and the spiritual leader ` Bongthing' or 'Athing' used to occupy important position in the political and socio-religious life of the Lepcha community. A.R.Fonning though does not support the theory of Lepcha rulers and contends that the Lepchas do not believe in the system of gradation or ranking,[47] a sixteenth century document[4]5 granting permission to the Tsongs (Limboos) to settle in the Mayel Lyang (i.e. Sikkim), however, is indicative of the presence of a determinate source of authority whose position in the Lepcha society was undoubtedly superior to others.

The Lepchas, however, lost their authority with the solicitation of a legendary brotherhood pact with the migratory Bhutia patriarch, Khye Bumsa. In 1642[49] Phuntshog Namgyal, a Bhutia peasant, was consecrated as the first Bhutia king, called Chogyal (Dharmaraja), of the Tibetan origin at Yoksum in west Sikkim. He was described as the descendant of the brave ancestors of the Khan' province in eastern Tibet

The system of government during the Namgyal dynasty was essentially based on absolute monarchy with feudalistic root. The king was aided by an assembly of monks and laymen, called Lhade-Mede' (the Assembly of Elders) composed dominantly by the Bhutia lamas. "['he Lhade-Mede had no fixed numbers. Initially the members were nominated by the Kazis and later by the Private Secretary to the Chogyal. Lhade-Mede's jurisdiction was extended to everywhere from marriage of the member of the Royal family to issues of national importance. In all these mailers Lhade-Mede used to advice the Chogyal. The advice was not legally binding on the Chogyal though rejection was not the convention. The meeting of Lhade-Mede was generally held at the Palace at the request of the Chogyal at any time the latter deemed necessary.[51] Reportedly, the last meeting of the Lhade-Mede was convened in order to consider the marriage proposal of the last Chogyal of Sikkim, Palden Thondup Namgyal, with an American lady, Hope. Cooke.

The politico-administrative structure underwent further evolutionary refinement under the first political officer of Sikkim, John Claude White. He usurped the authority of the Chogyal Thutop Namgyal and brought the administration of the State under his complete control. After the convention of 1890 between Great Britain and China relating to Sikkim and Tibet, the British Political Officer became the virtual ruler of Sikkim exercising powers both in internal and external affairs of Sikkim.[52] He introduced Advisory Council, later called the State Council, composed mainly of Kazis and landlords considered faithful by, the British government. It is stated "Members of the Council have continued to attend regularly at the Palace. Their attendance at the meeting of the Council held by the Political Officer has been particularly good. The Maharaja was present on each occasion...." [53]

The Council grew both in terms of maturity and in its content gradually with the progress of time requiring it to meet thrice a year.[54] J. Claude White tried his best to establish a modern system cif administration in Sikkim. After the return of the Maharaja Thutc0 Namgyat from confinement in 1895 he was restored the charge ofJudiciary. Gradually he took over the Council and shared administrative power with the Political Officer with the power of reviewing any transaction vested with the latter. Sidkeong Namgyal Tulku, son of Thutop Namgyal, was trained'and educated in Oxford. After his return to Sikkim in 1908, he was appointed the Vice-President of the State Council and given the charge of Education and. Forest Departments in addition to Ecclesiastical.[55] With the growing confidence between the Chogyal and the British Government in India, the Chogyals gained much of their lost authority. During the reign of. Tashi Nan¯igyal, certain departments like Excise, Income Tax, Police and Jail were transferred to the Chogyal in addition to Education, Forest and Ecclesiastical affairs over which he had independent contro1.[56] Later, the departments like. Revenue, Stamps, Printing Press, Co-operative Societies etc. were also transferred to the Chogyal. The Chogyal was assisted by K.P. Dewar, the then Chief Executive Officer, in his day-to-day administration. In April 1918 the Chogyal Tashi Naingyal was conferred full power of administration of Sikkim by Charles Bell, the then Political Officer of Sikkim.[57]

Thus, the Chogyal once again became the fountain of all authority in so far as internal administration of the State was concerned. The government was directly under the control of the Chogyal who used to receive functional assistance from the secretariat. The administration was trying to adapt itselfto modern form of government but owing to the presence of conservative elements, it basically served the interests of the influential clergy and landed class. During the late 1930s the strength of the nominated State Council was raised to '.9 and the incumbents remained in the post during the pleasure of the Chogyal. The working of the Council was systematically organized and definite functions were assigned to it including that of budget preparation to which the final approval of the Chogyal was required. The Chogyal enjoyed prerogatives to pass any order independently of the Counci1.[58] But in all matters of adrninistrative importance the Chogyal was to consult the British Political Officer. In other words, even if the powers were transferred to the Chogyal, the ultimate authority was, in fact retained by the Political Officer

After the departure of the British from India in 1947, the successor government, i.e. India, had no treatv obligation with Sikkim. The void was, however, filled up by concluding a Standstill Agreement on 27 February, 1948 between the Sikkim

Darbar and the government of India. Both agreed to continue all agreements, relations and administrative arrangements which existed between the British Crown and the Sikkim State before 14th August, 1947 pending the signing of a new agreement or treaty. In December 1950 the. Indo-S ikkim treaty was signed continuing the status of Sikkim as the Protectorate State of India. Accordingly, the Chogyal was given autonomy regarding internal affairs subject to ultimate responsibility of the government of India for maintenance of good governance and law and order; the government of India was responsible for Sikkim's external: relations, defense and communicationa° besides being the most important source of planned revenue.

With the increasing association with. India and birth of the political parties in the nineteen forties the demands for democratic government and economic reforms gained momentum. In order to accommodate the interest of the agitating people the Chogyal introduced certain legislative reforms on an experimental basis. The State Council was made representative in its composition by including six more members from the agricultural class but soon after attending few sessions these representatives realized the futility of their presence in the governmental machinery.[61] There were no proper rules regarding sharing of powei's between the Ministry and the Chogyal.

The resignation of the Ministry unleashed a fresh agitation which resulted in the appointment of an. Indian Officer as Dewan with effect from 11 August, 1949. The appointment of an Indian administrative officer, John Lal, as Dewan, was primarily to facilitate increasing association of the Sikkimese people with the government of India.[62] With this development the Chogyal and the. Dewan became the joint alithorities of political/administrative power of the State with the divided State Council in the middle to act as pawns in the hands of either of them. According to the Agreement of 1950, an Advisory Committee was formed to initiate measures for establishing Panchayati Raj Institutions, providing training in the art of popular government and holding elections for forming future State Council. A Tripartite Agreement between the Chogyal and two other major parties (Sikkim National Party & Sikkim State Congress) of Sikkim was reached in. May 1951 in which the "Parity" system as a basis for distribution of seats between the Bhutia-Lepcha and Nepalis in the State Council was evolved.[63] Under the Parity system the minority Bhutia-Lepcha and majority Nepalis were allotted equal seats in the State Council. The. Parity system denied separate representation to the Lepchas while seats allocated for the Nepalis were inadequate to the majority community. The Proclamation ofJanuary 1952 laid`down the mode of election to the Sikkim State Council[64] while the constitutional proclamation of. March 1953 provided rules of governance and powers of the State Council.[65]

On August 7,1953, the Chogyal promulgated a constitutional proclamation raising the members of the State Council to 17 in which six seats were reserved for the Bhutia-Lepcha and six seats for the Nepalis with a provision of five nominated members by the Chogyal. The provision of five nominated members was introduced with an intention to maintain domination of the Chogyal and his supporters in the legislative institution. Thus, the ethnic considerations continued to receive major attention at the political decision making process.

The proclamation of 1953 also postulated the powers and functions of the State Council and the Executive Council. A system of diarchy was established to share the powers between the Chogyal and the State Council. The Chogyal was in command of the Reserved Subjects which included the items like Ecclesiastical, External Affairs, State Enterprises, Home and Police, Finance. Land Revenue, Rationing, Establishments etc. The Dewan appointed by the Government of India was the administrator of the Reserved subject. The Transferred Subjects namely Education, Public Health, Excise, Press and Publicity, Transport, Bazars, Forests and Public Works etc. were managed by Executive Councillors chosen from among the elected members of the State Council. They held office during the pleasure of the Chogyal and were responsible to the latter. However, the Chogyal had the right to veto any decision made by the. Executive Council and to substitute his own decision thereof [66] 'Me Executive Council was composed of the Dewan, who was the ex-officio President of the State Council, and such other Councillors appointed by the Chogyal on parity basis from the elected members of the Council from time to time The formation of the government was peculiar in the sense that the members of the State Council were elected on party basis whereas formation of the Ministry was not Both the legislative and executive wings of the government were headed by the Devvan appointed by the government of India in consultation with the Chogyal. Moreover, the nominated mernbers could also be appointed as the member of the Executive Council. The number of Executive Councillors varied between two in 1953[67] to six in 1970[68] and 1973.[69] Iliere was also a practice of appointing two" or three:[7'] Deputy Executive Councilors since 1959.

In 1958 the members of the State Council was increased to 20 with a provision of separate seat reservation i.e. 6 seats for the Bhutia-Lepcha, 6 for the Nepalis, 1General, 1 Sangha and 6 'nominated by the Chogya1.[72] In order to contest the General seat, a person was required to have permanent habitation in Sikkim and such other qualifications necessaly for becoming the member of the State Council 13 In principle, the General seat was meant for any person having fixed habitation in Sikkim, but the Indians settled in Sikkim were not eligible to participate in the elections. Fixed habitation was presumed to mean habitation before February 1, 1958; and consequential termination of fixed habitation in the countiy of 060'1.[74] Thus, mere owning of house or making a living in Sikkim were not sufficient fora person for enjoying voting right and to contest elections.

In 1967 the total membership of the State Council was enhanced further to 24 of which 7 seats were reserved each for the Lepchas Bhutias and the Nepalis and one each for General, Tsong, Scheduled Caste and Sangha and :6 nominated seats. Those who possessed Sikkim Subjects Certificate and were of 30 years of age were eligible to be the member of the State Council. The normal tenure of the State Council was three years unless otherwise dissolved sooner by the Choyal. It was to meet at least twice a year in six months interval counting from the date of the last sittine though the Chogyal was empowered to summon special sessions at any time he deemed necessary. The Chogyal could also address the Council, send messages[77] and postpone election of the State Council. In the absence of the Presiding Officer, i.e. the Dewan who was the Principal Administrative Officer or. Sidlon, the Chogyal could appoint any other person to preside over the meetings. For example, the Chogyal appointed Rai Bahadur T.D.Densapa in the absence of Mr R.N. Haldipur in 1967, Mr. M.P. Pradhan in the absence of Mr. I.S.Chopra in 1972.[78]

Diarchy as the principle of division of powers between the Chogyal and the. State Council continued in 1967 also The Reserved Subjects, which contained all the important items of State interests, continued to remain tinder the prerogatives of the Chogyal. The State Council enjoyed powers with regards to the Transferred Subjects such as education, forest, agriculture, public works, health etc. subject to the assent ofthe Chogyal The State Council was restricted from holding discussion on, or, asking any question or dealing in any manner on matters involving the Maharaja or members of the ruling family, external relaticins, including relations with the Government of India, the appointment of the Dewan and the members of the judiciary and any matter pending before the court of law.[8o] The State Council could discuss and east vote regarding the annual budget, but if the budget estimate was rejected by it, the Chogyal enjoyed power to certify it and consider it sanctioned. The Council could not vote on certain expenditures made out of the State fund namely expenditure on civil list, including household expenditure of the Chogyal, pay and allowances of the. Dewan, members of judiciary and officers on deputation from the government of India.

In the executive field too the Chogyal exercised authority, through the Principal Administrative Officer who was also the President of both the State Council and the Executive Council. The executive councilors enjoyed limited power. Under 'financial power' the Executive Councilors and Deputy Executive Councilors could spend Rs. 500 and. Rs. 200 respectively which was later increased to Rs. 5000 and Rs. 2500 subject to approval of the Chogyal. Regarding legislation on the Transferred Subjects, the proposal to that extent was required to be passed unanimously in the Executive Council as far as possible; in case of difference among them or between the Councilors and the President, the matter was to be decided by the Chogyal. The Executive Councilors were to keep the Chogyal informed on all matters of importance through the Principal Administrative Officer. They were to submit their tour programmes to the Chogyal for approval and were eligible to sanction leaves, with or without pay, to classes 11 and III officials but regarding, gazetted and class 1 officers, the councilors were to refer the matter to the Establishment department.

The Dewan was the most powerful man in the administration of Sikkim. He was the President of both the State Council and Executive Council as well as the chief administrator of the Reserved Subjects. It was true that the power of the Chogyal was clipped neither by the constitution nor by legislature, but the administrative complexities emerging over a wide field of administration required the expertise and experience of the Dewar'. He was called Sidlon or the Principal Administrative Officer to whom other administrative officers like the Chief Secretary, Secretaries and Directors were subordinated.

The Councillors were far weaker as a decision maker or lawmaker than expected. During the debate on the Sikkim Subject Regulation in 1961, one of the members of the Executive Council compared their status with an office clerk.[81] The office of the Principal Administrative Officer was• abolished in 1972[82] and thereafter the Chogyal assumed the administration of the State by himself In December 1972, the Chogyal appointed an ad-hoc Couneil, called Special Council, composed of senior bureaucrats to deal with matters of urgent national importance, including the general elections, in his absence.[83] The Sikkim Government Gazette announced that "All decisions taken by the Special Council would be of interim in nature subject to the Chogyal's review and/ or ratification."[84]

In 1973 Council election the grudges over counting of votes between the two rival candidates Was fdlloWedi by a communal frenzy[85] and agitation by virtue of ethnie affiliatiOn of the candidates involved At the intervention of the Dewan the agitation : was, hdWever, put Off and a Tripartite Agreernent Was signed on May 8, 1973, between theiChogyal,i the government of India and the represefitatiVeS of the three pOlitical parties of Sikkitn.[86] 'Me Agreettent pOstulated for wider legislative and executive poWers.: lbr the elected representatives, an adult. franchise with one Man one vote principle as a basis of eleCtiOn to be cOndtitted· for the first:time under the Supervision of the. Election' Coinmissibn of India and constitution of the Assembly in four: years interval in place of the State:· Counci ComMenting on. the Agreement, 1,:B.Basnet:wrote',. 'The povyerS of the ChOgyal, even though he; fernains the 'Head Of the State', have been drastically redtteed: The preponderant ascendancy of the Bhutias in every field has been rudelY shaken: The Nepalese people of Sikkith, who had risen in revolt,. have been assured of a fairer deal. The govermnent. of India has gained emliThously. :rhel Indian› hold oiler Sikkim has becoMe'firiner:The. internal administration:of Sikkim haS; to all intents. and purpose,: taken over by India".[87] The 'Tripartite: Agreement eases transformation of a: Protectorate State; as mentioned in 1950:Treaty; into an AssOciated State:of India."

In the following Year, i.e. Febrtiat•,Y 1974, the Proclamation of Representation; Of Sikkim StibjectS Act, 1974 was issued enhancing the numerical strength of the Assembly to 32 out Of. which 15 seats were reserved for the Lepcha-Bhutia, 15 for the Nepalis, I for the Seheduled Caste and I. for the Sangha.1 he seats reserved for the TSOngs cOmmunity.was unfortunately done aWay. with The Proclamation alSo Stipulated 25 years as a qualifying age and the Sikkim: Stibiect Certificate mandatory for the Members of the AsSembly.. In April 1974 the clectio4 to theAssembly:Was held under the new PrOCIamation.l'he Sikkim National CongreSs Swept the poll by winning 31 seatS. The Sangha seat went in favour of the NatiOnal Party. The Chogyal addressed the·rieW. Assembly on May 10;: 1974. On May 11, the. AsseMbly adopted' resolutions reaffirming the principles, purposes and provisions of the 8th May Agreement and requesting the government of India to take immediate steps for Sikkim's participation in the political and economic institution of India.[89] In another resolution, the Assembly resolved to request the government of India to depute a constitutional expert to give a legal and constitutional framework to the objectives of its resolutions.[90]

The resolutions of the State Assembly for Sikkim's participation in the political institution of a separate country of India and framing of a new constitution for Sikkim by India indicate Assembly's intention for merger. Accordingly, at the instance of the Chogyal, the government of India deputed G.R.Rajagopal, former Secretary in the Ministry of Law, Government of India, to prepare a draft constitution for Sikkim, called Sikkim Bill. The draft constitution which was ready by June 20, 1974, provided for a unique division of powers intending to maintain India's legitimate control over the affairs of Sikkim. Under the proposed Sikkim Bill the Chief Executive, who was the appointee of the government of India, was the chief administrative head in Sikkim with the responsibility to ensure total compliance with any decision taken or orders or directions issued by the government of India in relation to Sikkim [91]

The Assembly adopted the draft constitution unanimously but the Chogyal was constrained to accept the status inferior to that of the Chief Executive in a country of his own. He also opposed the Sikkim Assembly's request for participation in India's political and eOonomic institutions. The Chogyal refused to give his assent to the Bill and even contradicted the statement that he had ever agreed to accept the draft constitution earlier.[92] He was of the opinion that "the draft constitution violated the Endo-Sikkim Treaty of 1950 under which Sikkim had its separate identity and international personage as a protectorate of India.[93] In his communication to the government of India, the Chogyal firmly maintained that Sikkim had never been a part of India geographically, ethnically or rauially.`3`The Chogyal contended that three basic principles, which he considered important should be included in the proposed Sikkim Bill of 1974 namely (a) establishment of a fully responsible democratic government; (b) safeguarding legitimate rights and responsibilities of the government of India; and (c) the preservation of separate identity and internal autonomy of Sikkim.[95] 'fhe Chogyal feared that the Chief. Executive who being the nominee of the Government of India and responsible to it could not be impartial in his functioning whenever the interests of the two countries were involved. Though genuine the concerns had been, a spate of statements published by him in foreign press embarrassing India perhaps crippled him in winning favour of the government of India to come to terms.

The conservative pro-Chogyal elements like the. Sikkim National Party and the association of the Lamas, called Denzong Lhade Tsogpa, had lost much of their organizational strength since the end of 1960s. The growing demand for democracy and popular government during this time, made them apprehensive of the fate of the Chogyal and the status of Sikkim as a Buddhist state. Some prominent members of the Denzong Lhade Tsogpa tried to influence the people on the need for protecting the status of Sikkim. They also appealed to the Buddhist Association of Calcutta and other parts of India for using their influence on India for protecting the identity of Sikkim.% Some members of the Sikkim National Party too formed an ad-hoc committee and requested the constitutional expert for introducing safeguard measures in the interest of the Bhutia and Lepcha communities in, the proposed constitution. They also urged to carry out census of the Bhutia-Lepcha population in order to counter the false propaganda that their number in Sikkim was only a few thousand, demanded continuation of the Parity formula' as a basis for seat distribution in the Assembly, safeguards against the influx of the Nepalis and others from outside Sikkim, preservation of distinct identity of Sikkim and the Bhutia-Lepcha communities etc.[97]

Kazi Lliendup Dorjee was relentless in his effort for seeking. Chogyal's approval to the Sikkim Bill, 1974. On. June 28, 1974, the Assembly endorsed the Bill for the second time and issued a 48-hour ultimatum to the. Chogyal for his assent to the Bill. Again on June 30, 1974 he urged the Chogyal to come to reason and respond to the 48-hour ultimatum for the promulgation of the. Sikkim Government Bill, 1974".[98] On July I, 1974, the Chogyal returned to Gangtok from Delhi and finally agreed to give his assent to the Bill. 'The Assembly was reconvened on 3 July but the Chogyal did not attend the emergency session. His message was read out by the Chief Executive which stated that "the clause 30 of the Bill, instead of safeguarding Sikkim's separate identity under the Treaty of 1950, would badly affect it".[99] Under Chapter VI, article 30 of the Sikkim Bill 1974 states, "For speedy development of Sikkim the social, economic and political fields the Government of Sikkim may (a) request the Government of India to include the planned development of Sikkim within the ambit of the Planning for the economic and social development of India and to appropriately associate officials from Sikkim in such work; (b) request the Government of India to provide facilities for students from Sikkim in institutions for higher learning and for the employment of people from Sikkim in the public services of India (including All India Services), at par with those available to citizens of India; and (c) seek participation and representation for the people of Sikkim in the political institutions of India. On July 4, 1974, the Chogyal gave his assent to the original Sikkim Bill, i.e without modifying the relevant clause of the Sikkim Bill over which he had reservations.

The Government of Sikkim Act, 1974 was finally passed upholding the legal status of Assembly formed as a result of the elections held in April 1974, as the first Assembly duly constituted under this Act. Later, the cabinet made two formal requests to the government of India to provide representation for the people of Sikkim in Indian Parliament and to merge Sikkim with India.

After detailed and careful study of the request the Union Cabinet on August, 29, 1974, took a crucial decision to accord Sikkim a status of an "Associated States" of. India. Accordingly the Constitution (Thirty-fifth Amendment) Act 1974 was: passed in the Indian Parliament on September 3, 1974, to provide legal constitutional framework to Sikkim as an "Associated State" of

India by inserting article 2A and X Schedule in the Constitution. In another'development the Sikkim Assembly on April 10, 1975, passed a resolution abolishing the institution of the Chogyal and declaring Sikkim as a' constituent part of India. A referendum was conducted on April 14, 1975, and the people's verdict went in fav'our of the Assembly's resolution for merger. fact the political situation was such that thee people had to choose between the Chogyal and Kazi Lhendup Dorji Khangsarpa, the symbols representing monarchy and democracy respectively. The mandate favouring Kazi was meant for the institutionalization of dentocracy in Sikkim. The government of India was apprised personally by the Chief Minister, Kazi L.D. Khangsarpa, about the verdict of the referendum on April 16 & *17,* 1975 and urged for taking necessary action. The Lok Sabha, accordingly, passed the Constitution (Thirty-sixth Amendment) Bill on April 23, 1975, to include Sikkiiri as the 22nd State of the Indian Union. The Rajya Sabha passed the Bill on April 26. On May 16, 1975, President Fakhruddin Ali Ahmed gave his assent to the Thirty-sixth Constitutional Amendment Bill and with it Sikkim became the twenty-second state of India. Article 371F was inserted in the constitution of India to provide and preserve political, social and cultural distinctiveness of Sikkim. The President appointed Mr.B.B.Lal, formerly the Chief Executive of Sikkim, as the first Govemor of Sikkim who then administered the oath of office to the first Chief Minister, Kazi Lhendup Dorjee Khangsarpa, and to his four other cabinet colleagues.

Thus, in the post-merger scenario the executive authority vvas vested in the Governor who was an'appointee of the President of India. The Chief Minister along with the. Council of Minister became the real ruler of the State Government. The State Secretariat headed by the Chief Secretary and other Secretaries taken from the Indian Administrative Service, was established. All the four districts were put under the District Collectors drawn frorn the Indian. Administrative Service. The office of the Development Commissioner continued with an objective to push through development projects and planning in close collaboration with the heads of several other departments.

The uniform proceduiv in politico-administrative structure, including the system of election, was lacking in Sikkim since the beginning. Earlier, the franchise system was discriminatory in nature. By amending the Representation of the People Act, 1950 the erstwhile communal voting system was removed but by reserving seats in the Assembly on ethnic ground it led to perpetual ethnic division, competition and confrontation among various communities. The political parties though secular in constitution. could not prevent themselves from becoming the party addressing and representing community interests. Even though they fought elections on party basis, their share in the government was based heavily on ethnic consideration.[100] Parity formula was continued as the principal basis for distribution of seats in the Assembly between the Bhutia-Lepcha and Nepali population, including old rules favouring the erstwhile ruling sections of the Sikkirnese population. The office of the Chogyal was abolished but much of the schemes designed by him continued, including his cherished idea that the government should be carried on equally by the two major communities-the Bhutia-Lepcha and the Nepalis respectively) °I irrespective of the fact that the constitution of India justifies rule of the majority.

Economy of Sikkim:

Tike other Himalayan states the economy of Sikkim has been basically agrarian in·character based on terrace farming system. The Bhutias, W110 were mainly traders, and the Lepchas who made poor farmers, the agricultural economy is the contribution of industrious Nepalis who by virtue of historical antecedents had acquired immense knowledge on terrace'farming. The topography of the state of Sikkim, however, is such that even in 1991 hardly 16 per cent of the total land was put under operational holding. As such control of agricultural land has been the principal means to wealth, stability and power and, thus, a prime factor in determining social relationship.

Traditionally, the Chogyal, including members of the royal family, Was the sole owner of lands and, obviously, was not a primary source of State revenue system. Historically speaking, during 1740's Rabden Sharpa, a Tibetan monk who accompanied Phuntsog Namgyal 11 from Tibet and served as regent to the young king for five years, introduced a system of crude form of assessment and collection of revenue, called Zolung, to be collected in kinds (grain and wine) or cash although the actual rate of duty on trade is unknown. The ryot was to pay a basketful of rice and a rupee annually during the normal time and during extraordinary situation, like war, the payment was to be as much as possible.[102] The economy was possibly a self-sufficient agricultural system with little surplus though detail information about the state of economy is not available. The notion that there. was limited agricultural surplus can be deduced from the fact that Sikkim was not a prosperous kingdom. The condition of the , peasantry during this period cannot be accurately ascertained. However, the incidents of revolt by peasants at Rabdentse and Pemayangtse during the late 18th century are indicative of presence of peasant's discontent.

A new system of assessment and collection of revenue was introduced in 1889 by John Claude White, the first political officer of Sikkim with an objective to enhance the revenue of the government. He along with Phodong Lama and Khangsa Dewan facilitated some Nepalis of Darjeeling, especially Laximidas Pradhan and his uncle Keshab Narayan Pradhan, to get the thikadarship for cultivation and mining, as the Bhutias were averse to digging earth for their religious belief. By 1913 the family members of Laximidas Pradhan could be found all over Sikkim. Some important members of Laximidas's family were Rai Saheb Lambodar Pradhan, Rai Saheb Laximi Naryan Pradhan, Suriaman Pradhan, Dalbahadur Pradhan, Ratnabahadur Pradhan, Sherbahadur Pradhan.[103] They also operated a number of copper mines like Tuk Khani near Turuk in South Sikkim, Rinchi Khani in Rinchingpong in West Sikkim, Bhotang Khani near Rangpoo in East Sikkim, Pachey Khani near Rhenock in East Sikkim and Rathok Khani in Manthang in South Sikkim.'°4 The family is also credited for minting coins in Sikkim.

By the beginning of the twentieth century Sikkim witnessed a steady change in the land holding pattern and collection of revenue. Out of a total of 104 estates in Sikkim 15 estates were managed by the Maharaja as Private Estate and were divided into 62 revenue blocks, Monasteries had 5 Estates consisting of 38 revenue blocks, 13 estates were under Managers appointed on commission by the Durbar and the rest 71 estates were with the Kazis and Thikadars.[105] Altogether there were 71 landlords, of whom 13 were Lamas, 21 were Kazis and 37 Thikadars.[106] Within their territorial jurisdiction the landlords enjoyed certain degree of civil and administrative power, including magisterial power.

The land at the block level was further distributed among some people called Bustiwallas and Mandals who became the first intermediaries between the Kazis and ryots. The second type of intermediaries was the Kazis and Thikadars between the Mandals and Bustiwallas, and the Chogyal. The difference between the Mandals and Bustiwallas depended on the area of land they held. A Bustiwal could hold 20 acres of land whereas 30 acres was fixed for the Mandals.[107] They, however, did not usually cultivate the land by themselves but further leased out to tenants, known variously as Adhiadars, Kootidars, Chakhureys and Pakhureys, under certain conditions. The right of the Bustiwallas was hereditary and transferable.[108] The Kazis and Thikadars were to assess the land revenue to be paid by the tenants and the Bustiwal las and Mandals were responsible for collection of revenue from the tenant fixed at the time of commencement of lease and deposition to the Kazis and Thikadars who in their turn paid a fixed amount to the State treasury.[109] Tenants like Chakhurey and Pakhurey were found in Monastery Estates. Besides tilling the land, one member of the tenant was to render compulsory labour daily in the households of individual lama or the monastery.

From the management point of view, monastery estates were grouped under two types - Private Estate like Rumtek and Phodong, and Udor Tsosum like Pemiongtse, Relang, Tashiding and Phensang. The revenues collected through the block mandals was to be deposited in the monastery concerned to be used for the maintenance of gompas and religious performances in the monasteries. The mandals would not get commission for their services but were exempted from payment of land revenue for the land they held as their personal holdings.[11o] The monasteries under Udor Tsosum also collected rents of various types directly through the respective block mandals and maintained settlement record.

Regarding the Private Estates of the Maharaja, his own agency collected revenue from 18 blocks while the revenues of the remaining'44 blocks was to be collected by the government through respective district officers and •deposited in the Private Estate account after deducting 7 per cent Mandals' commission and 10 per cent supervision charges. However, on cardamom khazanas the 7 per cent mandals' commission was not to be deducted.[111] At present the sales tax from the traders located within Private Estates are collected by the department of Income tax and Sales Tax, government of Sikkim, to be refunded to the Private Estate after deducting 10 per cent as supervision charges.

The lessesse landlord system introduced by J.C.White proved so successful that in 1889 land revenue constituted as high as 67 per cent of the total revenue of Sikkim [112] The growth in economy led to competition and social confrontation, and in 1897 restriction on transfer of Bhutia-Lepcha land to others, including the Nepalis, was imposed. In 1917 the land prohibition law was redefined as Revenue Order No. 1. Apart from this, inequality regarding payment of revenue also prevailed. For the same amount of land the Bhutias and Lepchas used to pay less than the Nepalis. The rate of Ilouse Tax between the Bhutia-Lepcha and Nepali subjects was also unequal, i.e. Nepalis used to pay Rs. 6 while it was Rs. 2 for the. Bhutia-Lepcha. The new revenue policy benefited the Kazis and Thikadars immensely but the condition of the tenants deteriorated further due to the presence of intermediaries and their extortionist behavior, besides insecurity of tenure. Correction measure was introduced in 1925 by making the provision of collection of revenues directly by the collectors but its effect on the condition of the tenant was marginal. An economic reform was urgently needed. In 1949. after the democratic movement for greater civil rights, the lessee system was abolished without disturbing the Private Estates and the Estates of the Morutsteries.

'he best view of the socio-economic conditions of the people of Sikkim under the feudalistic regime of the Chogyal can be found by referring to the document entitled 'A Few Facts About Sikkim State' written by Tashi Tshering in 1947. The document reads, "The landlords are vested with magisterial powers in both civil and criminal matters. They are also empowered to register docurnents for the sale or transfer of landed properties. There are no effective checks on these powers and the landlords are free to abuse them for their own gains. The more fine a landlord can impose, the larger his share of spoils, for he receives one-half of the collection as his fees and the other half goes to the State. A grabbing landlord has no difficulty in dispossessing an uncompromising ryot of his cherished possession, be it a paddy field or a herd of cattle. Most of the landlords live away from the estates and their powers are exercised by ignorant and rapacious underlings who have no scruples about filling their own pockets besides extracting as much as they can for their masters."

The document then highlights the form of oppression under forced labour (Jharlangi), which was rampant in Sikkim. "There are various forms of forced labour to which the ryots are subjected. About twenty years ago, a notification was said to have been issued by the State, based on International Conventions announcing the abolition of forced labour. This notification was never explained to the ryots and the practice was never stopped, let alone abolished. It is carried on to this day ....Forced labour with minimum, often without any compensation, is usually exacted by the landlords when cultivating their extensive, mostly ill-gotten, private fields and when harvesting their crops...such exactions of late have become manifold on account of the ever—increasing farming and gardening interests of the landlords, which allow the roots scarcely any time to attend to their on iffairs. Most of the influential landlords....live in Gangtok. Their estates may be two or three days journey away. From there the ryots have to come all the way to Gangtok and serve their landlords in turn in various menial capacities. The ryots get no wages or compensations for such services, and they are lucky if they escape cruelties."

Those landlords whose estates were in and around Gangtok " the forced labour is often requisitioned on behalf of the State for carrying loads across the passes (over 15000 feet) into Tibetan territory......What he will earn as wages under the prescribed rates for forced labour, would barely suffice to buy his meager meal for the journey to and from. The landlord bleeds him to the limit and sends his own private pack mules to carry the loads, for which he is doubly recompensed. A greedy landlord often seizes upon his chance of making further easy money and calls for double the number of men required."

This state-requisitioned forced labour was commonly known as "Kalo Bhari" (black loads) in Sikkim. The document continues, "Kalo Bhari was the name given to a special consignment compactly packed in black tarpaulin, which gave the name. Huge quantities of these loads were transported overland to China via Tibet during the later part of the war (World War II). Such was the demand for transport for this purpose that the wages offered reached unprecedented heights.

The cupidity of the landlords rose in unison and they stooped to swindle. They falsely requisitioned 'force labour on the authority of the State' to carry these loads. A very large number of these loads belonged to private concerns..... The landlords charged the private concerns the highest rates, paid the ryots the prescribed rates, and pocketed the rest....Such blatant deception could not, however, remain concealed for long. When they learnt about it, the victims of the swindle approached the powers- that-be for redress.

As the culprits were all 'high born' Kazis, the matter was hushed up, and the aggrieved ryots were sent away with the facile advice to 'let bygones be bygones and to forgive and forget." The publication of the article incited peasants' resent-ment which resulted in the peasants' movement of 1949 for economic reforms.

After merger, the Lhendup Dorjee Government constituted a Committee under the Chairmanship of Mr. N.B.Khatiwada to look into the problems of land revenue and to recommend measures for land reform in Sikkim. Among others, the Committee in its report recommended for fair rent and heritable rights of tenancy, non-eviction of tenants and allocation of at least 3.5 acres of land under unavoidable circumstances, fixation of upper ceiling at 16 acres on agricultural holdings, maintenance of land records of Private Estates by the government and abolition of Private Estates and the Monastery Estates.

The government responded by enacting the Sikkim Agricultural Land Ceiling and Reform Act, 1977. But contrary to the Khatiwada Committee recommendation the Act of 1977 came out with some striking differences. The Act did not abolish the Monastery Estates but classified the monasteries into 'Group A' Schedule and 'Group B' Schedule and fixed the ceilings as 60 acres and 25 acres respectively. Similarly, for an adult unmarried person or only surviving member of a family the ceiling was six and a half acres while a family with a minimum of five members was to have twelve and a half acres as the upper ceiling. An addition of two acres was allowed for each person in excess of five but not to exceed twenty and a half acres in aggregate.

The Land Reform Act, 1977 had many loopholes. The ceiling was applicable only on agricultural holdings. And since the entire land records of the Estates were in the hands of Private Estates Organization manipulation for showing agricultural land as non-agricultural one was very much possible. Moreover, there were problems regarding distribution of vested land and land confiscated by the government in excess of ceiling due to the existence of Revenue Order No. 1 of 1917 which prohibited alienation of land to other communities other than the Bhutias and Lepchas.[113] In 1989 two separate Bills, namely the Sikkim Alienation of Land (Regulation) Bill, 1989 and the Sikkim Transfer of Land (Regulation) Bill, 1989 were passed by the State Legislature with an objective to restrict alienation of land by the members of Bhutia and Lepcha communities of Sikkimese origin to others and also by Sikkimese in favour of non-Sikkimese. However, the Governor, Shri S.K. Bhatnagar, reserved both the Bills for further consultation with the President of India. It is to be noted here that the regulation in question, i.e. Revenue Order No.1, is applicable even in cases that could conceivably be in the larger interest of the State in terms of providing employment opportunities. At present the tribal land can be obtained on lease after obtaining permission from the State government or the State can take over a tribal land by paying compensation.

According to the report published by the Department of Land Revenue, the percentage of land owned by the Nepalis in 1983 was 59 per cent of cultivable land while the land shared by the Bhutias and Lepchas in the same year was 20 per cent each.[114] It is important to mention here that though the Nepalis own the largest amount of cultivable land, the Bhutias have the highest amount of excess land. Thus the detection of excess land and its acquisition is likely to escalate tension with political overtones.[115]

Table 2.1: Communitywise Distribution of Land in Sikkim – 1976-83 (Area in Hectares)

Communities	Total Paddy field (Area %)	Total Dry land (Area %)	Wasteland (Area %)	Cardamom (Area %)	Total Cultivable land (Area %)
Bhutia	21.12.	16.13	24.18	27.05	20.32
Lepcha	14.97	--	17.53	32.72	20.38
Nepali	57.19	64.95	62.00	22.37	58.66

Source: Land Record Section, Department of Land Revenue, Govt. of Sikkim, Gangtok.

The distribution of operational land holding in Sikkim reflects unequal distribution pattern. The marginal landholders, who form the lowest type of landholders and represent about 50 percent of landholdings, possessed 10.3 percent of the total operational land area in 1990-91. Their concentration was highest in the East district, both in terms of number of holdings (56 per cent) and area (12.8 per cent). In comparison to this, farmers with large holdings, i.e. above 10 hectares, were about 2.3 percent of the landholdings, but owned 20.2 percent of the operational area. The North district had the highest number of large farmers who, with 5 per cent of the operational holdings, owned over 30 percent of the operated land in the district. Except in the East district, land holdings and operated area were more or less evenly distributed among the small and semi-medium farmers.

Table 2.2: District-wise and Size/Class-wise Distribution of Landholdings - 1991

Category	North Holdings		East Holdings		South Holdings		West Holdings	
	No. %	Area %	No. %	Area %	No. %	Area %	No. %	Area %
Marginal	49.0	8.5	56.0	12.8	44.3	9.7	46.0	10
Small	10.0	5.1	22.0	22.0	25.0	18.5	21.0	17
Semi Medium	18.0	20.0	14.0	23.0	18.0	24.0	20.0	28
Medium	17.0	36.0	6.4	23,0	10.0	26.0	11.2	31
Large	5.3	30.0	1.3	17.0	3.0	22.0	2.1	14
Total in Hectares.	4,942	14,407	19,666	32,936	12,548	28,575	13,971	31,088

Source: Sikkim Human Development Report, 2001, Govt. of Sikkim Publication.

Inequality regarding land distribution also prevailed among the Scheduled Caste farmers. The large farmers, who consisted of less than 1 per cent (0.4 per cent) of the total Scheduled Caste farmers, possessed nearly 10 per cent of the operational area. The marginal farmers, on the other, who constituted of 70 per cent of Scheduled Castes farmers, operated 27.2 per cent of the operated area. The situation among the small farmers, i.e. 19 per cent, was quite encouraging with almost 28 per cent of the operated area.

Among the Scheduled Tribe farmers, the distribution of land was more or less in equilibrium. The percentage of the marginal farmers among the Scheduled Tribes was relatively low and the Medium and Semi-Medium farmers together held more than 35 per cent of the operated holdings and over 57 per cent of the operated land. But, in this case too, the large farmers, who consisted of less than 5 per cent, held over 28 per cent of the land. This is indicative of the fact that the land reform measures have been largely ineffective and the traditional pattern of land holding is still persisting.

Table 2.3: Land Distribution within the SC & ST Population (1991)

Category of Holdings	Scheduled Castes		Share in		Scheduled Tribes		Share in	
	No.	Area Hect.	No.	Area Hect.	No.	Area Hect.	No.	Area Hect.
Marginal	1366	547	70.0	27.2	7073	3425	42.3	7.2
Small	370	558	19.0	27.7	2901	4384	17.4	9.2
Semi Medium	164	468	8.4	23.3	3421	10497	20.5	22.0
Medium	43	247	2.2	12.3	2487	15962	14.9	33.5
Large	7	191	0.4	9.5	827	13362	4.9	28.1
All	1950	2011	100	100	16709	47630	100	100

Source: Sikkim Human Development Report, 2001, Govt. of Sikkim Publication.

Uncertain land tenure rights, insignificant public investment and over-dependence on obsolete technologies characterized the agriculture sector in pre-merger period. However, different land reform measures, agricultural credit and marketing, and provisions of inputs like better quality seeds, fertilizers, and better irrigation along with extensive plan outlay have induced a new vigour in the sphere of agriculture. From subsistence farming, agriculture now has become an economically viable venture. The total food grain production in the State has increased from nearly 62,000 tonnes in 1980-81 to 103,000 tonnes in 1997-98 to nearly 111,000 tonnes in 1999-2000.[116] However, in 2000-01 the food grain production remained more or less unchanged at 111,000 tonnes.

Developments in the field of horticulture, floriculture, animal husbandry, fisheries etc. are also worth mentioning. Horticulture production includes fruits vegetables, potatoes, other tubers, cardamom, ginger and turmeric. By and large this sector is making a steady progress. In 1995-96 the total horticulture production was 92,700 tonnes which during the Ninth Plan (1997-2002) has risen to 1, 31,000 tonnes.[117] The South district reigns number one position in terms of horticulture production. Sikkim also has great variety of flowers. Efforts are being made in recent past to augment quality production of cut flowers and bulbs along with the infrastructural facilities. A model floriculture garden has been set up at Namchi and a 'cymbodium' orchid centers at Pakyong and Assam Lingzay.

Animal husbandry as a traditional occupation forms an integral part of the household economy of the State. Almost every family earns income through rearing of some livestock. It is estimated that about 50 per cent of Sikkim's total area is used for livestock farming. In the last 20 years the livestock products has risen but has not been able to meet the local demands. Fish production has remained stagnant at 140 tonnes since1997 though the revenue earned has increased from 0.48 lakhs in 1997-98 to 0.76 in 1999-2000.

The first ever industrial development planning under the Seven Year Development Plan was initiated in 1954 as a result of the understanding reached between the Prime Minister Nehru and the Chogyal. For providing stability to rural economy, the cottage industry was given first priority. The Second Five Year Plan, however, stressed emphasis on medium scale industries like tea industry. These industries were given subsidy up to 15 per cent of the total investment. The upper limit of the grant was fixed at Rs. 5 lakhs. Apart from this subsidy on transport, on interest, on power, pre-operative expenses and facilities for getting machines on hire purchases were also provided. The Directorate of Industries and Industrial Training Institute were set up in 1976 to monitor trend of progress and provided adequate training for industrial purposes. In the following year (1977) a financial institution, called Sikkim Industrial Development and Investment Corporation (SIDICO) was established with two-pronged objectives- a) to work as a composite developmental corporation and b) to provide financial assistance to small and medium scale industries. It provides loan up to Rs. 90 lakhs for individual units apart from granting loan for expansion, diversification and modernization. The loans are sanctioned for: (a) Industrial activity- manufacturing, processing or preservation of goods; b) Hotels and Restaurants; c)Tourism and related activities; d) Transportation of passengers and goods; e) Service sector- like computer and software development; (f) Diagnostic Centre, Nursing Home, Medical Equipments, Pathological, Clinical laboratories, Health Care Center etc; (g) Assembling, Repairing or Packing any articles with the aid of machine or power; (h) Such other activities which may be made eligible by IDBI/SIDBI from time to time.[118]

Besides, the Institution also provides loans up to 50 thousand to the artisans and craftsman, upto 10 lakhs for women, upto 15 lakhs for ex-servicemen, widows of ex-servicemen and disabled persons, upto 10 lakhs with 1 per cent service charge for people having technical skill and to purchase vehicles to ply as taxis. The interest rate is fixed at 12 per cent, 13.5 per cent and 19 per cent depending upon the amount of money loaned.[119] Loans are also granted by ST/SC/OBC Development Corporation Ltd., established in 1996, for setting up Poultry Farming, Piggery etc. upto the limit of Rs. 30 lakhs.

Table 2.4: Registered Small Scale Industries / Tiny Units in Sikkim (1999)

Period	East	North	South	West	SSI/Tiny Units Total
1975/76 - 79/80	7	X	2	1	10
1980/81 - 84/85	7	X	4	2	13
1985/86 - 89/90	56	1	14	9	80
1990/91 - 94/95	84	2	18	11	115
1995/96 - 98/99	60	X	13	6	79

Source: Government of Sikkim, Department of Industry, Gangtok.

Under the Sixth Five Year Plan emphasis was given to the Small Scale Industries and Cottage Industries. Accordingly, District Industrial Centers were set up at Jorethang and Gangtok to provide information and guidance and to work as a facilitator.[120] In 1983 Sikkim Industrial Licensing Act was promulgated for regulating a systematic development of Industries. This Act no longer exists today.

The industry sector in Sikkim is still at a nascent stage. According to 1992 data the industry contributed a negligible one percent towards employment generation. Most importantly many small-scale industries are going sick. In recent study of PSU performance in Sikkim, the Indian Institute of Cost and Management Studies and Research (INDSEARCH) recommended for the closure of four public sector units like Sikkim Mining Corporation, Sikkim Industrial Development and Investment Corporation Ltd., State Bank of Sikkim and Sikkim Nationalized Transport.[121] Sikkim flour mills and the Chandmari Workshop are also facing loses. However, among the consumer enterprises Sikkim Jewels Ltd. and Sikkim Time Corporation are profit-making units.

The factors inhibiting industrial development have been physical remoteness, difficult terrain, lack of raw materials and markets, and high transport and marketing cost. Under the New Industrial Policy, 2007 the government of Sikkim has given highest priority for setting up eco-friendly industries particularly agro-horticulture and floriculture, animal husbandry and dairy products, minor forest based products, handlooms and handicrafts, precision oriented high value low volume products, information technology, hydropower, tea, health, education and tourism.[122]

In view of the pristine panoramic surroundings, diverse culture and religious practices of the people, the tourism industry has been considered having a huge potential to expand availing income generation opportunities not only for those who are directly engaged but also to those who are engaged in allied sectors like hoteliers, transporters, retailers and those associated with telecommunications.

Every year the visitors to Sikkim are increasing. For instance, in 1997 about 120821 domestic and 8812 foreign tourists visited Sikkim. In 1998 it was 120103 domestic and 8985 foreign; in 1999 the number was 135273 and 9821 respectively. In 2000 there was a slight increase in domestic tourists (140151) but the number of foreign tourists had fallen (i.e. 8794) as compared to preceding year. This trend continued in 2001 also (i.e. 144278 domestic and 7757 foreign). In 2002, about 136506 domestic and 8539 foreign tourists visited the state as compared to 133247 domestic and 6947 foreign in 2003. The trend is marked by constant ups and downs but as compared to pre-1994-95 era the flow of tourists is increasing. In 2009 the domestic tourists crossed five lakh mark.

Similarly, a steady progress has been seen in the field of tea production, herbal medicine and fruit processing. A better farming method, modern technology, improved transportation and distribution would prove blessing to these sectors. The Temi Tea Estate has already become a household name in many a house in India and abroad. The climate is suitable for tea cultivation and the experience of the Sang-Martam area needs to be utilized for future expansion of the tea industry. Production of drugs and herbal medicine may prove equally effective and a viable economic activity to venture. The reoperationalization of the fruit-processing unit at Singtam and establishment of a new unit at Ravangla have greatly benefited the local farmers. Under the new industrial policy (2007), the sectors like floriculture and horticulture are expected to do well.

The work opportunities in Sikkim seem to be precarious. According to the census data between 1981 and 1991 the absolute number of workers have increased from 153,000 to 169,000 while the percentage of total workers to the total population have decreased from 48.4 to 41.7 which is among the highest level of decline in India.[122] The income distribution, at the same time, is also very much skewed. Despite high levels of per capita income, the proportion of population living below the poverty line has gone up from 36 per cent in 1987-88 to 41 per cent in 1993-94. In the same year about 8 per cent of the urban people and 45 per cent of the rural population were living below poverty line.[123] The benefits of excellent growth rate have not percolated down to the people at the lower rungs of the economic ladder.

The Marwaries and other trading families from the plains control the major urban commercial establishments. According to 2003-05 reports on contractors in the department of Energy and Power about 79.26 per cent of the contracts were done by the north Indian families. Being a consumer state, the government depends on import from outside creating minimal income generation and employment opportunities within apart from a particular problem of beneficiaries parking funds outside the State. In terms of annual bank deposits and credit amount in Sikkim one can have a fairly good idea about the quantity of money that the beneficiaries are parking outside. For example, in 2002 the aggregate bank deposits show Rs. 808 crores and the credit amount was Rs. 129 crores.

Table No. 2.5: Community/Caste-wise total numbers of employees - 2002

Community/ Caste	Regular	Work-Charged	Ad-hoc	Muster Roll	Others/P SU	Total
Bahun	2578	166	20	771	115	3650
Bhujel	63	8	1	50	7	129
Bhutia	4275	229	40	1070	361	5975
Chettri	2674	286	18	1484	218	4680
Damai	242	28	3	180	11	464
Gurung	1385	107	18	895	190	2595
Jogi	5	2	-	7	-	14
Kami	761	95	3	479	66	1404
Lepcha	1902	72	19	789	171	2953
Majhi	7	-	-	9	3	19
Mangar	436	22	3	274	41	776
Pradhan	1394	127	8	428	54	2011
Rai	2629	172	20	1229	346	4396
Sarki	17	2	-	27	3	49
Sherpa	610	33	4	435	76	1158
Subba (Limboo)	1328	63	12	827	230	2460
Sunuwar	82	16	-	88	100	286
Tamang	1350	78	14	705	105	2252
Thami	5	-	-	2	-	7
Others	1936	72	15	240	-	1723
Total	23139	1578	198	9989	2097	37001

Source: Sikkim – A Statistical Profile-2004-05, Government of Sikkim.

It shows that about Rs. 679 crores have been siphoned out of the state during this period. Thus, the public sector has been the propelling force as far as employment is concerned. In per capita terms, Sikkim has the highest public sector employment in the country. There are over 11,000 employees on the muster roll in various government offices.[124] Almost half of the total government expenditure gets exhausted on wages and salaries (including pensions) and interest payments. To reduce the burden, the Government of Sikkim, under the new economic policy, has issued directives to private investors to provide compulsory employment to local candidates in their establishments, besides creating employment opportunities through effective management of State resources like tourism and hydro electricity.

Demographic Profile:

Sikkim's strategic geographical position has been the major determining factor in the demographic composition. Its territorial contiguity with four international borders viz. Tibet, Nepal, Bhutan and India along with intermittent military expeditions from different directions in the past have brought about a kind of cultural and demographic upheaval upon which the present day Sikkim, as a pluri-cultural society, is embedded. In the absence of documentary evidences it is difficult to come to a conclusion about the original inhabitants of Sikkim but it is generally acknowledged that Lepchas and some other tribes which now constitute Nepalis were among the early inhabitants of the State. At present Lepchas, Bhutias and Nepalis form the three major communities of Sikkim. The socio-cultural interactions among the three communities have rendered a kind of a "Salad Bowl" culture, yet maintenance of separate identity and social distinctiveness have remained groups' priority.

During the Chogyals' rule the maintenance of the Bhutia domination, whether cultural or political, was emphasized. The Bhutia rulers had always seen to it that no other community rise to such formidable a position as to pose a threat to their power. They had been able to subjugate the Lepchas quite conveniently through the myth of blood brotherhood, religious conversion, matrimonial alliances and appointment of some prominent Lepcha figures to formal governmental capacities. The Mangars were driven away to the south and the west, and Limboos and other Kirati tribes had been contained to a significant extent. The establishment of the British predominance, effectively from 1817, had been the beginning of erosion of Bhutia hegemony and also the beginning of settlement by other Nepalis. There were incidents of clashes between the rulers of Sikkim and the British India mainly due to the involvement of Tibetan interest over Sikkim, but the settlement process continued unabated notwithstanding the use of repressive and regulative measures by the ruling elites. They sought to counter-balance the increasing Nepali settlers by encouraging settlement of the Tibetans and Bhutanese in Sikkim.

Table 2.6: Community-wise Distribution of Population of Sikkim – 1891.

Caste/Communities	Males	Females	Children	Total
Lepcha	2362	2399	1001	5762
Bhutia	1966	1960	968	4894
Limbu (Limboo)	1255	1159	942	3356
Gurung	1108	1047	766	2921
Murmi (Tamang)	801	778	1288	2867
Rai/Jimdar Etc.	742	691	587	2020
Khambu	726	648	589	1963
Kami	626	464	580	1670
Brahman	521	372	521	1414
Mangar	363	346	192	901
Chhetri	303	253	273	829
Newar	240	183	304	727
Darji	102	92	93	287
Slaves	124	99	103	326
Miscellaneous/ including soldiers.	350	72	99	521
Total	11589	10563	8306	30458

Source: H.H.Risley: The Gazetteer of Sikhim, 1894/1993.

The earliest unofficial information regarding the population of Sikkim can be obtained from the writings of C.R.Markham. According to him there were about 7000 population in Sikkim in 1840 in which the Lepchas were 3010 (43 per cent), 1995 were Limboos (28.5 per cent) and Bhutias were also 1995 (28.5 per cent).[125] However, it is difficult to ascertain whether the total was that of the whole of Sikkim or a particular tract or region. The first ever official census was taken in February 1891 according to which the total population of Sikkim was shown as 30,498 persons including 5762 Lepchas, 4,894 Bhutias and various Nepali communities / groups, including Tsongs/ Limboos, taken together were registered as 18,955 persons.

The Rais and Khambus, though represent a single community, were enumerated separately. If the two communities are merged together, as they should have been, then the Rais will become the largest among the Nepalis followed by the Limboos (11.0 %) and Gurungs (9.6 %). In 1909 J.C. White unofficially mentioned the population of the Lepchas as 6000, Bhutias as little over 6000 and the Paharias/Nepalis as nearly as 50,000.[126] The figures do not provide a precise picture of the population yet it clearly indicates that there had been a steady growth in the population of the Nepalis and the Bhutias.[127]

A cursory look at the decadal population growth rate of Sikkim gives us an inconsistent result. During 1901-1911 the growth rate had been the highest while in 1911-21 there had been a fall of 6,199 persons. The reasons behind the fall could be attributed to either because of the influenza of 1917 or the First World War or the slower rate of migration as was mentconed by J.C. White in the Administrative Report of 1910-1911.[128] In 1921-1961 the population of Sikkim had increased steadily but at a slower rate though the population of Nepali had fallen by 0.83 per cent in 1931-1951.[129] The 1931 census gives us the following details of composition of the population of Sikkim.

The population figures of many communities like Gurung, Rai/Jimdar/Khambu, Mangar, Chhetri and Kami, had been shown 'Not Available' which undoubtedly indicate that these communities had been clubbed with 'others' for some enumeration difficulties.

In 1951, statistics based on religious affiliation presented an overall increased population of 1,37,725 persons with 39,397 Buddhists (largely the Lepchas 13,625 and the Bhutias 15,626) and 97,863 Hindus, including 15,991 Limboos. In 1951 Sikkim did not have urban areas in the sense that there was no municipality, corporation, notified town area, engagement of about 75 per cent people in non-agricultural occupation and others which are generally required for an area to be classified as urban areas.

Table 2.7: Community-wise Distribution of Population, 1931

Community / Caste	Total Persons
Lepcha	13,030
Bhutias of Sikkim	11,070
Bhutias of Tibet	560
Bhutias of Nepal (Sherpa)	3,645
Limboo	10,536
Gurungs	N.A.
Murmi / Tamang	7,617
Rai / Jimdar	N.A.
Khambu	N.A.
Magar (Mangar)	N.A.
Newar	3,911
Brahmin	8,530
Chhetri	N.A.
Kami	N.A.
Darji / Damai	1,866
Others	49,043
Total	1,09,808

Source: Census of India, 1931.

In 1961 the total population, taken on the basis of the mother tongue spoken by at least five hundred persons, was shown as 1,62,189 in which 88,916 were Nepalis, 14,847 Lepchas and 47,339 Bhutias including the Bhutia unspecified and 6,690 Tibetans.

Table 2.8: Mother tongue-wise Distribution of Population, 1961

Mother Tongue	No of Speakers
Nepali	74,319
Lepcha	14,847
Sikkim Bhutia	36,577
Bhutia Unspecified	10,762
Tibetan	6,690
Limboo	4,955
Sherpa	3,997
Rai	2,965
Tamang	1,423
Subba	1,257
Others	4,397
TOTAL	1,62,189

Source: Census of India, 1961, Vol. XVI, West Bengal and Sikkim Part 1-A, Book ii, Population and Society, P. 198.

Since the speakers of Gurung, Newar and Mangar languages were not available, they must have been amalgamated with the Nepali speakers.

In 1961 only the east district, i.e. the capital town Gangtok, was recognized as urban area having 12.08 as urban inhabitants. The East District had 85,621 persons followed by the West, South and North with 58,023, 53,185 and 13,014 persons respectively. The 1971 census once again taken on linguistic basis, had shown the total population as 2, 09,843 persons in which the Lepcha speaking people were accounted as 22,306 (10.63 %), 23,565 (11.23 %) were Bhutias and 1,34,237 (63.97%) were Nepali speakers inclusive of Limboo, Khambu/Rai, Gurung, Tamang, Sunwar, Mangar, Newar, Sherpa, Bahun, Chhetri, Kami, Damai etc. By 1971 North, South and West districts had been classified as urban areas with 2.5, 2.3 and 1.9 urban dwellers respectively. The East district had 19.9 per cent urban dwellers. The decennial population growth per every thousand persons in 1961-1971 was +334, +510, +162 and +0 in the North, East, South and West districts respectively.

In 1981 the total population of Sikkim was 3,16,385 persons out of which the speakers of Nepali language were 1,92,995 (61 %), the Lepchas were 22,147 (7. %), 21,514 Bhutias (6.8 %), 15,819 Limboos (5 %), 10,757 Sherpas (3.4 %), 4,240 Tibetans (1.34 %) and 48,914 others (15.46 %). The East district had been recorded as the most populated district among the four with 1,38,762 persons and a density of 145 persons per Sq. Km., followed by South (101 persons), West (64 persons) and North with meager 6 persons per Sq. Km.

The North district, which was prohibited for Nepali settlement, represents 59.56 per cent (4226 Sq. Km.) of the total area of Sikkim (7096 Sq. Km.) but due to inhospitable climate, rugged and perpetually snowcapped mountain ridges makes the place unsuitable for human habitation.

Table 2.9: District-wise Distribution of Population in Sikkim - 1981

District/ State	Area in Sq. Km	%	Urban	Rural	Total	%	Density per Sq. Km
North	4226	59.6	780	25,675	26,455	8.4	6
East	954	13.4	43,242	95,520	1,38,762	43.9	145
South	750	10.6	5.365	70,495	75,976	24.0	101
West	1166	16.4	1,697	73,495	75,192	23.8	64
Sikkim	7096	—	51,084	2,65,301	3,16,385	—	45

Source: District Census handbook-1981, Directorate of Census Operation, Sikkim.

The overall growth rate of population during 1971-81 has been very high in the North district which is 103.28 per cent followed by East (62.07 %), South (42.85 %) and West (29.59 %) in descending order. The increase in North district may be attributed to increasing Tibetan migration after the merger of Sikkim with India in 1975 and road construction. The East district obviously has the highest density of population per square kilometer by virtue of being the capital of Sikkim, Gangtok, and all the major business centers like Singtam, Rangpo are located in this district.

In 1978 the Constitution (Sikkim) Scheduled Caste and Scheduled Tribe Order was promulgated according to which Damai Kami, Majhi and Sarki of Nepali castes were recognized as Scheduled Castes of Sikkim while the Lepchas and the Bhutias including Chumbipa, Dopthapas, Dukpas, Kagateys, Sherpas, Tromopas, Yolmos and Tibetans were declared Scheduled Tribes of Sikkim. A separate table was included in 1981 in order to enumerate the number of SC/ST population of Sikkim.

In 1981 there were 18,281(5.78%) Scheduled Caste and 73,623 (23.27 %) Scheduled Tribes population with its highest concentration in the North District but with 30,540 persons they were largest in the East District in terms of absolute number. The district wise distribution of Scheduled Caste and Scheduled Tribe populations in 1991 and 2001 are given below.

In table no. 2.10 both Scheduled Caste and Scheduled Tribe populations are highest in the East district (absolute) whereas in terms of percentage and concentration of Scheduled Tribes population, the North District top the list with more than 53 percent both in 1981, 1991 and 2001. As in the earlier instances, the Scheduled Caste populations continue to be lowest in the North district whereas the Scheduled Tribe is lowest in the South district. However, the number of Scheduled Tribe population in Sikkim has changed recently with the inclusion of Limboos and Tamangs in the Scheduled Tribes list of Sikkim in 2003.

Table 2.10: District-wise Distribution of SC/ST Population in Sikkim - 1991 & 2001

	1	9	9	1	2	0	0	1
District /State	SC	%	ST	%	SC	%	ST	%
North	1,111	3.55	17,301	55.38	879	2.14	21,772	53.06
East	12,482	6.99	37,632	21.09	14,277	5.82	45,321	18.49
West	4,927	5.02	19,297	19.66	5,747	4.66	23,829	19.33
South	5,564	5.64	16,671	16.91	6,262	4.76	20,483	15.57
Sikkim	24,084	5.93	90,901	22.36	27,165	5.02	1,11,405	20.61

Source: Census of India, 1991 and Sikkim Statistical Profile, 2004 -05 (DESM & E), Govt. of Sikkim, Gangtok.

According to the 1991 census, the total population of Sikkim were 4, 06,457 persons of which 22.39 per cent (90,901 persons) were Scheduled Tribes and 5.93 per cent (24,084 persons) were Scheduled Castes. The decennial population growth rate of 1981-91 was 28.47 percent, which indicates a sharp fall in the decadal growth rate except in the West district where an increase of.96 per cent was registered. As usual the highest density of population was recorded in the East district (187 persons per sq.km.) followed by 131 in the South, 84 in the West and 7 in the North. In 1991 the percentage of ethnic Bhutia to the total population was about 16 per cent (65,033), the Lepchas as 14 per cent (56,904) and the Nepalis, including the plainsmen, constituted 70 per cent (2,84,520).[130]

The 2001 census has shown the total population of Sikkim as 5,40,851 persons of which 2,88,484 are males and 2,52,367 are females. The density per square mile has been 76. The Scheduled Caste constituted 5.02 per cent (27,165 persons) while the Scheduled Tribes are 20.61 per cent (1,11,405). The decadal growth in 1991-2001 in the Scheduled Tribes population is 20,504 persons absolute while the Scheduled Caste population increased by meager 3,081 persons. In other words unlike the 1991 census there has been a fall in the Scheduled Caste population while the Scheduled Tribes continue to show an upward trend even in 2001.

Table 2.11 District-wise Distribution of Population in Sikkim- 2001

District/State	Area in Sq. Km.	%	Urban	Rural	Total	%	Density per Sq. Km.
North	4226	59.6	1248	39,782	41,030	7.6	9
East	954	13.4	52,852	1,92,188	2,45,040	45.3	256
West	750	10.6	1,824	1,21,432	1,23,256	22.8	164
South	1,160	16.4	3,946	1,27,579	1,31,525	24.3	112
Sikkim	7,096		59,870	4,80,981	5,40,851	100.0	76

Source: Calculated from census data, 2001.

The distribution of population in the State, reflect wide variations owing to topographical factors. The North district, which comprises of 60 per cent of the total geographical area, accounts for hardly 8 per cent population. The majority of the population of North district belongs to Scheduled Tribes, while Scheduled Castes form 4 percent only according to 1991 census. In 1971-81 the North district recorded the highest decennial increase of almost 104 per cent but has registered the lowest increase of 18 per cent in 1981-91.

The East district is the most densely populated among the four districts of Sikkim with a density of 187 persons per square kilometer. According to 1991 census, it has less than 14 per cent of the total geographical area of the State (13.44 Sq. Km.) but provided shelter to about 44 per cent of the total population. In 2001, the East district represented about 45.3 per cent of the total population of the State with a density of 256 persons per square kilometer. (Table no. 2.11).

Table 2.12: District-wise Decennial Change of Population, 1971 2001

District/Year	Population	Absolute increase	Percentile increase	Annual Growth Rate
NORTH				
1971	13,014	-	-	-
1981	26,455	13,441	103.28	7.35
1991	31,240	4,785	18.09	1.68
2001	41,030	9,790	23.86	2.76
EAST				
1971	85,621	-	-	-
1981	1,38,762	53,141	62.07	4.95
1991	1,78,452	39,690	28.60	2.55
2001	2,45,040	66,588	37,31	3.22
SOUTH				
1971	53,185	-	-	-
1981	75,976	22,791	42.85	3.63
1991	98,602	22,628	29.78	2.64
2001	1,31,525	32,923	33.38	2.92
WEST				
1971	58,023	-	-	-
1981	75,192	17,169	29.59	2.63
1991	98,161	22,969	30.55	2.70
2001	1,23,256	25,095	25.56	2.30

Source: Calculated from various census data available.

The study of demographic composition of the State of Sikkim is indeed a challenging one because of the fact that the population figure prior to 1891 is not an official figure. It is equally difficult to ascertain that whether figures provided by C.R.Markham is that of a particular tract or whole of Sikkim. Similarly, in the post-1951 period the community-wise census figures are not available. The census enumeration on the basis of the religion or language cannot always provide exact account of the ethnic community, least in the case of Sikkim. However, after having studied the demographic composition of the state of Sikkim since 1840 certain striking features have been noticed such as:

a) That there has been a steady increase in the population of the Nepali community due to gradual inclusion of all other tribes, enumerated separately earlier, in the Nepali fold;

b) That Limboos who are regarded as Nepali tribe in other parts of India have always maintained a separate identity in Sikkim and have been enumerated in census as a separate linguistic group except in recent days;

c) That Lepchas who constituted the single largest group in 1891 have been relegated to numerical minority with only 14 per cent of the total population in 1991 though it does not mean a fall in their absolute number;

d) That the number of Bhutia population is also increasing substantially though not in the same proportion as the Nepali population is increasing. However, there has been a sharp fall in 1981 (21,514 persons) perhaps due to administrative callousness as the figure in 1991 has shot up to about 65,033 persons, i.e. 16 per cent of the total population.

e) That this disproportionate rise in the population of three communities is often perceived as a bone of contention though adequate safeguards (social, political and economic) have been devised favouring the Lepcha-Bhutia communities.

f) The population of Plainsmen is increasing since 1975 but official record is not available. According to an unconfirmed report their population in Sikkim is about 10 percent of the total population in 2001.

FOOTNOTES AND REFERENCES

1. D. Dahal : *Sikkim Ko Rajnaitik Itehas*, Part I, Subba publication, Gangtok, 1984, P.2.
2. Ibid, P. 3.
3. K.P.Tamsang: *The Unknown and Untold Reality about the Lepchas*, Mani Printing Press, Kalimpong, 1983, P. 42.
4. H.H.Risley: *The Gazetteer of Sikkim*, Low Price Publications, New Delhi, 1993 (reprinted), P 10.
5. A.R.Fonning: *Lepcha My Vanishing Tribe*, Chya-Pandi Farm, Kalimpong, 1987, P. 9
6. N.C.Sinha: *The Chogyal of Sikkim*, Bengal Past and Present, Vol. XCIII, Part I, No. 175, January-April, 1974.

7. Saul Mullard: "*A History From the Hidden Land: Some Preliminary Remarks on a Seventeenth Century Chronicles*", Bulletin of Tibetology, Vol. 41, No.1, May 2005, P.72.
8. Op cit. No. 5 P. 9.
9. *The Gazetteer of Sikkim*, Edited in Bengal Government Secretariat, first published in 1894, reprinted in 1972, Manjushri Publishing House, New Delhi, P. 39.
10. Op. cit. no. 8, Pp. 77-78.
11. Op. cit. No. 2, P. 24.
12. Op. cit. No. 11, P. 78.
13. *Footnote:The law of the agreement read as follows: "If your Lepcha (i.e. a Lepcha under your administrative authority) is male, his sons will belong to you (i.e. they will belong to you as servants). If the male Lepcha has only one son he will be retained by his family. Your wife will obtain whatever female Lepcha descendants that may exist, but if there is only one, she will be retained by the Lepcha family. If the male Lepcha is without male issue, he can receive a son from someone else", S.Mullard's 'A History From The Hidden Land: Some Preliminary Remarks On A Seventeenth Century Sikkimese Chronicle', published in Bulletin of Tibetology, Vol. 41, No. 1, May 2005, P. 79, Namgyal Institute of Tibetology, Gangtok, Sikkim.*
14. B.S.Das: *The Sikkim Saga*, Vikash Publication, 1983, P.5.
15. George Kotturam: *The Himalayan Gateway-History and Culture of Sikkim*, Sterling Publication, New Delhi, 1983.
16. L.B.Basnet: *Sikkim: A Short Political History*, S. Chand & Co. (Pvt.) Ltd., New Delhi, 1974, P.5.
17. L.A.Waddell: *Among the Himalayas*, Published by Pilgrims Book House Pvt. Ltd., 1989, P 432.
18. C.U.Aitshison: *A Collection of Treaties, Engagements and Sanads Relating to India and Neighbouring Countries*, Revised upto 1929, Mittal Publications, New Delhi, 1909/1983, Vol. 12, pp. 51-52.
19. Ibid, P. 311.
20. *Frontier and Overseas Expedition from India*, compiled by

Intelligence Branch, Division of Chief of Army Staff, Army Headquarters of India, Vol. IV, P. 128.

21. C.D.Markhan: *Narratives of Mission of George Bogle to Tibet and the Journey of Thomas Manning to Lhasa*, p. 202.
22. P.R.Rao: *India and Sikkim (1840-1970)*, Sterling Publication, New Delhi, 1972, PP.1-2; Alistair Lamb: *Britain and Chinese Central Asia: The Road to Lhasa (1767-1905),* London, 1960, P 41.
23. The text of the *Treaty of Titalia-1817* signed between the British and Sikkimese officials.
24. Op. cit. No. 17, P. 32.
25. V.H.Coelho: *Sikkim and Bhutan*, Vikash Publication, New Delhi, 1971, P. 17: Op.cit No. 4, P. 19, and Op cit No. 15, P. 52.
26. Sunanda K. Dattaray: *Smash and Grab-Annexation of Sikkim*, Vikash Publication, Delhi, 1984, P.23.
27. T. Namgyal and Yeshi Dolma: *History of Sikkim*, typescript, pp 114-15.
28. B.H.V.Bayley: *Dorje-ling*, Bengal Military Orphan Press, Calcutta, 1838, P.3.
29. Most historians like E.C.Dozey, O'Malley,A.J.Dash, Aitchison and others agree with 1st February 1835 as the date of transfer of Darjeeling but the circumstances which led to the transfer and absence of date on the original deed of transfer of Darjeeling tend to obscure the claim.
30. Op. cit No. 29, Pp. 8-9.
31. Fred Pinn: *The Road of Destiny-Darjeeling Letters 1839*, Oxford University Press, Calcutta, 1986, P.121.
32. Ibid, P. 287.
33. Ibid, p.121-22; also read S.B.Wangyal: *Sikkim and Darjeeling-Division and Deception*, KMT Press Pvt. Ltd., Pheuntsholing, Bhutan, 2002, P. 45.
34. Ibid, Pp 288-89.
35 Ibid, P. 288.

36. S.B.Wangyal's '*Sikkim & Darjeeling-Division and Deception*, Pheuntsholing, Bhutan, 2002, P.49.
37. Op cit. No. 19. Pp. 60-61.
38. Op cit. No. 36. P. 123.
39. Ibid; Also read Op.cit. No. 34, P. 66.
40. P. Melville: *Bengal Political Consultations*, 14th November, 1846, No. 29.
41. Alistair Lamb: *Britain & Chinese Central Asia: The Road to Lhasa (1767-1905)*, 1960, P. 138.
42. Op cit. No. 5, Introduction P Viii.
43. *Convention between Great Britain & China Relating to Sikkim & Tibet, 1890.*
44. *The Constitution of India,* Published by the Ministry of Law, Justice and Company Affairs, Government of India, May 1981.
45. Ibid.
47. Ibid.
47. Op. cit. No. 6, P.8.
48. J.R.Subba: *The Limboos of the Eastern Himalayas*, published by Sikkim Yakthung Mundhum Saplopa, Gangtok, 1999, P. 93.
49. Saul Mullard says that Phuntsog Namgyal, the first Bhutia king of Tibetan origin, was consecrated in 1646. His claim is based on the 17th century compilation volume entitled *"sBas yul 'bras mo ljongs kyi gnas yig dang rgyal rabs mdor bsdus bzhugs so"* by Gung rdorje. Op. cit. No. 14.
50. Op. cit. No. 26, P. 5.
51. N. Sengupta: *State Government & Politics in Sikkim*, Sterling publication Pvt. Ltd., New Delhi, 1985. P.197.
52. Op. cit. No. 7, P. 4.
53. Op. cit. No. 52, P. 197.
54. *Administrative Report of the Sikkim State for the year 1935-36.*
55. Op. cit. No. 54, P. 1.

56. *Administrative Report of the State of Sikkim for the Year 1915-1916*, Chapter I, P.1.
57. *Administrative Report of the State of Sikkim for the Year 1918-1919*, Chapter I, P.1.
58. *Administrative Report of the State of Sikkim for the Year 1934-35 & 1935-36,* P.9.
59. P.P.Karan & W.M. Jenkins Jr: *The Himalayan Kingdoms – Bhutan, Sikkim and Nepal*, Princeton Publication, 1963, P. 59.
60. Press Note of the Ministry of External Affairs, Govt. of India, dated 20 March 1950; The Text of Indo-Sikkim Peace Treaty, dated 5 December 1950.
61. Tashi Tshering*: A Few Facts about Sikkim.*
62. Op. cit. No. 51, P. 28.
63. *Sikkim –A Concise Chronicles*, Government of Sikkim Publication, 1962, P. 28.
64. Ibid, P. 28.
65. *Proclamation of H.H. the Maharaja of Sikkim*, dated 23.03.1953.
66. Ibid.
67. *Sikkim Darbar Gazette, Ex. Gazette*, No. 2, dated 26.02.1959.
68. *Sikkim Darbar Gazette, Ex. Gazette,* No. 3, dated 05.07.1970.
69. *Sikkim Darbar Gazette, Ex. Gazette*, No. 31, dated 26.03.1973.
70. *Sikkim Darbar Gazette, Ex. Gazette*, No. 21, dated 31.05.1967.
71. Op. cit. No. 63.
72. *Sikkim Darbar Gazette*, Extraordinary Gazette, Vol. VII, No. 5, dated 17.03.1958.
73. Ibid.
74. Schedule B, a supplementary copy attached to the Proclamation of Maharaja, dated 01.12.1957.

75. *Sikkim Darbar Gazette*, Extraordinary Gazette, No. 9, dated 21.12.1966.
76. *Proceedings of the State Council*, dated 08.08.1953.
77. Op.cit No. 67.
78. *Sikkim Darbar Gazette*, Ex. Gazette, No. 5, dated 4.8.1967 and No. 20, dated 28.11.1972.
79. Op. cit. No. 78.
80. Ibid.
81. Op. cit. No. 52 P. 228.
82. S*ikkim Fortnightly*, Vol. VI, No. 5 & 6, dated 10.07.1972.
83. *Sikkim Government Gazette, Ex. Gazette, No. 22*, dated 05.12.1972.
84. Ibid.
85. Op.cit. No. 25.
86. Ibid.
87. Ibid, P. 188.
88. Sunanda K. Datta Ray: *The Indo-Sikkimese Treaty – Contradictions in Tripartite Agreement*, an undated manuscript.
89. P.R.Rao: *Sikkim – The Story of its Integration with India*, Cosmo Publications, New Delhi, 1978, P. 49.
90. Ibid, P. 50.
91. *Text of the Sikkim Bill, 1974*, Clause 28, i & ii.
92. Op. cit. No. 90, P. 89.
93. Ibid, P. 53.
94. Ibid, P. 69.
95. Ibid, P. 56.
96. Op. cit. No. 82, P. 128.
97. *Representation of the Sikkimese Leaders to the Constitutional Advisor*, dated 11.06.1974.
98. Op. cit. No. 93, P. 57.

99. *Address by the Chogyal to the Sikkim Assembly*, Emergent Session, Gangtok, dated 03.07.1974.

100. Note: With reference to 1958, 1960, 1967 scenarios of the Executive Councilors of the State Council.

101. Op.cit. No. 69, & note issued by the Darbar with reference to the Proclamation of 16.03.1958.

102. P.K.Jha: *History of Sikkim-1817-1904*, OPS Publication, Calcutta, 1985, P. 68.

103. *Report of the Committee of Land Reforms, 1975*, Department of Land Revenue, Government of Sikkim, PP 104-07.

104. Unpublished family papers of Late Motichand Pradhan of Kalimpong, the Ex-Chief Magistrate of Sikkim.

105. Op. cit. No. 104.

106. M.P.Lama: *Sikkim Human Development Report, 2001*, IPR, Government of Sikkim publication in association with Social Science Press, New Delhi, 2001, P 84.

107. Revenue Order No. 8554/G, dated 26.10.1924.

108. Op. cit No. 106.

109. Op. cit. No. 16.

110. Manas Dasgupta: *Sikkim-Problems and Prospects of Development*, Indus Publication, New Delhi, 1992, P. 42.

111. Sitaram Sah: *Problems of Rural Development in Sikkim with Special Reference to agriculture*. (Unpublished Ph. D. Thesis, 1987, P. 89.

112. J.C.Debnath: *Development of Sikkimese Economy under Planning-1954-71*. (Unpublished Ph.D Thesis, 1974, N.B.U.

113. The Sikkim Code, Vol. II, Part I, Department of Law, Government of Sikkim, Gangtok, PP. 3-4.

114. Land Record Section, Department of Land Revenue, and Government of Sikkim.

115. Prof. D.J.Bhowmic & Ranju Dhamala: *"Land Reforms in Sikkim*, Seminar paper read in the Department of Sociology, 1987; Also read S.K.Chaube (Ed.) 'The Himalayas: Profiles

of Modernization and Adaptation, Sterling Publication, New Delhi, 1985, Pp. 113-125.

116. *Sikkim-A Statistical Profile, 2002*, published by Directorate of Economics, Statistics, Monitoring and Evaluation, Government of Sikkim, Gangtok; also refer Op.cit. No. 68

117. Ibid.

118. Information booklet published by SIDICO, Gangtok, 1996.

119. Ashok Lahiri & Others; *Sikkim-The People's Vision*, Government of Sikkim publication, 2001, P. 40.

120. Department of Industry, Government of Sikkim, 1991.

121. Op. cit. No. 120.

122. New Industrial Policy & Other Concessions for the State of Sikkim, 2007, Department of Commerce and Industries, Govt. of Sikkim.

123. Op. cit. No. 107.

124. Ibid.

125. Op. cit. No. 120, P. 40.

126. Op. cit No. 19, P. xc.

127. J.C.White: *Sikkim and Bhutan – Twenty-one Years on the North–East Frontier, 188 – 1908,* Low Price Publications, Delhi, 1999 (Reprinted), Pp.7-9.

128. A.C.Sinha, in *'Politics of Sikkim – A Sociological Study'*, 1975, has given a total of 80,000 persons but the same could not be found in the book quoted by him.

129. Census of India – 1931 & 1951.

130. Op. cit No. 124, p. 7.

3

Major Ethnic Groups of Sikkim: Their History and Identity

Humans as social animals achieve both real and ideal concepts of self partially out of a sense of belonging to a group. In an occupationally undifferentiated society a sense of social identity vis-à-vis political community rarely result in an antagonistic environs because it provides little basis for divergent concepts of belongingness. On the contrary, a more complex social formation, i.e. pluri-cultural societies, with their occupational divisions and amalgamation of groups maintaining a sense of diverse origin generally exhibit signs of tension, real or perceived, emanating from an overall sense of belongingness. This happens irrespective of having either an open (Democratic) or closed (Totalitarian/ Monarchical) system of political organizations or constitutional system.

The process of identity is not static, but at the same time community's self-definition is to be found. Group identity develops through self-definition and definition by others. The two may be same but at the same time contradictory too. Through the exchanges between self-definition and definition by others community identity emerges. Further, as a dynamic process community identity includes and excludes people as members of the group and non-members/others. Interestingly a particular section may be sometimes included and excluded another time. A section may demand inclusion and may be denied and, in another occasion, a section may emphasize exclusiveness/ separateness and yet may be included. Hence, understanding of community self-definition and self-perception is important. For this, a brief analysis of different ethnic groups and their identity is demanded.

Sikkim, a tiny Himalayan state of the Indian Union, is a multi-cultural society cohabited by a multiple cultural-linguistic groups of which the Lepchas (also called Rongs/Monpas), the Bhutias (also called Denzongpas /Lhopas) and the Nepalis (also called Gorkhas/Paharias) constitute major/prominent communities in Sikkim. Lamaist Buddhism and Hinduism are the two major religions with 27.15 percent and 68.37 per cent followers respectively as per the 1991 census. Besides, a small fraction of the population is still continuing with animism, found particularly among the Lepchas and mongoloid stocks of the Nepalis. In recent past the percentage among the followers of the Christianity is also rising with 3.30 per cent in 1991. Over the years social mobility among the three ethnic communities has increased along with the events of inter-community marriages and social interaction though maintenance of distinct ethnic identity is also emphasized. The government headed by Mr. Chamling has shown special concern over the importance of preserving ancient cultures and has been providing all necessary support for the preservation, continuation and development of this cultural heritage.

As stated above the major ethnic groups of present day Sikkim are the Lepchas, the Bhutias and the Nepalis. According to the first ever official census taken in 1891, the Nepalis were about 56 per cent and constituted a majority followed by the Lepchas (19 per cent) and Bhutias (16 per cent). More than hundred years after the share of the Lepchas has declined to 14 per cent whereas the Bhutias have maintained more or less the same proportion. The population of the Nepalis, however, has increased significantly. A separate account of the Nepalis is not available but generally gives an impression that they consist of 75 per cent of the total population which, however, also includes the plainsmen population. Another point, which deserves mention, is that the decline in the percentage of the Lepchas or that of stagnation of the Bhutias to total population does not mean decline or stagnation in absolute number. Besides, the communities like Sherpas, Yolmos (Kagatey), Limboos (Tsongs) etc. are also important in any analysis of ethnicity and identity formation mainly in view of what the communities think and what others say about them. Certain other Nepali tribes/castes like Mangars, Tamangs (Murmi), Gurungs, Rais etc. also deserve special mention in view of the ethno-political scenario of Sikkim.

The history of Sikkim is smeared with personal preferences and rejections. This was possible because of the disappearance or absence of recorded documentary evidences. It is believed that the Tibetan lamas have burned the documents when they first came into contact with the 'Monpas' or the inhabitants of the lower Himalaya.[1]

Paradoxically some anthropologists believe that there were three different tribes inhabiting Sikkim before the advent of the Lepchas in Sikkim. H. Siiger writes, "… There are ancient traits of various kinds contributing to the suggestion that the Lepchas originally came from the east. On entering Sikkim the Lepchas found three tribes already in possession of the country, viz. the Na-ang or Na-ong, the Chang, and the Mon, of which the Na-ong were the earliest inhabitants.[2] Risley too acknowledges the existence of the tribe called Na-ong, by which he means "the blind fools" and associates the tribe with the popular feat of building a legendary tower (Babel) at Daramdin in west Sikkim.[3] He considers the tribe extinct.[4] The New Encyclopedia Britannica also mentions "The Lepchas were early inhabitants of the region, apparently assimilating the Naong, Chang, Mon, and other tribes."[5]

The tribes in question may be the product of misrepresentation of the source [6] but Mainwaring considers "Na-ong" as one of the foolish sections of the Lepchas.[7] He further writes that other two tribes, i.e. Chang and Mon, as mentioned by Siiger, are most probably the "Tsong", by which name Limboos in Sikkim were/are known, and "Mon" should have meant the Lepchas.[8] "Mon" is the term used by the Tibetans for the inhabitants of the lower Himalayas.[9] The term, therefore, could be used to refer to all those lowland inhabitants, including the tribes mentioned above, the Lepchas and many other groups who are identified by the generic cognate term 'Kiratas' including the Mangars, Rais, Gurungs, Tamangs etc. In fact the wandering nature of socio-economic lifestyle of ancient tribes of the eastern Himalaya and absence of clear evidence make it difficult to identify any group or community as autochthons of Sikkim. We only have some evidences of early settlement/ settlers and vague references to them in the oral traditions and folklores.

These communities, though different in many respects, have developed a sense of belongingness and togetherness among themselves due to their long association. The intercommunity marriage, which was once considered a social taboo, is a common happening and a new Sikkimese culture, a sort of a fusion of all the cultures, is a reality. Having said that these communities also believe in maintaining specific group identity and refuse to be treated as part of a broader or combined form of identity though, under certain circumstances, such broader identity is also emphasized.

For instance the Bhutias and Lepchas have lived together for centuries as a combined community and under a common B-L identity but, off late, the Lepchas, through various activities and propaganda, emphasize on the maintenance of a separate Lepcha identity. Same is true with regards to the Limboos also. Limboos do not identify themselves with the larger Nepali identity. Similarly, different sub-cultural groups within the larger Nepali community also speak in terms of respective group identity. There are associations/organizations of almost all these little communities through which they articulate respective group interest and group identity. Thus, it is necessary that these identities of different communities, including the little communities, should not only be studied but it is also important to find out where the identity of the Sikkimese lies amidst plethora of identities.

The Lepchas or Rongs:

The Lepchas call themselves "Rong" or "Rongkup" which means "the son of the snowy peak".[10] The Tibetans, Bhutanese alike, call them "Rong-pa" which means the "the ravine folk" According to Waddell the title "Lepcha" was an anglicized version of the contemptuous name 'Lapchey' (vile speaker) given by the Nepalis.[11] The word 'Lapchey' is not a Nepali word and hence Waddell's contention seems to be a product of hearsay. Moreover, no one can say it for certain that the word is contemptuous in meaning. Rather there is a more convincing indication that the word 'Lepcha' or "Lapchey' is originated from the Lepcha word "Lapcho" which means a rough stone altar laid for the purpose of offering to the "semi-divine" spirits, called 'Lungzee' by the Lepchas. Fonning also subscribes to this viewpoint. He writes, "We call these altars 'Lapcho', and hence, seeing the autochthones so much concerned about these Lapchos, they started calling us Lapcho people, and ultimately, our tribe became the "Lepcha" tribe for them. Then when the British and the plains folk met us, we were known as Lepcha, the name by which our tribe is known to the outside people now".[12] Major places initially populated / inhabited by the "Lepchas" are, as of now, bear the same tribal names, viz. Lapcho near Peshok in Darjeeling district, or Lepsep in west Sikkim etc.

Amidst obscurity and plethora of contradictory views on the origin, tradition and history of Lepcha community, one school of thought believes that the Lepchas have migrated from Assam and Upper Burma and belong to Tibeto-Burman tribal family.[13] George Kutturan too has subscribed to this view.[14] Mrs. Beauvir Stocks, a veteran anthropologist, has traced their home in Southern Tibet1.[15] There have been references to connect the origin of the Lepchas with those three warriors of Alexander who remained in India, or with the missing tribes of Israel on the basis of their physical features, their artifacts and events, and linguistic similarity. Haffden Siiger writes, "if a straight line is drawn from the north to the south through Sikkim and Darjeeling and compare the Lepchas with other people of the west and the east, the Lepchas are much similar with the eastern people as such, the Lepchas may have migrated from the east to Sikkim and Darjeeling in the dim past".[16] Mackean also writes that the Lepchas came from the east with the Jimdars (Rai /Khambu) who went on to Nepal and settled there. The Meches who also came along with the Lepchas settled in the foothills.[17] Risley writes, "though the Lepchas claim to be the autochthones of Sikkim their physical characteristics stamp them as members of the Mongolian race, and certain peculiarities of language and religion render it probable that the tribe is a very ancient colony from southern Tibet".[18] While exploring further on the origin and identity of the Lepchas, Thakur and Lepcha (1981) conclude, "We have here attempted to offer four-fold explanations to the origin of the Lepchas based on (i) habitational, (ii) linguistic, (iii) divinical and (iv) historical-anthropological evidences. Yet it seems difficult to give a conclusive answer to the problem of the origin of this tribe".[19]

The Lepchas, on the other, consider themselves as autochthones of Sikkim, called "Mayel Lyang", which means "the land of the hidden paradise", or "the delightful region" and then later migrated to other places.[20] Such an explanation may be viewed as an indication of psychological attachment of the Lepchas with Sikkim and is rarely found in other interpretations. The government of Sikkim has recognized Lepchas as the primitive / indigenous tribe of Sikkim and a resolution in the State Legislative Assembly has been passed seeking concurrence of the Government of India.

Thus, it is very difficult to come to a definite conclusion on the origin of the Lepchas. On the basis of available Lepcha manuscripts, traditions, folklores and life experiences of old individuals, both the Lepchas and other, the following legend seems important. The present Lepcha families are the direct descendent of the ten sons of Fodongthing (Father) and Nazaongnyo (Mother), the first primogenitors of the Lepchas to whom God created from the snows of mount Kungtsuomzaongboo Choo (Kangchanjunga). Their descendants are called 'Rong – Kup

– Kati' or 'Rongkati' which means 'Ten Rongs' (Lepchas). Their customary rules are called 'Rong – Kati – Tyum' which means 'the laws of the Ten Rongs'. The different Lepcha clans claim their association with the 108 Lepcha ancestors who rescued the community from the domination of Laso Mong, a Tibetan invador, by killing him at the foothills of mount Pandim. In course of time the title which these warriors earned got transformed into number of clans such as Tamsangmoo, Soongootmoo, Sangdyangmoo, Samickmoo, Munlomoo, Lutsommoo, Brimoo, Fyungtalimoo, Sampumoo, Numchyomoo, Sadamoo, Adenmoo etc.[21] Further divisions, i.e., Rongboo (Patrician) and Mongboo (Plebeians) took place as social divisions between the nobility or aristocratic and the commoners began primarily on the basis of functional pursuit. Though, there exists cultural and linguistic homogeneity among the Lepchas, geographically they are divided into four sects namely Renjyongmoo, Illammoo, Damsangmoo and Promoo. The Lepchas of Sikkim, Darjeeling, Kurseong and Siliguri are called Renjyongmoo whereas their brethrens in Illam, Kalimpong and Bhutan (Bhutan in Lepcha is called Pro) are respectively called Illammoo, Damsangmoo and Promoo.[22]

In Lepcha society the king is called "Panu" and Pohartak Panu is considered the first Lepcha ruler of Sikkim.[23] Mentions about Turvey Panu, another Lepcha ruler in succession, may be found in the writings of Mainwaring (1876), Sinha (1975), and Chaube (1987) also. According to Sinha, Turvey Panu ruled Sikkim sometime around 1425 A.D. He was succeeded by Tuv Athak.[24] He further writes that last Lepcha Panu was born in 1686 and ruled for a period of 25 years[25] A.R. Fonning, however, does not subscribe to the theory of Lepcha Panu.[26]

Lepchas have their own language and perhaps it is the oldest language of all the hill dialects. However, its origin is obscured and nobody can say for certain from where it originated and how it became the mother tongue of the Lepchas. According to philologists the language belongs to the Tibeto – Burman group of languages to which the other languages of other tribes of the sub-Himalayan region also belonged. According to the Lepcha mythology, the Lepcha language is the language of God, i.e., the language of Fodong Thing and Nazaong Nyo, to whom the Lepchas owe their origin.[27] Others have claimed that the language was invented by Thekong Mensalong, a legendary seventeenth century Lepcha leader[28] but, Fonning considers such a claim as a product of glorification of the legendary hero.[29] Gorer, paradoxically, contends that the Lepcha alphabet was invented by the Chogyal Chador Namgyal of Sikkim at the end of the seventeenth century or the beginning of the eighteenth century.[30] Once again, Fonning does not agree with the contention of Gorer on the ground that Chador Namgyal had the most hectic time, both mentally and physically, during his short span of nine years rule (1707-1716), i.e., after his return from the exile. Such a highly intellectual peacetime work such as invention of a script of a foreign language could have been possible only when Chador Namgyal was a superhuman being'.[31]

The Tibetan sources revealed that Lhatsun Chhempo, one of the three Lamas who anointed and consecrated the first Bhutia king (Chogyal) of Sikkim in 1642, gave the language to the Lepchas. This source is believed to have been mentioned in a book written by Lama Khajon Ngawa. Last but not the least is a Gorkha theory, which relates its origin to the Kirata king Maw-rong or Mohorong of the seventh century. The Lepchas, who formed a section of the Kirata tribes, was called by the name 'Imay' then. Whatever may be the contentions on the origin of the Lepcha language, it certainly has undergone certain modifications under the influence of various other languages of the sub-Himalayan tribes. Among them the Tibetan influence on the Lepcha language seems to be most profound. This is because that most of the Tibetan religious books, including the Tashay Namthar, also called Tashay Sung, the oldest among the Lepcha Namthar, were said to have been translated in the Lepcha language by the Tibetan lamas. This is suggestive of the fact that the Bhutia Lamas knew the Lepcha language very well. It is believed that the despotic Bhutia king and dogmatic lamas burned down the Lepcha manuscripts saying that writings and records contained nothing but superstition, lies and evil.[32]

According to an unconfirmed record Lepchas were approximately 3010 persons out of a total of 7000 populations in 1840. In 1873, Edgar in his travelogue recorded the Lepcha population as 2,500 persons out of a total of 5000 population. In 1891, the figures increased to 5,762 of which 2,362 were males, 2399 females and 1,001 were children. Below, an attempt is made to provide an overall figure of the Lepcha population in Sikkim since 1840.

Table 3.1: Number of Lepcha Population during 1840 – 1991

Census year	Numerical figure	Percentage to total population
1840	3010 (Approx.)	43
1891	5762	19.1
1909	6000	9.7
1931	13,060	11.89 (12 %)
1951	13,625	9.89
1961	14,847	9.8 (10 %)
1971	22,306	12.4
1981	22,147	8.3
1991*	56,904	14.0

Source: From various books and census reports. * Source: Sikkim Human Development Report, Govt. of Sikkim, 2001.

The figures given in the above table indicate a steady increase in the numerical strength of the Lepcha population in absolute term except in 1981, though percentage-wise the population shows a downward trend. Today, the Lepchas are in the minority among the three ethnic communities of Sikkim.

On the basis of the investigative works carried out by various authors on the occupational habit of the Lepchas, we know that initially the Lepchas led a semi – nomadic economic lifestyle depending mainly on forest products –fruits, roots and tubers- and hunting and fishing. Besides, they used to grow two varieties of dry-land paddy (Dunbra and Ongroyzo), millet (Mongbru) for preparation of Chee (a Lepcha beverage) and Maize (Kunchung) through the practice called shifting cultivation. Abundant forestlands provided ample scope for such a simple economic formation to sustain.

The contacts with the Tibetans during the fifteenth and sixteenth century had a great influence on the economic lifestyle of the Lepchas along with exposer to political domination, subjugation and cultural transformation with which the Lepchas were possibly unfamiliar of. They were confined in the Dzongu protected area and lost contact with the outside world. This basically proved detrimental for community's political and economic advancement. Gorer, who worked with the Lepchas of the Dzongu reserved area, writes that orphans and children of poor Lepcha parents used to be kept as slaves.[33]

Another important phase is characterized by political unrest, with conflicts and tension. The contacts with the Nepalis introduced a new variety of crops, viz. cardamom and wet-paddy, along with the system of terrace farming. This has a significant influence on the occupational habit and settlement process of the Lepchas.

The British got involved in Sikkim's affairs due to the latter's involvement in wars with Nepal and Bhutan. Along with the British there came people from Nepal and trading family from Indian mainland. Gorer writes about the extortionist and dishonest aptitude of the Kanyas (Indian traders) settled in Mangan. He writes, "an application was made to the court in the spring of 1937 to have the Kanyas (Indian traders) removed because their proximity (with the Lepchas) was the chief reason for the indebtedness and distress. Some years ago the court sent out an order that people were not to borrow so much and the Kanyas were not to cheat so much; but with the shops on the spot and with cunning and insinuating salesman, the Lepchas are unable to resist."[34]

After the occupation of Darjeeling and later Sikkim by the British, many Christian missionaries came into contact with the Lepchas. The Lepchas who were poor and ignorant became a convenient proposition for the missionaries to propagate Christianity among them. But Sikkim being a theocratic State the expansion of Christianity and subsequent conversion of the Lepchas into Christianity were not so easy. As such Christianity became more predominant in Darjeeling than in Sikkim. As a result the Lepchas of Darjeeling and Kalimpong had excelled far beyond than their Sikkimese brethren in terms of conversion to Christianity, access to modern and secular education, economic well-being, political consciousness and perhaps in the field of hygiene and sanitation too. In this context Fonning writes, "Among our people, those who have received modern education, and those holding important positions in the government and other services, the vast majority are invariably found from within this Christian group."[35] Dr. Yen Tshing Sitling was politically active during the agitation of the Hillmen's Association of the thirties in Darjeeling. Some educated Christian Lepchas, like Rev. Gyen Tshering Sitling, Anyu Azen Rebecca etc. were active in the field of social activities and had been the founder member of an organization, called Mutanchi Rong Shezum (The General Lepcha Association) in Kalimpong during 1940s. The objective of this voluntary organization was to educate, protect and ameliorate the poor Lepchas from the condition of abject poverty and mental darkness.

While the Lepchas in Darjeeling and Kalimpong were working for the overall development of the Lepcha community, the socio-political condition in Sikkim was not conducive for such an endeavour as yet. The indifferent attitude of the Lepcha landlords and Kazis towards their own Rongfolk further impaired their socio-economic progress. Besides, any attempt on the part of the Lepcha leadership or elites to raise voices for the emancipation of the Lepchas was promptly suppressed by the Sikkim government dominated by the Bhutias with a king of Bhutia descent. For instance, Ruth Karthak, a socially and political conscious lady and the founder of Sikkim Independent Front party in Sikkim in 1966, was removed from Sikkim allegedly for hatching a conspiracy against the Chogyal.[36] Kazi Lhendup Dorji Khangsarpa, despite the allegation for money laundering, survived the repression perhaps for being an incarnate Lama and the overwhelming support which he enjoyed from the majority Nepalis.

A common notion found in books and anthropological reports about the Lepcha is that they are the dying race. Fonning too used the notion as the title of his book 'Lepcha My Vanishing Tribe'. According to Fonning, the 'vanishing' condition of the Lepchas was created, firstly, due to the forceful conversion of the Lepchas into the Lamaist Buddhism during the Bhutia rule in Sikkim and, later, due to propagation of Christianity during the British. Thus, by vanishing tribe Fonning actually means the depleting socio-cultural, linguistic and religious condition of the Lepchas rather than the absolute figure of the Lepchas, which is increasing at a slower pace. Gorer also shares Fonning's apprehension when he writes, "As a society with its unique conglomeration of attitudes the Lepchas are certainly disappearing for their culture presupposes a homogeneous interlocking community and this as well as their complete suppression of competition and aggression, cause an inevitable break down of culture in any mixed community."[37] While, Morris considered it psychological to a great extent associated with the habit of too much of drinking[38] the depleting condition of the Lepcha population could be also the case of malnutrition.

In 1977 the Lepcha language has been recognized as one of the State languages of Sikkim. Renjyong Mutanchi Ringmom Kurmom (Sikkim Lepcha Literary Organization) was formed in 1978 with a primary objective to develop and promote the Lepcha language and literature in Sikkim. At present the language is taught up to the Under-Graduate level in North Bengal University. This was accomplished in 2000. The contributions of the Chamling government along with the Lepcha literary personalities, including some foreign writers, have been immense in the publication of extensive literary materials. Notable among the Lepcha writers in Sikkim are D.K.Luksom, Sonam Tshering Lepcha, D.C.Luksom, Lha Tshering Lepcha, Norgain Tshering Sangdyang, Nima Lhamu Lepcha, Dhendup Lepcha, Ongdi Tshering Lepcha.

In 1978, the community has been recognized as one of the Scheduled tribes of India. The State Government of Sikkim has reserved about 33 per cent seats for the Tribals, including the Lepchas, both in services in the State Government and the Public

Sector undertakings, and in allotment of quota in educational institutions for professional courses.[39] Despite reservation, their participation, however, is very much dismal in service sector. In 16 different services, both All India Services and State, the participation of the Lepchas is meager 4.87 per cent out of the total of 1273 posts. The domination of the Bhutias over the Lepchas in terms of their share in the coveted administrative services viz. IAS, IPS and IFS (Forest), is continuing with the ratio of 22:1 out of a total of 99 officers.[40] It is to be noted that there was not a single IAS, IPS and IFS officers among the Lepchas until very recently.

Table 3.2: Community-wise share in various services, August- 2005

	Ethnic Communities / Affiliation						
Services	**Nepali**	**Bhutia**	**Lepcha**	**Sherpa**	**Other***	**Un-Identified**	**Total**
I.A.S	9	13	1	1	22	-	46
I.P.S.	4	3	-	-	18	-	25
I.F.S.	6	5	-	-	17	-	28
S.S.A.S.	83	39	7	-	12	-	141
S.S.S.	21	8	1	1	2	-	33
M.G.S.	7	4	2	1	-	-	14
S.S.N.S.	18	7	8	-	-	-	33
M.D.	133	70	11	5	4	-	223
S.F.A.S.	105	27	7	2	4	2	147
A.H.&V.S.	40	21	3	-	6	-	70
S.C.E.S.	107	26	5	1	17	-	156
S.C.S.	29	22	1	-	-	-	52
S.M.E.S.	31	10	1	2	3	-	47
S.E.E.S.	72	25	6	1	4	1	109
S.S.E.S.	34	13	4	1	6	-	58
S.D.M.S.	44	32	6	2	6	1	91
TOTAL	743	326	63	17	121	4	1273

Source: Website of Sikkim Government, 2005. Note: * Indians from the plains.

The younger generation educated Lepchas are politically conscious and articulate demands through various means. The Representation of the People (Amendment) Act, 1980 has reserved 12 seats for both the Lepchas and the Bhutias of Sikkimese origin in the State Assembly. However, the absence of governing formula regarding seat sharing between the Lepchas and the Bhutias has mostly favoured the Bhutias in having larger number of representation in the Assembly. Various Lepcha socio-cultural organizations namely Renjyong Mutanchi Rong Tarjum (Sikkim Lepcha Progressive Association), Renjyong Mutanchi Rong-Ong Shezum (Sikkim Lepcha Youth Organization) have been demanding fifty per cent reservation out of the 12 seats reserved for the Bhutia-Lepcha communities in the Assembly and fifty percent in quota allocated for the tribals in employment and educational institutions for professional courses outside Sikkim. Further, the Sikkim Lepcha Youth Association has also demanded for legal protection banning the sale or purchase of their land by others, including the Bhutias, and compulsory use of 'Lepcha' title by the members of the community, particularly reflect the level of ethnic and identity consciousness among the younger generation of the community. It must be noted here that according to the provision of the Revenue Order No. 1 of 1917 the purchase of Bhutia-Lepcha land by others is forbidden but Bhutias can purchase the Lepcha land and vice-versa. Bhutias being economically better off are in advantageous position. Hence, by raising such demand the Lepcha Association wants legal protection of their land from the Bhutias also. Apart from this, the association also show concern over the practice of changing title due to inter-community marriage and the way that some Lepchas write names without surname (this makes difficulty in identifying a Lepcha from a Bhutia) which has affected the enumeration process and very often the cause of misrepresentation or under representation of the Lepchas.

Considering the spirit of blood brotherhood pact signed between the Lepchas and Bhutias at Kabi Lungtsok and by virtue of living side by side for years, one could presume that there should have been no social alienation between the two. The communities, however, have some delicate problems. From the findings of Chie Nakane it can be said that the Bhutias consider themselves socially and culturally superior race than the Lepchas.[41] The statement is corroborated by Gorer and Das also. Perhaps it was due to this social prejudice that 'when a Lepcha achieved a higher status and became Kazi, he used to identify himself as a Bhutia'.[42] The Bhutia community attaches overwhelming importance to the legendary blood-brotherhood pact which occurred between Lepchas and Bhutias. Lepchas, however, now perceive such a pact as a new leash of domination and assert their separate existence independently of the Bhutias. For example, the Lepcha Youth Association has categorically asked the convener of the Sikkim Bhutia-Lepcha Apex Committee (SIBLAC) to drop 'L' (symbolizing Lepcha) from the name of the organization.

The Bhutias:

The word Bhutia is derived from the name of the place "Bhot", i.e. Tibet, to which the Bhutias of Sikkim originally belonged. The migration of the Bhutias into Sikkim probably have begun during the fifteenth and sixteenth century.[43] Maharaja Thutop Namgyal and Maharani Yeshey Dolma Namgyal have also subscribed to this viewpoint and added further that the migration took place continuously in many ways and through different routes, from the northern and western passes of Sikkim.[44] According to a popular version the religious strife between the Yellow-Hat-Sect (Gelukpas) and the Red-Hat-Sect (Nyngmapas) in Tibet forced many followers of Red-Hat-Sect to flee Tibet along with their leader Khye Bhumsa after their defeat. They settled in the Chumbi Valley, an inalienable part of Sikkim then. Initially the nature loving and friendly Lepchas did not object but as the migration continued the Lepcha Athing, Thekong Tek, advised the Panu Hyum to take stock of the situation. It is said that the Lepcha Panu was treacherously murdered.[45] According to the folklore/legend Khye Bhumsa later sought hospitable relationship with the Lepcha spiritual leader (Athing) Thekong Tek which was then solemnized by a 'blood-brotherhood' pact at Kabi and solicited blessing for son. Having realized their bleak future in Tibet, they made Chumbi Valley their permanent settlement and gradually spread to other parts of Sikkim. These early settlers from Tibet presently are known as Dezongpa or Lhori while those who have migrated to Sikkim during the eighteenth and nineteenth centuries were called Khampa or Pu-pa and considered different from the Denzongpa or Lhori. Those who migrated in the twentieth century, especially after Chinese occupation of Tibet, are referred to as Tibetans. The distinction, however, has been narrowed down due to the use of all embracing generic term "Bhutia" in the Scheduled Tribes Order of 1978.

Following the classification given by Risley, the Bhutias of Sikkim may be grouped under three categories. Firstly, the six families descended directly from Khye Bhumsa. They are Yul-Thenpa, Lingzerpa, Zhantarpa or Sangdarpa, Tshegyu Tarpa, Nyungyepa and Tshepa. The last four families (clans) are also called Tungdu-Rusi or 'the four families of a 1,000 collections'. The second category includes those who migrated after the exodus of Khye Bhumsa. They are called Khampas or Bebtsen Gye by virtue of having founded eight families (Clans) namely Gansapa, Namchangopa, Chungiopa, Ethenpa, Phenchungpa, Phempunadik, Namnakpa and Nachingpa. The third category is comprised of those who migrated at various times since the establishment of the Bhutia rule in Sikkim. They are called Rui-Chhung or the little families with eight important branches, the Chumbipa (immigrants from Kham in Tibet and Ha in Bhutan and settled near Chumbi Valley), and Lopen Lhundub (migrated from Ha and Paro in Bhutan and settled in Lachen and Lachung valleys). Each of these families or clans is further subdivided into several sub-families.

The Sikkimese Bhutia language was a spoken dialect and for all literary, cultural and educational pursuits, Tibetan was used in the past. It was also the official language of Sikkim before the merger. All government gazette notifications were brought out in Tibetan language, including the official newsletter 'Sikkim Herald'. After 1975 efforts have been made to develop Sikkimese Bhutia as a distinct language in Sikkim, and in 1977 the status of Official language has been accorded to it. The social-cultural organization of the Bhutias like Bhutia Kay-Rab-Yargay Tsogpo, is dedicated in conserving and developing the culture, tradition, religion, language and literature of Bhutias of Sikkim. It was established in 1983. It has conducted many seminars, workshops and meetings with the objective of contributing towards the promotion of the Bhutia language and their rich culture. The organization also helps publication of books and dictionaries besides encouraging people who are engaged in the promotion of the Bhutia culture, art, literature and language by felicitating them. Almost all the Bhutias of Sikkim are bilingual/trilingual and speak Bhutia language as well as Nepali and Lepcha languages fluently. The language is taught upto the under-graduate level. The University of North Bengal introduced the Bhutia language as one of the elective subjects in 2001. Some of the prominent writers of the Bhutia language are Pema Rinzing Bhutia, Palden Tshering Gymtso, Norden Tshering, Dorji Rinchen Lama & others. The first Bhutia-English dictionary, co-authored by Norden Tshering and Pema Rinzing Lama, was published in 2001.

The majority of the Sikkimese Bhutias are the followers of Lamaist Buddhism but sympathizer of Christianity is also rising in recent past. Bodhisattva is their chief deity followed by guardian deities, including local deities, family deities, village deities and also mount Kanchenjonga. Monastery or Gumpa is their place of worship and the Bhutia lama (spiritual leader) performs all customary rituals. Their main concentration is in the North district, especially in Lachen and Lachung villages but, of late, they are numerically the largest among the tribes of Sikkim in the East district, especially in Gangtok.

In 1840 the Bhutias were approximately 1995 out of a total of 7000 populations. In 1873 they were 1500 persons out of a total of 5000 population. In 1891 the figure shot up to 4,894 persons among whom 1,966 were males, 1,960 females and 968 were children. The following table (table no. 3.3) will provide an overall view on the growth of the Bhutias in Sikkim. During 1901-1911, there has been a substantial growth, while a decline is recorded in the year 1911-21. The fall has been partly attributed to deaths resulting from the great influenza epidemic of 1917. Since then the increase is maintained steadily except in 1981.

Table 3.3: Number of Bhutia Population in Sikkim from 1840-1991

	COMMUNITIES		
YEAR	**Sikkimese Bhutia**	**Bhutia unspecified**	**Tibetan Bhutias**
1840	1995	N.A.	N.A.
1891	4894	N.A.	N.A.
1909	6000	N.A	N.A.
1911	10411	12433	N.A.
1921	9639	9639	N.A.
1931	11070	15130	560
1951	15626	15626	N.A.
1961	36577	10762	6690
1971	36760	29875	33931
1981	21548	N.A.	4149
1991*	65033	N.A.	N.A.

Source: various books and census reports. * Sikkim Human Development Report, Government of Sikkim, 2001.

The Bhutias were mostly the traders and herdsmen earlier but a sizable number were also engaged in cultivation. They generally preferred hilly terrain, high altitude and cold climate for habitation. With the consolidation of political power and establishment of religious hegemony after 1642 not only the settlement pattern was changed but the social stratification too began to take shape in the form of Royal family, Lamas, Kazis and the commoners.

The Lamas (spiritual leaders), who often belonged to the noble families of Tibet[46] were the custodian of the important monasteries of Sikkim like Dubdi, Pemiongchi, Tashiding etc., besides exercising significant influence, as advisers to the Chogyal, in the political-administrative affairs of the State. The monasteries were in possession of huge landed property over which the Lamas enjoyed both revenue and administrative control. The Kazis, on the other, were landlords / zamindars, mostly belonging to the Bhutia-Lepcha groups, who enjoyed immense economic and political power in a feudal bureaucratic and economic set up under the Chogyal. Within their territorial jurisdiction they also exercised power of adjudication.

The involvement of the British in Sikkim's affair (more explicitly after 1861) saw a reduction in the political and economic powers of the Kazis and Lamas, on the one hand, and settlement of certain Nepali businessmen and peasants and economic prosperity of the protected State of Sikkim on the other.

The economic prosperity led to competition over resources and growth of resentment against the policies of the British Political Officer in general and Nepalis in particular. The resentment, however, led to introduction of certain legislative measures in favour of the Bhutias and Lepchas in the form of prohibition of transaction of the Bhutia-Lepcha land to the Nepalis and other communities (Revenue Order No. 1, 1897/1917), differential rate of revenue between the Bhutia-Lepcha and the Nepali peasants (1915) and settlement laws.

In the wake of demands for abolition of Zaminadari system followed by peasants' movement of 1949-50, certain economic changes were introduced such as abolition of the Zamindari system (excluding 15 private estates of the Chogyal and 5 monastery estates) and payment of revenue directly to the State. Though the effect of the economic reform on the land share pattern was marginal (due to continuation of the Revenue Order No. 1 and absence of ceiling and tenancy reforms), but their source of income had been drastically reduced. They, however, were apprehensive of the government notification no. 3082/L.R., 1954 which had the intention to detect the excess land over the upper ceiling of 20 acres and distribution of the same among the landless masses. They desired for protecting their hereditary right over land and since they exercised influence at the decision-making level, the successive land reform measures to a large extent have remained ineffective.

In 1978 Bhutia community has been recognized as one of the Scheduled Tribes of Sikkim. The 1978 Order included eight other

Bhutias namely Tromopa, Dopthapa, Sherpa, Yolmo, Kagatey, Drukpa, Tibetans and Chumbipa within the definition of the term Bhutia.

Though these groups have been recognized as Bhutias they are not benefited by the Revenue Order No. 1 which prohibits sale or purchase of Bhutia-Lepcha land by other communities, including the Nepalis. However, they can contest elections from the 12 Bhutia-Lepcha seats reserved in the Legislative Assembly of Sikkim.

Traditionally, Bhutias are assertive and industrious people. The young generation Bhutias are well educated, well informed and are conscious of their rights and privileges both as a Sikkimese and as a citizen of a democratic country.

Their access to best available educational institutions in the country and abroad together with the facilities extended to the Scheduled Tribes community, the Bhutias are overwhelmingly represented in the top level bureaucratic posts and in other decision making institutions. Their representation in such institutions often benefited the community immensely in terms of employment and other economic opportunities as compared to other communities of Sikkim.

According to the statistical data provided by the department of Personnel and Administrative Reform & Training, Gangtok, there were as many as 28.76 per cent Bhutias in the highest administrative jobs in 1999, i.e. 44.5 per cent in IAS, 17.4 per cent in IPS and 21.7 per cent in IFS (Forest) in Sikkim.

The percentage is slightly reduced in 2005 mainly due to increasing number of bureaucratic personnel from the plains. Similarly, according to an unpublished report of the Economic Census conducted in 2005-06 by the State government, Bhutias have been ranked as richest among the three communities of the State. Table 3.4 gives us a glimpse on ethnic backgrounds of the bureaucrats in 1999 and 2005 in Sikkim.

Table 3.4: Ethnic Background of the Bureaucrats in Sikkim -1999 & 2005

Ethnic Communities	Number of Cadres and Percentage							
	1999				2005			
	IAS	IPS	IFS	Total	IAS	IPS	IFS	Total
Lepchas	-	-	-	-	01 (2.1)	-	-	01
Bhutias	12 (44.5)	04 (17.4)	05 (21.7)	21	13 (28.3)	03 (12.0)	05 (17.8)	21
Nepalis	06 (22.2)	05 (21.7)	06 (26.1)	17	9 (19.6)	4 (16.0)	6 (21.4)	19
Sherpas	-	-	-	-	01 (2.1)	-	-	01
Others	09 (33.3)	14 (60.9)	12 (52.2)	35	22 (47.8)	18 (72.0)	17 (60.7)	57
Total	27	23	23	73	46	25	28	99

Source: Department of Personnel & Administrative Reform & Training, Government of Sikkim, December 1999 & August 2005.

Being the ruling community, the Bhutias did not have a political organization of their own before 1947 as their interest were adequately protected and represented through various proclamations issued by the Chogyal from time to time. However, some pressure groups of the traditional landlords (Kazis) and Lamas of monasteries were present from the very early days in Sikkim. Being parties to the ruling clique these groups played important roles both in creating channels for articulation of their demands and influencing political decision in favour of the group.

The non-associational group of the Kazis (landlords) was very powerful and enjoyed both administrative and judicial authorities within their territorial jurisdiction. The officials of the Darbar were mostly chosen from among the Kazis and by virtue of their proximity with the Chogyal, they used to influence decision in their favour. It is said that the Kazis were instrumental in denying the status of "hereditary subjects" of Sikkim to the Limboos even when one seat was reserved for them in 1967".[47] In 1978, out of 13 Bhutia-Lepcha candidates who were taken in the IAS cadre selection 10 belonged to the Kazi group.[48]

Similarly, the Bhutia spiritual leaders, called Lamas, also used to form a formidable pressure group in Sikkim. Their activities extended from advising the ruler in political affairs of the country to management of monasteries, including the monetary allocation for monasteries and selection of religious performances out of the State treasury. The custom was that the Chogyal could not avoid the advice tendered by the Lhade Mede, the Council of incarnate Lamas. Their influence in the political affairs of the State was such that in March 1958 one seat was reserved for the monasteries in the State Council as Sangha seat. It was politically very active during the 1970's as the members of the organization were apprehensive of the fate of the Chogyal and the status of Sikkim as a Buddhist State after its merger with a democratic secular India.[49]They were instrumental in maintaining the socio-cultural and political identity of Sikkim even after the merger.

The first ever political organization of the Bhutias, called Sikkim National Party, was formed in 1948 with an objective to oppose the demands of the Sikkim State Congress for accession with India, establishment of responsible government and abolition of the Zamindari system. It was communal in its propaganda and feudal in its outlook, and, as such, failed to function as a political party. Sengupta writes, "The Sikkim National Party has sprung up with a curious programme which may be called the very anti-thesis of the policy of Sikkim State Congress".[50] For the Sikkim National Party, also called Chogyal's party, the Lepchas and Bhutias alone were indigenous Sikkimese whereas Nepalis were considered immigrants from Nepal.

The political and other social organizations that are formed after the merger in 1975 differ from their earlier counterparts in terms of composition and the group to which they appeal for support. Genuinely, they cannot be considered ethnic organizations of the Bhutias but are tribal organizations dominantly led by the Bhutias. The Denzong People's Chogpa (DPC), a registered political party, the Denzong Tribal Yargay Chogpa (DTYC), Sikkim Tribal Welfare Association (STWA), the Denzong Lhaday Yangki Chakchen (Association of Buddhist Monks of Sikkim), the

Bhutia Kay-Rab-Yargay Tsogpo (BKRYT) are such organizations to name a few. The Bhutia Kay-Rab-Yargay Tsogpo is a social organization dedicated in conserving and developing the culture, tradition, religion, language and literature of Bhutias of Sikkim. It was established in 1983.

It conducts seminars, workshops and meetings with the objective of contributing towards the promotion of the Bhutia language and their rich culture. The organization also helps publication of books and dictionaries besides encouraging people engaged in the promotion of the Bhutia culture, art, literature and language by felicitating them. The Association of Buddhist Monks of Sikkim and 'Concerned Citizens of Sikkim' became popular during 1994 in respect to the protest movement unleashed against the construction of Rathang Chu Hydro Electric Project on religious – environmental grounds. The project was abandoned in 1997. Thus, religion has been an important factor and strength which binds the tribals together but in spite of several attempts unification at the ethnic level is yet to be accomplished mainly due to existence of separate organizations of the tribal communities with distinct ideological belief and propaganda. The Bhutia way of life, which is generally highlighted as Sikkimese identity, is something that irks other tribal groups.

The Nepalis:

Nepalis constitute ethno-linguistically the majority group in Sikkim. But before going into the details of the subject there are certain ambiguities associated with the word 'Nepali' which required clarification in the first place. Firstly, who is a Nepali? Is he a citizen of Nepal or a member of an ethnic group or a caste or one who speaks Nepali language? To an average Sikkimese or for Indians as such, Nepali means those who have migrated from Nepal and speak the language which is identified as Nepali / Khaskura or Gorkha and belonging to Aryan languages group as distinct from Tibeto – Burman languages or dialects like Bhutia, Tibetan, Lepcha, Limboo etc. Over the past decades there have been attempts to undermine the history of the existence of various groups who are now known to the outsiders as Nepalis. The Sikkimese Nepalis belong to Sikkim in the same way as the Bhutias and the Lepchas do.

Secondly, Nepali is not a complete homogenous group like that of the Lepchas. It is a conglomeration of different and distinct tribes and communities which can be broadly classified under two basic groups: Mongoloids and Aryans. Thirdly, there is a lack of cohesion between "those who are considered as Nepalis" and "those who consider themselves as Nepalis".[51] For example, the Limboos in Sikkim are called Nepalis but they themselves do not consider so. Similarly, Sherpas or Yolmos are subsumed constitutionally as a Bhutia group but they acknowledge themselves as Nepalis. Fourthly, an identity of a Nepali cannot be established only because he speaks Nepali language. A Bhutia or Lepcha or Marwari may not know any language other than Nepali yet he is never considered as Nepali but a Limboo or Rai or Gurung may speak no Nepali but his own language or dialect, yet he is a Nepali to the outside world.[52] So, Nepali identity is not just linguistic, but also racial and above all historical.

Nepali is just an umbrella term under which various tribes and communities find a homogeneous representation. The following groups are generally included as Nepali such as Bahun (Brahmin), Thakuri, Chhetri, Newar, Rai, Gurung, Tamang, Limboo, Mangar, Jogi, Bhujel, Thami, Yolmo, Sherpa, Dewan, Mukhia, Sunar, Sarki, Kami and Damai. Except those who belonged to Aryan stock and basically Hindus by religion like Bahun, Chhetri, Thakuri, Kami, Sarki and Damai who represent north Indian physical features, rest of the Nepali sub-cultural groups have their own languages or dialects, traditions, cultures, heroes and habits, religion and belong to Mongoloid racial stock. If taken together, they consist of roughly about 50 percent of Sikkim's total population. The Bahun, Chhetri etc. speak Nepali language which belongs to Indo-Aryan group of languages with Nagri script like Hindi while the Mongoloid stocks are mostly bi-lingual, i.e. speak their own language/dialect other than Nepali language. Nepalis, therefore, is a mixture of Aryan and Mongoloid racial groups.

In the history of settlement of different ethnic groups in Sikkim the Nepalis seemed to have followed a natural process due to the prevalence of free intercourse between the people of Nepal and Sikkim, the territorial contiguity existing between the two neighbours, porous and flexible borders and, of course, war. From the writings of many eminent social investigators and anthropologists like Subba, Mackaen, Risley, Hooker, Sinha etc. it is safely established that some of the Nepali tribes or communities belonging to Mongoloid (Matwali) groups like the Limboos (Tsongs), the Mangars, the Gurungs, the Tamangs, the Rais etc. either lived in Sikkim or in places contiguous to it even before the arrival of the Lepchas or were contemporaries of the latter. R.K.Sprigg writes, "the Limboos were living in Sikkim before there was Sikkim for them to live in".[53] Mangers, now a constituent of the larger Nepali community, are among the early inhabitants of Sikkim and are often referred to as contemporary of the Lepchas. According to J.D.Hooker, Mangars were the aborigines of Sikkim, but were driven by the Lepchas to further westwards into the country of the Limboos, and this latter further to the west.[54] The ruins of forts built by the Mangars, called Dzongs, are still found in many parts of Sikkim.

The astounding similarity in the numerical system of the Lepcha and Mangar languages like Nat, Nees, Som, Buli etc.[55] not only indicate influence on each other but it is also a proof that these two communities lived together side by side in the ancient past. The Mangars share some religious, cultural and linguistic similarity with the Gurungs also.[56] In Hooker's writing Murmis (Tamangs) finds a special place as one of the native tribes of Sikkim. He writes that the Murmis (Tamang) are the only other native tribe remaining in any numbers in Sikkim.[57] They are the scattered people of Tibetan origin, and called 'Nishung' named after the two districts of Nimo and Shung, the places of their early inhabitation, situated on the way to Lhasa.[58] They were originally called Bhote, meaning Tibetans, but later they assumed the title 'Tamang' indicating their traditional occupation as "horse riders". The word "Tamang", it is claimed, is derived from the Tibetan word 'Tamakh' meaning "mounted guard" of the king. In Tibetan language 'Ta' means 'horse' and 'Makh' means 'mounted guard'. In course of time the word 'Makh' is believed to have been corrupted as 'Mang'.[59] The Rai community, which is a constituent of the larger Kirata family, is also considered as the ancient inhabitants of Sikkim. A special reference to the Rai tribal community as contemporary of the Lepchas is found in the writings of W.G.Mackaen.[60] Chaudhuri also writes that the Rais have come to Sikkim along with the Lepchas from the Assam hills.[61] A.C.Sinha writes, "In Sikkim there are three main sub-cultural stocks" of the Nepalis community namely "the Kiratis, the Newaris and the Gorkhas." Among the Kiratis, the Limboos, the Rais, the Lepchas, the Gurungs, the Tamangs and the Mangars constitute the autochthonous inhabitants of Sikkim."[62] He further adds that with the growing assertion of the Bhotia rulers, the Limboos, the Mangars, the Lepchas and other Kirati tribes were pushed westwards to Nepal and southwards to India.[63] Risley also writes " the Limboos, Gurungs (Tamus), Murmis (Tamangs), Khambus (Rais / Zimdars) and Mangars are more or less allied, while the others, excepting the Lepcha and Bhutia, are later immigrants from beyond the Arun in Nepal."[64] Haimendrof in his classic work 'Himalayan Traders' has described Gurungs and Rais as tribal communities of Sikkim.[65] The Gurungs of Chakung are called Taksari Gurung and were associated with copper mining. In 1891 the Gurung community constituted the fourth largest community of Sikkim after the Lepchas, Bhutias and Limboos.

Risley, while reflecting on the population of Sikkim in 1891, had used different nomenclatures, such as Rai, Khambu and Jimdar, considering each one as separate community but, in reality, they belong to a single community, i.e. Khambu, the inhabitants of Khambuan. It is said that after the occupation of the Khambuan by Prithibi Narayan Shah in 1832, the Khambu tribal chief was given the honorific title 'Rai'.[66] 'Jimdar', on the other hand, is a corrupted version of the word 'Jimmadar' or 'Jimmidar' or 'Jamindar' (land lords) which probably means the 'functionary with official responsibility' (Jimma = custody or hold + Dar = custodian or holder of land). Taken both the Khambus and Rai/ Jimdar together, the community formed the largest constituent among the Nepali community in 1891 and continues to be so even in present day Sikkim. Presently, only the Rai community uses the title Kirata though etymologically it also includes Limboo, Gurung, Mangar, Tamang, Sunuwar, Lepcha.

The bulk of the Nepalis, particularly those belonging to the Aryan stock, appear to have migrated in the middle of the 19th century. Scholars like T.B.Subba relate the migration with the territorial conquests. He explains that a large chunk of territory of Sikkim, i.e. eastward of Mechi River to the westward of Teesta River, was under Nepal for about thirty-seven years since 1780. Many Nepalis living in that territory are known to have come and settled in Sikkim since then.[67] Not only Sikkim, the present day Tarai belt consisting of Siliguri and adjoining areas was permanently inhabited by the Nepalis and Adhibashi people, there is no record of the Bengali population in Siliguri.[68] In fact the name Siliguri (actually Silagadi = Stone Fort) itself is originated from the Stone Fort constructed by the Gorkha Army at the time of invasion of Sikkim.

Secondly, the scholars like P.K.Rao and B.S.K. Grover consider that Nepalis were particularly encouraged to settle in Sikkim by the British for two important reasons: (a) to accelerate the economic growth, and (b) to counteract the supremacy of the Sikkimese royal family and the Bhutia councilors.[69] Yet other scholars like Karan and Jenkins, Lall and, later on, Datta-Ray consider J.Claude White, the first British political officer of Sikkim, predominantly responsible for the large-scale migration of the Nepalis.[70] Before assuming his new administrative responsibility in Sikkim as the Political Officer, J.C. White had spent a year or so in Nepal and thus had the experience of working and understanding the Nepali way of life. He justified the Nepali migration on the economic ground saying that "the un-enterprising, lazy and unthrifty aborigines would not respond to the strong inducements held out to them to open up this new land."[71] In the Administrative Report of 1905-06 he writes, "The Nepali ryot is hardworking and thrifty as a rule, pays his taxes regularly and at the same time is a law-abiding and intelligent settlers."[72] In 1906 he expressed his willingness to open up hitherto forbidden North district for the Nepalis in the interest of Sikkim. During 1910-11 he regretted that "immigration from Nepal continues but not on as large a scale as formerly."[73] Equally responsible were those Lepcha councilors and landlords who always favoured settlement of Nepalis in Sikkim for economic benefits. The prominent among them were Tseepa Lama, Khangsa Dewan, Phodong Lama and Lasso Athing[74]

Apart from the economic reason, there is a political dimension also associated with the process of migration. In the context of Sikkim the British interest had always met a fitting challenge from the pro-Tibetan forces within Sikkim and Tibet as a whole. Sikkim, in fact, proved to be a common bone of contention between the British and the Tibetan rulers. The Tibetans had always considered Sikkim as an extension of Tibet, and the successive Chogyals, except for Sir Tashi Namgyal, looked towards Tibet as an ultimate source of guidance in all respects, including management of monasteries and religious matters.

Thus, in order to combat against such a strong contender and challenger it was obvious for J.C.White to turn towards the Nepalis who had already proved their being sui generis both in times of war and peace. In this connection Basnet writes, "The Gorkhas (Nepalis) made as good a peasant in peace-time as he made a soldier in war. The Bhutias and Lepchas made poor farmers partly because of their ignorance of the methods of cultivation and partly because of a natural indolence. The Lepchas had always been used to easy-going ways and was averse to hard labour or, for that matter, any other form of strife and struggle. The Bhutias, while having natural aptitude for trade, was loath to physical labour."[75]

Another factor which seemed to have worked for Nepalis was the changing socio-political scenario in the Himalayan Kingdom. The military expeditions intending to consolidate Nepal politically under Prithivi Narayan Saha and his successors, the population explosion and its effect on land holdings, declining economic conditions and food deficiency in Nepal are specially highlighted by scholars as indigenous factors, also called push factors, responsible for Nepali migration.

Whereas, various treaty agreements such as Anglo-Nepalese Friendship Treaty of 1850, the Indio-Nepal Peace and Friendship Treaty of 1950 etc. served as legal political framework in the process of migration and are considered external factors or pull factors. For instance article 7 of the Indo-Nepal Treaty of 1950 states; "The Government of India and Nepal agree to grant, on a reciprocal basis, to the nationals of one country in the territories of the other the same privileges in the matter of residence, ownership of property, participation in trade and commerce, movement and other privileges of a similar nature."[76]

Another element, which should be taken into cognizance, is that all Nepalis who have settled in Sikkim might not be migrants from places of Nepal. As mentioned earlier many tribal communities, who are presently included into the Nepali fold, inhabited the western and southern parts of Sikkim long before the country got its present name. Sikkim of the 18th or 19th centuries cannot be considered as the land of economic opportunity or socio-politically enticing for settlement purposes. Thus, many groups who were known by their own individual calling were living in Sikkim from the very early days but the term Nepali is of later origin. They are so used to their individual calling that even today during the census enumeration they err by writing group's title instead of Nepali.

According to the unconfirmed report the Nepalis were perhaps 1995 persons in 1840 out of a total population of 7000 persons. According to Edgar the total population of Sikkim in 1873 was 5000 persons out of which Nepalis, including the Limboos, were 1000. The populations gradually increased with the passage of time and under various historical / political circumstances. Table 3.5 provides detail of the Nepali population in Sikkim since 1840.

Table 3.5: Nepali Population in Sikkim during 1840-1991

YEAR	TOTAL POPULATION
1840	1995
1891	18,981
1909	50,00
1931	36,105*
1951	97,863**
1961	88,916***
1971	1,34,236
1981	1,92,295
1991	2,84,520****

Source: Various books and census records. Note: *Separate enumeration of groups like Gurung, Rai, Mangar, Chhetri, Kami are not available for this period.

** Taken on the basis of religion (Hindus) inclusive of Indian plainsmen.

*** On the basis of language spoken. ****Inclusive of "others".

The above table is indicative of the fact that the population of Nepali community increased gradually over the decades. In 1931 the population has been shown only 36,105 persons due to the unavailability of the data regarding the Gurungs, Rais/Jimdars/Khambus, Mangar, Chhetri and Kami sub-cultural groups of the larger Nepali community. Due to some enumeration difficulties these communities perhaps have been included in 'others' which is shown over 49,043 persons in 1931 census.

Nepalis are predominantly Hindus by religion and linguistically different from that of the Bhutias or Lepchas. For being one of the premier communities of Sikkim, they assert their own separate identity and resent any propaganda undermining their interest and existence/identity. The Bhutias, on the other, are apprehensive about the Nepalis because of their numbers, economic well-being and assertive nature. In her article, Chie Nakane attempts to highlight areas of disagreement by saying that "the ruling class (Bhutias) of Sikkim is much concerned, not only about the Nepali economic exploitation of the Lepcha and Bhotia community, but also about the increase of the Nepali population as opposed to the decrease of the Lepcha-Bhotia population."[77] Nepalis seemed to have shown great resilience despite the use or misuse of legal – political apparatus against the community in the past. The differential treatment against the community actually strengthened the feeling of togetherness or belongingness among various sections of Nepalis, on the one hand, and emergence of new class of educated individuals, on the other. These new breed of Nepalis were not only employed in various governmental capacities but were also active in the field of politics and were at the helm of corridors of power. C.D.Rai, Kashi Raj Pradhan, D.B.Gurung, R.P.Alley, D.B.Tiwari, Raghubir Singh Basnet, Nahkul Pradhan, Nagendra Singh Gurung, P.B. Khati etc. belong to this group.

In 1941 the first ever social organization of the Nepalis, called Member Party, was born at Namthang with objectives to oppose the oppressive rules and the practice of forced labour, called Zharlangi. Later in 1947 three other socio-political organizations by the name of Praja Sudharak Samaj, Praja Sammelan and Praja Mandal were born predominantly led or with the support of the Nepalis. In 1948 these three organizations were merged to form a full fledged political party by the name of Sikkim State Congress with objectives to abolition of Zamindari system, formation of interim government and accession of Sikkim with India.

After the establishment of a democratic government in India in 1947 Sikkim entered into an interim agreement with India in 1948 and a full-fledged treaty in 1950. With the signing of these treaty-agreements the prospects for extension of democratic values in Sikkim became a reality. Gradually changes in old laws and system of governance had been introduced accommodating the interests of the Nepalis. In 1951 six seats were reserved for the Nepalis in the State Council which was further raised to 16 in 1974. In 1975 Sikkim was merged with India and with it the Nepali seats had been converted into 17 General seats in 1979. In 1979

Mr. N.B.Bhandari became the first Nepali Chief Minister of Sikkim followed by three other Chief Ministers namely B.B.Gurung (1984), S.M.Limboo (1994) and P.K.Chamling (1994, 1999, 2004, 2009).

Nepali language became one of the official languages in 1977 though the language had been the lingua-franca of the state from the very early days. The first ever coin minted in Sikkim in 1880's was engraved in Nepali. The first Nepali Boarding School was set up at Gangtok in 1906 which in 1925 was merged with Bhutia Boarding School to form Tashi Namgyal High School of the present day. In 1921 Nepali language was used as the medium of instruction in this school and in the following year it became an optional paper and compulsory paper since 1924. From 1925 Nepali became the medium of instruction in all the schools of Sikkim. At present, apart from Nepali, languages spoken by various other constituents of the larger Nepali community like Newar, Gurung, Rai, Sunuwar, Mangar, Limboo and Tamang languages have been recognized as official languages and are taught at the school and under-graduate levels in Sikkim.

Nepalis in Sikkim are classified into four groups namely Scheduled Tribes (Limboos and Tamangs), Most Backward Classes (Gurung, Rai, Manger, Thami, Sunuwar, Bhujel, Dewan etc.), Other Backward Classes (Bahuns, Chettris and Newars) and Scheduled Castes (Kami, Damai, Sarki etc.).

Other communities / groups:

In this section, discussions about certain racial groups of the Nepalis have been presented in view of the ambiguities currently surrounding the groups and their ethnic identities. The ambiguities basically revolve around what do the groups in question think, or others think about their ethnic affiliation. For instance, the Limboos in Sikkim are called Nepalis but they themselves (at least organizationally) do not consider as Nepalis. Similarly, Sherpas or Yolmos are subsumed constitutionally as the Bhutia group but they generally acknowledge themselves as Nepali. Such developments in recent years indicate the presence of a dichotomy between self-definition of the group and generally perceived notions about the group; and also indicate the evolving nature of cultural and ethnic identities. A group or a sub-group under certain historical circumstances may try to redefine their self-identity and claim distinctiveness. For this reason, it is felt that the groups which in recent years have attempted to assert their separate identity, contrary to prevailing perception about their identity, deserve separate treatment.

The Limboos (Tsongs):

The community is known as Tsongs or Chongs in Sikkim, and 'Yakthumba' – a term which is popular in Nepal is an endogamous term generally used by the Limboos themselves. The honorific title 'Subba', which means Chief, is also often in use as synonym which was perhaps given by the Gorkha rulers after the conquest of the Limbuan, presently eastern Nepal, the principal settlement area of the Limboos.

Etymologically, the term "Limboo" means "archer" or "bow shooter" and the community is carrying this name since the split of Limbuan into ten districts / thums.[78] Yakthumba, on the other, most likely means inhabitants of hill or hill men (Yak=Hill, Thum=Place/District and Ba or Pa = people / inhabitants.)[79] According to another version, Yakthumba means Yak herders[80] which seems relevant in case of the Lhasa Gotra Limboos who, as some writes have put it, have migrated from the Tibetan region of Tsang where Yak is found in abundance. The Limboos, however, do not subscribe to the idea of Gotra classification which they consider predominantly a Hindu practice. They consider it as an attempt to identify the Limboos within the Hindu fold. According to J.R.Subba "Yakthungba" got currency only after the division of Limbuan into ten provinces or Thums. To him the word "Yakthumba" is composed of three Limboo words namely "Yiok, Thum and Ba" which means "fort, Province and from" respectively and when taken together it becomes "from the fort of the province". It is quite a common practice among the Limboos to ask to which province a Limboo man or woman belongs to. The common question is "Adangba (si) Atti Thum Keyungba (si) Be?" The answer to this query can be "Tambar Yiok Keyungba Ro" or we are from Tambar fort of Tambar Khola. 'Yiokthumba' in course of time corrupted to 'Yakthungba'.[81] Since Limboos are predominantly found in and around Yaksum, there is a strong possibility of having the word "Yaksumpa" corrupted into "Yak-thum-ba/pa" in the distant past. The Purana also gives reference to a group of people called 'Yak-sa' whose kingdom was in the Himalayas. The Limboos belong to the Kirata tribal family whose earliest reference is found in the Puranas.[82] Their original homeland was supposed to be in the Tsang province of Tibet from where they migrated to a place lying on the eastern or the left bank of the Arun and extending from it to Sikkim (i.e. Sikkim of 1858), was referred to as Limbuan or the country of the Limboos. It formerly belonged to Sikkim, but was conquered and permanently annexed to Nepal by the descendants of Prithivi Narayan Shah of Nepal.[83] Their migration from Tsang province is believed to have been due to the increasing influence of the Lamaism over their religious way of life.[84] The title "Tsong", as the Bhutias of Sikkim preferred to use, links them with the province of Tsang in Tibet.[85] The lexicon meaning of the term "Tsong" in Bhutia language is 'to sell'[86] which associates the Tsong (Limboo) people with their occupational trait as 'merchants'.

Thus, the present two districts namely Gyalsing (Geyzing) in the west and Namchi in the south and a part of the north district of Sikkim lying on the western bank of the Teesta river were originally peopled by the Limboos. The territorial area, called Limbuan, was divided into 10 districts or thums headed by their respective chiefs, called Subba. From this division into 'Ten' the Limboos were henceforth referred to as 'Das Limboos' (Ten Limboos) and derived clan names either from locality or from the 'thars' or septs or sub-divisions.[86]

According to R.K. Sprigg, "The Limboos were living in Sikkim before there was a Sikkim for them to live in! By this paradoxical remark I mean that Limboos have inhabited the area in which they now predominate (or in which they predominated till very recently) from time immemorial; but Sikkim has been in existence only since 1642, a Water Horse Year, and in the year in which Phuntsog

Namgyal ascended the throne as the first Chogyal at Yoksum Norbugang in what is now western Sikkim."[87] They (Limboos) seemed to have shared with the Lepchas the Western half of Sikkim, before the advent of the Tibetans and other Nepali tribes.[88] Risley too has mentioned about the Limboos as one of the early inhabitants of Sikkim and their coexistence with the Lepchas to the extent that they share common clan names like Sangmipo, Luksom etc.[90] The Bhutias and Lepchas call them 'Tsongs' which etymologically means 'merchants'.

That the Limboos (Tsongs) were one of the early inhabitants of Sikkim is conspicuous by the fact that in the treaty of "Lho-Mon-Tsong-Sum", believed to have been signed in the middle of seventeenth century, also mentioned 'Tsong' (Limboos) along with the 'Lho' (Bhutias) and the 'Mon' (Lepchas). The treaty signed in water hare year is the historical testimony of a blood relationship among the three communities of Sikkim and a pledge to "abide by the commands of the king, his Guru and his sons and will never let arise a bad thought against Sikkim".[90]

The text further adds, "we the ministers and leaders of Sikkim including those of the eight communities of Lhopas (Bhutias) hereby pledge that Lho-Mon-Tsong-Sum will have one destiny and one government. They will fight together with their foes and ...... feast together with their friends......... If any among the Lho-Mon-Tsong-Sum, would not abide by this pledge will be made to pay three ounces of gold as pledge breach fee and thereafter he will be punished according to the degree of crime he has committed from slight physical punishment to the extent of death penalty. No hesitation will be made in execution of this punishment so that all may keep this in their minds."[91]

Understandably, the Treaty was designed to ensure political stability to the Namgyal dynasty, established in 1642, from the potential threat from both the Lepchas and Limboos. If the translation is authentic, the apprehension of the Bhutias is noted as "during the last Mongpa (Lepcha) war some people's action were noted and let them be beware of now from this year of water hare onwards we will abide by the King, his Guru and his sons and will never let arise a bad thought against Sikkim"[92] It also suggests that the treaty was accorded after the establishment of the Namgyal dynasty. The enactment of the treaty was followed by grant of autonomy to the Limboos by the king Phuntsog Namgyal as "The Tsong or Subba or Limboo Chiefs are hereby authorized to rule their districts under the title of 'Subba' with all the facilities of enjoying their tribal rites in social and religious functions by beating the royal band called Negara (Perlge) or cattle drum."[93]

In all its likelihood, the Treaty of Lho-Men-Tsong-Sum was never implemented in the sense there is no record suggesting that Limboos (Tsongs) were ever appointed as Dzongpens during the rule of Phuntsog Namgyal. Kutturan writes that there is no record to indicate that such a council had ever existed.[94] However, the conclusion of the Treaty helped the Bhutias in winning the support of the Limboos in future military expeditions and consolidation of Sikkim. Later Nepal succeeded in occupying the whole of Limbuwan area up to the Teesta River for thirty-seven years since 1780. As per the condition of the Treaty of Titaliya of 1817, the portion of the land occupied by the Gorkhas were restored by the British to Sikkim which now form the west district of Sikkim including the present district of Darjeeling in West Bengal. It is said that the Limboos were one of the ethnic groups who had witnessed the consecration ceremony of the first Chogyal of Sikkim in 1642 at Yaksum.

Similarly, the name of the country Sikkim itself is the conspicuous testimony of the Limboos (Tsongs) being the ancient inhabitants of Sikkim. According to Risley the word 'Sikkim' is derived from the two Limboo words "Su" (new) and "Khin" (a house or place) and is associated with a new palace built at Rabdentse by Phuntso Namgyal.[95] L.B.Basnet also considers the word Sikkim originating from Limboo vocabulary "Su-Him" (new house) and the name was first got currency when a Lepcha Chief married a Limboo girl.[96] According to the Limboo legend when the bride entered her husband's house she exclaimed in her own tongue "Su-Him", and thus, in course of time, corrupted into Sukhim,

Sikhim and then to Sikkim.[97] However, from the writings of Hamilton and Kirkpatrick, it is clear that the name was originally given to a place and not to a country.[98] This also suggests that the Limboos have the tradition of inter-marriage with other tribes particularly with the Lepchas and in many respects their habits are found to be similar to those of the Lepchas.

Scholars differ in their viewpoints regarding the Limboo religion. Campbell admits that the Limboo religion is neither Hindu nor Buddhist but at the same time it is very difficult to "give a name to the one they practice".[99] Dalton too has similar difficulties and adds that they have "obstinately adhered to their primitive paganism."[100] Risley calls the leading principle of the Limboo religion as animism.[101] Some other scholars like Swami Prapannacharya and Gambhir Rai Arya have linked Kirati tribes with the Aryans (not mongoloids) and their religion with the Vedic origin.[102] In this context, it is worth mentioning that the Limboos of Sikkim have been worshiping three important deities: Theba Samang (literally Grandfather God), Yuma Samang (Grandmother God), and Him Samang (Household God).[103] besides worshiping Tagera Nyingmaphuma, which is often personified as Lord Shiva. Hence any clear relationship with either Hinduism or Buddhism cannot be established.

The manner of worship, however, differs depending upon the clan and locality but sacrifice of male animals and birds are common among them. Limboos have a tradition of "mundhums", a sort of rituals chanted orally while performing various kinds of religious performances. The priests are variously called as Phedengma or Samba or Yebe-Yema and Yuma depending upon the kind of ritualistic functions they perform. Generally Phedengma is supposed to perform more sober and cleaner religious duties than the Yebas and the Yemas. The Sambas are believed to possess immense powers of controlling and driving off the evil spirits.

The Limboo language belongs to the Tibeto – Burman family like many other mongoloid languages. The script is called "Siri Jonga", originally taken from Brahmi script prevalent in North India and evolved through the 6th century A.D.[104] The script is named after its creator Siri Jonga who was the Limboo king of Limbuwan. During the eighteenth century another Limboo linguist, Teyongsi Siri Jonga Sing Theba, spread the language among the Limboos of Limbuwan and Sikkim. His mission was considered dangerous by the Tibetan authority in Sikkim and was killed by the Lamas of Pemiongchi monastery in 1741 at Martam, West Sikkim. Teyongsi in Limboo language means re-incarnation and he is considered as the re-incarnation of Siri Jonga of Limbuwan. The third phase in the history of evolution of Limboo language began with Lasor Sendang (1840-1926) who was born at Atharai Thum of Limbuwan.

He taught Limboo language to the villagers of Western Sikkim.[105] It was due to his relentless and inspirational effort that a Yakthung Hang Chumlung Sabha was held on 26th July, 1925 at Kalimpong and later the Sabha was converted into Akhil Baratiya Kirant Chumlung Association to cover greater areas of Darjeeling and Sikkim. The social movement started by Mahaguru Phalgunanda Lingden during the middle of the 20th century contributed immensely towards the promotion of the Limboo language and script including social reforms and religious awakening among them.[106] The movement was especially successful in bringing the Limbos of Limbuan, Darjeeling, Kalimpong and Sikkim (west, south & north Sikkim) under a single platform of "Satya Dharma ko Muchulka" (Conscious Document of True Religion). Since Mahaguru Lingden was the follower of Josmani sect of Hinduism which believes in prohibition of animal sacrifice, non-vegetarian diet and consumption of liquor etc., it was considered antithetical to the Limboo way of life in general and hence his influence remained confined to a small section of the Limboo population.

In 1942 Iman Singh Chemzong arranged for teaching Limboo language in Geyzing (now Gyalsing). He wrote Limboo-English dictionary besides publishing many books on Limboo literature and culture. Harkadhoj Limboo also used his influence as the Councilor to teach Limboo language as additional subjects upto class II and in 1979 it was taught upto class VIII. In 1981 the language was recognized as one of the State Languages of Sikkim and in 1982 Limboo programmes were broadcast through All India Radio, Gangtok. In 1985 it was introduced as main subject in the syllabus of Central Board of Secondary Education (CBSE)[107] and in 2000 the University of North Bengal gave permission to teach the language as main subjects at the under-graduate level.[108]

Though the Treaty of Lho-Mon-Tsong-Sum mentioned Limboos as sons of Bhutias, the Limboos continue to receive unequal treatment from the successive Bhutia rulers. The Revenue Order No. 1 of 1917 did not include Limboos as one of the protected members of the Chogyal's subjects. They were treated at par with other Nepalis and paid higher revenues. In 1958 Shri Barnadhoj Limboo contested the Council election from the Pemayongtse constituency but owing to the complicated and communal system of voting introduced under 1958 proclamation, he was not elected despite securing 684 votes as against the third successful candidates, Shri Galden Tashi Bhutia, who secured 623 votes. In 1961 the Chogyal promulgated the Sikkim Subject Regulation identifying the Limboos as one of the indigenous subjects of Sikkim. The proclamation embroiled into controversy allegedly for creating a rift within the Nepali community. Though all references to communities were removed from the Subjects Regulations with effect from 16 January 1962[109] it was successful in raising doubts whether Limboos were Nepalis. In 1967 one seat was reserved for the Limboos in the Sikkim Council and in 1968 royal permission was granted for teaching Limboo language in government schools.[110] The Limboo seat in the Sikkim Council continued till 1973. The Representation of Sikkim Subjects of 1974, however, unceremoniously abolished the provision of a separate Tsong (Limboo) seat and for all practical purposes the community was clubbed with the Nepali community.

In May 23, 1973 the Akhil Sikkim Kirat Limbu (Limboo) Chumlung was established at Tharpu in West Sikkim. The organization in its first meeting held on 19 July 1973 at Soreng bazaar in west Sikkim adopted resolutions declaring 'Chongs'

(Tsongs/Limboos) as one of the indigenous tribes of Sikkim and were not Nepalis.[111] In 1976 the Kazi government did not recommend Limboos as the Scheduled Tribes of Sikkim even though the Central Home Ministry had particularly asked for clarification from the State Government as to why Limboos (Tsongs) could not be included in the list of Scheduled Tribes of Sikkim.[112] In November 1977 the then Governor of Sikkim, Shri B.B.Lall, wrote to the central counterpart demanding restoration of seats reserved earlier for the Limboos in Sikkim Legislative Assembly in concurrence to article 371F(f) of the constitution of India.[113] However, Limboos were neither recognized as tribes of Sikkim in 1978 nor seat was restored when the Presidential Ordinance seeking to amend the Representation of People Act 1950 and 1951 was issued in 1979. Since then the Limboos, through its various forums, have been highlighting the concept of Lho-Men-Tsong-Sum in support of the claim as aboriginal Sikkimese and their just demand for inclusion in the list of Scheduled Tribes and restoration of seats in the Assembly. In August 1987 the State government submitted the following explanations in favour of the Limboo community in the conference of the Union Ministers held for comprehensive revision of the list of Scheduled Castes and Scheduled Tribes as "Limboos: They claim their existence right from the time of that of the Lepcha in Sikkim. They were one of the members of the Lho-Mon-Tsong-Sum. They have their separate language complete with script, which the State Government has described as one of the State Languages and is being taught up to class XII in schools. They have their different theory of god/goddess and ritual indicating trait of distinct culture and tradition. Their case for inclusion in the list of Scheduled Tribes has already been recommended by the State Government of Sikkim".[114] Though there were sufficient recommendations in favour of the Limboo community for Scheduled Tribes status, the then Bhandari government reserved the special recommendation by stating "We cannot separate the demands. We do not want divide and rule policy. All Sikkimese are one".[115]

According to the report of the Economic Survey carried out by the Bureau of Economics and Statistics, Government of Sikkim, in 1994-95 the Limboos constituted about 10.71 per cent (6842 households) of the total households (63,878) of Sikkim. While classifying the Limboo households under seven economic categories the Report concluded that the Limboos were economically poorer as compared to the general households of Sikkim. About 80.32 percent (5,496) of the Limboo households had less than Rs. 11,000/- while 91.94 percent (6,260) had less than Rs. 20,000/- annual income indicating that the majority of Limboo households were below the poverty line.

Table 3.6: Limboo Households by Economic Categories, 1994-95.

Households Income per annum	Limboo Households (Absolute)	Percentage of Limboo Households categories	Total Households (Absolute)	Percentage
Below Rs. 4,000/-	2592	37.80	18,655	29.20
Below Rs. 6,000/-	3662	53.52	28,933	45.20
Below Rs. 8,500/-	4775	69.79	38,869	60.84
Below Rs. 11,000/-	5496	80.32	46,581	72.92
Below Rs. 20,000/-	6260	91.94	55,258	86.51
Below Rs. 50,000/-	6801	99.40	62,747	98.22
Above Rs. 50,000/-	41	0.06	1,131	1.77
Total	6842	-	63,878	-

Source: Bureau of Economics and Statistics, Government of Sikkim, 1994-95, Gangtok.

The Bureau highlighted the following factors responsible for such a dismal economic condition of the Limboos in Sikkim. They are:

a. Political and administrative suppression by the ruling class for nearly 353 years. (1642-1995 A.D.);

b. Social and economic exploitation by the ruling class for about 333 years (1642-1975);

c. Faulty culture and traditions of Limboos themselves;

d. Low level of literacy, awareness, simple mindedness and peace loving nature;

e. Lack of political, economic and social awareness.[116]

Table 3.7: Number of Limboos in Government services, 1994-95

Employment Class	Limboos	Others	Total	(%) of Limboos	(%) of Others
Class I	7	352	359	0.03	1.95
Class II	33	750	783	0.18	4.14
Class III	524	9,183	9,707	2.89	50.74
Class IV	450	6,797	7,247	2.48	37.56
Total	1014	17,082	18,096	5.60	94.40

Source: Bureau of Economics and Statistics, Government of Sikkim, 1994-95, Gangtok.

According to the table 3.7. Limboos occupy a small section of the total workforce in the State Government. Their percentage at the higher administrative and decision-making level is negligible while at the lower levels (class III and IV employees) the members of the community are employed in large numbers i.e. 2.89 and 2.48 percent respectively.

In 1990 the community was included in the list of Other Backward Classes (OBC) of Sikkim by the central government but the State government headed by the Chief Minister Bhandari refused to implement the Mandal Commission recommendations in Sikkim.[117] The community was also denied opportunity to be recognized as Scheduled Tribes of Sikkim in 1990 for ethnic and political reasons.[118] In 1994 the Chief Minister, P.K.Chamling, implemented the Mandal Commission recommendations and Limboos, besides other, were recognized as the Other Backward Classes of Sikkim. Chamling also wrote to the central government for the (a) recognition of the Limboo language in the Eighth Scheduled of the constitution of India; (b) inclusion of the Limboo community in the Scheduled Tribes list of Sikkim; and (c) reservation of seats for the Limboos in the Legislative Assembly of Sikkim.[119]

The Report of the Other Backward Classes Commission submitted to the State Government in 1998 provides following details (Table 3.8) on the economic position of the Limboos in respect of other communities. The data was compiled from 38 government departments.

Table 3.8: Caste/Community-wise Employment Status in 38 Departments, 1998.

Sl. No.	Communities	Selection IAS/IPS/IFS	Gazetted Grade I	Gazetted Grade II	Non-Gazetted	Class IV
1	Scheduled Tribe	23	95	120	888	1115
2	Scheduled Caste	2	7	15	143	450
3	Bahun/Sharma	2	25	42	372	739
4	Chhetri	6	11	35	318	752
5	Pradhan/Newar	7	17	44	245	301
6	Gurung	-	8	17	180	524
7	Mangar/Thapa	1	1	16	74	208
8	Tamang	1	5	12	158	555
9	Limboo	2	3	14	151	586
10	Rai	1	12	28	81	789
11	Sunuwar	-	2	9	50	23
12	Dewan	-	2	3	5	2
13	Giri/Sanyasi	-	1	1	16	44
14	Jogi	-	-	-	2	13
15	Thakuri	-	-	1	4	3
16	Bhujel	-	-	1	10	29
17	Bengali	-	1	4	16	1
18	Marwari	1	2	4	10	5
19	Bihari	3	3	6	20	15
21	Sweeper	-	-	-	-	5
22	Keralian	-	1	20	20	15
23	Rajasthani	-	1	-	2	-
24	Kashmiri	-	-	-	1	-
25	Mohamedan	-	-	-	2	-
26	Garali	-	-	-	1	-
27	AngloIndian	-	-	-	-	1
28	Thami	-	-	-	-	2
29	Karmakar	-	-	-	1	6
30	Oria	-	-	-	1	-

Source: Report of the OBC Commission, 1998.

In January 2003, the Limboos and Tamangs were recognized as the Scheduled Tribes of Sikkim without fixing the number of seats to be reserved for them in the State Assembly though notification in this respect is required under article 332 of the constitution of India. In the same year the Union Cabinet postponed all issues relating to delimitation of Assembly and Parliamentary constituencies to till 2026 and the delimitation commission formed in 2002 could not carryout separate enumeration of the Limboos as they were not Scheduled Tribes in 2001. Since then the Sikkim Limboo Tamang Tribal Forum and the Sikkim Limboo Tamang Joint Action Committee have been demanding for reservation of seats within the special provision of articles 371F and 332 (1) of the constitution of India. It must be mentioned here that article 371 (F) is non-obstante in nature. The recognition of the Limboos and Tamangs as Scheduled Tribes, however, has created an anomalous situation.

These communities are now recognized constitutionally as Scheduled Tribes but they cannot contest election from the 12 Bhutia –Lepcha seats in the State Assembly of Sikkim because these seats are reserved only for Bhutias and Lepchas not as Scheduled Tribes but as ethnic communities. In order to solve the problem the Delimitation Commission in its letter to the Government of India, vide letter no 282/DEL/2003, dated 11.06,2003, proposed for the need to amend Section 7 (1A) of the Representation of the People Act 1950.[120] In December 2005 the Government of Sikkim constituted a commission under the chairmanship of Prof. B.K.Burman. The Commission in its report submitted on 31st March 2008 recommended for reservation of 20 seats for the tribals,[121] including the Limboos and Tamangs and others who would be considered for inclusion as tribes in future. The Government of Sikkim has accepted the recommendation in its meeting held on 24th April, 2008 and forwarded to the government of India for necessary action but as of now no further development has taken place in this regard.

Thus, Limboos are one of the primordial ethnic communities of Sikkim and are generally identified with the larger Nepali entity. But, a substantial section of Limboo community resents to such identification. Almost all of them speak Limboo language beside the Nepali language. The community has been having, at least, one representation in the Legislative Assembly since 1974 and the same has been increased to four after 1999. They are one of the Scheduled tribes of Sikkim but seat in the Assembly is yet to be reserved.

The Sherpas:

The Sherpas are known all over the world for their virility as efficient mountaineers. The word "Sherpa" is a combination of two Bhutia words 'Shayar' (East) and 'Pa' (Residents or People). Thus, it is presumed that the name "Sherpa" was used by the Tibetans. According to Balchandra Sharma, a noted Nepali historian, the Sherpas have come down from Tibet and settled on the North Eastern part of Nepal especially in the region of Solo Khumbu.[122] The Sherpa legend, however, indicates their original place as Shera-Ta in the Kham province of Tibet. Following their tantric leader, named Shyr-Toong-Gyal, the Sherpas migrated to the regions of Solokhumbu in Nepal and some of them advanced further towards the hilly areas of Darjeeling, Bhutan and Sikkim.[123] In another version the Sherpas are considered to have originally lived "in the frontier of districts in the Tsing-Lai-Sechwan provinces of China[124] and possibly migrated to Sikkim and other parts of the region after Tibet's conversion to Buddhism in the middle of the 7th century.[125] Since the Sherpas were, and still are, by and large Buddhist by religion, their occupational indulgence as porters and guides in mountain expeditions till date provides a valuable basis for migration into the hilly areas of Darjeeling and Sikkim. They are also seen having leadership and organizational qualities.

The Sherpas are divided into number of endogamous clans which can broadly be divided into two groups - Khadev and Khamedu - the former holding a higher status than the latter.[126] Further, there are subdivisions or sub-clans or branches within these two bigger clans. A few of them are – Gajra, Goporma, Golay, Pang Karma, Pang Dorjay, Pal Dorjay, Pinasa, Nay Jungba, Rong Sherpa etc.

The early accounts of the Sherpa population in Sikkim are not available. The census taken in Sikkim in 1891 does not provide details about the Sherpa population but the passing remark made by Risley in the Gazetteer of Sikhim (1928/1993) suggests that most probably the Sherpa community was enumerated and shown as Bhutias.[127] At present the Sherpa population in Sikkim is around 20,000 to 25,000[128] with 3,340 households[129] spread in all the districts of Sikkim. The areas inhabited mostly by the Sherpa population in Sikkim are Ribdi, Bareng, Sangkhu, Okhrey, Seprey Nagi (Sombarey), Bega and Bermoik in the West district, Bermoik Thangsing, Palk Naya Busty, Damthang, Jowbari, Perbing and Soreng in the South, Phademchen, Agamlok, Subaney Dara, Sumin, Dokchen, Thokchey and Yali in the East district and Kabi in the North district.

The Sherpas in general are the followers of Buddhism of Ningmapa sect; but spirit worshipping, called Bonpo, which too is influenced by the tenets of Buddhism, is also common among them. Like the Tibetan lamas the Buddhist Sherpa lama performs rituals based on the teachings of Padmasamvava (Guru Rimpochey) along with the main mantra as "Om-Mani-Padmay-Hum-Ray". While the Bonpo Lama follow the teachings of Bonpa Serab and initiate puja ceremony with "Om-Manti-Muyey-Saydo" as key mantras.

The Sherpas observe various social and religious festivals and are mostly organized in Gumpas. Their festivals, culture, food habits and traditional attire, except for 'Gametil', a piece of striped cloth worn over the Bakhu, which the married Sherpa women wear at the back while the Bhutia women wear the same piece of cloth, called 'Pangden', on the front, bears much resemblance with Bhutias. Lochar (New Year) is their most important festival besides Manirindu, Dumji and Osho etc.

The Sherpas speak in Sherpa language among them and use Tibetan script. Sherpa language falls under the Tibeto-Burman group of languages but Dawa Gyatso Sherpa, the Sherpa translator in the Sikkim Legislative Assembly, contends that "Sherpa language is based on Tibetan language but it differs from Tibetan in pronunciation. Only ten percent of Sherpa words resemble Tibetan words".[130] The language is accorded recognition in Sikkim as a State language in 1995 and since 2000 it is being taught upto the senior secondary levels in government schools. Besides rendering Assembly proceedings in Sherpa language, the deliberations can also be made in the Sherpa language in the State Legislature as was done for the first time by Mingma Tshering Sherpa, legislator from the Rakdong-Tintek (BL) constituency, in 2002 Budget Session.

In Sikkim, the Sherpas are mostly engaged in agricultural activities. Land is their main source of income but since the Revenue Order No. 1 does not provide protection, the number of landless among them is on the rise. The subsidiary sources of income include labour, service and guides on mountain expeditions. In earlier days the Sherpas, for being natural climbers, were mostly employed as porters by the White Sahibs in their mountain expeditions. Over the years many of them have become heroes of the Himalayas and have engaged as guides and instructors in mountaineering institutions in India and abroad. However, their participation in the service sector is as low as 1.33 percent out of a total of 1273 posts in 16 different services of the State. (Table 3.9)

In Sikkim the Sherpas enjoy scheduled tribes status as one of the Bhutia sub-tribes since 1978.[131] However, since seats in the State Assembly are reserved as per the Representation of People Act 1950, i.e., when Sherpas were not recognized as Bhutia tribes, the Sherpas are denied with the privilege of seat reservation in the State Legislature. It must be mentioned here that the Representation of People Act, 1950, as amended in 1980, provides for a broader definition of the "Bhutias" including the Sherpas and other Bhutias.[132] Over the years it was given an impression that the 12 seats reserved for the Bhutias and the Lepchas were not meant for other tribals included within the corpus Bhutia in 1978 though vide. Representation of People (Amendment) Act, 1980 (8 of 1980) seats reserved for the Bhutia-Lepcha are also meant for those groups included within the larger Bhutia definition in 1978.[133] In other words Sherpas can have representation only as a Bhutia and not as a separate Sherpa community. And since Sherpas are recognized as Bhutias, it is contended that they do not need separate seat in the Assembly.

Table 3.9: Service-wise figure of Sherpa Community in Sikkim, August 2005.

Sl. No.	Services	Sherpa	Total Posts.
01	Indian Administrative Service	01	46
02	Indian Police Service	00	25
03	Indian Forest Service	00	28
04	Sikkim State Agriculture Service	00	141
05	Sikkim Statistical Service	01	33
06	Mines and Geology Service	01	14
07	Sikkim State Nursing Service	00	33
08	Medical Doctors	05	223
09	Sikkim Finance & Acct. Service	02	147
10	Animal Husbandry & Veterinary Service	00	70
11	State Civil Engineering Service	01	156
12	Sikkim Co-operative Service	00	52
13	State Mechanical Eng. Service	02	47
14	State Electrical Eng. Service	01	109
15	Sikkim State Educational Service	01	58
16	Sikkim Directorate and Misc. Services	02	91
17	Total	17	1273

Source: Department of Personnel & Administrative Reform & Training, Govt. of Sikkim, August 2005.

Since 1994 the community has been contesting election from reserved Bhutia-Lepcha constituencies. The community has their own socio-cultural organization, called Sikkim Sherpa Association, which has been working for the promotion of culture, language and over all development of the Sherpa community. Despite adversities, the Sherpas have maintained their own cultural identity. With the gradual advancement in the field of education the Sherpas have become economically better off and conscious of their interest and political rights, and assertive too, while maintaining a healthy understanding with other communities. Despite being Scheduled Tribes, the Sherpas, in general, have not been able to come up at par with other tribes of Sikkim and this is where both the concerned Association and government should give a serious thought.

Yolmos/Kagatey:

It is believed that they have migrated to Sikkim from eastern Nepal. The name "Kagatey" is derived from a Nepali word "Kagaj" meaning paper and associated with their traditional occupation of paper-making. However, they preferred to call themselves 'Yolmos' though both nomenclatures are found in the list of Bhutia Scheduled Tribes included by the Constitution (Sikkim) Scheduled Tribes Order, 1978. Earlier they used to be treated as one of the Tamang groups.[136]

They speak Kagatey language or dialect and use Tibetan script for writing purposes. They speak Nepali language quite comfortably and often hold having closer social and cultural ties with the Nepalis than the Bhutias. The Bhutia organizations like Survival Sikkimese and Sikkim Bhutia-Lepcha Apex Committee consider them as one of the Nepali sub-cultural groups.

They are Buddhist by religion. Their chief deities include the Buddha and the Padmasamvava (Guru Rimpochey). They go to Gumpa (monastery) for worshiping but since there is no separate Gumpa of the community in Sikkim, they have been seen visiting Gumpas of other Bhutia communities of Sikkim. Earlier, they had a binding rule of having one of the sons trained in Lamaism to become a Lama afterwards, but such a custom is no longer adhered to. Their major festivals include birthday of Padmasamvava, Buddha Purnima, and Lochar (New Year) etc. They celebrate the Lochar festival separately with rituals of their own.

The socio-cultural organization of the Yolmos/Kagatey is not known in Sikkim. They have also never been seen or heard raising demands in public. It seems either they have been completely assimilated within the Bhutias or their numbers are too few to form organization. No ethnographic details of the community are available in Sikkim. Economically they are yet to make substantive progress, though after 1978 few of them have emerged in the field of hotel business, service sector, creative arts and politics at the state village levels.

The Question of Identity:

In a multi-cultural society ethnic conflict/tension generally occurs due to the feeling of marginalization or alienation, real or perceived, of one group or groups by other or others. This feeling is apparent in a multi-ethnic society which is characterized by the presence of a dominant and dependent culture. For instance, during the Chogyal's rule the Tibetan way of life was emphasized to such an extent that it led to the feeling of marginalization among other ethno-cultural groups of Sikkim. And in the post-merger era the Bhutias feel in the same way in presence of the dominant Nepali culture. Such feelings, more often than not, will lead to emergence of groups and mobilization resisting assimilation and asserting distinct identity of their own. In a liberal democratic polity such actions of resistance often appeal with the ideas of freedom, equality and justice, and attach special attention regarding preservation or conservation of ethno-cultural symbols of the group like dress, language, religions, customs, historical antecedents, legendary heroes, geographical sites and related beliefs etc. Thus, a multi-ethnic society presents a tendency of conflict between the forces intending to develop a common identity based on the cultural ethos of the dominant group while the smaller groups owe their allegiance or loyalty to their own group identity. The phenomenon is well explained by Amalendu Guha as 'Little Nationalism'.[135]

The question of identity or feeling of loss of identity is not new in the political history of Sikkim. In fact it is as old as the state itself. But in the present perspective the identification process, however, is not as easy as it seems to be mainly due to the prevalence of various levels/layers of identities and their political uses. Different groups and individuals in Sikkim present the question of socio-cultural/ community/political identity in diverse ways: sometimes the identity of Bhutia-Lepcha as opposed to Nepalis received importance; sometimes the issue of the Bhutia domination over the Lepchas is highlighted and sometimes even the issue of the interest of the "real" Bhutias vis-à-vis the Tibetan Bhutias or other Bhutias is raised. Hence any attempt at creating a common or civil-political identity on the basis of ethno-cultural affiliation is not only contentious but also a major issue in Sikkimese politics though the trend is universal in dimension.

During the Chogyal's rule conscious attempts had been made to provide Tibetan identity based on cultural affiliation of the ruling class. Tibetan language, religions and the way of life was imposed through legal-political means on the people belonging to other ethno-cultural groups in order to achieve the objective. This also included the attempt to write their own history and legends while destroying the historical antecedents of the early inhabitants of Sikkim. The impact was colossal especially on the Lepchas and Limboos but it was not so profound on the Nepalis in general owing to their numerical strength and organized Hindu religion.

During the reform movement of the late 1940's the identity question vacillated between the two extremes – whether Sikkim should remain as a monarchical and theocratic State or embrace democratic system. The Sikkim National Party defended Sikkim's independence in terms of history, society, culture, language, religion and ethnicity of the ruling community.[136] The ruling Bhutia elites were apprehensive of being ousted from power in a democratic state of Sikkim while the majority Nepali saw in it the end of discrimination and hegemony of the minority over the majority.

The political transition in 1975 called for massive restructuring of the system affecting the erstwhile pattern of governance and resource distribution system. This had raised a certain level of anxiety more intensely among the Bhutias than the other two groups, and to combat with this new perceived menace the priorities were accordingly reoriented / designed to suit the immediate purposes. Henceforth the question of identity revolved around the question of ethnic identity of particular group/groups, including the question of preservation/protection of the rights and privileges of that group or groups.

In a pluri-cultural society the political decision makers generally faced with an onerous responsibility of maintaining a balance while accommodating or representing, as far as possible, the interests and aspiration of all the sections of the people, whether majority or minority. In the context of post-merger Sikkim the fears and apprehensions of the minority have been perhaps lavishly exaggerated for no culture can become extinct or get submerged simply because of the fact that some other culture has overtaken it. In reality, the feeling of being overtaken or subsumed under another group or culture rather add more vigour for consolidation or preservation of cultural identity of the minority provided that it does not voluntarily give up but which is seldom desired. For instance take the case of the Lepchas or Limboos in the early period of Sikkim. Despite conscious effort to obliterate the Lepcha or Limboo language or religion, they survived the assimilation process under monarchical theocratic system and flourished further in presence of another dominant, i.e. Nepali culture. In fact, the political decision-making process should be, as far as possible, accommodative or neutral in its dealing with promotional and delivery responsibilities.

The Bhutias, once belonging to the ruling elite, mainly feared or apprehend that they would be relegated to a subordinate position in the political hierarchy after the merger of Sikkim with India. The Sikkim Tribal Welfare Association (STWA), formed in 1978, was apprehensive that the unhindered influx of the Nepalis would pose a threat to their culture and existence and would fight against any economic or political policies of the government which the association would think detrimental to the interest of its member. It suspected the policies of the government which was/is dominated, at least numerically, by another cultural group.

The real threat, however, on the identity of the Bhutias is due to the enactment of the Constitution (Sikkim) Scheduled Tribes Order, 1978. The Order declared Bhutias and Lepchas as Scheduled Tribes but many other tribes of Bhutia origin were also included in the definition of Bhutia, who, according to the Bhutia organizations like Survival Sikkimese, do not merit inclusion in the definition of the Sikkimese Bhutia – such as the Chumbipas, Dopthopas, Kagatey, Sherpas, Yolmos, Drukpas, Tromopas and Tibetans. This had actually aggravated the sense of insecurity among the Bhutias.

The inclusion of Limboos and Tamangs as scheduled tribes in 2002 is yet another cause of concern to them. Though the government is committed to preserve the seats reserved for the Bhutia and Lepcha, these tribal communities, by virtue of being greater in number and assertive too, would be sharing the economic and educational benefits which until recently had been dominated by the Bhutias. The 33 percent reservation in government departments and public sector undertakings, and for allotment of seats in educational institutions for professional courses are meant for the Scheduled Tribes[137] which, until substituted, also included the share of the Limboos and Tamangs.

The Bhutia-Lepcha communities are also more resentful of the present electoral system and delimitation of constituencies. Due to the demographic composition and settlement pattern, the Bhutia-Lepcha candidates have to depend on the Nepali voters for winning election in BL reserved constituencies. They want genuine representation of the candidates from the reserved Bhutia-Lepcha seats and hence they proposed for continuation of the election system existed in1958.

The Bhutia-Lepcha tribals are also apprehensive towards the issue of the land reform. Being the erstwhile ruling community, the Bhutia-Lepcha tribal community even today possesses extensive landholdings. According to the Agricultural Census, 1990-91 about less than 5 per cent (4.9 %) of the Scheduled Tribes possesses over 28 per cent (28.1 %) land area under their possession.[138] Besides, the monasteries, which are the symbols of their cultural identity, also possess huge estates received as rewards or donation either from the Chogyals or the Kazi landlords. Earlier, such estates enjoyed tax exemption and the income from them was utilized for the maintenance of the monasteries.

However, in order to implement various welfare policies, various legislations were passed in the post-merger era by the State government namely Sikkim Agricultural Land Ceiling and Reform Rules, 1978 (amended in 1979 and 1985), Sikkim Cultivators Protection Act, 1985, Land Registration and Acquisition Rules, 1978, which were viewed as measures designed to alienate or dislodge them from their hereditary rights over land. The Bhutia being the ruling community, the effect of the land reform measures would be obviously colossal on them than other communities. In fact, Sikkim has the tradition of protecting the land of the Bhutias and Lepchas since 1897 when J.C. White became the political officer of Sikkim in 1889. The rule was further strengthened in 1917 as Revenue Order No. 1 and now enjoys constitutional sanction under article 371 F (k).

But despite existence of such laws prohibiting alienation of Lepcha-Bhutia land to others, including other tribals, they feared that the amount of land confiscated by the government in excess of upper ceiling would be distributed among the non-tribals. In fact, a resource scrapped and industrially unviable State like Sikkim has its own compulsions and challenges within which it has to implement various welfare policies, build infrastructure facilities and create scope for employment generation. This is where the onus of all tensions lie – the interest of the State is viewed as the interest of the majority Nepalis and considered contradictory to the interest of the ethnic minority group/groups. When the government proposes, somebody somewhere will be dispossesses. It is to be noted that the issue is not that of cultural assimilation or domination, but it is most likely an issue of feeling different and such feeling is present not only between the majority and minority cultures but also found among minority ethnic groups i.e., Bhutia and Lepcha, and even within the Bhutias and majority Nepalis themselves.

Over the years it so happened that the Lepchas and Sherpas feel that they have been left out far behind their Bhutia brethrens in all respects. The 12 seats reserved for the Bhutia-Lepchas have been monopolized by the Bhutias. The Lepcha Youth Association wants parity to be maintained between the two communities and enactment of legal provision prohibiting transfer of land to others, including the Bhutias. On the other hand, the Sherpas too want separate seat to be reserved for the community in the Assembly and modification in the Revenue Order No. 1 so that they being the Bhutia, as per the constitution (Sikkim) Scheduled Tribes Order, 1978, should be allowed to buy tribal (Bhutia-Lepcha) land.

Nepalis too are apprehensive of their identity in view of allegation made in different occasions challenging their identity as Sikkimese Nepali. At various point of time they have been referred in ignominious terms like 'coolies' and 'immigrants' despite the fact that all Nepalis were neither immigrant nor coolies. They have been threatened eviction and metaphorically told to leave Sikkim on several occasions in the past.

In 1975, many Nepalis of Sikkimese origin were denied Indian citizenship since the cut off year was based on the Sikkim Subjects Regulation of 1961. The Nepalis feared that they would be rendered stateless. Similarly, in 1979 the 16 seats reserved for the Sikkimese Nepalis, symbolizing community's ethnic-political identity, were abolished. The Nepalis also feel apprehensive at the presence of influx of more articulated and assertive outsiders. Their fear seemed to have been justified in view of 1985 Assembly election when one non-Nepali candidate was elected from the Gangtok General Constituency and the way their numbers in the highest administrative jobs like IAS, IPS, IFS are sinking so rapidly.

Nepalis do not contemplate threat of assimilation or cultural domination but fear political and economic alienation and marginalization. They seemed to be perplexed when they find the economic and service sectors being dominated by the outsiders. The difference between the Nepali and plainsmen in services like IAS, IPS and IFS (Forest) is approximately 19 (19.19) percent is to 58 (47.94) percent respectively in August 2005. In 1999 the difference was approximately 23 (23.28) percent is to 48 (47.94) percent respectively. The percentage of the Nepalis in these elite services was even lower than that of the Bhutias both in 1999 and 2005.

In addition to this is the presence of traditional rules almost all of them discriminate against the Nepalis barring perhaps only three namely Income Tax Manual, Notification regarding land holding which is 20 acres for Bustiwalas, 30 acres for Mandals and 100 acres for Kazis, and Sikkim Subject Certificate.

Another noteworthy continuum in dominant-dependent scenario is found within the majority Nepalis of Sikkim that further adds confusion to the question of identity. It must be mentioned that the mongoloid Nepalis, which roughly formed about 50 per cent of the total Nepali population in Sikkim, are ethno – culturally different from the Aryan Nepalis and believed to have lost their distinct cultural identity during various historical-political circumstances in the distant past. Besides demanding for revival of cultural identity they also complain that the upper caste Nepalis (Aryan stock) have appropriated the major part of the privileges intended for the Nepalis as a whole. They alleged that the upper caste Nepalis have denied them the status of Other Backward Classes in 1990. Some mongoloid Nepalis like Tamang, Limboo, Gurung, Mangar, Rai, Sunuwar etc. hold the former Chief Minister, belonging to the upper caste, responsible for doing nothing to push forward their just claim for the tribal status. Though there is no manifest tension between the two groups but the formation of separate organizations such as Sikkim Tamang Buddhist Association, All Sikkim Gurung (Tamu) Buddhist Association, Sikkim Sunuwar (Mukhia) Koinchbu, Akhil Sikkim Chhetri-Bahun Kalyan Sangh, Scheduled Caste Welfare Organization, Akhil Bhujel (Khawas) Sangh, Akhil Sikkim Mangar Association, Akhil Kirat Rai Sangh of Sikkim, Sikkim Newar Guthi, Akhil Sikkim Kirat Limboo Chumlung, Dewan Yakkha Chhumma etc. with objectives to promote and protect group interests and identity is indicative of the apparent diversities within the larger Nepali community. Amidst plethora of identities and apprehension relating identity of one against the other, the common identity, i.e. Sikkimese identity, has remained dormant if not lost forever.

FOOTNOTES AND REFERENCES

1. Footnote: It is said that long before the rule of the Rong/ Lepcha community in Sikkim this region was under the sway of Chandrapalla of Palla dynasty and was called Vijaypur Sikkim. *District Census Handbook, Census of India 1981, Parts XIII, A-B, Directorate of Census Operation Sikkim, P.5*
2. H.Siiger: The Lepchas – Culture and Religion of a Himalayan People, Part I, the National Museum of Denmark, Copenhagen, 1967, P. 27.
3. H.H.Risley: The Gazetteer of Sikhim, Low Price Publication, New Delhi, 1993 (Reprinted), Pp. 34-38.
4. Ibid. P. 42
5. The New Encyclopedia Britannica, Vol. 21, 15th Edition, Chicago, 1974/2003, Pp 148 – 49
6. T.B.Subba: Socio – Cultural Aspects of Sikkim – Chie Nakane Re-examined, Man in India, Vol. 65, No. 1, March 1985, P. 91.
7. G.B.Mainwaring: Grammar of the Rong (Lepcha) Language, Baptist Mission Press, Calcutta, 1976, P. 189.
8. Ibid, P. 189.
9. L.A.Waddell: Among the Himalayas, Pilgrim Books, Delhi, 1899/1998, Pp. 92 – 93.
10. K.P.Tamsang: The Unknown and Untold Reality about the Lepchas, Mani Printing Press, Kalimpong, 1983, P. 1.
11. Op. cit. No. 9, P. 433 (see footnotes)
12. A.R.Fonning: Lepcha My Vanishing Tribe, Chyu-Pandi Farm, Kalimpong, 1987, Pp.57-58.
13. S. K. Chatterjee: Kirata Janakriti – Indo-Mongoloids: Their Contribution of the History and Culture of India, Royal Asiatic Society, Calcutta, 1951.
14. George Kutturan, The Himalayan Gateway: History and Culture of Sikkim, Sterling Publication, New Delhi, 1983.
15. C.D.Beauvoir Stock, Sikkim: Customs and Folklore, Cosmo Publication, New Delhi, 1975.

16. Op. cit. No. 2, P. 66.
17. W.G.Mackaen, Sikkim: Encyclopedia of Religion and Ethics, Vol. II, 1920.
18. Op. cit. No. 3, P. i. (See introduction).
19. R.N.Thakur & S.W.Lepcha: Who Are The Lepchas? The Eastern Anthropologist, Vol. 34, No. 3, 1981.
20. Op. cit. No. 11, P. 1.
21. Ibid, P. 39.
22. Ibid, P. 41.
23. D. Dahal: Sikkim Ko Rajnaitic Itihas, Subba Publications, Gangtok, 1984, Pp. 2 – 3.
24. Ibid, P. 3.
25. A.C. Sinha: Politics of Sikkim – A Sociological Study, Thompson Press, Faridabad, 1975, P. 12.
26. Op. cit. No. 13, P. 7.
27. Op. cit. No. 23, P. 11.
28. Op. cit. No. 27, P. 154.
29. Ibid, P. 154.
30. Geoffrey Gorer: The Lepchas of Sikkim, Gyan Publishing House, New Delhi, 1996 (reprinted), P. 38.
31. Op. cit. No. 30, P. 155.
32. Op. cit. No. 28, P. 22.
33. Op. cit. No. 31, P. 44.
34. Ibid. P. 115.
35. Op. cit. No. 32. P. 303.
36. L.B.Basnet: Sikkim – A Short Political History, S. Chand & Co., Delhi, 1974, Pp. 148 – 51.
37. Op. cit. No. 35, P. 37.
38. A.K.Das: The Lepchas of West Bengal – A Socio-Economic and Cultural Profile, in M.K.Raha (Ed.) "The Himalayan Heritage, Gyan Publication, Delhi, 1987, P. 103.

39. Sikkim Government Gazette, Extraordinary No. 307, dated 17.09.2003.

40. Department of Information Technology, Government of Sikkim, Gangtok, 2005.

41. Chie Nakane: A Plural Society in Sikkim – A Study of the Interrelations of Lepchas, Bhutias and Nepalese" in C.Von.Furer Haimendorf (Ed.) 'Caste & Kin in Nepal, India and Ceylon, Asian Publications, Bombay, 1966/1978, Pp.245-49.

42. Statement of Chuksung Lepcha, Joint Secretary of Renjyong Mutanchi Rong Tarzum, cited in Sandhya Thapa's "Ethnicity, Class and Politics in Sikkim", unpublished Ph. D. thesis, NBU, 2002, P. 269.

43. Op. cit. No. 37, P. 11; Op. cit. No. 42, Pp. 215.

44. Thutop and Yeshey Namgyal: The History of Sikkim 1908 (transcript). It is believed that the manuscript was written during the period of incarceration in the 1890s at Kurseong and Darjeeling. Dawa Kazi Samdup later translated the original Tibetan version into English.

45. Op. cit. 25, Pp. 21 – 22.

46. Op. cit. No. 45.

47. N. Sengupta: State Government and Politics in Sikkim, Sterling Publication, New Delhi, 1985, P. 125.

48. Legislative Proceedings, Autumn Session, September 1978, Sikkim Legislativ Assembly Secretariat, Government of Sikkim, P. 20.

49. Op. cit. No. 48, P. 128.

50. Ibid, P. 9.

51. T.B.Subba: Dynamics of A Hill Society, Mittal Publications, New Delhi, 1989, P. 8.

52. Ibid, P. 8.

53. R.K. Sprigg: read 'Preface to the Limboos of the Eastern Himalayas with special reference to Sikkim', by J.R.Subba, Sikkim Yakthung Mundhum Saplopa, Gangtok, 1999, P. v.

54. J.D.Hooker: The Himalayan Journals, Vol. 1 & 2, Today and Tomorrow, New Delhi, 1969 (Reprinted), P. 130.
55. Subhas Deepak: Sikkim Study Series – Language and Literature, Vol. V, IPR publication, Government of Sikkim, Gangtok, 2004, P. 81.
56. Sikkim Herald (English version), Vol. 10, No. 61, dated 25th April 1969, p. 2.
57. Op. cit. No. 55, P. 130.
58. Ibid, P. 130.
59. K.M.Tamang: Tamang Community of Sikkim, Sikkim Tamang Buddhist Association, April 29, 2002, P. 1.
60. Op. cit. 18.
61. B.Chaudhuri, "Crafts of Sikkim and Social Identity" in M.K. Raha (Ed.) 'The Himalayan Heritage, Gyan Publishing House, Delhi, 1987, Pp. 75-76.
62. Op. cit. No. 26, P. 7.
63. Ibid, P. 7.
64. Op. cit. No. 19, P.27.
65. C.V. Haimendorf: Himalayan Trade, 1975, P. 5.
66. Kumar Pradhan: The Gorkha Conquests: The Process and Consequences of the Unification of Nepal with particular reference to Eastern Nepal, Calcutta, OUS, 1991, P. 52.
67. Op. cit. No. 53, P. 1.
68. Sashibhusan Dutta: Final Report on Darjeeling Tarai Settlement, Calcutta Secretariat Press, 1898.
69. P.K.Rao: India & Sikkim – 1814-1970, Sterling Publications, New Delhi, 1972, P. 65; B.S.K.Grover: Sikkim and Bhutan - Storm and Consolidation, Jain Publications, New Delhi, 1974, Pp. 23-24.
70. Karan & Jenkins: The Himalayan Kingdoms – Bhutan, Sikkim and Nepal, Princeton Publications, 1963, P. 69: J.S.Lall (Ed.): The Himalaya – aspects of Change, OUP, Delhi, 1981, P. 218: S.K.Datta-Ray: Smash and Grab – Annexation of Sikkim, Vikash Publications, New Delhi, 1984, Pp. 37-39.

71. J.C.White: Sikkim and Bhutan – Twenty-One Years on the North-East Frontier 1887- 1908, Low Price Publications, Delhi, 1909/1999.

72. Sunanda K. Datta-Ray: Smash and Grab – Annexation of Sikkim, Vikash Publications, New Delhi, 1984, Pp. 37-38.

73. Ibid, P. 38.

74. Op. cit. No. 44, Pp. 43 – 44; S. Dutta: Migration and Development – The Nepalese in North – East, EPW, Vol. 16, 1981, P. 1054.

75. Ibid, Pp. 42 – 43.

76. Copy of the Treaty of Peace and Friendship between the Government of Indian and the Government of Nepal, 1950.

77. Op. cit. No. 42, P. 259.

78. Iman Singh Chemzong: History and Culture of the Kirant People, Chandraw Hang Zobegu, Fidim, 1966, P. 63.

79. T.B.Subba: Politics of Culture – A Study of Three Kirata Communities in the Eastern Himalayas, Orient Longman, Chennai, 1999, P. 32.

80. George Louis Van Driem: a Grammar of Limboos, Ph. D. thesis, University of Leiden, 1987.

81. J. R. Subba: The Limboos of the Eastern Himalayas, Sikkim Yakthung Mundhum Saplopa publications, Gangtok, 1999, P. 84.

82. H.H.Risley: Tribes and Castes of Bengal, Ethnographic Glossary, Vol. 2, Firma KLM. Publications, Calcutta, 1981 (reprinted), P. 14.

83. Op. cit. No. 65, P. 2.

84. Op. cit. No. 46, P. 12.

85. Op. cit. No. 83, P. 38.

86. Op. cit. No. 54, P. v. (Read the preface).

87. Op. cit. No. 12, P. 119.

89. Op. cit. No. 87, Pp. 34 – 38.

90. Tripartite Treaty of Lho-Men-Tsong – Sum as translated by Prof. Ringu Tulku, Sikkim Government College, Gangtok, dated 31/08/1984.

91. Ibid.
92. Ibid.
93. Op. cit. No. 81, P. 128.
95. Op. cit. No. 15.
95. Op. cit. No. 90, P. 40.
96. Op. cit. No. 74, P. 5.
97. Ibid, P. 5.
98. Op. cit. No. 96, P. 40.
99. C.A. Campbell: The Darjeeling Guide Including a Description of the Country and Its Climate, Soil and Production, Samuel Smith & Company, Calcutta, 1845, Pp. 76-77.
100. Edward T. Dalton: Descriptive Ethnology of Bengal, Office of the Superintendent of Government Press, Calcutta, 1872, P. 102.
101. Op. cit. No. 99, P. 18.
102. Swami Prapannacharya: Vedma Ke Chha, Chirinjivi Dharma Prakashan, Pryag, 1981; Gambhir Rai Arya: Hindu Dharma – Kirant Jati Ra Eshai Mat, Himalayan Observer, Kalimpong, 1980.
103. Op. cit. No. 79, P. 97.
104. M. Gurung & R.P.Lama: Sikkim Study Series, Culture, Part I, Vol. III, IPR, Government of Sikkim, Gangtok, 2004, P. 165.
105. Ibid, P. 166.
106. Op. cit. No. 81, P. 268.
107. Vide Letter No. Acad./11/F1 (2)/83/49983, dated 17.12.1983.
108. Vide Letter No. 312/U-G-2000, dated 17.07.2000.
109. Home Department, Government of Sikkim, Notification No. S/277/61, dated 16.01.1962.
110. Memo No. 62/990, Education, dated 11.03.1968.
111. I.S.Chemzong: Kirat Sahitya Ko Itihas, Published by Manishankar Sering Limboo, Terethum, 1973, Pp. 34-35.
112. D.O.No. BC/12016/24/75-SCTV, dated 21.07.1976, Ministry of

Home Affairs, Government of India, Shastri Bhawan, Room No. 604, A-Wing, New Delhi.

113. Excerpt from the letter written by the former Governor of Sikkim, B.B.Lall, to Shri T.C.A.Srinivasavaradan on 5th November 1977.

114. Copy of the Report submitted by Passang Namgyal, Secretary, SC/ST Welfare Deptt., Government of Sikkim, to Shri Sahchaman Limboo, Minister, SC/ST Welfare Deptt, Government of Sikkim, Dated 19.08/1987.

115. Chief Minister's noting on the Report submitted by the Secretary, SC/ST Welfare Deptt., Government of Sikkim, dated 22/08/1987.

116. Op. cit. No. 107, P. 179.

117. Sikkim Observer, dated 08/09/1990.

118. Copy of the letter written by Mata Prasad, Additional Secretary, Ministry of Welfare, Government of India, to the Chief Secretary, P.K.Pradhan, Government of Sikkim, dated 18.12.1991.

119. Letters of the Chief Minister, P.K.Chamling, to the Prime Minister of India from 25.08.1995 to 1997.

120. Copy of the letter of Secretary, Delimitation Commission of India, Nirvachan Sadan, New Delhi, to the Secretary, Ministry of Home Affairs, North-Eastern Division, North Block, New Delhi, Letter No. 282/DEL/SC-ST/2005, dated 14.03.2005.

121. Burman Commission Report, March 2008.

122. Op. cit. No. 105, P. 257.

123. Ibid, P. 257.

124. M. Hermanns: The Indo-Tibetans – The Indo-Tibetan and Mongoloid Problem in the Southern Himalaya and North-Eastern India, Published by K.L. Fernandes, Bombay, 1954, P.23.

125. A Draft proposal on the Sherpa Community of Sikkim, Published by Department of Law, Government of Sikkim, Gangtok, 2002, P. 10.

126. Op. cit. No. 68, Pp. 46-47.

127. Op. cit. No. 99, P.38.

128. Denzong Sherpa Association, Gangtok (Now defunct).
129. Social Welfare Department, Government of Sikkim, 1997.
130. Op. cit. No. 56, P. 91.
131. Constitution (Sikkim) Scheduled Tribes Order, 1978.
132. Letter of the Under Secretary, R.K.Bajaj, Lok Sabha Secretariat, to Birbal Limboo, President, Sikkim Limboo Tamang Joint Action Committee for Tribal Status, Gangtok, D.O.No. 53/CI/2004/R-32, dated 22.11.2004.
133. Read explanation of Clause 7 (1A) of the Representation of the People (Amendment) Act 1980 (8 of 1980).
134. Op. cit. No. 126, P. 46.
135. Amelendu Guha: Little Nationalism Turns Chauvinist, EPW, Vol. 15, Nos. 41 & 42, Special No. October 1980.
136. Petition of the Sikkim National Party, dated 01.05.1948.
137. Sikkim Government Gazette, Extraordinary No. 307, dated 17.09.2003.
138. M.P.Lama: Sikkim Human Development Report 2001, IPR, Government of Sikkim, Gangtok, 2001, P. 44.

4

State Policies, Political Parties and Ethnic Question Before 1975

A plural society inhabited by different ethno-cultural or linguistic groups often exhibits antagonistic tendencies due to the presence of competition among them over various things which they consider valuable. Such antagonistic tendencies, which otherwise remain dormant, act under certain situations in a particular way impairing social cohesion and development itself. The political institutions, which are expected theoretically to act as arbiters in a conflict, also often act as instruments of promoting interest of a particular ethnic community. Moynihan and Glazer believe "the strategic efficacy ethnicity as a basis for asserting claims against government has its counterpart in the seeming case whereby government employs ethnic categories as a basis for distributing its reward."[1]

The problem with such a measure is that government tends to favour a particular ethnic group or groups and deprive others which in the long run, may normally lead to ethnic polarization or ethnic divide in the society and subsequently it affects political mobilization. For instance, in his recent analysis Dipankar Gupta writes that the Sikh identity in India and subsequent demand for a separate Sikh State have developed not only because of its opposition to Hindu identity but also in relation to the community's perception of a government which has discriminated the Sikhs.[2] Similarly, Susana Devalle argues that the movement for a separate state of Jharkhand was basically a political manifestation of the ethnic resentments of the people of Jharkhand against the 'deku' (the outsiders). She believes that Jharkhandi identity and politics developed together gradually through a historical process which in the long run resulted in an antagonistic relations between the two.[3] In the context of Sikkim, a careful analysis of those different historical events as well as perceptions of different ethnic groups about the government may prove helpful in understanding the reasons behind ethnic segregation and development of ethnicity oriented consciousness among the various ethnic groups. At this stage a brief analysis of the demographic composition of Sikkim is required.

Major socio-cultural groups or communities of Sikkim before its merger with India and even today are the Lepchas, the Nepalis and the Bhutias (for details see Ch. III). The Bhutias and Nepalis have their sub-groups, some of which often claim to have distinct culture, social values and racial origin. Such groups demand for a separate recognition as a distinct community and not just as either Bhutias or Nepalis. For instance, the Tsongs (Limboos) and Tamangs claim that they constitute separate socio-cultural community and therefore should not be confused with Nepalis. Interestingly, the two sub-cultural groups are regarded as Nepalis in the adjoining Darjeeling hills. In fact, the Nepalis do not constitute a single homogenous group. From the racial point of view Nepalis may be broadly classified into two major categories – Aryans and Mongoloids, the latter constitute the bulk of the larger Nepali community. Similarly, among the larger Bhutia community, the 'real Bhutias' and Sherpas assert their separate identity. Besides, there are fairly good number of plainsmen, called 'Byaparis' in Sikkim. Among the three major ethnic groups, the Lepchas, also called 'Rong', are fairly established as the original inhabitants of Sikkim.[4] Similarly, scholars who have accomplished research works in this field are unanimous in their contention that certain sub-groups of Mongoloid Nepalis such as Tsongs (Limboos), Mangars, Rais, Gurungs, Tamangs etc. are also among the aboriginal tribal communities of Sikkim. The Bhutias and a certain section among the Nepalis are, however, the later migrants. The Bhutias have probably migrated to Sikkim during the fifteenth and sixteenth century from Tibet as a result of the religious strife between the Red-Hat-Sect and the Yellow-Hat-Sect.[5] It is believed that the Bhutia patriarch, Khye Bumsa, sought hospitable relationship with the Lepcha Athing (Priest), Thekong Tek. The occasion was then solemnized by a blood-brotherhood pact at Kabi and the Lepcha priest also blessed Khye Bumsa for a son. According to the legend, Phuntsog Namgyal, who was consecrated in 1642 at Yaksum as the first Bhutia[6] ruler of Sikkim is described as descendant of Khye Bumsa though some writers have expressed reservation in the light of the circumstances which necessitate Tibetan migration into Sikkim.

Scholars differ quite extensively on the issue of Nepali migration into Sikkim. The confusion is mainly owing to the presence of two separate racial groups – Mongoloid and Aryan – within the corpus Nepali. Following the remarks made by various eminent scholars like Chatterji, Sprigg, Risley, Hooker, Mackaen, Choudhuri, Sinha, Mainwaring and others it can be said that Nepalis of Mongoloid race were among the early settlers in the same way as Lepchas and Bhutias. These tribal communities were known by their group names like Limboo (Yakthumba), Mangar, Gurung, Murmi (Tamang), Rai (Zimdar/Khambu) or by cognate reference 'Kiratis' which, according to some writers, also includes the Lepchas. The Nepalis of the Aryan stock, however, have started inhabiting Sikkim in the later half of the nineteenth century both as a result of the military expeditions and territorial occupation or at the instance of the local Sikkimese authorities, particularly the political officer, J.C.White, and other Lepcha Kazis and landlords who, as a part of the national policy, either duped or persuaded the Nepalis to settle in Sikkim for political and economic reasons. The scholars like Subba, Rao, Grover, Karan & Jenkins, Lall, Datta-Ray and others subscribed to this version. Over the years, it became quite common among the scholars to consider Nepalis as a homogeneous entity and conveniently called them as later migrants from Nepal completely ignoring historical evidences of the presence of various sub-cultural groups who are now pass by the name Nepalis even before the establishment of the Bhutia rule in Sikkim. Such sweeping remarks about the Sikkimese Nepalis is not only far removed from the facts but also have blurred the true identity of the Nepalis in Sikkim. In fact, all Nepalis were/are neither migrant from Nepal nor were they poor or landless as some writers have so erroneously put.

State Policies and Ethnic Divide:

Information scattered in various books and manuscripts are suggestive of a most cordial relationship between the Lepchas and various other constituents of the Nepalis. Inter-group marriages were quite common among the Lepchas and the Tsongs. The Tsongs and the Mangars adorned the court of the Lepcha Panu "Turvey"[7] It is said that the relationship between the Lepchas and the Tsongs prospered with the defeat of the notorious marauding Tibetan invader 'Lhaso Mong', believed to have ruled over the Lepchas for 12 years, by the joint effort of the Lepchas and Tsongs sometime in 666 A.D.[8] The absence of competition for resources and generally peace-loving nature of the two communities might have also helped the relationship to foster and grow further.

In 1642, Phuntsog Namgyal of the Tibetan descent was appointed as the Chogyal of Sikkim by the three Tibetan lamas at Yaksum, west Sikkim. With Phuntsog's appointment the political and religious suzerainty of the Tibetan ruler was established in Sikkim.[9] The Chogyal and members of ecclesiastical body used to look towards Tibet for ultimate guidance on political as well as religious matters concerning Sikkim. A convention to have Tibetan girl for marriage in Sikkim's royal family was established including the son born out of the Tibetan wife alone as successor to the throne. The influence of Tibetan authority began to be so overwhelming that by 1733-34 even the regent for minor Chogyal, Phuntsog Namgyal-II, was selected from among the Tibetans in Tibet and sent to Sikkim to rule as long as Tibet wanted.

Attempts were put in place to legitimize the rule of Bhutias through the myth of 'blood-brotherhood' between Bhutias and

Lepchas. Under various pretext like the 'blood brotherhood' pact or 'Lho-Men-Tsong-Sum' etc., the ruling Bhutias had always attempted to justify their rule as historically predetermined and advocated forceful conversion of the Lepchas and other Nepali tribal communities into the Lamaist (Nyangmapa) form of Buddhism, the chief religion of the ruling hierarch. The recalcitrant Lepcha and Tsong chiefs/patriarchs were often eliminated surreptitiously. For instance, in December 1826 the Lepcha Prime Minister, Bholod Kazi or Tshongot Bholek, along with his pregnant wife and two sons, was treacherously murdered at Tumlong by Tung-yek Menchoo Bhutia, the father of Dunya Namgye who is better know as Pagla Dewan (mad Chief Minister) in the history of Sikkim.[10] Later in 1828, Tsong Tsang-thung and Gyamu (both were Lepchas) gave eye-witnessed testimony of the murder.[11] Bholek's youngest son, Gebu Atchuk, who later became the Athing of Pakyong, was also killed in 1856 allegedly by Meche Dolma, the first wife of Tsugphud Namgyal, in connivance with the Dev Raja Jigmi Topgye of Bhutan.[12] Later Iklathup, the cousin of Bholek Kazi, also fled to Nepal with 800 Lepcha households contemplating threat to his life.[13] The settlement of those Lepcha refugees figured prominently when the talks on transfer of Darjeeling took place between the Sikkimputi Raja and Lord Bentinck in 1834-35.[14] Similarly, the Tsongs (Limboos) believed that the Tibetan Lamas of Tashiding and Pemayangtse monasteries were involved in the murder of Tsong (Limboo) linguist and a preacher, Guru Teyongsi Sirijonga (Singthebe), who is revered even today by the Tsongs (Limboos) as an incarnation of Siri Junga, the creator of the Tsongs (Limboo) script.[15]

Scattered information from different sources also reveal that the Lepcha and Tsong (Limboo) people often were waging localized wars or revolts against Bhutia domination and expansion of Bhutia control over land. According to R.K.Sprigg after the murder of Bolot or Bholod, the Lepcha Prime Minister of Sikkim, in 1826 the Lepchas were involved in Kotapa insurrection and made several raids into Sikkim.[16] Sprigg also provides information regarding the involvement of Changzod Karwang in the suppression of rebel by the Tsongs (Limboos) against the Bhutia Chogyal.[17] The policy of elimination of important Lepcha personalities continued even in the later half of the 20th century. Ruth Karthak, a Lepcha lady, who founded Sikkim Independent Front party in 1966 in order to articulate socio-economic and political grievances and asserting a separate identity of the Lepcha community, was banished from Sikkim allegedly for questioning the legal basis of Bhutia rule in the land of the Lepchas.[18] The emerging Bhutia rulers and elites in Sikkim pursued a policy of systematic elimination of important Lepcha and Tsong (Limboo) people of important families, lords and functionaries. Thus, in spite of matrimonial linkages and blood brotherhood pact, a deep seated mistrust prevailed in their relationships.

Thus, slowly but steadily the Lepchas and the Tsongs lost their leaders, their land and most importantly their freedom. The condition of the Lepchas is well described by B.S.Das in the following words, "The dominance of the Bhutias was so overwhelming that the Lepchas remained the poorest and the most neglected of the people... Mostly confined to the northern belt of Sikkim in an area called Djongu, they lived their life of indolence and negligence contributing little against the aggressive exploitation by the Bhutias of the riches in land and forest."[19] The territorial confinement of the Lepchas in the seemingly barren and desolate area of Djongu, though in the name of protection, has ruined the community in diverse ways, most significantly in the field of economic and educational advancement. The Tsongs (Limboos) too suffered intermittent looting and killing at the hands of the royal soldiers in the vicinity of Rabdentse which alienated the Tsongs forever.

The Gorkha invasion in Sikkim in the eighteenth century generated an antagonistic relationship between Nepal and Sikkim. Its effect was also reflected in the relationship between the Nepali subjects and Bhutia rulers in Sikkim which was characterized by mutual suspicion and xenophobia. Hence, the Gorkha soldiers who had occupied the western parts of Sikkim, including the capital Rabdentse, received support from the local Lepcha and Tsong populace. The growing intimacy between the Gorkhas and Lepcha-Tsong subjects of western Sikkim, including latter's revolt expressing displeasure against the Chogyal Gyurmed Namgyal for marrying a Tibetan girl, further evoked resentment of the ruling community against the Nepalis. On the contrary, the Lepchas and Tsongs seemed to have been contended with the way the Gorkhas had given them administrative autonomy over their respective fiefdom.

The available sources do not in any way indicate antagonistic relationship between the Nepalis and Lepchas, but the relationship between the Bhutias and Lepchas or between the Nepalis and Bhutias was marked by the relationship of domination and dependence and thus not always cordial. The settlement of the Hindu Nepalis, excluding the Tsongs (Limboos) and other mongoloid sections who now constitute Nepalis, under the tutelage of the British policy makers in conjunction with some influential local Lepcha Kazis for their own political and economic interests naturally became the cause of concern and apprehension for the Bhutia ruling elite. The Bhutia rulers who constituted a numerical minority always remained suspicious of the subjects who were in majority. This suspicion naturally prompted the minority rulers to view Nepali settlements of the late 19th century and early 20th century with reservations. This view is supported by the expression that the Lamaist Buddhism which had wide influence on social, political and economic life of Sikkim would be confronted Hinduism coming up with the overwhelming Hindu Nepalis in Sikkim.[20] In the Gazetteer of Sikkim H.H.Risley also writes, ".... race and religion, the prime movers of the Asiatic world will settle the Sikhim difficulty for us, in their own way. We have only to look on and see that the operation of these causes is not artificially hindered by the interference of Tibet and Nepal."[21]

Thus, the legacy of ethnic division and occasional ethnic outburst was as old as Bhutia Namgyal dynasty itself; the British functionaries simply ensured that the forces responsible for such division were not interrupted. The governing principle of the British Political officers in Sikkim, which also reflected the interest of the Bhutia ruling elite, was guided by the objective to keep the ethnic communities at bay. The prevalence of ascriptive collective identities, in this case religion and race, in them are not always adequate for ethnic division or tension but the way the State or political party uses such identities very often create ethnic mobilization and tension. An attempt is made here-below to show how such policies contribute in the enhancement of ethnic division and ethnic mobilization.

Revenue Order No. 1, 1917:

The erstwhile ruling elites had always perceived Nepalis as a potential threat. The growing demands for representative government and presence of numerically overwhelming Nepalis had been the greatest cause of concern for the Bhutia rulers. The condemnation of the Nepalis as 'non-Sikkimese' or 'immigrants' and introduction of various discriminatory legal-political arrangements were all but manifestation of those perceived fear and a part of the strategy for maintaining Bhutia domination over the Nepalis though, as a matter of fact, "neither community was indigenous and were only early settlers."[22] The first ever recorded policy intending to restrict the expanding influence of Nepalis was promulgated in January 2, 1897 prohibiting the Bhutias and Lepchas from selling or subletting their lands to other communities.[23] The updated version of the notification was issued in May 17, 1917, popularly called "Revenue Order No. 1" which is in vogue even today. Further, a general direction was issued to all Elakadars, Managers of Elakas and the Chief Court reiterating that " no Nepali can purchase Bhutia or Lepcha land" unless special permission to that effect was granted by His Highness.[24] These notifications were issued in the interest of the minority Bhutia and Lepcha communities but until 1969 the Tibetans and Bhutanese were not debarred from buying the Bhutia-Lepcha land in Sikkim[25] while other indigenous Nepali tribes who had been living rule in Sikkim long before the establishment of the Bhutia in Sikkim, were denied such benefits.

Similarly, the land revenue imposed on the farmers belonging to the three ethnic communities, namely the Bhutias, the Lepchas and the Nepalis, was also discriminatory. For the same acre and quality of land the Nepalis had to pay a higher rent than the Bhutia or Lepcha farmers. The policy remained operative till 1966[26] when the policy was revoked under pressure from the Nepalis who were demanding abolition of discriminatory revenue system since the days of the peasants' movement in 1949. The differential rate of revenue between the Bhutia-Lepcha and Nepali subjects is shown below in table no. 4.1

Table 4.1: Rate of revenue to be paid by the Nepalis and B-L peasants.

Class (In Rs. & Anna)	Nepali (In Rs. & Anna)	Lepcha-Bhutia (In Rs. & Anna)
Paddy – Class I	Rs. 2	Rs. 1 – 8 – 0
- Class II	Rs. 1- 8 – 0	Rs. 1 – 2- 0
Dry field (No Class)	Rs. 14	Rs. 8

Source: P.K.Jha: History of Sikkim – 1817-1904. Unit of measurement was Pathy which was equivalent to 4 sheers.

This system was intended to deny the fruits of labour to the Nepalis. The revenue chart clearly was differential and was in favour of the Bhutia-Lepcha community. But the most important part of the revenue structure was the very high rate of taxes on dry fields. Nepali subjects had to pay almost double as compared to the tax paid by the Bhutia-Lepcha subjects. It was possibly done to restrict accumulation of land in the hands of the Nepalis. Similarly, the Nepali subjects used to pay Rs. 6 as House Tax as compared to Rs. 2 by the Bhutia and Lepcha subjects. But under the prevailing socio-economic conditions of the peasants even those who were favoured by the government policies, i.e. Bhutias and Lepchas, were incapable of paying such a high rate of revenues and were subjected to various forms of exploitation at the hands of the Kazis and landlords. Apart from the forceful confiscation of their land, they were subjected to compulsory voluntary services like 'Kuruwa', 'Zharlangi', 'Kalo Bhari' etc. Such inhuman practices were banned in 1937 and 1947 respectively but the Kazis and landlords continued to exploit the gullible poor farmers.

Further, Nepalis were considered as 'non-hereditory' subjects and were not allowed to settle beyond the Dikchu river in the north. The Administrative Report of the State of Sikkim for the year 1931-32 states, "A portion of the country lying in the Teesta Valley north of Dikshu has not been thrown open to Nepali settlers and is specially reserved for the 'hereditary' inhabitants of Sikkim such as Lepchas and Bhutias; recently Tamangs and Sherpas, who are Nepali Buddhist were allowed to settle there, and own land…..A law prohibiting land alienation by hereditary State subjects (i.e. Bhutias and Lepchas) in favour of non-hereditary subjects such as Paharias (Nepalis) or domiciled plainsmen is in force and acts as a very useful check on the former class, which is poor and improvident, getting speedily replaced by the latter, who are more subtle and shrewd."

The content of the Administrative Report 1931-32 was repeated in 1934-35 and 1935-36 administrative reports of the State of Sikkim also.[27] The rationale behind the policy was to protect the interest of the minority Bhutia-Lepcha communities, but the intention to segregate the Nepali subjects on religious ground was distinct when the Tamangs and Sherpas of the Nepalis were allowed to settle and own land in the forbidden north just because they were Buddhist by religion. The policy differentiating communities either on grounds of ethno-cultural identity or religious belief had adverse effects on the communities' social mobility besides strengthening of aggressive ethnic consciousness among them. Karan and Jenkin (1963) attempt to justify the Durbar's view as "…Through the ebb and flow of political maneuvering, the government of Sikkim has had one firm consideration- the preservation of Sikkim from internal political strife. Bhutias and Lepchas may be in minority, but they are the original people, and their character is largely that of Sikkim. Accordingly, the administration has endeavored to safeguard their rights. The administration's policy is that the Nepalis, who are in the majority, should live as partners of the indigenous population".[28] Under the prevailing circumstances, the Nepalis had no objection to the idea of 'living as partners', but were apprehensive to the way that Nepalis were subjected to various types of discriminations including the allegation that Nepalis were grabbing Bhutia-Lepcha lands though such alienation was prohibited since January 1897. On the contrary, there were instances of individual Lepchas who complained about their lands being taken over by some affluent and powerful Bhutias. Secondly, the land rights of the Nepalis like Tsongs and Mangers who had been enjoying territorial autonomy even after the consolidation of the Bhutia rule in Sikkim, were not respected. Thirdly, those Nepalis who came to Sikkim under the tutelage of some Bhutia-Lepcha Kazis and the British Political Officer had settled in the barren land or not in the areas traditionally inhabited by the Bhutia and Lepcha communities. They converted the barren wasteland or forest land into agriculturally productive land and practiced terrace farming. Lastly, owing to their religious belief, the Bhutias and Lepchas were averse to digging for agriculture or mining purposes, and hence by tradition they were not cultivators.

On the religious front forceful conversion of non-Buddhist continued. Numerous monasteries were built at the expense of the government though the Lepchas and other converts were prohibited admission in some monasteries. Being the ruling community the Bhutia cultural festivities used to receive subsidy from the government. Rustomji, one of the closest friends of the last Chogyal, P.T.Namgyal, once remarked that the intention behind the construction of the Institute of Tibetology in Gangtok was an effort to dislodge the dominance of the Nepalis who were basically Hindus by religion.[29]

Since the beginning of the theocratic regime, the influence of the Tibetan Lamas and aristocrats over the administration of Sikkim had been overwhelming. Phuntso Namgyal appointed 12 Kalons (Ministers) from the Tibetan migrants and 12 Dzongpens (Administrator of the Fort) from the Lepchas. There is no recorded evidence to suggest that Tsongs too were appointed as Kalons or

Dzongpens. Over the years, the political scenario changed but the bureaucracy, including the recruitment pattern, continued to be traditional, i.e. relatives of Royal family and members of ruler's religious and political clique, feudal elements and individuals supporting the Royal interest for personal gain continued to dominate the bureaucracy. The Nepalis, who had least possibility of fulfilling the criteria, had been effectively marginalized.

A study conducted in 1970-72 by Dr. Sinha (1975) with a view to analyzing the social background of the bureaucrats of Sikkim observed that "recruitments to the higher civil service are made on personal considerations through certain networks of influence at the highest level."[30] The study further revealed that out of the 72 bureaucrats interviewed for the purpose about 56.77 per cent (41 approx.) belonged to the Bhutia-Lepcha community while the Nepalis formed 31.44 per cent (22 approx.).[31] The alienation of the Nepalis in the elite service took place despite the fact that the Nepalis had better or higher educational qualification than the Bhutias or Lepchas. The former Dewan of Sikkim, N.K.Rustomji (1987), wrote "unqualified Bhutias and Lepchas were appointed to posts which Nepalis, by virtue of their higher qualifications, had a stronger chance."[32] This practice of appointing civil servants on personal whims continued till the merger of Sikkim with India in 1975.

The Parity Formula:

The end of the British rule in India in 1947 was the beginning of a new era in the political history of Sikkim. This was the era of democratic movements, of rights and freedoms, and of political agitations calling for amelioration from the bondage of exploitation. The peasants' agitation of 1949 was followed by the short-lived 'Popular Ministry' of Tashi Tshering together with the support of the Government of India for 'progressive association' of the people of Sikkim in the Government accentuated the demand for representative governance in Sikkim. Along with the question of 'association' of the people, the problem of representation of different communities in the government acquired importance among the parties concerned. The Darbar, quite obviously, wanted to maintain equilibrium between the two major communities irrespective of their numerical strength. Accordingly, in May 1951 the Chogyal called for a tripartite conference to sort out the problem of representation in the proposed State Council. The Maharajkumar Palden Thondup Namgyal represented the royal interest, Sonam Tshering represented the Bhutia-Lepcha interest and the Nepalis were represented by Capt. Dimik Singh Lepcha and Kashi Raj Pradhan. It was in this tripartite conference of 1951 that the "Parity Formula" as the governing principle for equal seat sharing between the minority Bhutia-Lepcha and majority Nepalis was worked out and accordingly adopted. The concept of Parity Formula was a true copy of the 1896 scheme agreed between Sayyid Mahmud, son of Sayyid Ahmed Khan of Allahabad, and Theodre Beck, the Principal of the Aligarh College. They drew up the scheme of 'Parity' representation between the muslim minority and Hindu majority on behalf of the association called Muhammedan Anglo-oriental Defence Association founded by Sayyid Ahamed Khan in 1893. The major theme of the scheme was to protect the political interest of the Muslims in higher councils, districts, municipalities where the Muslims were 25 per cent of the total population. Moreover, the Muslim representatives of such councils, districts shall have to be elected only by the Muslim voters. Nari Rustomji who was a Persian muslim and the Dewan of Sikkim was the man behind for adopting this communal scheme in Sikkim. Thus by using the same formula in Sikkim the supremacy of the ruling community was established in the name of the protection of minority ruling community. According to this Formula the State Council was made a 17 member legislative body in which six seats were reserved for the Bhutia-Lepcha community and six seats for the Nepali community, and the remaining five seats were the nomination of the Chogyal. In spite of the clear instruction by the party President, Tashi Tshering, the Sikkim State Congress nominee, Kashi Raj Pradhan, failed to negotiate for more seats for the majority Nepali. Condemning the Formula as murder of democratic principle, Tashi Tshering tried to renegotiate on the seat sharing formula but failed to yield any response from the

Chogyal. It was rumoured that the representatives of the State Congress were forced to sign in an intoxicated condition. Thus, with the blessings of the government of India the "Parity Formula" was signed under which the 25 per cent Bhutia-Lepcha population was given equal representation with the 75 per cent Nepali population.[33] Besides, since the Lepchas were not awarded any separate representation the Bhutias who constituted only 10 to 12 per cent of the population now exercised control over 50 per cent of seats in the Council. The proposal of the Sikkim State Congress to have at least one representation each from the three communities was, however, opposed by the Bhutias.[34] The Nepalis resented the Parity Formula for some additional reasons: the Formula was arbitrarily extended to every conceivable area like scholarships, employment, stipends etc. where the Bhutias-Lepchas had equal claim with the Nepalis though the latter constituted the numereical majority. Hence, being in majority the Nepalis were ultimately the loser. It reduced the opportunities available before the Nepalis as regards to employment, stipends, scholarships etc. The outcome of the Parity Formula was conspicuous. In 1999 the ratio between the Bhutias and Nepalis in the IAS was 12:6 while in 2005 it was 13:9. Interestingly, the parity formula was not implemented in cases of settlement or land transaction between the two communities. Mr. C.D.Rai once remarked that "under what impression Kashi Babu (Kashi Raj Pradhan) signed the agreement we do not know. But this Parity Formula has been the festering wound for the Nepalis".[35] Politically, the Parity Formula was the first ever official attempt to restrain the influence of the majority Nepali subjects in the political institution of Sikkim.

On the basis of the 1951 agreement, the Maharaja issued a Proclamation in January, 1952 laying down the rules regarding the electorate and the method of election[36] The Proclamation was not only communal in intent but the method of election too was very complicated and confusing. The Proclamation, which was a perfect replica of 1896 scheme agreed between Sayyed Muhammed and Theodore Beck, stated, "Whereas each of the Nepali seats was to be returned by the whole electorate of the constituency concerned, the Bhutia-Lepcha candidates were first to be elected by only the Bhutia-Lepcha voters of the constituency concerned and thereafter to be voted again by the whole electorate of the constituency."[37] The arrangement contained special safeguards for the Bhutia-Lepcha candidates but it also was intended to reduce the influence of Nepalis in determining electoral results as no such safeguard was offered to candidates contesting for the seats reserved for the Nepalis. The Proclamation of March 1953 postulated the composition and functions of the Executive Council and the State Council.

Elections were held for four different territorial constituencies like Gangtok, North-Central, Namchi and Pemayangtse in two different dates starting from March to May. The election result clearly reflected sharp ethnic division among the voters. The National Party (also called Darbar Party) won all six Bhutia-Lepcha seats and confirmed its identity as the Bhutia-Lepcha Party whereas the Sikkim State Congress won all six Nepali seats and became a Nepali Party. Interestingly, all Bhutia – Lepcha candidates contesting from the Sikkim State Congress were defeated in the primary election which helped the Bhutia – Lepcha candidates contesting from the Sikkim National party to have an absolute control over the reserved Bhutia – Lepcha seats. Table 4.2 shows the party position in the first election of Sikkim State Council.

Table 4.2: Party position after the first State Council Election, 1953

Name of the Political Party	No. of seats contested	No. of seats won
1. Sikkim State Congress	6	6
2. National Party	12	6
3. Rajya Praja Sammelan	5	0
4. Scheduled Caste League	2	0

Source: N. Sengupta's 'State Government and Politics in Sikkim, 1985.

Sources close to the Darbar believed that the Chogyal viewed the Parity system as an interim solution to the problem of minority representation and was optimistic about its disappearance with the emergence of the feeling of Sikkimese nationalism. But the way the system was extended to other areas and the way Lepchas were denied separate representation, it effectively generated a feeling of deprivation among the majority Nepali and the minority Lepcha subjects. Expressing dismay over the idea of Sikkimese nationalism, Mr. C.D. Rai questioned 'How could people generate a feeling for Sikkimese identity when the government itself is engaged in devising means for keeping the people perpetually divided?'[38] The Nepalis believed that the Parity scheme was a special strategy manufactured to protect the interest of the minority ruling Bhutia community at the cost of the rights and privileges of the Lepchas and the Nepalis.

Sikkim Subjects Regulation:

The Administrative Report of the Sikkim State for the year 1934-35 and 1935-36 justified the anti-Nepali approach of the government as an effective means for checking the influence of the Nepalis and plainsmen, described as non-hereditary subjects, over the Bhutias and Lepchas, defined as hereditary subjects.

The Sikkim Subject Regulation of 1961 was yet another mechanism invented by the government to keep the Bhutia-Lepcha subjects separated from the Nepalis and other communities. Unlike in the earlier instances, interestingly, the Tsongs (Limboos) were treated at par with the Bhutia-Lepcha subjects this time. The Sikkim Subject Regulation was promulgated on July 3rd, 1961. It stated;

a. All persons of Sikkimese domicile, if born in Sikkim and resident there, or if ordinarily resident in Sikkim for not less than fifteen years prior to the promulgation of the regulation;
b. Persons not domiciled in Sikkim but of Lepcha, Bhutia, or Tsong origin whose father or grand-father was born in Sikkim; and
c. Person not domiciled in Sikkim but whose ancestors have deemed to be Sikkimese subjects before 1850.[39]

Subjecthood by naturalization was allowed on fulfillment of residential qualification of minimum fifteen years and subsequent renunciation of citizenship of the country of his/her birth / origin.

The Regulation was significant for three reasons. Firstly, it categorically recognized the Lepchas, Bhutias and Tsongs (Limboos) as the bonafide subjects of Sikkim while such ethnic reference in case of the Nepalis was avoided. The segregation of the Tsongs (Limboos) from the Nepalis was viewed as an attempt to split the Nepali community and subsequently harm their political interest. Secondly, the Regulation recognized all those Sikkimese who were alienated due to realignment of political boundaries prior to 1946 as Sikkim Subjects. The Clause 'C' of the Regulation of July 1961 was explicit in the sense that it intended to accommodate the population of Darjeeling of 1850 as subjects of Sikkim. Thirdly, the Regulation though maintained 1946 as the cut off year but for all practical purposes the cut off year was actually pushed to 1936. The Land Survey Report of 1950-51 was the basis for registration of names in the Subject Register and the 'Bustiwals' were the least eligible subjects for enumeration in the Survey Report.[40] Thus only those who had landed property were considered eligible to be registered as Sikkim Subjects while the ordinary peasants without any substantial landed property in 1936 were left out. Owing to the nature of land ownership system and settlement rules prevailing then in Sikkim, it was obvious that many were denied registration in the Land Survey Report and subsequently in the Sikkim Subject Regulation of 1961.

The promulgation of the Regulation was considered inevitable in view of the growing influx of population from outside Sikkim. It must be noted here that there has been a general tendency among the scholars to associate influx with the Nepalis but the influx of the plainsmen and Tibetans has seldom attracted attention of the scholars. For example between 1931 and 1951 the Nepali population had fallen by 0.8 percent and in 1961 the speakers of the Nepali language were only 88,916 persons, including the Tsongs and all other tribes and castes which now constitute the larger Nepali community. On the contrary, during 1961, the Bhutia population of Sikkim had been 54, 029 persons, including the

Tibetans.[41] Besides, the population of others in 1961 was 4,397 persons. Considering the circumstances leading to promulgation of Sikkim Subject Regulation in 1961, and not in 1947, it is logical to say that the Chogyal was not only desirous of inclusion of the Tibetans in the Bhutia fold but also provided refuge to thousands of them in Sikkim in spite of resentment expressed by the Bhutias and Lepchas against the decision of the Chogyal. The Regulation of 1961 possibly was an attempt to legalize the status of Tibetans and Drukpas who immigrated into Sikkim during the 1950s particularly after China intensified its activities over Tibet.

Various political parties criticized the Sikkim Subject Regulation of 1961. The political parties, namely Sikkim State Congress, Sikkim National Congress, Scheduled Caste League and a faction of the Sikkim National Party, held a joint session at Gangtok on the 26th July, 1961 and passed a proposal to request the Chogyal to withhold the enforcement of the Regulation of 1961 pending determination of public opinion.[42] Since the Regulation was promulgated without consulting the members of the State Council, C.D.Rai demanded certain amendments in the Regulation in the Council meeting in which the Sikkim Subject Regulation was placed for discussion.[43]

While considering the demands of various political parties for amendment and in view of possible political backlash, the proclamation of the 3rd July 1961 was amended.[44] The relevant portions of the Sikkim Subject Regulation, 1961 (as amended in 1962) are provided below;

1. Short title and extent:
   - (i) This Regulation may be called the Sikkim Subjects Regulation, 1961.
   - (ii) It shall extend throughout the territory of Sikkim.
2. Commencement –

   This Regulation shall come into force on such date as may be appointed for the purpose by The Chogyal of Sikkim.

3. Certain persons domiciled in Sikkim territory at the commencement of the Regulation be Sikkim subjects -
   (1) "Every person who has his domicile in the territory of Sikkim immediately before the commencement of the Regulation shall be a Sikkim Subject if he
   a) Was born in the territory of Sikkim and is resident therein, or
   b) Has been ordinarily resident in the territory of Sikkim for a period of not less than fifteen years immediately preceding such commencement; or
   c) Is the wife or minor child of a person mentioned in clause (a) or clause (b).[45]

The Sikkim Subject status was denied to certain persons namely:

a) Any person who renounces his status as a Sikkim Subject, or voluntary acquires the citizenship of any other country, or takes an oath of allegiance to a foreign country or ruler thereof without the consent of the Chogyal's government; or
b) Any person who severed his connection with Sikkim such as by parting with his property in Sikkim and migrates to a place outside Sikkim andIndia after the commencement of this Regulation, or has not been ordinarily resident of Sikkim for a continuous period of seven years shall thereupon ceased to be a Sikkim Subject; or
c) Any Sikkimese women who marries a person who is not a Sikkim Subject.

A Committee was constituted under section 3 (3) of the Sikkim Subject Regulation, 1961 (as amended in 1962) by the Chogyal for the purpose of enumeration of names in the register and subsequent grant of certificates subject to fulfillment of the above conditions and favour of the Chogyal.[46] It could not be known as to how many actually applied for registration and how many of them were issued Sikkim Subject Certificates. But, there were allegations ranging from denial of the Certificate to some to issuance to those who actually did not merit or deserve to get it. To sum up, names of many people could not be registered and hence they were denied the status of the Chogyal's subjects.

The Sikkim Subjects Certificate once again became a subject of controversy in 1975 when Sikkim became the 22nd State of the Indian Union. The Sikkim Citizenship Order of 1975 under clause 2 stated "Every person who immediately before the 26th day of April 1975, was a Sikkim Subject under the Sikkim Subjects Regulation 1961, shall be deemed to have become a citizen of India on that day".[47] As a result, those who did not have their names in the Sikkim Subject Register were denied Indian citizenship too. In regard to 'stateless persons' or 'left-out persons' it was stated that "many persons had applied for registration but their applications were not considered for immediate registration for want of verification of antecedents due to lack of proper administrative machinery prevalent at that time. Besides, the political considerations which guided the Chogyal's administration also delayed the process of verification and subsequent grant of Subject Certificates. It was further stated that the registration of names in the Sikkim Subject Register was not mandatory. Therefore, only those who desired for government services or get scholarships or acquire immovable property, for which submission of Sikkim Subject Certificate was necessary, actually applied and procured the subject certificate. Thus, thousands belonging to the three ethnic communities – Nepalis, Bhutias and Lepchas - mostly living in rural areas, were left out and this resulted in wide-spread discontentment among the people of Sikkim."[48] An interesting debate in the State Legislative Assembly over the administrative lapses and subsequent denial of registration of names in the Sikkim Subject Regulation revealed indifferent attitude of the Panchayat Officials and Mandals as the primary cause of the problem. It was said that the officials ".... would not do anything unless some gifts (butter/ghee or Rs. 10/15 per person) were given".[49] The members also expressed the view that the Panchayat officials not only misguided the villagers but there was no provision for re-

registration of the names of those who were left out in the first time.[50] The legislators condemned the Regulation of 1961 as undemocratic and a black act of the Chogyal regime, and emphasized to keep the year of merger of Sikkim with India, i.e. 1975, as the cut-off year for the award of citizenship to the left out person of Sikkim as it was done in case of the people of Goa, Daman Diu and Dadra Nagar Haveli.[51] Bhandari contended that if the 'left out' persons were denied inclusion in the subject list then Sikkim's merger with India would be questioned.[52]

The Sikkim (Citizenship) Order, 1975 was amended in 1989 to include the names of the 'left-out' persons of Sikkimese origin without obliterating the mandatory clause of the Sikkim Subjects Regulation of 1961 as the basis for the grant of Indian citizenship. Hence, the Sikkim Subject Regulation of 1961 (as amended in 1962), continue to remain an important document which distinguishes a Sikkimese from others. It is the symbol of identity and passport to public appointment and other political-economic opportunities in Sikkim. For being the old laws in force immediately before the merger, it enjoys protection under article 371F (k) of the Indian constitution. As of now, the office of the District Collector issue 'Certificate of Identification'[53] to the descendants of the Sikkim Subject Certificate holders.

At present, the controversy surrounding the Sikkim Subjects Regulation, 1961, revolves around the constitutional validity of the Regulation. In 1984, the then governor of Sikkim, Homi J. H. Taleyarkhan was reported to have written in his official file 'Sikkim Subject', dated the 3rd June, 1984 that "Clear order must be passed. There is nothing like 'Sikkim Subject' since May 1975 and that everyone since the merger of Sikkim with India is an Indian National.......At present even those who have been here for generations harassed. The two separate merit Identity Cards, one to 'NL' (non-local) and other to 'L' (local) shall be withdrawn immediately as it smacks of 'apartheid' within our own country on this account".[54]

In yet another development the then Chief Secretary, Mr. K.S.Rao, reportedly told the local journalists that Sikkim Subject

Certificate would gradually loose significance with the extension of the Employment Exchange (Compulsory Notification of Vacancies) Act, 1959, in Sikkim.[55] Amidst public outrage and protest movements the government was forced to roll back its policy in 1997. Perhaps it is because of these emerging controversies and also due to the urgency of identifying real sikkim from the fake subject holders "Pink Card" is being issued at present.

Legally speaking, article 15 (1), which does not provide 'residence' as grounds for discrimination, State can confer special benefits upon its residence in matters other than those in respect of which rights are conferred by the constitution upon all citizens. Apart from this, article 371F, which is a non-obstante article, also provides constitutional sanctions to the old laws of Sikkim. But same article under clause (l) also authorizes the union parliament/ central government to amend or repeal the provisions contained in the said article.

After the expiry of the Public Employment (Recruitment as to Residence) Act, 1957 [enacted under article 16 (3) of the constitution] in 1974, the government of India is not legally bound to continue with such provisions. Hence, even if the people of Sikkim disagree on many other issues, they find reason to agree on selective issues like the Sikkim Subject document or extension of Employment Exchange (Compulsory Notification of Vacancies) Act, 1959 or extension of Central Income Tax Act, 1961 and defend it as symbols of their separate identity as Indians of Sikkimese origin from dilution and discontinuation.

Emergence of Political Parties and Ethnic mobilization:

Sikkim basically represents traits of a traditional society. In such a traditional society political parties and other political organizations do not always represent ideological and policy divisions. Political parties, in such circumstances, often are organized on the basis of traditional bonds, networks and relations. The political parties seek to expand their support base and often appeal, including raising ethnic demands, are made on the basis of traditional bonds in order to be electorally successful and capture

capture political power. On the other hand, ethnic groups or communities seek better share of the State resources and articulate groups' interest or aspirations, and adopt strategies, including extension of support to political party or parties, in order to achieve their objectives. In other words, political parties and ethnic groups often are engaged in symbiotic relationship in fulfillment of their respective objectives.

Thus, when political mobilization of ethnic community or group takes place the traditional community consciousness is strengthened. During the late 1940s through to 1970s the Sikkim National Party had clearly demonstrated the creation of a modern political organization on the basis of traditional ethnic-cultural identities to expand its support among the members of target group. The Sikkim State Congress too had similar agenda in operation. Political parties and social organizations are also engaged in the process of articulation and aggregation of interests in a society. The demands raised by social organizations and also political parties are transformed into political issues which represent the aspirations of a group of people. But more importantly, through the function of raising and mobilizing support for an issue or demand, parties and social organizations generate consciousness regarding the demand and indirectly legitimize the demand. Hence, the activities of political parties and social organizations supporting and raising a particular demand tend to legitimize the demand socially and influence popular perceptions.

The authoritarian rule of the Chogyal, the feudal socio-economic structure, the poor, suppressed and illiterate masses, lack of political awareness and leadership can be cited as formidable reasons for the non-existence of a political organization in Sikkim till the early nineteen forties. Although reform measures were started in various fields since the consecration of Sir Tashi Namgyal in 1914, they were yet to make a noticeable progress. The practice of forced labour, locally called Zarlangi, was continued to be in operation through covert means causing great social and economic stress on the masses.

A single event at Namthang in which Mahasing Limboo and Passang Tshering Lepcha revolted against the practice of forced labour and against the practice of making the Lepchas as palanquin bearer, proved to be an eye opener for peasants who had long groaned under the boots of Kazis and the Landlords. Soon a secret organization, called Member Party, was formed in 1941 at Namthang at the initiative of Trilochan Sapkota, Jainarayan Sapkota, Jaimurn Lepcha and Dida Lepcha.

They were inspired by the leaders of the Indian freedom struggle based in Darjeeling. They opposed the Zamindars and their oppressive rules, and told people not to co-operate and obey them or their exploitative rules. Later, Tashi Tshering published a pamphlet entitled "A Few Facts about Sikkim" in 1947 detailing the nature of exploitations and emphasizing need for a strong political organization to address basic issues affecting peasants and common people. This initiative was largely responsible for converting individual resentment into a mass movement in Sikkim. Excerpts taken from the document are given below for better understanding of the situation responsible for the emergence of political organization.

"Sikkim is a small Indian State tucked away in a corner of the Himalayas. Its ruler, Maharaja Sir Tashi Namgyal, K.C.S.I., is of Tibetan descent, and so are his personal adherents called 'Kazis', who formed the majority of the landlords of Sikkim. His Highness has State Council consisting entirely of landlords and a Secretariat, which is largely controlled by landlords... The subject people or ryots have no voice in the administration and they have long groaned under the pernicious yoke of landlordism.

"The Kazis, who are the leading landlords, claim to belong to the old nobility and compare themselves with the barons of the feudal system...They form an exclusive and influential coterie around the ruling family and are able to impose their will on all and sundry. The rest of the landlords, called 'Thikadars', are content to play second fiddle to the Kazi party and thus share in the loaves and fishes of office and other privileges... Bound by a common policy to oppress the ryots, the 'Thikadars', especially the most influential one, have proved as bad as any of the Kazis. Landlordism… has enabled the landlords, through coercion and intimidation, to acquire for themselves the best holdings of the ryots. The landlords pay no taxes which consequently fall with greater severity upon the ryots. On the other hand the landlords receive large unearned commissions from the state as a reward for carrying on a thoroughly corrupt administration."

Talking about the modus operandi of the landlords, the document further writes, "The landlords are vested with magisterial powers in both civil and criminal matters. They are also empowered to register documents for the sale or transfer of landed properties. There are no effective checks on these powers and the landlords are free to abuse them for their own gains. The more fine a landlord can impose, the larger his share of spoils, for he receives one-half of the collection as his fees and the other half goes to the State. A grabbing landlord has no difficulty in dispossessing an uncompromising ryot of his cherished possession, be it a paddy field or a herd of cattle. Most of the landlords live away from the estates and their powers are exercised by ignorant and rapacious underlings who have no scruples about filling their own pockets besides extracting as much as they can for their masters."

The document then highlighted the form of oppression under forced labour (Jharlangi), "There are various forms of forced labour to which the ryots are subjected. About twenty years ago, a notification was said to have been issued by the State, based on International Conventions announcing the abolition of forced labour. This notification was never explained to the ryots and the practice was never stopped, let alone abolished. It is carried on to this day….Forced labour with minimum, often without any compensation, is usually exacted by the landlords when cultivating their extensive, mostly ill-gotten, private fields and when harvesting their crops…such exactions of late have become manifold on account of the ever-increasing farming and gardening interests of the landlords, which allow the ryots scarcely any time to attend to their own affairs. Most of the influential landlords….live in Gangtok. Their estates may be two or three days journey away. From there the ryots have to come all the way to Gangtok and serve their landlords in turn in various menial capacities. The ryots get no wages or compensations for such services, and they are lucky if they escape cruelties."

Those landlords whose estates were in and around Gangtok " the forced labour is often requisitioned on behalf of the State for carrying loads across the passes (over 15000 feet) into Tibetan territory......What he will earn as wages under the prescribed rates for forced labour, would barely suffice to buy his meager meal for the journey to and from. The landlord bleeds him to the limit and sends his own private pack mules to carry the loads, for which he is doubly recompensed. A greedy landlord often seizes upon his chance of making further easy money and calls for double the number of men required." The document continues, "Kalo Bhari was the name given to a special consignment compactly packed in black tarpaulin, which gave the name. Huge quantities of these loads were transported overland to China via Tibet during the later part of the war (World War II). Such was the demand for transport for this purpose that the wages offered reached unprecedented heights. The cupidity of the landlords rose in unison and they stooped to swindle. They falsely requisitioned 'force labour on the authority of the State' to carry these loads. A very large number of these loads belonged to private concerns..... The landlords charged the private concerns the highest rates, paid the ryots the prescribed rates, and pocketed the rest....Such blatant deception could not, however, remain concealed for long. When they learnt about it, the victims of the swindle approached the powers- that-be for redress. As the culprits were all 'high born' Kazis, the matter was hushed up, and the aggrieved ryots were sent away with the facile advice to 'let bygones be bygones and to forgive and forget."

This document acquired statewide appreciation but the people, in general, were too ignorant and unorganized for carrying out any unified action against the powerful Kazis and Thikadars.

The independence of India in 1947 together with the utterances of Pandit Jawaharlal Nehru and other leaders of the Indian National

Congress had been the greatest source of inspiration for the leaders like Tashi Tshering and C.D.Rai. Nehru was a strong supporter of republicanism and would frankly confess that "I am a socialist and a republican, and am no believer in Kings and Princes……[56] It was, therefore, natural for Tashi Tshering and others to demand for democratic system of governance and mobilize the people in the struggle for their own salvation.

Soon three separate social organizations were born in three different parts of Sikkim in 1947. The Praja Sudharak Samaj was formed at Gangtok, the Praja Sammelan at Temi Tarku in south Sikkim and the Rajya Praja Mandal at Chakhung in west Sikkim.[57] Among the three the Praja Sudharak Samaj was formed with an objective to work for reforms[58] while the Rajya Praja Sammelan was in favour of accession of Sikkim with India and union of the Gorkhas of Sikkim and North Bengal.[59] The third organization, the Praja Mandal, stood for the protection of rights and promotion of communal harmony among the three ethnic groups, i.e. the Bhutias, the Lepchas and the Nepalis, of Sikkim.[60] Though these organizations were basically social, they also had some political demands.

In a meeting held in the house of Captain Dimik Singh Lepcha on 9 October, 1947, the Sikkim Praja Sudharak Samaj was formed for the welfare of all the three ethnic communities of Sikkim.[61] The majority of those who attended the meeting being government servants, Babu Tashi Tshering, Babu Sonam Tshering (who became the President of Sikkim National Party in 1948) and Babu Raghubir Singh Basnet were selected to head the organization. The meeting also decided to form a working Committee by taking the representatives of the ryots of Sikkim.[62]

The Rajya Praja Sammelan was formed under the leadership of Gobardhan Pradhan and Dhanbahadur Tiwari at Timi Tarku (south Sikkim) with objectives to work for the accession of Sikkim with India and union of Gorkhas of Sikkim and North Bengal.[63] The third organization, called Praja Mandal, was formed at Chakhung by Kazi Lhendup Dorji Khangsarpa, who himself belonged to a landlord family. The party claimed to have been formed in 1945.[64] It stood for the promotion of welfare of the ryots and communal harmony among the three ethnic groups, i.e. Bhutia, Lepcha and Nepali, of Sikkim.[65] However, all these organizations were, more or less, formed as welfare bodies, committed to the promotion of interest of the ryots, but clearly lacked well-defined programmes, cohesive course of action and a set of political goals.[66] Thus, the need of a strong political party was felt immediately by none other than Tashi Tshering "who alone had good education, good understanding of politics and administration, and had the gifts of being able to articulate his views.[67] Accordingly, under Tashi Tshering, the leaders of the three premier organizations met at Palzor Stadium in Gangtok on 7 December, 1947 for a public meeting. By the end of the day, the three parties merged into one to form a strong political organization, called Sikkim State Congress.[68] It was in this meeting the pamphlet "A Few Facts About Sikkim", composed in English by Tashi Tshering and translated into Nepali by C.D.Rai, another highly educated leader from Namchi, was distributed among the people.

Tashi Tshering and C.D.Rai, irrespective of their ethnic affiliation, were elected as the President and the General Secretary of the party respectively. Other notable figures of the Sikkim State Congress were D.B.Gurung, Capt. Dimik Singh Lepcha, Sonam Tshering, Kazi Lhendup Dorji, Raghubir Singh Basnett, Dhanbahadur Tiwari and Gobardhan Pradhan. The most important feature of this party was, in spite of the Durbar's allegation that the emergence of Sikkim State Congress was the handiwork of the disgruntled Nepali peasants, that members of all the three ethnic communities were given adequate representation in the party.

On December 9, 1947 a five-member committee was formed to give representation to the Chogyal, Sir Tashi Namgyal. The memorandum highlighted three basic demands;

a) The abolition of land-lordism;
b) The formation of the interim government as an essential precursor of the democratic government to come; and
c) The accession of Sikkim to the Indian Union.[69]

The demands were basically the expression of the 'call of the downtrodden and suppressed ryots of Sikkim consisting of the Lepchas, the Bhutias and the Nepalis'.[70] The idea underlying the demand for accession was to acquire support of the government of India for the establishment of democratic system of governance in the theocratic and monarchical Sikkim.

The Maharaja, Sir Tashi Namgyal, agreed to the demand for abolition of landlordism in phased manner.[71] The Maharaja also agreed to appoint three nominees of the Sikkim State Congress as Secretaries to the government.[72] The State Congress in its meetings of 2 and 3 February, 1948 selected Tashi Tshering, Sonam Tshering and Raghubir Singh Pradhan. But later Tashi Tshering was replaced with Captain Dimik Singh Lepcha to give equal representation to the three communities,[73] subject to recall the members.[74] They were appointed secretaries after the party recommended their names to the Darbar.[75] Regarding the last demand of the State Congress, the Chogyal summoned five State Congress leaders in the palace on 9th December and told them that the union of Sikkim with India was out of the question.[76]

In the meanwhile, the Sikkim National Party was formed on 30 April 1948 under the leadership of Sonam Tshering. This party was sponsored by the Chogyal as an alternative to democratic agitation and to utilize communal and racial differences as backwaters to democratic development.[77] No force can be stronger than one which is based on ethnic or racial or religious elements. The leaders of the Sikkim National Party used racial-cultural issues to malign the demands of the Sikkim State Congress, in general, and interests of the Nepalis, in particular.

The Nepalis, who were dominant in the Sikkim State Congress, were alleged for being "later migrants, while the Bhutias and the Lepchas, by virtue of their having already settled in Sikkim when the Nepalis were unknown, were classified as indigenous people".[78] In a concerted attempt of the ruling house, the landlords and the

Lamas, the National Party projected itself as the party of the Bhutia-Lepcha community and the Sikkim State Congress as the Nepali party. The Sikkim State Congress by virtue of having majority supporters among the Nepalis came to be regarded as the party representing the Nepali interests, though it did not have any clear sectarian objective to achieve.[79] The National Party had been also successful in drawing a line that one who supported 'accession' were "ushering in the rule of the Dhotiwallas" and one who opposed 'accession' were for "independence of Sikkim".[80] Thus, according to Sikkim National Party's logic the Nepalis were anti-nationals and anti-Sikkimese too. This labeling also led to dissention within the leaders of the Sikkim State Congress. The birth of the National Party, therefore, facilitated ethnic and ideological polarization among the Sikkimese both at the social and party levels.

Politics of the Sikkim National Party clearly reflected its effort to polarize Sikkim into two camps: the Nepalis on the one hand and Bhutia-Lepcha community on the other. By this division the Sikkim National Party intended to retain and perpetuate not only the monarchy (as against any movement for democratization) but also the privileges enjoyed by the Bhutia landlords and elites. Democratization, therefore, was perceived by the Sikkim National Party as a threat to prevailing privileges. Thus, the struggle between monarchy and feudal system on the one hand and forces of democracy on the other was transformed into a struggle between Bhutia-Lepcha and Nepalis due to the manipulation of the Sikkim National Party.

The National party in its resolution adopted on 30 April, 1948 assured gradual demolition of the institution of landlordism and also justified as to why accession of Sikkim with India was impossible;

a) "Historically, socially, culturally and linguistically, Sikkim has closer affinities with Bhutan and Tibet;

b) "From the geographical and ethnic point of view Sikkim is not a part of India. She has only political relations with the latter, which was more or less imposed on her;

c) "The religion of Sikkim is 'Mahayana Buddhism' which is

the established religion of Tibet and Bhutan. Hence from the religious point of view also, she is quite distinct from India.

d) "The Policy of the Party is to implement their voice by all means to maintain intact the indigenous character of Sikkim and to preserve its integrity. The Party would make all out efforts to establish a separate entity and to remain outside the Indian Union even at the teeth of opposition from any political counter party;

e) "Taking into account the various vital points specified above, the Party firmly resolved that necessary arrangement should forthwith be made to revise Sikkim's political relation with the Indian Union on the basis of equality."[81]

It is to be noted that Sikkim National Party maintained that Mahayana Buddhism as the religion of Sikkim in spite of the presence of the Hindu Nepalis. By stating that in ethnic terms Sikkim was analogous to Tibet and Bhutan, the Sikkim National Party completely ignored the existence of the language, culture and religion of the Nepalis in Sikkim.

The Sikkim State Congress members visited Delhi in December 1948 and met the Prime Minister and other leaders of the Indian National Congress. Prime Minister Nehru had been reported to have told Tashi Tshering and C.D.Rai that the voice of the people would always reign supreme in shaping the destiny of Sikkim.[82] Nehru, however, had declined to support State Congress's demand for accession on three grounds: a) it would internationalized the issue; b) a nation which fought for its own independence could not immediately think of merging another nation and c) India's distinct relationship with the three neighbouring Himalayan kingdoms of Bhutan, Nepal and Sikkim.[83] After returning from Delhi, the Annual Conference of the party was called at Rangpo in February, 1949. In the gathering of about 5,000 people Tashi Tshering launched the "No Rent" and "No Tax" campaign and told people not to pay land revenue and other taxes until the Darbar considered their just demand for popular government. C.D.Rai and some other leaders were arrested on charges of violation of notification, issued some days ago, banning the assembly of people for political purpose but arrest warrant against Tashi Tshering was not executed.[84] The sympathizers of the party marched towards Gangtok.[85]

Apprehensive of public disorder, the government imposed curfew in Gangtok on 9 February. The leaders of the State Congress were released on 12 February unconditionally after the intervention of the Political Officer, Harishwar Dayal.[86] The business community also observed indefinite strike in support of the State Congress.[87] The negotiation, which was followed after the incidence, at the initiation of the Political Officer, however, failed. The Congress leaders resorted to Satyagraha. On 1 May, 1949 the agitation started in Gangtok and some three thousand party workers went up to the palace shouting anti-landlordism and pro-democracy slogans. For the first time Maharajkumar, P.T. Namgyal, addressed the crowd in Nepali language and assured to concede to their demand.

The movement was followed by the formation of the so called "popular Ministry" by the Chogyal and Tashi Tshering was sworn in as the Prime Minister of Sikkim on 9 May, 1949. The other members of the Ministry were C.D.Rai, Dimik Singh Lepcha from Sikkim State Congress and Dorjee Dadul and Reshmi Prasad Alley were appointed as nominees of the Darbar.[88] Representation-wise there were two Nepalis, two Bhutias and one Lepcha in a five-member ministry. The ministry could not last long 'due to the lack of unity within the ideologically segmented members of the Council itself and dissident clash over party politics"[89] The situation is explained by Datta-Ray as "The Prime Minister had no experience of administration and looked to the (Indian) residency for guidance in all matters..... Sir Tashi Namgyal did not think of delineating areas of jurisdiction and Tashi Tshering did not ask for a framework of governance."[90]

The political situation deteriorated further. The government of India sent Dr. B.V.Keskar, Deputy Minister for External Affairs, to Sikkim to resolve the impasse amicably but, despite his hard-pressed effort, the deadlock continued. Dayal, the Political Officer, also failed to resolve the problem. The Maharaja eventually dissolved the twenty-nine day old Ministry and the Political Officer was appointed as the interim administrator till the appointment of the Dewan, John Lall, on 11 August, 1949.[91] The sudden change in the attitude of the government of India was perhaps due to the increasing activities of the Chinese government on Tibet.

In July 1949, a delegation of the State Congress, headed by its President Tashi Tshering, went to Delhi and held discussions with the central leaders. "The delegation was informed that the government of India's sole wish was to ensure a stable government in the State of Sikkim and that under no condition could India tolerate chaos and disorder."[92] The absence of well-defined agreement between India and Sikkim along with India's intention to work closely with the government of Sikkim also figured in the discussion.[93] It was in this background that an all party convention, including Sikkim State Congress, Sikkim National Party, faction of Praja Sammelan and the Maharaja himself, was held in March 1950 in Delhi which ultimately resulted in the signing of the Indo-Sikkimese Treaty. However, the negotiation had failed to satisfy the demands of the Sikkim State Congress and the Prime Minister Nehru, though sympathetic towards their aspirations, told them not to demand for accession of Sikkim with India.[94] The disappointed State Congress leaders once again visited Delhi and met the Prime Minister and the Foreign Secretary. The burden of their complaint was that too little was done, and that there was too much philandering which was stalling the realization of a responsible government in Sikkim.[95]

On the basis of the convention of 1950[96] an Advisory Committee, under the Presidentship of the Dewan, was formed with the representatives of the major political parties like Tashi Tshering, Kashi Raj Pradhan, Captain Dimik Singh Lepcha from Sikkim State Congress, and Gyaltshen Tshering and Sonam Tshering from the National Party, as constituent members. The faction of Praja Sammelan declined to join the Committee alleging that the Committee did not represent all regions and all communities.

The Indo-Sikkim Treaty was signed between the Indian Political Officer, Harishwar Dayal and the Maharaja, Tashi

Namgyal, on 5 December 1950 at the Shuklakhang Monastery. Disappointed Sikkim State Congress members boycotted the State banquet hosted to celebrate the occasion. With the signing of the Agreement the idea of accession of Sikkim with India was put off for sometime though the Sikkim State Congress maintained that by keeping the administration in their hand the Government of India had accepted the demand in principle.[97] The party also promised to voice continuously for the establishment of democratic system of governance in Sikkim.[98] Meanwhile, the Advisory Committee was preparing to hold election for Panchayat and State Council. The vexing problem before the Committee was to decide over the distribution of seats among the three ethnic communities, the Nepalis, the Bhutias and the Lepchas. The Panchayat election which was held in December, 1950 was boycotted by the National Party on the ground that it failed to provide proper safeguards to the interest of the "indigenous population", i.e. the Bhutias and the Lepchas.[99] By raising the issue of indigenous population, the National Party was actually expressing its dissatisfaction over the Panchayat System, which was alien and un-indigenous, as against the traditional Bhutia system of rural administration called Dzumsa. The party perhaps did not want Indian system of village management to be introduced in Sikkim as well as it did not like Nepalis to hold official posts which were coming to their way through the Panchayat election. Hence, leaders of the National Party contended that the Nepalis were later immigrants while the Bhutias and the Lepchas, by virtue of their having already settled in Sikkim when the Nepalis were unknown, were the indigenous population of Sikkim.[100] The position taken by the Sikkim National Party is suggestive of the fact that how this party from the very beginning attempted to ethnicize political issues like decentralization of rural self government.

Considering the importance of holding elections for both the Panchayats and State Council, both the political parties were required to put on an extra effort in order to arrive at consensus over the system of representation but every time they failed.[101] In fact, the Sikkim State Congress had suggested for a three-member Council taking one representative each from the three ethnic communities[102] to which the National Party had reservation. Eventually, the Parity formula, as an interim solution to the problem of ethnic representation in the State Council, was worked out. According to the formula seats in the Council was to be shared equally between the (minority) Bhutia-Lepcha on the one hand, and (majority) Nepalis on the other.[103]

Tashi Tshering refused to ratify the agreement signed by his party's nominees and unsuccessfully tried to renegotiate on the issue.[104] Proclamations were issued in January, 1952 and March, 1953 detailing the composition, procedures, powers and functions of the Sikkim State Council and the Executive Council. In a seventeen member State Council the Bhutia-Lepcha as a combined group had six seats and Nepalis had six seats. The remaining five seats were to be nominated by the Maharaja in his discretion.[105] An interesting feature of the Proclamation was the method of election under which the Nepali candidates were to be directly elected by the voters during the elections while the Bhutia-Lepcha candidates were required to be elected first by the Bhutia-Lepcha voters in a primary election. The Bhutia-Lepcha voters were to elect four candidates each from the Gangtok and the North Central Constituencies and two candidates each from the Namchi and the Pemayangtse constituencies. The candidates so elected would then contest the final election. In the final election also, all the Bhutia-Lepcha voters, registered in the respective constituencies, were to cast vote.[106] Through such election rules it was always projected that Bhutia-Lepcha were different from that of the Nepalis and deserved preferential treatment. As the system of voting was designed on ethnic priorities, the voting pattern, including the result, was reflective of ethnic bias and preferences. Without such arrangement the National Party could not have been so successful in electoral politics.

In a country with low literacy and extreme all round backwardness the combined forces of the National Party, the ruling house, the landlords and the Lamas succeeded in garnering support in favour of the party's slogan that supporting them meant to support the indigenous Bhutia-Lepcha and for independent Sikkim.[107] The National Party always emphasized its identity as the Bhutia-Lepcha party and to that effect it wanted the Bhutia-Lepcha to understand that "about two-thirds of Sikkim's present population is now found to be of Nepali origin... that there was danger of their ultimate extinction, that their language would be swamped and submerged in the swelling Nepalis flood."[108]

The elections were held on different dates e.g. 1st, 8th, 15th and 22nd May for Gangtok, North-Central, Namchi and Pemayangtse constituencies respectively. The Sikkim State Congress won all the six Nepali seats whereas the National Party secured all six Bhutia-Lepcha seats. The performance of the two major parties in elections indicated the nature of ethnic-cultural polarization as a result of which the so-called Nepali party won all the seats reserved for Nepalis while the Sikkim National Party exercised absolute monopoly over Bhutia-Lepcha seats. Interestingly, the Sikkim State Congress did not even put up any candidate from the Bhutia-Lepcha reserved seats. The Scheduled Caste League and Rajya Praja Sammelan did not win any seat. Both Tashi Tshering and Lhendup Dorji Khangsarpa of the Sikkim State Congress were defeated. Kazi Lhendup Dorji replaced Tashi Tshering as Party's Presidnent.[109]

A 17 member State Council was formed in August 1953. The Executive Council was composed of three members namely Kashi Raj Pradhan (SSC) and Sonam Tshering (SNP) with the Dewan as Durbar's nominated member[110] The Lepchas had no representation in the Executive Council. The tenure of the State Council was initially fixed at three years but it was extended to till December, 1956 by a separate Proclamation.[111]

In view of the second Council election, a Proclamation was issued in 1957.[112] No changes were made in territorial constituencies and other requirements prescribed in 1953 proclamation. The State Congress contested election for establishing a representative government with the Chogyal as a constitutional head and removing communal pattern of election system introduced in 1953.[113] However, the proclamation of 1st December 1957 was not implemented. Rather after having obtained the consent of all the parties, the Dewan, N.K.Rustomji, modified the proclamation of 1953 and a fresh notification was issued on the 16th March, 1958.[114] The new proclamation enlarged the strength of the State Council from earlier 17 to 20 in which six seats were reserved for the Nepalis and six for the Bhutia-Lepcha. The number of nominated members was also raised to 6. One seat was reserved for the Sangha to be elected by an electoral college constituted of the Lamas of monasteries of Sikkim and one General seat to be elected by the whole electors of Sikkim serving as a single constituency. The 'General' seat, however, was not meant for the Indians settled in Sikkim.

The Lama community formed the most powerful pressure group in the theocratic State of the Chogyal. They assumed immense authority over the socio-cultural life of the Sikkimese as well as in the political-administrative fields. But as the democratic forces gained momentum particularly after the 1950s, there had been a gradual decline in the influence of the Lamas in the political sphere of Sikkim. By reserving seats for the Lamas in the political institution, the Chogyal provided a legal basis for the revival of their role in the political affairs of Sikkim. Thus, the society which was divided on ethnic considerations was divided on religious ground too.

The voting procedure laid down under clause 2 (i) (b) of the 1958 proclamation was very much complicated and communal. It stated that "the candidate securing the highest number of votes of the community which he represents will ordinarily be required to have secured also at least 15 per cent of the total votes of the other community for which seats have been reserved to entitle him to be returned. If, however, he fails to secure 15 per cent of the votes of the other community, the candidates securing the next highest votes of their own community and who have also succeeded in securing 15 per cent of the votes of the other community will be eligible to be returned, provided the difference between the number of votes of their own community secured by them and the highest candidates does not exceed 15 per cent of the total votes secured by the latter. If the difference is in excess of 15 per cent, latter will be regarded as returned, notwithstanding that he shall not have secured 15 per cent of the votes of the other community."[115] The example given below of Gangtok constituency explains the peculiarity of the voting system. The candidate securing the highest number of votes was not necessarily the winning candidate.

Table 4.3: Distribution of votes in Gangtok Constituency - 1958

Name of the candidate Candidates	Votes Polled			Total Votes	Remarks
	Nepali	B – L	Others		
1.Narendra Narshing (N)	2,102	295	89	2,486	Elected
2. Sonam Tshering (BL)	326	956	51	1,333	Elected
3. Kazang Wangdi (BL)	418	358	23	799	Elected
4. Thendup Lepcha (BL)	2000	162	48	2,210	
5. Chengpa Bhutia (BL)	1,944	173	57	2,174	
6. Haridas Pradhan (N)	324	450	38	812	
7. Kazi Narbu Dadul (BL)	156	294	83	533	
8. Karma Lama (BL)	126	323	09	498	
9. Dubo Bhutia (BL)	97	256	36	389	
10. Reshmi Prasad Alley (N)	416	332	24	772	

Source: Sikkim Darbar Gazette, Vol. VIII, No. 7, Oct. 1958 and other documents.

In the above constituency, by securing 15 per cent votes of the other communities and the highest votes of his own community, Narendra Narshing and Sonam Tshering were elected. Similarly, Kezang Wangdi who secured third highest vote of his own community and 15 per cent votes of other community was also elected in spite of the fact that Thendup Lepcha and Chengpa Bhutia secured the 2nd and 3rd highest number of votes secured by individual candidates.

In spite of the confusing and communal voting system, the State Congress won 8 of the 14 elected seats including one B-L and the General seat. The National Party won 5 B-L seats. These two parties were once established to facilitate democratic processes began to be recognized as parties of the two distinct communities despite the fact that the candidates of both the communities contested election from both parties. For instance, Hari Das Pradhan, a National Party candidate secured 450 B-L votes whereas of his won community he secured only 324 votes. Similarly, Thendup

Lepcha, a State Congress candidate secured 2000 Nepali votes while he secured only 162 of his own community.

In the General constituency Chuksum Bhutia, a Sikkim State Congress candidate, secured 7,444 Nepali votes and 1,168 B-L votes whereas Lakshmi Prasad Pradhan, a National Party candidate, secured only 1,068 Nepali votes and 1,364 B-L votes.[116] It seems that the Nepali candidates belonging to National party got little support from their own community but received a large percentage of Bhutia – Lepcha votes. Similar was the fate of most of the Lepcha – Bhutia candidates belonging to the Sikkim State Congress. Another noticeable feature of this election was though 6 seats were reserved for the Bhutia-Lepcha, none of the Lepcha candidate won election as they failed to secure requisite percentage of the B-L votes. The system of election together with the domination of the Bhutias in the National Party gradually alienated the Lepchas from the political institution. Similarly, neither the Sikkim State Congress, which had clear majority in the State Council, was allowed to form the Executive Council nor Mr. C.D. Rai was given the executive post who had returned after defeatng Kashi Raj Pradhan in the bye-election held after the Election Tribunal had declared Kashi Raj Pradhan, Nahkul Pradhan and Sonam Tshering as guilty of election malpractice.

The political developments continue to dissatisfy the leaders of the Sikkim State Congress. C. D. Rai, now the leader of the Sikkim State Congress (Progressive), Kazi Lhendup Dorji (Swatantra Dal) and Sonam Tshering (National Party of Sonam Tshering faction) criticized the growing undemocratic activities of the Durbar. They, along with D.B.Tiwari of Praja Sammelan and P.B.Khati of Scheduled Caste League, formed a new political party called Sikkim National Congress on 20 May 1960 at Singtam. The party demanded for responsible government and a joint electorate system. The National Congress had four seats in the State Council by virtue of amalgamation of four parties but had no representative in the Executive Council. The party sharply criticized the composition of the Executive Council and threatened to start Satyagraha movement.[117] At the advice of the political officer, the National Congress leaders like C.D.Rai, Lhendup Dorji and Sonam Tshering visited Delhi and apprised the Prime Minister with their grievances.

The election to the Third State Council was due in 1961 but political situation was not suitable for holding election due to the promulgation of the Sikkim Subject Regulation of July 1961 and the decision to enhance the strength of the Sikkim Guard. The Sikkim National Congress criticized the Regulation of 1961 as anti-Nepali designed to split the Nepali community by separating the Tsongs (Limboos) from the community.

The political parties, other than the Sikkim National Party, were unanimous in their criticism against the Darbar. They also criticized the government of India for approving it and for practicing double standard.[118] In a joint conference held at Gangtok on the 26th July, 1961 they requested the Maharaja to withhold enforcement of such an important regulation pending determination of public opinion.[119] C.D. Rai of Sikkim National Congress demanded amendment to the Proclamation before the Council when the issue was placed for discussion.[120] The National Congress also criticized Darbar's decision to increase the strength of the Sikkim guards and expressed apprehension that the force would be used to stifle political opposition.[121] However, in anticipation to public backlash, the proclamation was amended on 16 January, 1962[122] and all references to communities were removed. It was during this time that the Dalai Lama fled from Tibet reportedly with some 60,000 odd followers. The Chogyal expressed his desire to provide refuge to some 5,000 Tibetans in Sikkim against the desire of the Bhutia-Lepcha community of Sikkim. It was an act for strengthening the number of the Bhutia-Lepcha population to counter the Nepalis.[123] In view of the 1961 and 1971 census reports about the Tibetan population, accounted on the basis of the mother tongue spoken by 500 persons, it seems that the Chogyal had misled the people of Sikkim by showing only a small section of the Tibetan settlers.

Owing to the Indo-Sino conflict in 1962, the election to the State Council was put off sine die. The Sikkim State Congress and

Sikkim National Congress demanded creation of more elected seats, reduction of nominated members and introduction of joint electorate etc.[124] In 1965, the Darbar promulgated Panchayat Act, 1965 in order to hold Panchayat election together with the election of the State Council. Both the State Congress and the National Congress criticized the decision of the Darbar for introducing property or payment of land revenue as mandatory pre-condition for the voters or candidates contesting for the Panchayat election.[125] They also criticized introduction of two new seats, one each for the Scheduled Caste and the Tsongs, in the State Council. L.B.Basnet, the Joint Secretary of Sikkim National Congress, was arrested in the afternoon of 10 September, 1966 for reportedly saying "......the Sikkim Darbar assiduously applied itself to sowing the seeds of discord among the three communities......"[126] Kashi Raj Pradhan too was reported to have said, "attempts to remove communalism from Sikkim politics have been in vain, casteism has been introduced instead .... This trend, if not checked, will lead Sikkim one day to communal abyss."[127] The Sikkim State Congress accused the Darbar stating "out of the 18 elected seats 17 are communal, caste and class electorates."[128] The Chogyal, however, justified the reservation for the Tsongs and Scheduled Castes for being aboriginals and having a distinct identity.[129]

The Council election was held in scheduled time, i.e. March, 1967. Now the State Council had 24 seats of which 14 seats, including the Nepali and B-L seats, were to be elected from four territorial constituencies, three seats (Tsongs, General and Scheduled Caste) were to be returned by general constituencies and one (Sangha) by the electoral college of the monasteries. The remaining six seats were to be nominated by the Chogyal.[130] The Sikkim National Congress won 8 seats out of 18 seats, the National Party secured 5 seats and the State Congress secured only 2 seats. The other three seats went in favour of their respective candidate as they did not affiliate with any political party.[131] However, the ambiguous and complicated method of election introduced in 1958 once again created confusion in the East constituency regarding the election of Nahkul Pradhan (SSC candidate) and Chandralall Sharma (SNC candidate).

Just before the election Ruth Lepcha, a Sikkimese Lepcha women married to A. Halim, an Indian Muslim, formed a new political party called 'Sikkim Independent Front' in 1966 with objectives to protect the socio-economic and political interests of the indigenous Lepchas. The party fielded six candidates comprising of 1 Nepali and 5 Lepcha s for the 1967 election but their nomination papers were rejected for no specific reason. Ruth Lepcha, along with her husband, was arrested on 23 March, 1967 under the Sikkim Security Act.[132] Her husband was deported on 3 January, 1968 in accordance with provision of the Rule No. 10 (1) of the Sikkim Public Security Rules, 1962. According to the complaint filed by the Chief Secretary Ruth Lepcha was alleged to have said:

a) "The present ruler of Sikkim is not its real ruler... The Chogyal is a Bhutia, the real rulers of Sikkim were Lepchas;

b) "The present Chogyal, being a non-Lepcha, has no right to rule over Sikkim;

c) "The Lepchas are being suppressed in Sikkim. The Sikkim Darbar is intending to rehabilitate 5,000 Tibetan refugees in Sikkim. This move of the Sikkim Darbar is to harm the Lepchas."[133]

After her arrest and reported attempt of escape, she took refuge in the Indian House for safety. The Indian Political Officer, N.B.Menon, however, handed her over to the Sikkim authorities and was charged for additional offence, i.e. running away from legal custody. On 15 August, 1968, she was sentenced to two years' rigorous imprisonment by the Chief Magistrate of Sikkim, a retired Indian Magistrate serving the Sikkim Government. The judgement order read, "From the evidence of these witnesses it is clear that the accused was attempting to induce the ideas that the Chogyal and his government was (sic) a partisan one favouring one community against another and was obviously asking them not to obey the Chogyal and his government. And, she fully knew that by her telling these (things) to the simple villagers like these witnesses, a sense of discontentment would be created in them and stir up opposition to the Chogyal and the Government established by law in Sikkim and would incite them to insurrection and rebellion which is the object of sedition as contemplated in section 124A of the Indian Penal Code as applied to Sikkim. Further, from the evidence of these witnesses it is clear that the accused's criticism was not directed towards any individual officer of the governmental machinery but was directed towards the Chogyal and his government and as such towards the very foundation of the State."[134]

The charges, however, were neither made public nor were she tried under the Sikkim Public Security Rules, 1962 apparently in an attempt to show that she was not the subject of Sikkim after her marriage with an Indian man. But, the Sikkim Subject Regulation of 1961 (as amended in 1962) had no such provision that Sikkimese women would loose subject hood if married to non-Sikkimese. In the meanwhile the government issued a proclamation stating "A Sikkimese woman marrying a non-Sikkimese shall automatically lose her Sikkim Subjecthood."[135] Thus, by issuing a new proclamation she was declared a non-Sikkimese and was banished from Sikkim stating "It is necessary that Ruth Halim shall leave Sikkim, and the Government hereby orders that the said Mrs. Halim (Ruth Lepcha) shall remove herself from Sikkim and shall not thereafter enter Sikkim."[136] Ruth Karthak (Lepcha) hurriedly left Sikkim for Kalimpong, leaving behind her landed property and house. She hoped for a change in the order and could go back to the land of her birth and serve her people, i.e. Lepchas of Sikkim.[137] This recorded event was suggestive of the fact that the Lepchas under the Bhutia rules were subjected to various forms of dominations and their attempts for freedom were generally meted out with punitive actions.

Besides Ruth Karthak's anti-Chogyal activities, the political scenario of Sikkim was infested with intra-party squabbles. There was conflict between Kashi Raj Pradhan and Nahkul Pradhan in Sikkim State Congress, between B.B.Gurung and L.B.Basnet in the Sikkim National Congress and between Netuk Lama and Namgyal Tshering Bhutia in the Sikkim National Party. Removal from the party and formation of new party, at least a faction of the old, by the one who was removed became common during this period. On the whole, the aspiration and the trust of the people had been mercilessly sacrificed at the altar of leaders' self-centric political ambition. Referring to this political uncertainties V.H. Coelho observes, "The domestic political situation is, again, not very encouraging. Political life in Sikkim is almost stagnant. The Political parties have failed to enthuse the people...... The simple fact is that the political structure needs change and revitalization."[138]

In this political background the fourth Council election was held in April, 1970 on two different dates, i.e. on 9th and 14th of April, 1970. The National Party won 8 seats including the seats won by Netuk Lama faction, State Congress secured 4 seats, the National Congress won 5 seats, and the Tsong seat went in favour of an independent candidate. In fact, people's verdict was not in favour of any political party in particular because of growing factionalism, voters' distrust upon their leaders and division of votes due to formation of new parties like Sikkim Janata Parishad led by L.B.Basnet. A six-member Executive Council was formed by taking 2 from the Sikkim National Party, 3 from the Sikkim State Congress and 1 from Sikkim National Congress.

After the death of Sir Tashi Namgyal on December 2, 1963, the anti-Indian sentiment found resonance. Chogyal P.T.Namgyal's decision to approve national anthem of Sikkim to be played on important state functions, demands for revision of Indo-Sikkim Treaty of 1950, publication of article by Gyalmo (Hope Cook) claiming Sikkim's sovereignty over Darjeeling,[139] growing anti-Indian sentiments at the instance of the 'Study Forum' and Sikkim United Front led by K.C.Pradhan - all these activities heightened political tension in Gangtok. However, the Sidlon (Adminstrative Officer) I.S.Chopra, tactfully silenced anti-Indian voices by winning the confidence of the Chogyal on the pretext of revising the Indo-Sikkim treaty of 1950. The Sikkim National Congress wanted disclosure of the content of the ongoing confidential exchanges between the Chogyal and Mr. Chopra though it was forbidden under clause 15 (ii) of the 1953 Proclamation of the Chogyal. In the meantime, Kazi Lhendup Dorjee was dismissed from the Executive Council on 28th May, 1972 following the release of the Bulletin No. 2 on 26th January 1972 entitled "Sikkim at the Crossroads" accusing the Chogyal for being absolutist and denouncing the treatment of the Darbar towards its subjects.[140] While quoting from Kerensky's address to the Duma in 1917, the Bulletin warned the Chogyal "if you will not listen to the voice of warning, you will find yourself face to face with facts, not warnings".[141]

Kazi and his wife left for Europe while the publicity secretary of the Sikkim National Congress, D.B.Gurung, was given royal reprieve upon his pleading that he had no knowledge of the English language and must not be held responsible for the Bulletin published in English. Kazi was in a state of quandary after returning from Europe in August, 1972 as the Fifth Council election was due in January, 1973 and he was ineligible to contest the election because of release of the Bulletin No. 2. However, Athing-la (T.D.Densapa), with whom Kazi was related by marriage, persuaded the Chogyal that though troublesome Kazi was a safer bet than any Nepalis and no other Bhutia-Lepcha leader could command Nepalis loyalty than him.[142] Bajpai was also known to have advised the Chogyal "not to use a sledgehammer to crush a fly".[143] The apology of L.D.Kazi and his adopted son, N.B.Khatiwada, was accepted by the Chogyal on 21st October, 1972.

The public resentment against the Chogyal and the government of India continued. The Nepalis accused government of India for introducing a system which was anti-democratic in principle and communal in intent. The communal representation was the brain child of N.K.Rustomji, the then Dewan of Sikkim and the friend of the Chogyal, P.T.Namgyal. Rustomji, though considered Parsi Lama, had been instrumental in keeping the ethnic communities, i.e. Nepalis and Bhutia-Lepcha, politically divided. The Sikkim National Congress also came to know that the Proclamation of

1953 was drafted by the Indian officials and the Chogyal was merely asked to sign.[144] The Nepalis also accused the Chogyal for harbouring communalism by discriminating them in respect to employment, settlement, purchase of land, distribution of stipends and scholarship. 'Nepalis were eased out of jobs wherever possible and a hate-Nepali attitude was nurtured among the Bhutia students'.[145]

During the middle of 1972 there was a rumour that the Nepalis would be driven out of Sikkim. "Some highly placed Bhutia officials began to talk in terms of hastening the ouster of the Nepalis by adopting measures perfected by General Idi Amin of Uganda. There were rumours that the Bhutias were busy collecting sizable arsenal; the Bhutanese in Bhutan were being contacted; Khampas and other Tibetan refugees were being secretly armed; the Bhutias of Lachen and Lachung in North Sikkim, among whom communalism nurtured by ignorance, isolation and propaganda, were being armed with bows and arrows and some modern weapons."[146] Apparently, the Nepalis apprehended state sponsored persecution and the ethnic tension between the Nepalis and Bhutias deteriorated further.

On 26th October, 1972, the Sikkim Janata Congress was formed by merging the State Congress (Nahkul Pradhan faction) and the Janata Party (Kashi Raj Pradhan faction). The Janata Congress declared that Sikkim was not an Indian State but a separate country where the Janata was supreme.[147] The party also accused the Darbar for the injustice meted out to the Nepalis in Sikkim.[148] The party demanded for joint electorate system, a democratic form of government with Chogyal as the constitutional head and abolition of the parity formula. In order to garner support of the Nepalis, K.C. Pradhan supported aggressive action and advocated militant resurgence.[149] He regaled that "our national language is a version of Tibetan. The State religion is Tibetan Buddhism. There is no such thing as Sikkimese".[150] Speaking on the "Parity Formula", he claimed, "If we have parity then let it be taken to its logical conclusion. Sikkim should also have a Nepali king".[151]

In this background of utter political uncertainty, the Fifth Council election was held on two different dates - 10th January, 1973 for the South and West constituencies and 23rd January, 1973 for the remaining constituencies.[152] There were three important political parties in the election fray namely the Sikkim National Party, the Sikkim National Congress and the Sikkim Janata Congress, with almost identical political agenda. The treaty of 1950 and relations with India were not the election issues this time.[153] Shankar Bajpai had quoted to have compared Sikkim's national election with the local self-government elections elsewhere emphasizing on issues like roads, drinking water, irrigation etc. that would normally concern a small tehsil in India.[154] The National Party secured all the 7 B-L seats and two Nepali seats. The Sikkim National Congress secured 5 seats including one General and one Tsong seat. The Janata Congress won only 2 Nepali seats. The election result was suggestive of the fact that the election propaganda was unlikely to affect the election result due mainly to the prevailing system of communal representation and reservation of seats in the State Council. However, the allegation of rigging against the National Party candidate from Rabong led to ethnic disturbance between the Sikkim National Party and Sikkim National Congress candidates who, by coincidence, happened to be a Bhutia and a Nepali.

On the following day the Sikkim National Congress and Sikkim Janata Congress submitted a joint petition to the Chogyal demanding arrest of those officials involved in the election rigging at Rabong. Durbar's immediate reaction in the issue was to buy time. The two parties held a conference at Gangtok and demanded full fledged democracy, a written constitution, fundamental rights, universal adult franchise and abolition of Parity Formula.[155] A Joint Action Committee of the two parties was formed with L.D.Kazi as its Chairman, to pressurize the Darbar to concede to their demands but the Darbar did not budge.

The supporters of both the parties started gathering in Gangtok in batches since 3 April, 1973. The birthday celebration of the Chogyal, P.T. Namgyal, scheduled on 4 April, was differed by a day. The talk between the Joint Action Committee and the representatives of the Sikkim government failed. On the next day, more supporters of both the parties arrived in Gangtok and the police, in order to disperse the crowd, resorted to lathi charge and fired tear gas shots. Reportedly, many innocent people and milkmen were beaten up by the police who happened to dress in the Nepali attire.[156] Basnet writes, "Anyone wearing the Nepali dress, or just the Nepali cap, or just carrying a 'Khukuri' was beaten up and hauled off to a camp prepared for detaining demonstrators. Some 500 Tibetan refugees were hastily issued with lathis and asked to help the police. The refugees took their task seriously and joined their forces with the police in the lathi-charges."[157] In the evening the crown prince, Tenzing Namgyal, had wounded three women bystanders with his revolver at Ranipool.[158] As the day ended at least 60 people were injured among which some were seriously wounded. The renewal of violence on 5th April, 1973 left 150 injured and 6 dead.[159] Reportedly, Karma Topden too had acknowledged before the Chogyal that, "it's the first time in Sikkim that we had to fire on our people."[160] The Joint Action Committee apprised the Prime Minister of India, Mrs. Indira Gandhi, about the incident stating "the arming with lethal weapons and free use of Tibetan refugees and parading them within the areas under curfew to suppress the people's peaceful movement is indeed a matter of gravest concern to the safety and security of the Sikkimese masses."[161]

While the political situation was deteriorating and the people's movement gaining magnitude in Sikkim, the government in New Delhi was on the look out for an opportune moment to bring the administration of Sikkim under its complete supervision and control. Ashok Raina, exposing the design of New Delhi and its intelligence department in Sikkim, writes, "the people's uprising was the handiwork of the Indian intelligence personnel operating then in Sikkim.[162] The Indian intelligence persuaded the Chogyal to sign on the draft, prepared in advance, requesting the government of India to intervene and restore law and order. The army took over police function until relieved by the central Reserve Police Force (CRPF). On 7 April, the Political Officer once again persuaded the Chogyal to make a plea to the government of India for taking over the administration of Sikkim until some workable formula was evolved. The draft was endorsed by all the 20 members present, including Chogyal's trusted Jigdal Densapa.

B.S.Das took over the charge as the chief administrator of Sikkim on 9 April, 1973. Kewal Singh, the Foreign Secretary to the government of India, held talks with the representatives of the Joint Action Committee, the Sikkim National Party and the Chogyal. The J.A.C. submitted a list of 14 demands before the Foreign Secretary which included a new citizenship rules, an elected advisory council to assist the Indian administrator, eviction of all Tibetans, agrarian reforms, an inquiry into the distribution of the Indian financial aid, investigation of police conduct during the people's movement, release of political prisoners, summary dismissal of Dutta Chowdhury, investigation on the Ranipool shooting incident, a written constitution, fundamental rights, a full-fledged democracy, one man one vote system and abolition of 'Parity Formula', abrogation of the Indo-Sikkim Treaty of 1950 and signing of a new treaty strengthening the friendship between the people of the two countries."[163] The demands were popular in nature and no demand was made for the merger of Sikkim with India. The agitation was subsequently called off and tripartite agreement between the government of India, the Chogyal and the political parties of Sikkim was signed at Gangtok on 8th May, 1973. The agreement drastically reduced the powers of the Chogyal though he remained as the head of the government. The amenable monarch at the head of the government was more amicable for New Delhi for its future strategy.

In February 1974 the Assembly election was announced by the Chogyal. The total strength of the Assembly was decided to be 32 of which 15 seats were reserved for the Bhutia-Lepchas and 15 for the Nepalis. The Sangha and Schedule Caste had one seat each. The Tsongs (Limboos) were denied reservation of seat in the Assembly. The magic formula of one man one vote continued and public meeting on and preceding day of the poll was banned. After scrutiny about 81 candidates contested the election.

Table 4.4: Party Position in 1974 Assembly Elections

Name of the party	No. of elected candidate
1. Sikkim Congress	31 (Including 3 unopposed seat)
2. Sikkim National Party	01
3. Independents	00

Source: Sikkim Darbar gazette, Ex. Gazette, No. 55, dated 30.04.1974 and Ex. Gazette No. 29, dated 05.03.1974.

In spite of internal feuds within the leaders of the Sikkim Congress, formed out of the merger of the Sikkim Janata Party and Sikkim National Congress on 18 April, 1973, the party won 31 seats (16 Nepalis, 5 Bhutia, 9 Lepcha and 1 Sangha) in 1974 election. The Sikkim National Party won one seat. Table no.4.4 gives party position in the 1974 Assembly election.

The newly constituted Sikkim Assembly met on 10th May, 1974. On 11th May, 1974 the Assembly unanimously adopted a resolution for examining modalities for further strengthening of relationship with the government of India and to take immediate steps for Sikkim's participation in the political and economic institutions of India.[164] Regarding the Chogyal, the resolution stated that the "role and functions of the Chogyal cannot be more than those of the constitutional head of the government of Sikkim.[165] The Chief Minister, Kazi Lhendup Dorjee, warned the Chogyal that "in democracy….the people constitute the prime and vital factor that matters. Without the people there can be no government, no state, and no ruler. The voice of the people, therefore, is to be heard, honoured and respected." The Assembly also requested the Indian government to depute a constitutional expert to give a legal and constitutional framework to the objectives of its resolution. The resolution of the Assembly was a clear indication towards the merger of Sikkim with India, sooner than later.

In response to Kazi's invitation, the Government of India sent G.R. Rajagopal, a retired secretary in the Indian Law Ministry, to draft a constitution for providing a democratic set up for Sikkim. The draft constitutional Bill was ready by June 1974. During his visit to New Delhi, the Chogyal had assured the Prime Minister,

Mrs.Indira Gandhi, and the Foreign Minister, Shri Swaran Singh, of full cooperation to the members of the Assembly in the preparation of the new constitution. The Chogyal, however, not only failed to cooperate with the Assembly but his supporters also tried to prevent the legislators from entering the Assembly building.[166] The Assembly assumed its discussion at 10'clock at night and unanimously adopted the resolution endorsing the Government of Sikkim Bill, 1974. The new Bill provided for a popularly elected Assembly along with assurance to adequately represent the various sections of the populations. No single section of the population was allowed to acquire a dominating position in the affairs of Sikkim mainly by reason of its ethnic origin.[167] The Chogyal very strongly believed that the draft constitution violated the Indo-Sikkimese Treaty of 1950 under which Sikkim had its separate identity and international personage as a protectorate of India.[168] Reportedly, while in New Delhi he was advised by the Indian Prime Minister and the Foreign Minister to return to Gangtok and give his assent to the Constitution Bill and to respect the urge and aspirations of his people.[169]

On 28 June, 1974 the Assembly once again unanimously adopted the Bill and the copy of the resolution along with the ultimatum to put the Bill into effect within 48 hours was sent to the Chogyal. In case of the failure, the letter warned, that the Government of India would take steps for its enactment under the provisions of the 8th May, 1973 Agreement.[170] Meanwhile, the Assembly also requested the government of India to ensure representation of the people of Sikkim in the Indian Parliament and Supreme Court of India to have the appellate jurisdiction over the High Court of Sikkim. The Assembly also proposed for a change in the position and privileges of the Chogyal to suit his new position instead of "as hitherto enjoyed by him."[171]

The Chogyal returned to Gangtok on 1st July and expressed desire to address the members and convey his view on the Bill. The members of the Sikkim Congress, on the contrary, decided to boycott the session unless the Chogyal give his assent to the Bill. The Chogyal agreed to give assent to the Bill and the Assembly was reconvened on 3 July, 1974. He did not attend the Assembly session but his message was read in the Assembly. The Bill which was passed by 30 out of 32 members was assented to by the Chogyal on the 4th July, 1974. The Chogyal was of the opinion that article 30 of Chapter VI of the Bill would compromise the separate identity of Sikkim. The said article of the Sikkim Bill states, "For the speedy development of Sikkim in the social, economic and political fields the Government of Sikkim may;

a. Request the Government of India to include the planned development of Sikkim within the ambit of the Planning Commission of India, while that Commission is preparing Plan for the economic and social development of India and to appropriately associate officials form Sikkim in such work;
b. Request the government of India to provide facilities for students from Sikkim in institutions of higher learning and for the employment of people from Sikkim in the public services of India (including All India Services), at par with those available to citizens of India;
c. Seek participation and representation for the people of Sikkim in the political institutions of India.[172]

Thus, as per the Government of Sikkim Act, 1974 a five-member ministry led by the Chief Minister L.D.Kazi was formed on 23 July, 1974. Ethnic consideration was given due importance in the formation of the ministry. There were two Nepalis (Krishna Chandra Pradhan and Bhuwani Prasad Dahal), two Lepchas (Rinzing Tongden Lepcha and L.D. Kazi) and one Bhutia (Dorji Tshering Bhutia) in the ministry.

After the formation of the popular government, the Chief Minister Kazi made two formal requests to the government of India viz. to take steps as may be legally or constitutionally necessary to give effect to the government of Sikkim Act, 1974, and to provide representation for the people of Sikkim in Indian Parliament. Dorji Tshering Bhutia, Minister in charge of Public Health Department, believed that representation in Indian parliament would ensure a forum for the Sikkimese to raise their voice when something happened to the Sikkimese people.[173]

After having a careful and detail study of the requests of the Government of Sikkim, the Union Cabinet took the crucial decision to accord Sikkim the status of an "Associate State" of India on 29th August, 1974. The Constitution (Thirty-fifth Amendment) Bill, 1974 was introduced in the Parliament on 3rd September, 1974 to that extent. The Bill inserted article 2A which stated that Sikkim, which comprises the territories specified in the Tenth Schedule, shall be associated with the Union on the terms and conditions set out in that schedule.[174] The passing of the 35th Constitution Amendment Bill was the logical conclusion of the various events and developments that took place in Sikkim since 1950. In view of Chogyal's endeavour to internationalize the issue, the Sikkim Assembly, on 10th April, 1975, unanimously adopted a resolution abolishing the institution of the Chogyal and declaring Sikkim as a constituent unit of India. The State assembly also conducted a special opinion poll on 14th April, 1975 and, according to the verdict of the poll, the Government of India decided to accord the status of a full fledged state of India to Sikkim. On 23rd April, the Lok Sabha passed the Constitution (Thirty-sixth Amendment) Bill, 1975 providing the status of a 22nd state of India to Sikkim. The President of India, Fakhruddin Ali Ahmed, gave his assent to the Bill on 16th May 1975 ending the 332-year-old Namgyal dynasty in Sikkim. A special provision for the state of Sikkim was inserted under article 371F of the Indian constitution.[175]

The evolution of political and social history of Sikkim during the 19th and 20th centuries clearly indicate that unequal, more specifically, differential treatment of subjects was an accepted policy of the royal government of Sikkim. The basis of differential treatment was race, religion and culture, though often it was masked as categories like hereditary subjects and non-hereditary subjects. The categorization of the population of non-hereditary and hereditary subjects effectively was a racial-cultural categorization which placed the Bhutias-Lepchas under the category of hereditary subjects while the Nepalis and others were considered as non-hereditary subjects though many Nepali groups (Tribes and Castes) were living in Sikkim even before the formation of the Bhutia rule in Sikkim and hence should have included in the fold of hereditary subjects.

The position of the Tsongs (Limboos) who constituted a substantial part of the pre-Bhutia population of Sikkim was peculiar. Sometimes they were clubbed with the Bhutias and Lepchas as in the Sikkim Subject Regulation of 1961 or as in the popular expression 'Lho-Men-Tsong Sum', meaning Bhutia-Lepcha-Limboo. And sometimes, the Tsongs had to pay a higher rate of land revenue along with the Nepalis. The State policy towards the Tsongs was ambiguous and accordingly sometimes they were considered as original inhabitants and sometimes discriminated against because of cultural-linguistic reasons/differences.

In this context it is also to be noted that the Bhutia dominated monarchy was also pursuing a policy of differential taxation which clearly discriminated against the Nepalis who had to pay a higher rate of land revenue while lesser amount was imposed on the Lepcha-Bhutia subjects because of their cultural, racial and religious affinities with the ruling dynasty and elites. Similar discrimination was prevailed with regards to distribution of rewards and high government positions. Further, any mobilization of Nepalis and Tsongs was either forcibly suppressed or the leadership of such mobilization was eliminated through covert means in order to contain any challenge to the prevailing Bhutia domination. Even the Lepcha leadership whether Bholek in the 19th century or Ruth Karthak of late 20th century had to face state suppression if it challenged the domination of the Bhutia elites. The consequence of such differential policies was that the society was affectively divided on racial-cultural or ethnic lines. The vast multitude of Nepali subjects could not identify themselves with the monarchy and the government while the Bhutias considered the government as their own. Hence the differential policies initiated a social cleavage that sowed and buttressed the seeds of cultural or ethnic antagonism between the Nepalis on the one hand and Bhutias on the other. The natural consequence of such social cleavage was that the

Nepalis had remained in the forefront of democratic movement demanding reforms and changes in governmental structures or were sympathetic to the British government and, later, to the government of India (demanding accession with India). While the Bhutias rallied behind the monarchy and independent status of Sikkim. Thus, the political society was ethnically divided on the basis of cultural-religious differences and such division was indirect fallout of culturally biased differential state policy and regulation.

Such ethnic and cultural orientation, as mentioned in the preceding paragraphs, also affected the composition of political parties, mode of political mobilization and the political process as a whole in the later half of the 20th century particularly after the birth of the Sikkim National Party. The Sikkim State Congress was in favour of political reforms leading to democratic system of governance and accession of Sikkim with India. Though popular the demands had been they were clearly against the interest of the ruling elite and the Bhutia-Lepcha aristocracy. The Sikkim National Party, the brainchild of the Chogyal, naturally chose to counter the demands of the Sikkim State Congress by highlighting the racial and cultural differences between the Nepalis and the Bhutia-Lepcha subjects.

Through aggressive campaigning and political propaganda the National Party identified itself as the party of the Bhutia-Lepcha population while the Sikkim State Congress was dubbed as the party representing the interest of the Nepali community though many Lepchas were in the leading position in the State Congress than in the National Party. The ethnic division on party line had given way to ethnic tension whenever Sikkim went to polls on the one hand and political parties could never rise above ethnic issues on the other. The National Party continue to refer Nepalis in humiliating terms as migrants or non-indigenous and the latter, as a means of protection, rallied in support of the Sikkim State Congress or National Congress, as they were echoing the aspirations of the Nepalis, popular government and became sympathizers of the Indian administrator and remained in closer political ties with the government of India.

Political developments and state behaviour in Sikkim during the pre-merger days clearly indicates that the modern state system often works deliberately in favour of a particular community and attempts at limiting the space of another community. Sometimes the state-system may exclude a community completely. In Sikkim, the government of Chogyal defined the 'Sikkimese notion' in such a manner as to exclude the Nepalis including those Nepali tribes who were in Sikkim even before the establishment of the Bhutia rule in Sikkim. Land revenue systems, parity formula, definition of Sikkim Subjects Regulation etc., all are reflective of the exclusionist policies of the government. The Sikkim situation only confirms Andreas Wimmer's contention that modern institutions are systematically tied to ethnic and national forms of exclusion.[176]

FOOTNOTES AND REFERENCES

1. Glazer and Moynihan: Ethnicity – Theory and Practice, Howard University Press, Massachuset, 1975.
2. Dipankar Gupta: The Context of Ethnicity, 1997.
3. Susana Devalle: Discourses of Ethnicity – Culture and Protest in Jharkhand, 1992.
4. V.H.Coelho: Sikkim and Bhutan, Vikash Publications, New Delhi, 1983.
5. Namgyal and Dolma: The History of Sikkim, 1908, transcript.
6. Footnote: the Tibetans who migrated to Sikkim during the period of religious turmoil in Tibet are now called Sikkimese Bhutias or Dezongpa/Denzongpa.
7. D.Dahal: Sikkim Ko Rajnaitik Itihas, Subba Publications, Gangtok, 1984, P. 3.
8. Ibid, P. 8.
9. N.C.Sinha: The Chogyals of Sikkim – Bengal Past and Present, Vol. XCIII, Part I, No. 175, January-April, 1974.
10. H.H.Risley: The Gazetteer of Sikhim, Low Price Publications, New Delhi, 1993, P. 19; Op. cit. No.7, P. 52.
11. R.K.Sprigg: Shedding Some Light on the History, Language and Literature on the Lepchas, Published by Indigenous Lepcha Tribal Association, Kalimpong, 2005, Pp. 16-22.
12. Op. cit. No.7, Pp 51-53.

13. C.U.Aitchison: A Collection of Treaties, Engagements and Sanads Relating to India and Neighbouring Countries, Revised upto 1929, Mittal Publications, New Delhi, 1909/1983, Vol. 12, P.312.
14. Quoted in Bentinck's Minute of 8th January 1835, P. 23.
15. Birbal Limboo (Tamling): Teyongsi Sirijonga Sambandit Satya Kathaharo, Hee Gaon, West Sikkim, 2004, Pp. 20-21.
16. Op. cit. No. 11, P. 12
17. Ibid, P. 26.
18. L.B.Basnet: Sikkim – A short political history, S. Chand & Co. 1974, Pp. 148-50.
19. B.S.Das: The Sikkim Saga, Vikash Publications, 1983, P. 5.
20. N. Sengupta: State Government and Politics in Sikkim, Sterling Publications, New Delhi, 1985, P. 19.
21. Op. cit. No. 10, P. xxi.
22. Op. cit. No. 19, P. 84.
23. Notification dated 02.01.1897, The Sikkim Code, Vol II, Part I, P. 1, Government of Sikkim Publication.
24. Notification No. 660/G, dated 21/5/1931.
25. Notification No. 28/LR/dt. 21.04.1969.
26. Proclamation of the Chogyal, dated 30.08.1956.
27. Administrative Report of the Sikkim State for the year 1934-35 and 1935-36.
28. P.P.Karan and W.M.Jenkins: The Himalayan Kingdoms – Bhutan, Sikkim and Nepal, D.Van Nostrand Co., Princeton, 1963, P. 76.
29. N.K.Rustomji: Paper read at the Center of Himalayan Studies, North Bengal University, dated 10th March 1987.
30. A.C.Sinha: Politics of Sikkim: A Sociological Study, Thompson Press, Haryana, 1975, p. 56-58.
31. Ibid, P. 58
32. N.K.Rustomji: Sikkim – A Himalayan Tragedy, Allied Publisher, New Delhi, 1997.

33. L.B.Basnet: Sikkim – A Short Political History, S. Chand & Co., 1974, P. 173.
34. Kashi Raj Pradhan: Sikkim State Congress and Communal Problem, a Pamphlet.
35. Excerpts from the interview with Shri C.D.Rai on 17th September, 1996.
36. Sikkim Darbar Gazette, Extraordinary, Gangtok, dated 23.03.1953.
37. Op.cit. No. 33, P. 100.
38. Excerpts of the interview with Mr. C.D.Rai, Daragaon, Tadong, dt.17/09/2006.
39. Notification No. s/277/61, dated o3.07.1961.
40. Notification L.R. No. 12089/L & F 91950.
41. Technically and legally Tibetans in Sikkim are recognized as Bhutias vide the Constitution (Sikkim) Scheduled Tribes Order, 1978.
42. Op. cit No. 20, P. 161.
43. Ibid, P. 161.
44. Notification No. S/277/61, Dated 16/01/1962.
45. Sikkim Subject Regulation, 1961 (as amended on 16 January, 1961; 26 July, 1965 and 3 Dec. 1970)
46. Footnote: Section 3 (3) of the Sikkim Subjects Regulation, 1961(as amended in 1962): In any case of doubt as to whether a person has his domicile within the territory of Sikkim under this section, the matter shall be decided by The Chogyal with the assistance of Board consisting of persons to be appointed in accordance with the rules made under this Regulation.
47. Sikkim Government Gazette, No.11, dated 21.06.1975.
48. Sikkim's Basic Issues, Government of Sikkim Publications, Gangtok, 1986.
49. Legislative Proceedings, Special Session, Third Assembly, 1987, SLAS, P. 156.
50. Ibid, Pp. 157 – 58
51. Ibid, P 152.

52. J.N.Kazi: Inside Sikkim Against the Tide, Hill Media publication, Gangtok, 1993, P.264.
53. vide notification No. 65/Home/95, dated the 22nd November, 1995.
54. Chamla Tshering Bhutia: "Hamro Astha Sikkim Sangram Parishad", published by Government of Sikkim on the 9th Sangram Day, Gangtok, 1992, Pp. 39-41.
55. Himalayan Guardian, Vol. 6, No. 26, September 17, 1997: Also read "Appeal" a pamphlet published by Press and Publicity wing, SDF, Himal India Press, undated.
56. Sunanda K. Dattaray: Smash and Grab – Annexation of Sikkim, Vikash Publication, 1984, P. 55.
57. Op. cit. No. 27, P. 176.
58. Resolution of the Party, dated 09.10.1947, Gangtok.
59. V.H.Coelho: Sikkim and Bhutan, Vikash Publication, New Delhi, 1983, P. 47.
60. Interview with L.D.Kazi in January 2001, Chakhung Cottage, Kalimpong.
61. Resolution of the meeting, dated 09.10.1947 as cited in Op. cit. No. 42, P. 150.
62. Ibid, P. 151.
63. Op. cit. No. 59, P. 47
64. Op. cit. No. 162, P. 151.
65. Op. cit. No. 60.
66. Op. cit. No. 37. P. 36.
67. Ibid, P. 36
68. Namgyal Tshering, Sikkim: Aajako Sikkim, No. 4, September 1978, P. 2.
69. Sikkim State Congress petition to the Maharaja of Sikkim, dated 09.12.1947.
70. Tashi Tshering: A Few Facts about Sikkim, Gangtok, P. 1.
71. Sikkim: A Concise Chronicle, Government of Sikkim Publications, 1962, P. 27.
72. Ibid.

73. Kashi Raj Pradhan: Sikkim State Congress and the Communal Problems.
74. Interview with Mr. C.D.Rai, the former member of the Sikkim State Congress, dated the 17th September 2006.
75. Op. cit. No. 71, P. 27.
76. Op. cit. No. 56, P. 54.
77. Cited in Grover's 'Sikkim and India: Storm and Consolidation, Jain Brothers, New Delhi, 1974, P. 36.
78. Op. cit. No. 67, P. 55.
79. Ibid, P. 98.
80. Tashi Tshering: Sikkim At The Crossroad.
81. Petition of the Sikkim National Party, dated 01.05.1948.
82. Op. cit. No. 79, P. 85.
83. Op. cit. No. 74, P. 27.
84. Op. cit. No. 82, P. 87.
85. Op. cit. No. 59, P. 27.
86. B.S.K. Grover: Sikkim and India-Storm and Consolidation, Jain Brothers, New Delhi, 1974, P. 37.
87. Op. Cit. No.84, P. 87.
88. Letter of the Maharajkumar of Sikkim to the President of Sikkim State Congress, dated 08.05.1949.
89. Op. cit. No. 85, P. 27.
90. Op. cit. No. 76, P. 57.
91. Notification No. 836-1335/P.S. dated 11.08.1949.
92. Op. cit. No. 89, P. 28.
93. Ibid, P. 28.
94. Narendra Goyal: Political History of Himalayan States – Tibet, Nepal, Bhutan, Sikkim and Nagaland since 1947, New Delhi, 1966, P. 142.
95. Op. cit. No.93, P. 29.
96. Press Note issued by the Ministry of External Affairs, Government of India, dated 20.03.1950.

97. A Pamphlet issued by the Sikkim State Congress in April, 1950.
98. The Resolution adopted in the Fourth Annual Session of the Sikkim State Congress, 1950.
99. Op. cit. No.71, P. 27.
100. Op. cit. No.87, P. 98.
101. Op. cit. No.73.
102. Ibid.
103. Op. cit. No.95, P. 29.
104. Op. cit. No.100, P. 99.
105. Proclamation of H.H. the Maharaja of Sikkim, dated 23.03.1953.
106. Proclamation of H.H. the Maharaja of Sikkim, dated 28.12.1952.
107. Op. cit. No. 104, P. 98.
108. N.K.Rustomji, Enchanted Frontiers: Sikkim, Bhutan and India's North-Eastern Border Lands, Oxford University Press, London, 1973, Pp. 141-42.
109. Op. cit. No. 107, P. 105.
110. Op. cit. No. 103, P. 30.
111. Proclamation of the Maharaja, dated 26.09.1957.
112. Proclamation of the Maharaja, dated 01.12.1957.
113. B.B.Gurung: 'Sikkim Ma Chunao', Kanchanjangha, Vol. 2, No. 4, dated 25.12.1985.
114. Op. cit. No. 99.
115. Sikkim Darbar Gazette, Ex. Gazette, Vol. II, No. 5, dated 17.03.1958.
116. Election Office, Gangtok and other departments.
117. Op. cit. No. 110, P. 32.
118. Ibid, P. 32.
119. Proceedings of the meeting of representatives of SNP, SSC, SNC and SSCL, held at Gangtok on 26.07.1961.
120. Proceedings of the State Council, dated 29.09.1961.
121. Op. cit. No. 118, P.32.

122. Notification No. S/277/61, Sikkim Subject Rule, 1961.
123. Op. cit. No. 109. P. 120.
124. Asian Recorder, New Delhi, 1962, P. 4490.
125. Ranju Dhamala: Problems and Stratgegies of Development in the Eastern Himalayas (Ed.), Gyan Publishing House, New Delhi, 1993, Pp. 184-99.
126. Democracy in Sikkim – I, Now, dated 29.04.1966, P. 10.
127. National Herald, dated 29.01.1967, Locknow.
128. Sikkim: An Independent Fortnightly, Vol. I, No. 13, dated 06.01.1967, Gangtok.
129. National Herald, dated 22.01,1967, Locknow.
130. Sikkim Darbar Gazette, Ex. Gazette, No.9, dated 21.12.1966, Gangtok.
131. Op. cit. No. 121, P. 35.
132. Op. cit. No. 123, P. 148-50.
133. Ibid, P. 148-50..
134. Ibid, Pp 150-51.
135. Ibid, P. 148
136. Ibid, Pp. 148 – 50.Op. cit. No. 119, P. 169.
137. Ibid, Pp. 150-51.
138. Op. cit. No. 131, P. 51-52..
139. The Sikkimese Theory of Land Holding and the Darjeeling Grant, by Hope (Cook) Namgyal, Bulletin of Tibetology, Vol. III, No. 2, dated 21.07.1966, Namgyal Institute of Tibetology, Gangtok.
140. Op. cit. 137, P. 169.
141. Op. cit. No. 90, P. 160.
142. Ibid, P. 161.
143. Ibid, P. 161-62.
144. Op. cit. No. 140, P. 168.
145. Ibid, P. 173
146. Ibid, P. 173.

147. Op. cit. no. 141, P. 164.

148. Bulletin No.1 of the Sikkim Janata Congress issued by K.C.Pradhan & S.K.Rai.

149. Op. cit. No. 146, P. 174.

150. Op. cit. No. 147, P. 164.

151. Ibid, P. 164.

152. Sikkim Durbar Gazette, Ex. Gazette No. 12, dt. 23/09/1972.

153. Op. cit. No. 150, P. 166.

154. Ibid, P. 166.

155. Op. cit. No. 149, P. 180..

156. Ibid, P. 182.

157. Ibid, P. 182.

158. Ibid, P. 182.

159. Ibid, P. 184.

160. Op. cit. No. 153, P. 181.

161. Copy of the letter of the Joint Action Committee of Sikkim National Congress and Sikkim Janata Congress, dated 04.04.1973.

162. Ashok Raina: Inside Raw – The Story of India's Secret Service, cited in DattaRay's Smash and Grab: Annexaton of Sikim.Vikash Publicatopn.New Delhi, 1985,P. 186.

163. Op. cit. No. 160, P. 192.

164. P.R.Rao: Sikkim – The Story of its integration with India, Cosmos Publications, New Delhi, 1978, P. 49..

165. Ibid, Pp. 49-50.

166. Ibid, P. 50.

167. Text of the Sikkim Bill, 1974.

168. Op. cit No166, P. 53.

169. Ibid, P. 54-55.

170. Ibid, P. 55.

171. Ibid, P. 56

172. Op. cit. No. 148.
173. Op. cit. No. 168, P. 61.
174. Op. cit. No. 167.
175. The Constitution 36th Amendment Act, 1975.
176. Andreas Wimmer, Nationalist Exclusion and Ethnic Conflict, CUP, Cambridge, 2002, P. 5.

5

Parliamentary System, New Modes of Mobilization and Ethnic Politics

Political power in Sikkim before its merger with India, as it is evident from the discussion in the preceding chapter, in reality was in the hands of the minority Bhutia elites who attempted to establish their legitimacy by means of a legendary 'blood-brotherhood' pact with Lepchas who were inhabitants of Sikkim prior to the migration of Bhutias. The Lepchas were accommodated as minor partners in the ruling coalition. The Bhutia ruling group also accommodated some Nepali prominent personalities in the ruling coalition but latter definitely occupied a subordinate position like the Lepchas. A vast majority of the Nepali population was excluded from the governing process and they were treated as merely producers of revenue without any right. The policies of the Bhutia rulers offered little opportunity to majority Nepali population for participation in the government.

The Nepalis often were subjected to discriminatory rules such as the Revenue Order No. 1. The educated Nepali elites who were excluded from the centers of power perceived democracy and merger with India as the means for transforming such uneven distribution of power. Apparently, democracy and merger with India were unrelated! But given the circumstances prevailing in Sikkim then, it was inconceivable that the Bhutia rulers would transfer powers to a democratic government. While merger with India offered the prospect of introduction of Parliamentary Democracy as well as the support of the powerful protector. Being in majority and consolidated due to Durbar's discriminatory policies, they contemplated to bargain for fairer share in political affairs and initiate reform measures abolishing rules or policies which discriminated them. The Bhutia elites on the other perceived democratic government as a threat to their political domination and to the identity of a Buddhist State, including the fear of abolition of their political identity manifested in the institution of the 'Chogyal'. They also feared that they would be gradually ousted from the centre of power and privileges. With these apprehensions in mind, the Bhutias denounced democracy in the first place and emphasized vigorously for the need to protect and preserve the ethnic identity of the Bhutia-Lepcha community in Sikkim.

The introduction of parliamentary democracy as a consequence of merger in 1975 generated the expectation that ethnic / communal discrimination and ethno-cultural politics revolving around community interest would gradually make way for undifferentiated policies, rule of law and secular political mobilization. The constitution of India envisaged equality and individual rights irrespective of caste, race, religion etc. and it was expected that such a legal-constitutional framework would gradually minimize the prevailing inter-ethnic mistrust and conflict among Bhutias, Lepchas and Nepalis. But the expectation has not materialized. Rather ethnic cultural politics became a norm pursued and practiced by almost all political groups and parties to such an extent that even smaller communities and cultural groups which hitherto identified themselves with the larger cultural groups began to assert their separate political identity with a view to claiming larger share of resources and power. For example, the Lepchas started demanding for protection of their land from the Bhutias and maintenance of parity with the Bhutias in terms of Assembly seats, employment, educational facilities etc. The Bhutias, on the other, had been divided into the 'Real Bhutias' and the 'Other Bhutias' mainly on the basis of period of settlement and Nepalis too exhibited signs of split into the Other Backward Class (OBC) and Non-Backward Class (NBC) on racial origin. Similarly, the Limboos, at least organizationally, asserted their separate identity distinct from the general Nepali identity.

Actually, introduction of parliamentary system and majoritarian politics in a traditional society with sharp community divisions and cultural identity automatically may lead to political mobilization on the basis of available traditional community structures and affiliation. A clear demonstration of such a political mobilization in Sikkim was attempted by the Sikkim National Party before the merger and, as a consequence of which, the other political parties too, directly or indirectly, emphasized on traditional bonds, networks and relations in an attempt at strengthening traditional community consciousness for mobilization. In this situation intervention of political parties and political leadership becomes crucial for the replacement of community-oriented politics by secular democratic values. The new legal constitutional structure based on ideals of equality and freedom is also expected to facilitate this process. However, in Sikkim some of the legal provisions of the monarchical era had been retained even after the merger and continued to be the source of discontent among various communities. The process of political mobilization also remained, contrary to expectations, ethnicized and culture-centered. This chapter attempts to review political developments during the post-merger period with a view to assessing the role of legal-constitutional framework and party politics along with their methods of political mobilization in aggravating ethno-cultural tensions in Sikkim.

Certain legal-political ambiguities prevailed in the relationship between Sikkim and India after the departure of the British in 1947. Sikkim had been a protectorate state of the British India since 1890.[1] After independence of India, the government of India had no such treaty right of a protectorate over Sikkim. For being included in the list of Princely States of British India in 1921 and allocation of one seat to Sikkim by the Government of India Act, 1935[2] Sikkim was bound by the terms of Lord Wavell's declaration which stated "Political arrangements between the States on the one side and the British Crown and British India on the other will thus be brought to an end. The void will have to be filled either by the States entering into a federal relationship with the succeeding government or governments in British India or failing this, entering into particular political arrangements with it or them."[3] Accordingly, a two member delegation led by the crown prince, Palden Thondup Namgyal, and Rai Bahadur T.D.Densapa, discussed the matter with the Chamber of Princes and the new government of India at New Delhi. The general impression of both the government of India and the Constituent Assembly about Sikkim, as resolved on December 21, 1946, was in favour of according a special status to the latter. The Sikkimese delegation continued its discussion with the Indian counterpart leading to signing of Standstill Agreement on February 27, 1948. It stated "All agreements, relations and administrative arrangements as to matter of common concern existing between the Crown and the Sikkim State on August 14, 1947" were deemed to continue between the Dominion of India and the Sikkim Darbar pending the conclusion of a new agreement or treaty.[4] Later, a friendship treaty was signed on December 5, 1950 between the Chogyal Tashi Namgyal and Harishwar Dayal, the then Political Officer of government of India in Sikkim, declaring Sikkim as a protectorate state of India. While Sikkim enjoyed internal autonomy subject to the ultimate responsibility of government of India for maintenance of good governance and law and order, the government of India was held responsible for Sikkim's external relations, defense and communication.[5] Besides, the government of India also became the most important source of revenue for planned expenditures in Sikkim.

Subject to the conditions of the Treaty of 1950, the Chogyal and the Sikkim National Party, formed in April, 1948, always stood for the monarchy and relationship on the basis of equality with India while the Sikkim State Congress, formed in December 1947, demanded for a popular government, merger with India and socio-economic reforms.[6] Though reform measures were initiated the contradiction pertaining to ethnic issues/questions persisted despite efforts to accommodate grievances of the rival political parties. Political events which followed as a consequence of escalation of political strife between pro-democracy Nepalis and anyi-democracy Bhutia rulers ultimately convinced the government of India to take steps for merger. The 36th Amendment Bill proposed in the Indian

Parliament, seeking to accord Sikkim a status of the 22nd State of India, was passed in the Lok Sabha on April 23, 1975. In spite of the reservation raised by the opposition bench particularly regarding the discretionary powers of the Governor and virtual absence of reference to the Government of Sikkim Act, 1974 which protected the office of the Chogyal, the Rajya Sabha also passed the Bill on April 26, 1975 with a majority of 157 votes. On May 16, 1975 the President of India, Fakhruddin Ali Ahmed, gave his assent to the 36th Constitutional Amendment Bill with effect from April 26, 1975. The Amendment Act also repealed 2A and Scheduled X of the constitution inserted by the 35th Amendment Act 1974 when Sikkim was accorded the status of an Associated State of India. The President appointed B.B.Lal, formerly the Chief Executive Officer of India in Sikkim, as the first Governor of Sikkim who then administered the oath of secrecy to the first Chief Minister, Kazi Lhendup Dorji Khangsarpa and five other cabinet ministers.

The 36th Constitutional (Amendment) Act, 1975 also inserted article 371F in part xxi of the Indian constitution in order to protect and preserve the political, and socio-cultural distinctiveness of Sikkim. The noteworthy features of article 371F may be summarized as: (a) the Legislative Assembly is to be composed of not less than 30 members; (b) continuation of the unicameral Legislative Assembly formed in April 1974 with 32 members elected through direct election; (c) provision for reservation of seats in the Legislative Assembly for different sections (ethnic) of the population and delimitation of constituencies from which candidates belonging to such sections alone may stand for elections; (d) allocation of one seat in the House of the People and election of the candidate by the sitting members of the State Assembly; (e) power of special responsibility vested in the Governor for the maintenance of peace and for ensuring equitable social and economic advancement of different sections of the population; (f) continuation of the High Court as the High Court of the State of Sikkim; (g) continuation of all old laws in force immediately before the appointed day subject to amendment or repeal by the Legislative Assembly or by the President of India within two years from the appointed date; (h) extension of any law presently in force in State of India by the President of India by public notification; (i) the article 371F do not command the same constitutional status as that of article 370 applicable for the State of Jammu & Kashmir; and (j) the article 371F is a non-obstante article.

Government after the merger:

The Kazi government started functioning from May 16, 1975. As required by articles 371F(k) and (l), the government soon got into action to fulfill constitutional obligation for adapting and modifying laws of governance including rules of procedure and conduct of business in the Assembly in tune with the rules of the Lok Sabha. The rules delineating functions of the legislature and executive were formulated and training and orientation camps were held to make the functionaries fully conversant with the nature of responsibility they were supposed to carry out henceforth.

As stated earlier, the Governor under the new arrangement was vested with the power of special responsibility to act in his discretion for the maintenance of peace and for ensuring equitable social and economic advancement subject to such directions as the President may, from time to time, deem fit to issue. This special power of the Governor was perhaps given in view of the volatile condition prevailing then in Sikkim. According to constitutional norms of Union of India, the Governor during the normal time was to act on the advice of the Council of Ministers headed by the Chief Minister. But during the formative stage of democracy in Sikkim, B.B.Lal, the first Governor, always acted as the real executive head of the State. The Ministers, being novice, had limited know-how of the complex working of the democratic government which made them dependent on the wisdom of the ever-imposing Governor.

It was given an impression that the Governor also enjoyed overwhelming influence in the legislative business as well. As early as 1976, Mr. N.B.Khatiwada raised the issue of involving the Governor in each and every issue discussed by the Assembly.[7] The Governor was also alleged by the leaders of various political parties viz. Sikkim Janata Parishad, Sikkim Congress (R), Sikkim Prajatantra Congress etc. for being proactive in Legislative business as well as party politics during the October 1979 Assembly election.[8] Such interventions and special power of the Governor sometimes generated resentment among political leaders and ministers, and often the political parties exploited the issue.

After the merger, the circumstances prevailing in Sikkim was in favour of a visionary leadership and professional bureaucracy who could formulate policies and design plans and strategies for taking Sikkim into a new era of political stability and economic development. But not only the new breed of political leadership lacked adequate administrative experience, the local bureaucrats, which evolved through strict Darbari etiquette and parochial outlook, too were in need of structural overhauling and change in their attitude.

Thus, the Chief Minister Kazi was compelled to rely on the advice of State's Governor, B.B.Lal, and host of other bureaucrats posted in Sikkim on deputation. As a result the local senior officers were offended and often avoided the Chief Minister while the influence of the Governor and other bureaucrats upon the Chief Minister increased making him 'prisoner of indecision', as the opposition party used to call him. B. S. Das too acknowledged that Kazi's weakness lied in his lack of decisiveness and administrative acumen.[9] Though it was too early to expect drastic changes coming to their way, the people of Sikkim were, by and large, unhappy with the Kazi government. The rise in prices of essential commodities put tremendous pressure on the day to day life of the poor people. The priority laid on the industrial sector left the primary sector, where about 95 percent of the Sikkimese depended for livelihood, neglected which arouse public resentment against the government. The fruits of economic policy failed to trickle down to the needy for whom economic development often meant fulfillment of their immediate basic requirements. The land reform could not be implemented allegedly under the influence of big landlords and no effective measures were adopted to check corruption. In other words, gulf between the rich and the poor was ever expanding.

The political situation too was marred by inter-party and intra-party squabbles. In order to silence the dissenting voices within the ruling Sikkim Congress, Kazi effected merger with the Indian National Congress (I) in 1975. But, when the Janata party came to power at the centre in 1977, Kazi once again switched allegiance to the Janata Party. The frequent change of allegiance and dictating nature of national parties ruined Kazi's ability to lead the people of the State which incited split within the ruling party. Mr. N.B. Khatiwada left the ruling Janata Party in 1977 and formed Sikkim Prajatantra Congress (1977) owing to differences with the Chief Minister Kazi on the issue of non-implementation of the Land Reform recommendations, also called Khatiwada Committee Report, allegedly under the influence of the powerful landlords mostly composed of the Bhutias.[10]

In other words, community consideration, which had been the permanent feature of the pre-merger era, continued to get favour at the political policy-making level. Apart from this, the sense of insecurity of becoming alienated in the land of their own and feeling of uneasiness in view of the influx of outsiders further arouse respective community resentments against the State. Kazi government was also criticized for doing nothing in order to protect the Nepali seats in 1979. The apprehension of the Nepalis was so strong that R.C. Poudyal and some other MLAs left the ruling Janata Party and formed a new political party called Sikkim Congress (Revolutionary) in 1979. The emergence of two regional parties namely Sikkim Prajatantra Congress (earlier Congress for Democracy) of Khatiwada and Sikkim Congress (Revolutionary) by R.C.Poudyal formed more or less on the issues of deprivation of Nepalis were credited for continuing with ethnicity-oriented politics in the post-merger era.

Rise of anti-merger sentiment:

Palden Thendup Namgyal, the last Chogyal of Sikkim, always advocated for maintaining a distinct Sikkimese identity of Sikkim which became dormant during the massive pro-democracy movement leading to merger with India. But the failure of the Kazi government and ever-imposing attitude of the Governor and other officers paved the way for resurgence of Sikkimese identity within four years after the merger.

The Bhutia elite, who always stood by the view of the Chogyal for a separate identity of Sikkim, had constraint admitting merger as a fate accompli, while the Nepalis were largely disillusioned at the outcome of the merger when they found themselves alienated from the actual helm of the administrative affair which was controlled by officers coming on deputation from different parts of India. Hence, democracy was interpreted as the rule by plainsmen or simply as the 'Indian' rule. The anti-merger feeling gradually began to take root among the people. Political parties formed during this period namely Sikkim Prajatantra Congress (1977) of N.B.Khatiwada and Sikkim Janata Parishad (1977) of N.B.Bhandari, also contributed immensely towards escalation of anti-merger sentiment by raising it as the major issue of their political campaigns. Mr. Khatiwada, one of the signatories of the merger, questioned the way the 'Special Poll' was held and the result of the poll announced even of those areas from where ballot boxes did not reach at all.[11] He also condemned the 'Special Poll' as unconstitutional and illegal.[12]

In a letter to Morarji Desai, Khatiwada regretted that the method used by the government of India was 'the age-old methods of the imperialistic and expansionist nations of divide and rule, propagating false propaganda, creating an illusion that democracy was being introduced ....whereas, in reality, the trust of the simple and innocent people was being deceived, exploited and betrayed.'[13] The four signatories of the memorandum, including Khatiwada, requested the government of India to 'review' the status of Sikkim and restore rights to the Sikkimese to manage their own affairs. Mr. N.B.Bhandari, the then leader of the Sikkim Janata Party (later Sikkim Janata Parishad) also criticized the signatories of the merger as 'Battishay Chor' (Thirty-two thieves) or 'Desh Bechuwas' (persons who sold their country) and appealed to the people to 'not to be fooled again'. He stressed on the need for 'safeguarding the lost rights of the people of Sikkim'.[14] The slogans like 'Sikkim for the Sikkimese' and 'Sikkim Farkaunchoun' (shall bring back Sikkim) helped him and his party to gain quick popularity. Moreover, his anti-Kazi image had placed him in an extremely convenient position among the old guards of the Sikkim National Party, also called Chogyal's party, who had always stood against the merger with India.

The merger issue further gathered considerable attention with the publication of the statement of the Prime Minister Desai criticizing the manner in which the merger was effected.[15] Desai's observation was an extension of what the lawyer President of India, Mohammed Hidayatullah, wrote "in any event the Indian constitution cannot be relied upon to alter Sikkim's status.... The constitution binds India and not Sikkim."[16] Such an authoritative statement exposing legal implications of the Indian amendment validating merger was definitely stimulating for the anti-merger group. K.C.Pradhan, another architect of the merger, also stated that the resolution adopted by the Assembly in favour of merger had no mandate of the people.[17] The other signatories like N.B.Khatiwada, B.B.Gurung and R.T.Lepcha also regretted for being the victim of circumstances and believed that 'history would never pardon them'.[18]

It was in this background that the first election after the merger was held in April 1979. The political parties like Sikkim Prajatantra Party and Sikkim Janata Parishad used merger issue as a major political campaign to expose the failure of the Kazi government. Though the leaders of both the parties belonged to the Nepali community, Mr. N.B.Bhandari and his Sikkim Janata Parishad had an edge over Mr. Khatiwada and his Sikkim Prajatantra Party by virtue of not being a party to the merger. This image of him went well with the forces of anti-merger aspirants, particularly the pro-Chogyal Bhutia community; while a significant section of the Bhutia-Lepcha people were apprehensive of Mr. Khatiwada for his anti-Bhutia-Lepcha image. His land reform recommendation of 1977, demand for abolition of the private estate and Revenue Order No. 1 of 1917 which prohibited transaction of Bhutia-Lepcha land to others were viewed as against the interests of the landed Bhutia-Lepcha people.

Amendments to Representation of the People Act, 1950 and 1951 of India:

The election rules by which Kazi government was formed in May 1974 were based on the Proclamation of Representation of Sikkim Subject Act, 1974. After the merger the election rules prevailing in Sikkim needed adaptation or modification in accordance with the election rules prevailing in India. Accordingly, the Representation of the People Act, 1950 (43 of 1950) was amended in 1976 (Act 10 of 1976) and Section 7A in the said Act was included with retrospective effect from September 9, 1975. Section 7A, clause (1) & (3) provided for a 32 member Legislative Assembly chosen by direct election from Assembly constituencies and continuation of reservation of seats as provided immediately before the commencement of the constitution (Thirty-Sixth Amendment) Act, 1975.

Similarly, Section 25A was inserted validating Sangha constituency, including the election held in Sikkim in April, 1974 for the purpose. It also provided for preparation or revision of the electoral rolls for the Sangha constituency in such a manner as directed by the Election Commission of India, in consultation with the Government of Sikkim.[19] In other words, the amendment to the Representation of the People Act, 1950 legitimized the Assembly elections, including total number of Assembly seats and seats reserved for various communities/class, held in April, 1974 in Sikkim.

As all Assembly seats in Sikkim were reserved for one or other community / caste under the 1974 Act and as the system was allowed to continue even after the merger, the Representation of the People Act, 1950, as amended in 1976, was found to be inadequate in determining the eligibility of candidates contesting from the reserved constituencies. As such the Representation of the People Act, 1951, which provides rules pertaining actual conduct of elections to Parliament and State Legislatures, was amended and Section 5A was inserted in 1976 with retrospective effect from September 9, 1975. The section inserted, i.e. 5A of the Act of 1951, stated, "Notwithstanding anything contained in section 5, a person shall not be qualified to be chosen to fill a seat in the Legislative Assembly of Sikkim unless –

a) in the case of a seat reserved for Sikkimese of Bhutia-Lepcha origin, he is a person either of Bhutia or Lepcha origin and is an elector for any Assembly constituency in the State other than the constituency reserved for the Sanghas;
b) in the case of a seat reserved for Sikkimese of Nepali origin, he is a person of Nepali origin and is an elector for any Assembly constituency in the State;
c) in the case of a seat reserved for Scheduled Castes, he is a member of any of the castes specified in the Representation of Sikkim Subjects Act, 1974 and is an elector for any Assembly constituency in the State; and
d) in the case of a seat reserved for Sanghas, he is an elector of the Sangha constituency.[20]

The amendment to the Representation of the People Act, 1951 (as amended in 1976) was simply a legal-political formality seeking to legitimize the election held in 1974, but, by and large, it was against the true spirit and tradition of the parliamentary democratic constitution of India. By upholding and supporting Chogyal's method of delimitation based on ethno-cultural and religious elements, the government of India not only supported communal and ethnic politics in Sikkim but under parliamentary democracy such elements found a new scope for growth and deepening of their roots further.

In the eve of the first Assembly election after the merger, the electoral rolls became a major bone of contention between the political parties and the government owing to non-enumeration of names of about fifty thousand persons in the electoral rolls.[21] Political parties like Sikkim Janata Congress and Sikkim Prajatantra

Party demanded for inclusion of all Nepalis living in Sikkim since 1970 in the electoral rolls.[22] Apart from this, the political parties also expressed resentment over the proposal of the Election Commission of India and the Union government to extend voting right to the plains people living in Sikkim[23] and the proposal to amend the Representation of the People Act, 1951 in order to abolish 15 seats reserved hitherto for the Nepalis and subsequent reduction of seats reserved for Bhutia-Lepcha communities to 12 from 15 seats reserved earlier.

The Representation of the People (Amendment) Bill, 1979 (Bill No. 79) as proposed by the Janata Government in May 1979 could not be passed due to dissolution of the Lok Sabha. In the meanwhile, the President issued an ordinance, called the Representation of the People (Amendment) Ordinance, 1979, seeking to amend Section 5A of the Representation of the People Act, 1951. The basic features of the Ordinance were: (a) the Assembly was a 32 member legislative house out of which 12 seats were reserved for the Bhutia-Lepcha, 2 for the Scheduled Castes, 1 for the Sangha (monastery) and 17 seats were declared as General seats. The provision of seats reserved for Nepalis was abolished and the plains people were given the right to franchise and contest election for the first time. Apart from the 12 reserved seats, the Bhutia-Lepcha could contest election from the General seats as well. Similarly, article 332 (1) (3) of the constitution of India was extended to reserve 2 seats for the Scheduled Castes of Sikkim. After the Lok Sabha election of 1980, the Union Parliament passed the Representation of the People (Amendment) Bill, 1980 and subsequently section 7(1A) in the Representation of the People Act, 1950 and sub-section 2 in section 5A of the Representation of the People Act, 1951 were inserted as rules governing Assembly elections in Sikkim.

The apprehension shown against the Act by the Nepalis and the Bhutia-Lepcha people alike, therefore, was not without substance. Since the 17 seats had been declared an open seat, anybody who was an Indian citizen and having names in the electoral rolls of any constituency in Sikkim could contest election. Nepalis feared that "the people from the plains would gradually oust them from all position of importance."[24] Similarly, the Bhutia-Lepcha people resented reduction of seats from 15 to 12 seats. They contended that since eight other sub-groups like Chumbipa, Tromopa, Dopthapa, Yolmo, Kagate, Sherpa, Drukpa and Tibetan, were included within the definition of 'Bhutias', the seats actually should have been increased. They feared dilution of their original Sikkimese identity and further reduction of seats in case if these sub-groups of Bhutias became politically proactive and more demanding. The political decision, which was supposed to promote democratic ethos/ distribution of power, actually became the cause of social division and ethnic tension.

The Amendment (1979/80) therefore set the issue of identity in motion in two ways: it generated the perception of 'Sikkimese' identity and protection of Sikkimese culture vis-à-vis plainsmen migrated to Sikkim from various parts of India. Further, it increased the gulf between Nepalis on the one hand and Bhutia-Lepcha on the other. Nepalis became unhappy because their seats were abolished while seats for Bhutia- Lepchas were retained. The Bhutia-Lepcha on their turn lamented the end of "Parity" guaranteed in 1951 and subsequently in 1974. Besides, they were also apprehensive over the reduction of reserved seats and dilution of their identity due to inclusion of other Bhutias.

Election and Ethnicization:

The first election after the merger was rescheduled to be held on the 12th October 1979.[25] About 247 candidates contested the election out of which 131 belonged to various regional and national political parties and 116 were independent candidates. There were nine women candidates of which four were party candidates. Ruth Karthak Lepchani, who was removed from Sikkim in 1969, also contested election from three constituencies.[26] None of the political parties gave tickets to the plainsmen and hence, as many as 8 plainsmen contested election as an independent from the Gangtok constituency alone.

The crisis within the ruling Janata Party led by Kazi Lhendup Dorji had deepened further over the issue of reduction of Bhutia-Lepcha seats, abolition of reserved Nepali seats, and over the grant of political rights to plainsmen. The dissidents under R.C.Poudyal blamed the Chief Minister Kazi for the present political development in Sikkim. Through a signature campaign Poudyal mobilized a significant number of legislators in his support. A memorandum signed by at least 14 ruling party leaders and legislators (6 of them withdrew support later) was submitted to the Union Minister, Mr. P. Shiv Shankar, requesting him to reconsider the Bill No. 79.[27] The growing indiscipline within the ruling party necessitated Chief Minister Kazi to remove R.C.Poudyal from the Ministry in the middle of June 1979. The Chief Minister's offer to reserve 15 seats out of 17 general seats for the Nepalis could not satisfy the dissidents.

In a public meeting held at Gangtok on July 8, 1979 Poudyal justified "reservation of seats for the Nepalis as they were likely to be reduced to minority in near future, unless some safeguards were immediately provided."[28] He further clarified that "in 1975, people of Sikkim had accepted Sikkim's merger with India subject to certain conditions. One among these conditions was that only the people of Nepali, Lepcha and Bhutia origin of Sikkim would be able to contest elections to the State Assembly. This condition was also made a part of the Representation of the People Act by inserting a new provision in it in September 1975."[29] He questioned as to why this provision was now being changed by conferring electoral rights on the plainsmen.[30] On July 31, 1979, he circulated copies of a petition among the members of Parliament intending to draw their attention towards the resentment of the Sikkimese people against the Bill No. 79 which, according to him, was brought to the Parliament without the knowledge of the Sikkim Assembly or that of the State cabinet.[31] He maintained that the Bill was an attempt to invalidate and nullify the sacred commitments given to the Sikkimese people prior to the merger and emphasized that in view of the influx of the people from other States the seats for the Nepalis in proportion to their population should be reserved.[32]

In September 1979, he formed a new regional party, called the Sikkim Congress (Revolutionary). He condemned the Bill No. 79 as 'Black Bill' and personally did not contest the election, but he was the chief campaigner of his party. He also filed a writ petition in the Delhi High Court in September 18, 1979 questioning the constitutional validity of the seats reserved for the Bhutia-Lepchas on the basis of race or religion. The Bhutia-Lepchas considered his action as an attempt to completely annihilate their identity in Sikkim. The election manifesto of the Sikkim Congress (Revolutionary) stated, "We are opposed to the Black Bill No. 79. We are contesting this election under protest and have filed a writ petition before the Hon'ble High Court in Delhi against the undemocratic and non-secular features of the Bill. As long as the Bill is not withdrawn or a suitable amendment to it is not done, the Sikkim Congress (Revolutionary) will launch a sustained movement against it by legal, Parliamentary and legislative measures."[33] Moreover, his party's demand for recognition of the Nepali language in the 8th Schedule of the constitution and grant of citizenship to all those living in Sikkim till 1970 made him biased towards his own ethnic community, i.e. Nepalis.

Mr. N. B. Khatiwada and his Sikkim Prajatantra Congress (SPC) also raised the issue of Bill No. 79 and relative deprivation of seats of the Nepalis. He also condemned grant of political rights to the plainsmen.[34]

Mr. N.B.Bhandari and his Sikkim Janata Parishad party also expressed resentment over the extension of political rights to the plainsmen and did not give party ticket to them. He tactfully avoided public utterances on the controversial seat issue and mobilized the supporters of the Chogyal and Limboo voters by raising the issues of merger, restoration of Limboo seats and tribal status respectively considering the importance of the Bhutia-Lepcha and Limboo factors in determining political outcome. He effectively blended issues of Sikkimese identity with the requirement of the constituency from which he was contesting (Limboo dominated Soreng constituency). By raising issues like 'Sikkim for the Sikkimese' and 'Sikkim Farkaunchoun' (bring back Sikkim) Mr. Bhandari also tried to contain ethnic differences with issues of common concern.

The Sikkim Janata Parishad won election with 16 seats of which 8 seats belonged to the reserved B-L seats. The total seat was raised to 17 when the Sangha candidate, an independent, joined Sikkim Janata Parishad. The Sikkim Congress (Revolutionary) won 11 seats including 3 B-L seats and the Sikkim Prajatantra Congress secured 2 seats. However, Kazi's Janata Party was completely routed in the election. Later, Chamla Tshering Bhutia, elected from the Sikkim Congress (Revolutionary) ticket, defected to Bhandari's Sikkim Janata Parishad. It was said that its soft stand against the Bill No. 79, virulent attack on the Kazi government on merger issue and its inability to safeguard the rights and dignity of the Sikkimese actually helped Sikkim Janata Parishad to win majority of the Bhutia-Lepcha seats and an equal number of General seats with that of the Sikkim Congress (Revolutionary) which was solely banking on ethnic Nepali votes. Hence, the Bhutia-Lepcha and Limboo voters had been crucial for Bhandari's election victory in 1979.

The Presidential Ordinance of 1979 had been the central issue around which the 1979 Assembly election was contested. The loss of seats and inclusion of eight other Bhutias in the Bhutia fold made the Bhutia-Lepcha apprehensive and rallied behind Sikkim Janata Parishad of N.B.Bhandari and its slogan for 'bring back Sikkim'. The anti-merger sentiments, therefore, found resonance. On the other hand, the Sikkim Congress (R) propagated communalism in the name of protecting the interests of the Nepalis and played upon their emotions. Party's attempt to seek legal remedy on abolition of Nepali seats vis-à-vis opposition to continuation of 12 Bhutia-Lepcha and 1 Sangha (Monastery) seats aggravated social tension. This was also true with the Sikkim Prajatantra Congress of N.B.Khatiwada which opposed abolition of Nepali seats and extension of political rights to the plainsmen. Thus, during the monarchical regime prevalence of ethnic groups seeking egalitarian treatment seemed to be have caused social division, in the parliamentary democracy the political mobilization of ethnic communities for electoral gain became the cause of social tension.

Bhandari Regime: 1979-89.

By defection, the majority of the Sikkim Janata Parishad rose to 18 and the Governor, J. S. Lal, called upon Mr. Bhandari to form the government. An eight member Council of Ministers was formed on 18 October, 1979 with Mr. N.B.Bhandari as the Chief Minister. The party also won the lone Lok Sabha seat in January 1980 but lost bi-election of Khamdong and Chakhung Assembly constituencies.[35] No major departure in terms of issues was seen in this election too. The issues like Bill No. 79, issue of merger, rights of the Sikkimese vis-à-vis non-Sikkimese continued to dominate election propaganda and political campaigns.

After assuming power the Chief Minister Bhandari reorganized the administration as far as practicable to provide Sikkimese look to its structure and functioning. The Central Reserve Police Force (CRPF), which was present in Sikkim since 1973, was replaced with the Sikkim Armed Police. The number of central government officials on deputation to Sikkim was also considerably reduced. He even changed the name of his political party from Sikkim Janata Parishad to Sikkim Parishad in an attempt to keep distinct Sikkimese identity to the party and his leadership. The party was extremely critical of the Governor, Shri B.B.Lal, during the October 1979 election. The resentment continued even after the formation of the government and eventually succeeded in replacing him in 1981.[36] Homi J.H.Taleyarkhan, a veteran politician, succeeded Mr. Lal as the Governor of Sikkim in January 1981. Being a Congressman, the Governor engineered a regional adaptation of a national party. Bhandari and his colleague enbloc joined the Congress (I) party. In fact, since the return of the Congress (I) party at the centre after 1980 Lok Sabha election, the politics in Sikkim assumed an interesting shape over the issue of getting recognition of the Congress (I) party. The merger of Sikkim Parishad with the Congress (I) in 1981 was a political necessity intending to keep the united opposition at bay.

The choice of the Governor in Mr. Taleyarkhan, however, was a political blunder for Mr. Bhandari. The honeymoon between the two ended abruptly with the unconstitutional dismissal of the Parishad government in May 1984. It was believed that the Governor was not supportive of Bhandari's anti-plainsmen attitude while the Chief Minister disliked the politician governor allegedly for involving and inciting split within the Council of Minister often on ethnic grounds.[37] In fact, neither the governor could live up to the constitutional obligation[38] nor the Chief Minister Bhandari could restraint himself from punishing dissident voices within the Council of Minister. Besides political differences, the duo had stiff ideological differences too. Unlike Bhandari's call for 'Sikkim for the Sikkimese' and 'Son of the Soil' policy based on the Sikkim Subject Certificate, the Governor always maintained the view that "Sikkim Subject has no validity and all Indians should get permanent jobs in Sikkim".[39] One of the Ministers, Chamla Tshering Bhutia, also alleged the Governor for conspiring against rights of the Sikkimese by abolishing the Sikkim Subject Certificate.[40] The tribal (Bhutia-Lepcha) leaders who were instrumental behind Bhandari's political success, was also the factor in political alignment in Sikkim which the Governor seemed to have used effectively against Mr. Bhandari. Considering the inclination of the Bhutia-Lepcha legislators towards the Governor and also as being the representative of the Limboo dominated Soreng Assembly constituency, Bhandari wrote to the Prime Minister of India, Mrs. Indira Gandhi, for the inclusion of Limboos in the Scheduled Tribes list of Sikkim in 1981.[41] It must be noted that the Bhutias had always cherished a secret desire to have their own Chief Minister which, however, could not have been possible without the blessing of the Governor or through some political alignment at the top. Against the design of Mr. Bhandari to use anti-merger and Sikkimese identity for political bargaining, the Governor was on the lookout for a Chief Minister who was acceptable to the Sikkimese but would be able to contain the issue of Sikkimese identity to go beyond a point of no return. Mr. B.B.Gurung was appointed as the third Chief Minister of Sikkim on 11 May 1984 with this intention. However, his pro-Indian speech given on the State Day, dated 16 May 1984, created unhappiness among his supporters, both within and outside the government. The Assembly was suspended on 24

May 1984 and Sikkim was brought under the purview of article 356 of the constitution of India.

Soon after the dismissal, Mr. Bhandari resigned from the Indian National Congress (I) along with his colleague. He founded a new regional party, called Sikkim Sangram Parishad (SSP), in 1984 in New Delhi. In December 1984 Lok Sabha election, he made a heroic comeback by winning the lone Lok Sabha seat with thumping majority. His electoral victory was indicative of the fact that politics in Sikkim essentially revolves around either ethnic or regional issues. The people of Sikkim, in general, by virtue of past experiences, are skeptical about national parties and even deny that they have any role to play in the politics of Sikkim.

The domination of the party continued in the Assembly election held in March 1985. The Sangram Party won 30 out of 32 Assembly seats. Apart from Bhandari's personal charisma, he skillfully exploited affective issues like restoration of parity formula and reservation of seats for Sikkimese Nepalis, citizenship for the people rendered stateless in Sikkim, fixation of 1970 as the cut off year for granting of citizenship, preservation of local identity and implementation of the 'Son of the Soil' policy, constitutional recognition of the Nepali language in the Eighth Schedule of the Indian constitution, amendment of the provision of the constitution which justifies dismissal of the state government by the Governor on his/her pleasure.[42] As far as election manifesto was concerned, his idea of 'Sikkim for the Sikkimese' was heavily tilted in favour of the Sikkimese Nepalis to which he himself belonged. This departure may be due to the 1984 political development in which almost all the tribal leaders were involved in 'remove Bhandari' campaign. Though his slogan 'Sikkim for Sikkimese' was meant to criticize the policy of the government of India for granting political rights to the plainsmen, it too flared up into the issue of sikkimese verses non-sikkimese.

The contradictions prevailing between Mr. N.B.Bhandari and State's Governor, Homi J.H.Taleyarkahan, basically appeared to be a clash of two identities – Sikkimese identity vs. Indian identity. But when the protagonists of Sikkimese identity suffered from political setback, they resorted to mobilization of communities on ethno-cultural elements as a means for political resurgence. This added a new dimension in Sikkimese identity, i.e. Sikkimese identity is partly territorial and partly cultural.

Division within the Nepali community - Growth of New Identities:

The earlier two Chief Ministers compared the rule of Mr. N.B. Bhandari as the dictatorship of the worst type. Bhandari was alleged to have become arrogant and obsessed to falsities of vested interest. The continual loss of democratic values both within the cabinet and in party functioning, rampant corruption and spoil system, victimization of the opposition and above all politics of divide and rule characterized Bhandari's government in the post-1985 era. Unlike his 1981 stand[43] he later opposed inclusion of Limboos and Tamangs in the Scheduled Tribes list in 1987 even though the central government wanted the two communities to be recognized as Scheduled Tribes.[44] He perhaps was of the impression that the inclusion of Limboo and Tamang in the Scheduled Tribes list would lead to division within the Nepali community. But some old Sikkim Sangram activists believed that Bhandari did not want to displease the Bhutia-Lepcha tribal community with whom he was completely relying for safety and continuity of the government during those years. However, his decision alienated the Limboo and Tamang communities and with this the first crack appeared in the corpus Nepali. The Limboos, in disgust, reactivated their organizational activities and submitted a memorandum to the President of India requesting him to include Limboo community in the Scheduled Tribes list of Sikkim and restoration of the Limboo seat in the Assembly.[45] The Limboo Organization, called Akhil Kirat Limboo Chumlung (Estd. 1973), also demanded resignation of the Chief Minister, Mr. N.B. Bhandari.[46]

The major rift within the Nepali community, however, began with the passing of the legislation by the central government seeking to implement Mandal Commission Recommendation. In Sikkim, the communities like Rai, Limboo, Mangar, Tamang, Gurung and

Bhujel were included in the Other Backward Classes (OBC) list which, taken together, formed the majority of the State's population, and excluded other groups of Nepalis like the Bahuns (Brahmins), Chhetris (Kshatriyas) and the Newars. This obviously led to division within the larger Nepali community in terms of the 'backward' classes, also called Matwalis (one who uses liquor as part of traditional religio-cultural belief) and the 'forward' classes who belonged to higher castes Nepalis and economically affluent in the State as compared to the former.

Apart from the division in terms of classes, there had been attempts to highlight racial differences between the two sections of the Nepalis, i.e. Mongoloid (mostly animist and Buddhist) and Aryan (Hindus). Racially, the Other Backward Classes belonged to the 'Mongoloid' stock while the Forward section of the Nepalis were 'Aryan', with an exception of the Newars who dominated the State administration. There were as many interpretations and explanations about the communities as there were groups and organizations wanting to include or exclude communities into one or the other fold such as OBC, tribals and Newars on the one hand and Aryan Bahun and Chhetris on the other or Kiratis vs. non-Kiratis within the mongoloid fold. These divisions within the Nepali fold also had larger political ramification. Considering the fact that the Mongoloid population formed about 50 per cent of the State's population, it posed a serious threat to Bhandari's domination in the politics of Sikkim. Bhandari, an upper caste Nepali by birth and belonging to the Aryan fold, was quick enough to understand the outcome of polarization on racial or religious grounds and rejected the proposal of the Mandal Commission Recommendation. On 7 September 1990, the Assembly passed a resolution rejecting the central directives for implementation of the Mandal Commission recommendation in Sikkim.[47] It must be mentioned here that the list of Other Backward Classes in Sikkim was first prepared by Mr. Bhandari himself in 1980.

Apart from rejecting the Mandal recommendation, his selective use of derogatory or inauspicious remarks against the Other Backward Classes in public meetings such as "when people become mad, they become OBC" etc. further drifted the OBC sections away from the mainstream Nepali community. Once a single community, Nepali began to be referred to as NBC[48] and OBC. Invariably, the shape of the nose 'Thepche' (flat nose) and 'Chuchey' (pointed nose) were used for identifying the Mongoloid fold from that of the Aryan Nepali. In this context J.N.Kazi writes, "Elsewhere in the world politics may be decided by the colour of one's skin, or by the faith that one profess, but in this part of the region, the shape of things to come may ultimately be determined by the shape of one's nose. The traditional 'Thepche – Nepte' divide denoting their racial differences, is gradually surfacing and will definitely set the future political agenda in the Himalayan borderland."[49]

The OBC people with their inkling for benefit in terms of 27 per cent reservation in employment and other economic benefits were infuriated at the rejection of the implementation of the Mandal Commission's recommendation and articulated their resentment besides engineering electoral mobilization and formation of ethnic organizations. These ethnic organizations, including the Akhil Sikkim Kirati Limboo Chumlung, representing the Limboos of Sikkim, accused Bhandari of highhandedness and demanded for a 'review' of the State government's decision on the Mandal Commission issue. The Akhil Sikkim Kirat Limboo Chumlung also stated that the government's decision deprived the 'majority' Sikkimese Nepalis of their share in 'social and economic benefits' just to appease a 'very small' section of the Nepali community.[50] The Rais, by virtue of being the largest section among the Nepali population in the State of Sikkim and perhaps economically the most deprived too, conducted indoor meetings and formed association (e.g. Akhil Kirat Rai Sangh of Sikkim in June 1990) which led to the formation of the Mandal Coordination Committee headed by the veteran political personality, a retired civil servant and a journalist, Shri C. D. Rai. The Committee worked as the forum of the OBC communities and was instrumental in forging unity among them.

With the mongoloid consciousness gaining significance, the Nepali language, which had been the symbol of unity and strength during the pre-merger era, became another contentious issue between the two leading to a new interpretation of identity. Mr. Bhandari who used the term 'Arya Bhasa' (Arya language) as a synonym to 'Nepali Bhasa' (Nepali language) in the memorandum submitted to the visiting President of India, Shri P. Venkataraman, dated 21 October 1991, regarding constitutional recognition of the Nepali language[51] became the source of contradiction.

Truly speaking, the source of the Nepali language, like many other Indian languages, was/is the Sanskrit language, i.e. the language used by the Aryans for all purposes of communication in ancient India. But the use of the term 'Arya Bhasa' as a synonym for the 'Nepali Bhasa' was not acceptable to the mongoloid section of the Nepalis. According to them the Nepali language had never been the language of a single racial community but a conglomeration of several dialects/languages spoken by different sub-tribes of the larger Nepali community. Nepali as a language had passed through several evolutionary phases and called variously like Parbatey Bhasa, Pahari Bhasa, Khash Kura etc. before attaining the present form. A renowned Nepali litterateur and a linguist, Surya Vikram Gnewali, too subscribed to this view saying, "Every Nepali dialect or even language had contributed towards the development of the Nepali language".[52] In fact, the essence of the mongoloid resentment towards the Nepali language was/is that they considered it as a symbol of linguistic domination imposed by the ruling Aryan race, at the cost of their own dialects or languages, during the 18th century. They also held Nepali language chiefly responsible for disappearance or moribund condition of other languages/ dialects spoken by various other sub-groups of the mongoloid section of the Nepali community. The emphasis, therefore, had been on the preservation of other languages/dialects spoken by the majority section of the Nepali community while the Nepali language to remain as the lingua franca of the State of Sikkim.

This controversy surrounding the Nepali language alienated a substantial section of the Nepali community in Sikkim, particularly the Limboos, Tamangs, Rais, Gurungs, etc. who belonged to various hill tribes but gradually assimilated themselves within the larger Nepali-fold and identified as Nepalis. These tribes often are bi-lingual using Nepali in the public sphere while resorting to their tribal language in their homes and within community level. As the emphasis on Aryanism grew, the demand for recognition of languages/dialects spoken by these communities, including the demand for recognition of them in the Scheduled Tribes list also grew in magnitude. This development also had a tremendous affect on the electoral alignment.

The contemporary event like publication of a book entitled 'The Hidden Facts in Nepali Politics' by Shri Gopal Gurung seemed to have contributed immensely in the development of the mongoloid consciousness in Sikkim. The book, which was banned both in Sikkim and Nepal, was an attempt to expose the hollowness of Nepali politics which, it contended, was based on the exploitation of the majority mongoloid Nepalis by the minority Aryans/Hindu Nepalis. Apart from this, a certain section of the Limboo elites in Sikkim were also influenced by the activities of the Limbuwana Mukti Morcha (Limbuwana Liberation Front), a Limboo dominated political organization of the Eastern Nepal, led by Bir Nembang. It was believed that both Shri Gurung and Nembang frequented Sikkim and Darjeeling and made friends with some key figures and organizations in both the places.

The division in the Nepali community occurred in two ways: firstly, the State Government decided not to recommend for inclusion of the Limboos and Tamangs in the Scheduled Tribes list. The community felt alienated by the policies of the government which was taken in favour of the Bhutia-Lepcha community. This generated a sense of community resentment and consciousness as against the notion of belonging to Nepalis. Secondly, the communities belonging to Other Backward Classes too resented the policy of the government which denied them the status of OBC in 1990. The feeling of deprivation and differential treatment among the OBC communities, including the Limboos and Tamangs, gradually resulted in consolidation of consciousness for separate identity other than the larger Nepali identity. Thus, it appears very strongly that the nexus between the electoral politics and government policies have accentuated process of social divisions and created community consciousness in favour of smaller identities which hitherto were regarded as Nepali community.

Chamling and the rise of the OBC:

The Mandal Coordination Committee, under the leadership of Mr. C.D.Rai, had become a common forum of the OBC and gained enough strength to withstand any reprisal action from the government. But the significant section of the OBC leaders, including party leaders, were perceiving Mr. P.K.Chamling, who was not only politically popular within the ruling SSP party but also belonged to the majority Rai community of Sikkim, as the person to lead the OBC community.

It was during 1990-91 that Mr. Chamling, then a cabinet minister, was also beginning to have ideological differences with his political boss, Mr. Bhandari. His defiance was as much to do with his reelection with a record 97 per cent votes in 1989 Assembly election as with the emergence of the Backward Class politics in Sikkim. He was also the choice of the Congress (I) which was then engaged in 'remove Bhandari' campaign. As rumours had it, Mr. Chamling then was having the support of 12 M.L.As, including some Ministers. Mr. Chamla Tshering, another powerful Bhutia leader, had the support of 8 Bhutia-Lepcha M.L.As and the rest were with Mr. N.B.Bhandari. Considering the gravity of the situation, Mr. Bhandari removed Mr. P.K.Chamling first from the Ministry on 16 July 1992 and later from the primary membership of the Sikkim Sangram Parishad party. Mr. Bhim Raj Rai, M.L.A from Jorthang-Nayabazar constituency and belonging to Chamling's own Rai community, was appointed in Chamling's post in a bid to pacify his growing anti-OBC image. The government suffered no untoward damage due to the fact that Mr. Chamling declined to be in power through some unconstitutional and unscrupulous means. The constitutional recognition to the Nepali language in August 1992 further normalized the condition.[53] The Denzong Tribal Yargay Chogpa, an organization dominantly of the Bhutias, however was not happy with the inclusion of Nepali language in the Eighth Schedule of the Constitution and expressed resentment by alleging the Chief Minister Bhandari for working in favour of his own Nepali community.

After his removal from the Ministry and the SSP, P. K. Chamling formed a new regional party called Sikkim Democratic Front (SDF) in March, 1993. The SDF was initially considered as the party representing Mongoloid Nepalis or the OBC group, and the clash between SDF and SSP at Namchi (18 June, 1993) was viewed as the conflict between Mongoloid and Aryan Nepalis. The SDF party was declared a terrorist organization and its supporters were arrested. An arrest warrant was served against Mr. P.K.Chamling. This further antagonized the OBC segment of population and indirectly strengthened a sense of unity among the mongoloid Nepalis. The emergence of SDF, therefore, marks a new dimension in Sikkim's ethnic politics – a search for mongoloid identity.

About the same time (1993-1994) the government of India proposed to extend the Central Income Tax Act, 1961 to Sikkim effectively from April 1995. In other words Sikkimese, including those who were making a living in Sikkim, was exempted from central income tax and other direct taxes. In a letter dated July 24, 1993 Bhandari requested the central counterpart for tax exemption for the Scheduled Tribes of Sikkim in a manner that tribes of North-East India were exempted from the central income tax. The Sikkim People's Forum formed on March 18, 1994, demanded tax exemption for the Nepalis also along with tribals. Forum believed that any rule which was applicable only to the Nepalis who enjoyed protection under 371F (g) as 'different section of the population of Sikkim' would be unconstitutional, partial and discriminatory against the community.

The Rajya Sabha member, Mr. Karma Topden, reportedly told the People's Forum to wait till "we get what is being granted to us and then we will do for you".[54] Mr. Topden's statement antagonized the delegates of the People's Forum and communal tension flared up like a wild fire. The newly formed SDF party supported the demand of the People's Forum by calling a three-day strike from March 22, 1994. The strike was a complete success which also evoked strong reaction from the State Government. The government issued a press release in which the participating government employees were warned, the proposal for exemption to the tribals from the central tax was welcomed and stressed need for passing the Finance Bill (No. 15) without any delay.[55] The press release also emphasized "let the tribals of Sikkim avail themselves of the tax exemption in the first instance, thereafter steps for obtaining tax concessions for the other ethnic communities of Sikkim can also be taken up by all, with even greater zeal."[56] It divided the Sikkimese into tribals (Bhutia-Lepcha) and non-tribals (Nepalis).

The People's Forum, however, continued its agitation and met Dr. Manmohan Singh, the then Union Finance Minister, in April 1994. The Chief Minister Bhandari also met the President of India, S.D.Sharma, and the Prime Minister along with his party legislators and submitted a memorandum to the President requesting for the smooth passage of the Finance Bill No. 15 of 1994 seeking to extend Central Income Tax Act, 1961 to Sikkim while giving due recognition to the proposal of the State Government for giving exemption to the tribal communities of Sikkim. As a compromise, the memorandum also requested the President "to advice the government of India to take immediate steps to incorporate a provision in the present Finance Bill availing similar exemption to the Nepalis of Sikkimese origin also."[57] The Finance Minister, however, withdrew the Bill after receiving Bhandari's request letter. The Finance Minister stated that, "The Finance Bill seeks to exempt from the income of the members of the scheduled tribes residing in the state of Sikkim. However, the concession to the Schedule Tribe of Sikkim was introduced in the Finance Bill in accordance with the wishes of the Chief Minister of Sikkim. The letter has now come with the fresh request that not only Schedule Tribes but all the people residing in Sikkim should be exempted from the taxation….. This has raised examinations de novo, means a fresh examination.

Therefore I propose to withdraw for the time being the proposal in the Finance Bill ....”[58]

Bhandari, who already lost sympathy of the Nepalis, was accused of deceiving the Bhutia-Lepcha tribals also. In fact, the statement of the Finance Minister did not anywhere mention about imposition of the Income Tax on either community but the feeling that Bhutia-Lepcha alone should first enjoy the tax benefit generated apprehension among the Nepalis. Ethnic tension, which was brewing gradually since the People’s Forum was formed, further intensified after the withdrawal of the Finance Bill No. 15. Anti-Nepali or anti-Bhutia-Lepcha slogans (Nepali thieves, leave Sikkim / Bleed Bhutia-Lepchas etc.) echoed valleys and villages of Sikkim. Dressed in traditional attire a protest rally was organized at Gangtok by a certain section of the Bhutia-Lepcha community on May 7, 1994.

On May 5, 1994 about 18 M.L.As deserted Mr. Bhandari in favour of a new leader Mr. Sanchaman Limboo. Ethnic tension went on unabated and it became difficult to contain the situation. Democracy as an ideology and a force to restore peace and communal harmony was put to test. On May 15, 1994 Mr. P.K.Chamling called a public meeting at Singtam which in itself was a record in terms of public gathering. It was in this public meeting he declared, “if somebody wants to bleed any Bhutia or Lepcha to death, he should first chop off my head.”[59] Chamling’s extraordinary stand was finally able to restore normalcy and was successful in diffusing ethnic tension before it turned out to be a full-fledged ethnic violence. Chamling later recollected that, “the extraordinary rally called by the SDF party at Singtam was finally able to replenish the lifeblood of communal harmony and unity in Sikkim.”[60] This incident is a clear reminder as to how precarious the inter-community relation is and how state policies and organizations contribute to either containing or aggravating the situation in a plural society.

Bhandari lost the no-confidence motion held on May 17, 1994. Mr. P.K.Chamling though participated in the hour-long Assembly discussion, abstained from voting.[61] Mr. Chamling criticized the outgoing Chief Minister Bhandari for harbouring a false notion of communal harmony and for sowing the seeds of division within the Nepali community by making controversial statements in the White Hall like 'I was out of Sikkim for few days and the Nepalis in Sikkim were split into OBC and NBC."[62] Chamling believed that communal harmony could prevail only if the three ethnic communities were given liberty for self-growth.[63]

Sanchaman Limboo, the leader of the dissident group, was sworn in as the fourth Chief Minister of Sikkim on 18 May, 1994 but soon lost majority following the resignation of the two tribal ministers. Both Mr. Bhandari and Chamling, including some members of the Legislative Assembly, also resigned from the Assembly. The Limboo faction merged with the Congress Party (I), which was in power at the centre, and continued in office till the formation of the new government.

The fall of the Bhandari government ushered in a new phase in Sikkimese politics with community or cognate identity becoming a center of political alignment and mobilization. The rise of the Other Backward Classes (OBC) as a formidable political force in Sikkim not only changed the nature of politics but it also avail opportunity to reinvent nativist identity for various sub-groups of the Nepalis who were often ignominiously referred to as migrants, foreigners, influx, coolies etc. in Sikkim. It is worth mentioning that communities falling within the Other Backward communities like Limboos, Mangars, Gurungs, Rais etc. belonged to the early inhabitants of Sikkim but their identity remained mostly unreported and marginalized due mainly to the then prevailing political atmosphere, lack of education and awareness and indolent nature generally found among the members of backward communities.

The rise of OBC consciousness led to formation of various socio-cultural organizations bearing traditional community names like Gurung Samaj, Tamang Samaj, Rai Samaj, Chhetri-Bahun Samaj, Limboo Samaj, Mangar Samaj, Damai/Kami Samaj, Sikkim Newar Guthi etc. These organizations functioned both as agencies of unification and social control over its members. Since 1990 there have been a steady growth in the number of such ethnic organizations and are politically articulate and assertive too.

Assembly Election – 1994:

The 1994 Assembly Elections provide ample examples about the nature of alignments and symbiotic alliances occurring between the political parties and socio-cultural organizations with respect to the choice of the candidate and voters' strength of the candidate's own cognate group in a particular constituency. Apart from this, the 1994 Assembly election was also significant from the view point of initiatives taken at the family, social, peer group, media levels to influence the voters to cast vote either in favour or against a particular party or cognate group or individual candidate(s). For instance, a Nepali Weekly "Prajatantra", published from Gangtok, urged for unity between the mongoloid Nepalis and the Bhutia-Lepcha voters to bring to an end to the rule of N.B.Bhandari in Sikkim to whom the Weekly alleged for favouring only the high caste Nepalis.[64] Similarly, one Gram Panchayat member, Mr. M.Chettri, a higher caste Nepali and a supporter of Sikkim Democratic Front, was reportedly approached by his relatives and told him to support the Sikkim Sangram Parishad led by Mr. N. B.Bhandari, a higher caste Nepali, by saying, "time has come to see not the 'Party' but 'Jati'.[65] Apparently political parties too were very often identified and referred to by the identity of the leadership. For example, the Sikkim Democratic Front was called an OBC (Mongoloid) party, the Congress (I) party as a tribals' party, i.e. Bhutia-Lepcha party, and the Sikkim Sangram Parishad party was associated with the upper castes Nepalis.

In 1994, many important office bearers of the Sikkim Democratic Front Party (SDF), mostly belonging to upper caste Nepalis and tribals, left the party. On October 21, 1994, a month before the Assembly Election, the higher caste Nepalis and tribal leaders resigned en-masse from the SDF party. Notable among them were the publicity Chief Nandu Thapa (Chhetri), Jagat Bandhu Pradhan, Madan Chhetri. The Vice-President of the SDF party, M.M.Rasaily, and four other tribal leaders also deserted the party.

In a joint statement, the leaders alleged Mr. P.K.Chamling of favouring the Nepalis of Mongoloid stock and of failing to give proper representation to Nepali Bahun (Brahmin), Chhetri, Bhutia, Lepchas etc.[66]

Table 5.1 shows major changes in the voting pattern and selection of candidates before and after 1994 Assembly elections. It further explains that during the Bhandari regime the ratio of the Bhutia representatives in the State Assembly has been much higher as compared to the Lepchas. During his fourteen years of rule only 20 per cent Lepchas have been represented to the Assembly as compared to 80 per cent of the Bhutias. However, the difference between the Bhutia and Lepcha candidates in the Assembly is narrowed down significantly in 1994 and in 2004 Assembly elections parity between the two communities has been restored. The parity perhaps is the outcome of the representations that various Lepcha organizations have been making regarding fifty per cent seat reservation for the community out of the 12 seats reserved for the Bhutia-Lepcha (B-L) community in the Assembly since 1996.

Another significant feature of the 1994 Assembly election was that the Sherpa tribal community was provided a separate representation.

By fielding Mingma Tshering Sherpa from Rakdong-Tintek reserved B-L constituency, Bhandari seems to have punished the tribal legislators for their betrayal in 1994 which caused his fall from power. This situation led to formation of a communal organization like 'Survival Sikkimese' in 1995 by a section of the Bhutias. The organization claimed that Sikkim belongs to only the Bhutia and Lepcha communities and the Nepalis, including others, were neo-colonialist. Besides, the above table also shows the increasing number of the OBC candidates in the Assembly after P.K.Chamling assumed power in Sikkim.

As a firm believer in democratic values, Chamling after coming to power in 1994 charted out three pronged priorities of his government viz. to provide safeguards of all kinds to various ethnic communities, to undertake capacity building measures and to explore possibilities for ensuring better centre-State relation without compromising the basics of Sikkimese identity, both in thought and

Table No. 5.1: Community-wise Representation in Sikkim Legislative Assembly: 1974-2004

Communities Tribals	1974/79	1979/84	1985/89	1989/94	1994/99	1999/04	2004/09
Bhutias	8	11	10	10	7	8	6
Lepchas	8	2	3	3	5	4	6
Sherpas	X	X	X	X	1	1	1
Other Tribals Limboos	1	3	2	2	3	4	4
Tamangs	X	1	X	X	1	2	1
OBC Gurungs	2	4	2	2	2	1	2
Rais	3	1	4	5	5	5	4
Mangars	X	X	X	X	1	X	1
Upper Castes Chettri-Bahun	7	7	7	6	3	3	4
Newars	2	1	1	2	2	2	1
Scheduled Castes	1	2	2	2	2	2	2
Plainsman	X	X	1	X	X	X	X

Sources: Compiled from Election reports, various documents and newspapers.

actions. Safeguards to ethnic communities, according to Chamling, were inevitable to infuse confidence and new vigour, to provide dignified living and to inculcate spirit of responsibility in every Sikkimese.[67]

Chamling implemented Mandal Commission recommendation and ethno-cultural groups like Bhujel, Gurung, Limboo, Rai, Tamang, Mangar and Sunuwar were declared as the Other Backward Classes (OBC) in the state.[68] Apart from this, a list containing names of the above communities was also forwarded to the central government for the grant of scheduled tribe status.[69] Similarly, the Sikkim Official Language (Amendment) Act, 1995 (6 of 1995) was passed in the Assembly to include Newari, Rai, Gurung, Mangar, Tamang, Sunuwar and Sherpa languages in the list of official languages of Sikkim.

However, Chamling's pro-OBC policies alienated upper caste Nepalis on the one hand and his initiatives favouring certain OBC communities for the status of Schedule Tribes created apprehension among Bhutia-Lepchas on the other. There were attempts to topple the government headed by Mr. Chamling but were never materialized. Thus, in an attempt to accommodate grievances of the upper caste Nepalis, the OBC list was enlarged in 2003 to include Bahun (Brahmin), Chettri, Newar and Sanyasi in the list.[70]

The communities who were declared OBC earlier were now classified as the Most Backward Classes (MBC). He played an important role in the appointment of N.B.Khatiwada, an upper caste Nepali, as the Additional Advocate General of Sikkim High Court. Similarly, in 1995 'Dzumsa', a traditional Bhutia institution of village administration, was institutionalized as the lowest unit of the Panchayati Raj Institution in Bhutia dominated Lachung and Lachen villages (North Sikkim), recommendations were made to the central government for the inclusion of the Bhutia and Lepcha languages in the Eighth Schedule of the constitution, initiatives were taken to protect the socio-cultural, economic and political interests of the Bhutias and Lepchas, played an instrumental role in achieving the 'most primitive community' status for the Lepchas and provided adequate representation for the community in the legislative

Assembly of Sikkim. He once again played a decisive role in the appointment of Karma Topden Bhutia as the ambassador of India to Mongolia, first by any Sikkimese to hold such a dignified post. The construction of the Rathang Chu Hydel Project was abandoned in 1997 in view of the socio-cultural and religious belief of the Buddhist attached with the river.

In Chamling's economic policies, villages, which formed about 89 per cent of State's population, had a special place. Being a villager himself, he realized that conditions in the rural areas needed land reforms and alternative means of livelihood. He started Land Bank Schemes in 1995 whereby (a) surplus land owned by private parties were purchased by the government for distribution to the needy and poor landless Sikkimese; (b) Land under Khasmal, Jhora, Lease and Waste land under the forest department and land used for cattle grazing were acquired by the government and distributed freely to the needy homeless and landless Sikkimese. He allocated 70 per cent of the total budget of the government for the development of the rural areas with a purpose of alleviating economic condition of the villagers. Along with it the process of decentralization and organizational cohesiveness were also initiated at war footing to yield effective and efficient implementation of the welfare programmes. As required by the 73rd Constitutional (Amendment) Act, 1992, the State government enacted Sikkim Panchayat (Amendment) Act, 1995 with party-based election system. 33 per cent seats were reserved for the women in the Panchayat institutions and 30 per cent in government jobs. Similarly, seats were reserved for different sections of populations in government employment and educational institution of professional courses outside Sikkim, viz. 33 per cent for the scheduled Tribes, 6 per cent for Scheduled castes, 21 per cent for Most Backward Classes (Gurung, Dewan, Bhujel, Rai, Mangar, Sunuwar, Thami and Jogi) and 14 per cent for the Other Backward Classes (Bahun, Chhetri, Newar and Sanyasi).[71] On 16 September 2003, the State Cabinet took decision to reserve 2 per cent seat from the quota reserved for the Scheduled Tribes for sports persons of the concerned tribe and 5 per cent for the children of other business community and government employees.[72] In June, 2003 Limboo and Tamang communities were included in the Scheduled Tribes list of Sikkim. Though the Opposition condemned Mr. Chamling for being castiest and communal, his endeavour for providing the most representative face of the Assembly deserves wholehearted appreciation.

In fact, a society whose history was shaped by sharp ethnic divisions and differential treatment, any long-term policy seeking to eschew ethnic differences would be counterproductive. For instance, when a Sherpa candidate was given ticket to contest from Rakdong-Tintek (BL) constituency in 1994, the Bhutias accused Bhandari for subverting ethnic harmony. Similarly, Chamling's effort to maintain parity between the Bhutias and Lepchas has been considered as one of dividing unity and disturbing the cordial relationship existing between the Bhutias and Lepchas. The relationship between the Bhutias and Nepalis had been Perhaps shaped by their long historical interactions characterized by occasional wars and occupation of territories. To the Bhutias, the Nepalis had been basically 'migrants' from Nepal, Hindus by religion and 'troublesome as neighbours'. As a Nepali Chief Minister, Bhandari's policies, therefore, had been reflective of the need to malign such perceptions but in doing so he became unnecessarily pro-Tribal. In order to appease the Bhutias, he refused to recommend for inclusion of Limboos and Tamangs in the Schedule Tribes list of Sikkim in 1987.[73] and his anti-OBC stand in 1990 in favour of the upper caste Nepalis alienated the OBC communities. But ethnic preferences and priorities change, so are the alignments based on these elements. Bhandari's desire to be in power often by raising and manipulating community oriented issues actually helped in the growth of ethnic divisions into smaller parochial groups. Political mobilizations based on ethno-cultural elements or articulation of community oriented demands through political organization generally create an atmosphere of suspicion. This happens because ethnic politics, by nature, is partial in intention and the state which is both a source and distributor of resources, by and large, is viewed not as an agency pursuing equality or distributive justice.[74] Modern states are welfare states and pursue affirmative actions. Such affirmative actions in a socio-culturally divided society tend to generate euphoria for some and Parochial of community consciousness for others because of the fact that one who is not benefited by the state policies may develop a sense of alienation and discrimination compared to the one who is benefited. This feeling of deprivation also strengthens unity and solidarity within the members of a group and expresses group's resentment, firstly, against the government and, secondly, towards the community or communities which have been benefited or likely to be benefited by the political decisions.

This tendency is more likely to happen in Sikkim as the legal-political framework prevailing in Sikkim recognizes social differences in terms of ethnic or religious categories. In such circumstances political parties or organizations operating in Sikkim automatically depend upon issues either concerning ethnic group or groups (e.g. issues concerning Nepali, Bhutia, Lepcha or plainsmen) or some all encompassing issues concerning Sikkim as a whole (e.g. protection of the rights of the Sikkimese, protection of Article 371F, exemption from Central Income Tax Act etc.) for widening their support base and electoral gain. The political parties irrespective of their support base and ideology formulate strategies and policies provoking ethnic or regional sentiments for political gains. Mr. Chamling seemed to have realized this fact sooner than later when he says, "instead of staying divided on grounds of caste, religion, sex and class, today's age calls for mutual coexistence based on humanity, unity and brotherhood...It is imperative for every body to take responsibility to modernize Sikkim....The improvement and development of our place and our lives lie in our collective efforts".[75]

Citizenship and the Question of left out persons:

The citizenship issue was yet another example as to how policies and decisions of the government create ethnic division and tension in a multi-cultural society. After the merger the Government of India took a decision to grant citizenship to the erstwhile subjects of the Chogyal on the basis of the Sikkim Subject

Regulation of 1961. The grant of citizenship became imperative as the Indian Citizenship Act, 1955 under section 7 states, "If any territory becomes a part of India, the Central government may, by order notified in the official gazette, specify the persons who shall be citizens of India by reason of their connection with the territory; and those persons shall be citizens of India as from the date to be specified in the Order."

Accordingly, Government of India promulgated Sikkim Citizenship Order, 1975 stating "every person who immediately before the 26th day of April, 1975 was a Sikkim Subject under the Sikkim Subject Regulation of 1961 shall be deemed to have become a citizen of India on that day."[76] Thus, persons whose names were registered in Sikkim Subject Regulation of 1961 became citizens of India automatically from the 26th April 1975. However, a section of people who could not register their names in the Sikkim Subject register on account of ignorance, indifference, administrative lapses, political considerations etc., became stateless persons overnight following the merger. It must be noted here that the Sikkim Subject Regulation of 1961 itself had been the subject of controversy earlier owing to its provision regarding ethnic communities wherein any reference to the Nepalis was avoided though the Lepchas, Bhutias and Tsongs (Limboos) were mentioned in clear terms.

A certain section of the Sikkimese were unhappy with the way the Sikkim Subject Regulation of 1961 (now repealed) was adopted by the government of India as the basis for the grant of Indian Citizenship to the erstwhile subjects of the Chogyal. Theoretically, as per article 3 (b) of the Sikkim Subject Regulation of 1961 (as amended in 1962) the cut-off year for the qualification of Sikkim Subject Certificate was fixed at 1946, i.e., fifteen years immediately preceding the commencement of the Sikkim Subject Regulation, 1961 but effectively the cut-off year was pushed further back to 1936. The land Survey Report of 1950-58 was the basis for registration of names in the Sikkim Subject Register and the names of only those Bustiwallas (Secondary land holders) were enumerated in the survey report who had been continuously possessing the plot of land for a period of not less than 14 years.[77] Thus, persons who failed to qualify the minimum condition of 14 years as Bustiwallas were not registered in the Land Revenue Survey Report and subsequently in the Sikkim Subject Regulation of 1961.

Moreover, the registration of names in the Sikkim Subject register too was not mandatory. A government publication admitted that those who desired for government services or wanted government scholarships or acquired immovable properties for which submission of Sikkim Subject certificate was necessary alone applied for the Certificate.[78] The document further writes, "There were many who had applied for registration but were not considered for immediate registration for want of verification of their antecedents due to lack of proper administrative machinery prevalent at that time. Besides, there were political considerations which guided the Chogyal administration in the grant of Sikkim Subject Certificates. This was evident from the manner the Committee formed for granting certificates performed its task. There are documentary proofs to show utter indifference of the Committee towards applicants. Thus thousands were left out and this resulted in wide-spread discontentment."[79] Hence, determination of Indian citizenship on the basis of Sikkim Subject Regulation, 1961, generated discontent among a section of population, particularly Nepalis who were often not enumerated as Sikkim subjects by an indifferent Chogyal's government. The issue of citizenship became a source of tension between Nepali and Bhutia-Lepcha population.

Although the Union Parliament enjoys exclusive authority in all matters relating to citizenship, including acquisition and termination of citizenship, the decision of the Union Parliament regarding the grant of citizenship to the Sikkimese was contradictory to the decision taken earlier in case of the Goa-Daman-Diu Citizenship Order, 1962 which stated that every person who or either whose parents or any of those grandparent was born before the 20th December, 1961 in the territories now comprising the Union Territory of Goa-Daman-Diu shall be deemed to have become a citizen of India on that day. Similar stands were taken by the Union parliament regarding grant of citizenship to the people of Dadra-Nagar Haveli (Dadra Nagar Haveli Citizenship Order, 1962) and Pondichery (Pondichery Citizenship Order, 1962). Logically the Sikkim Subject Regulation of 1961 is one of the old laws of the Chogyal's era and by making the provision as the basis for grant of citizenship the government of India has lived up to the pledge that it guaranteed to the Sikkimese at the time of merger; it kept the nationalist element contended and put a check on non-Sikkimese from getting recognized as citizens of India.

The first Assembly election after the merger was due in October 1979 to be completed latest by October 16, 1979.[80] With the prospect of election underway and electoral rolls being prepared, the issue of citizenship received unprecedented attention of almost all the political parties. A section of the ruling Janata Party demanded grant of citizenship to all the Nepalis living in Sikkim. The citizenship issue was also one of the major issues of the Sikkim Prajatantra Congress of N.B.Khatiwada and Janata Parishad led by N.B.Bhandari. They demanded citizenships for all those people who were living in Sikkim for some years. It was claimed that those people were living in Sikkim for a long time and possessed necessary qualifications for inclusion as voters. Earlier, the Assembly adopted a resolution demanding Indian citizenship for all those who were in Sikkim till 1970. A delegation consisting of members of the State Legislative Assembly also visited Delhi in September 1978 and apprised the central leadership on the decision of the Sikkim Legislative Assembly on the question of citizenship.[81] The Janata Party in its Rangpo Convention in January 1979 adopted resolutions demanding 1974 electoral rolls as the basis for 1979 elections and citizenship for all those living in Sikkim till 1971.[82]

The Sikkim Prajatantra Congress also criticized Chogyal's administration for intentionally dropping out names of the genuine Sikkimese from the voters list and for indiscriminate inclusion of names of plains people in the voters list.[83] The President of the Sikkim Janata Parishad, N.B.Bhandari, alleged that a considerable number of genuinely Sikkimese Subjects had been left out of the electoral rolls.[84] In April 1979 the leaders of all political parties and the State Cabinet held separate discussions with the visiting Prime Minister of India, Morarji Desai, on citizenship issue. It was reported that N.B. Khatiwada asked the Prime Minister for setting up a Commission to ascertain the identities of the left out persons if the Prime Minister had any doubts about their claims.[85] He alleged that the people coming from other states like Haryana, Punjab, Bihar, Rajasthan etc. were easily finding their names registered in the voter's list without furnishing any document, while the Nepalis were asked to produce domicile certificates.[86]

In 1979, the Janata Parishad government led by N.B.Bhandari set up an All Party Citizenship Committee under the chairmanship of the then Deputy Speaker of the State Assembly, L.B.Basnet. The other members of the committee were Sherab Palden (Finance Minister, Govt. of Sikkim), Athup Lepcha (Forest Minister), T.R. Sharma (Agriculture Minister), Dorjee Tshering Bhutia (MLA, Ranka (BL) constituency), N.B.Khatiwada (MLA, Timi-Tarku constituency, K.N. Upreti (MLA, Rhenock constituency and B.R. Pradhan (Law Secretary, Govt. of Sikkim, acting as the Secretary of the Committee.) The Committee suffered from utter lack of cooperation from the members of the government. The Chairman was also reported to have threatened to quit the Committee owing to sharp differences over community considerations.[87] Despite difficulties, the Committee submitted its report recommending grant of citizenship to "every person who had been ordinarily resident in the territory of Sikkim for not less than five years immediately preceding the commencement of the Constitution (Thirty Sixth Amendment) Act, 1975 and every minor child of such a person born before such commencement shall be deemed to have become citizen of India on that day."[88] As such, the Committee maintained 1970 as the cut off year for the grant of citizenship. The recommendation of the All Party Citizenship Committee was, however, not implemented.

The citizenship issue once again became a major political issue during the March 1985 Assembly elections. The Sikkim Sangram Parishad (SSP), formed in 1984 by Mr. N.B.Bhandari, won 30 out of 32 Assembly seats by carefully manipulating citizenship issue among others like reservation of seats for the Sikkimese Nepalis in the State Assembly and inclusion of Nepali language in the Eighth Scheduled of the Indian constitution. Bhandari maneuvered series of political dialogues with the union government, including the Prime Minister Rajiv Gandhi and demanded grant of citizenship to all those left out Sikkimese who had voted at the time of merger of Sikkim with India. Bhandari, who first came to power in 1979 on the merger issue, had a distinction of conveniently viewing everything from the merger point of view.

He clarified that it was neither the question of stateless persons nor an attempt to provide citizenship to the stateless, but it was about those genuine Sikkimese subjects who were "left out" from the Sikkim Subject Regulation of 1961.[89] The legislators belonging to SSP warned that if the central government delayed the process further, the number of left out persons might increase to one lakh.[90]

On the other hand the Congress (I) Party and Denzong Tribal Yargay Chogpa (DTYC), a tribal organization, alleged that the Sikkim Sangram Parishad government was indulging in anti-Sikkimese activities by allowing thousands of non-Sikkimese to fill up the forms. Both Congress (I) and DTYC demanded grant of citizenship only for those genuine Sikkimese who possessed Sikkim Subjects Certificates and participated in the voting for the merger in 1975.[91]

In other words, the Congress (I) party and the tribal organization were advocating for Sikkim Subject Regulation of 1961 as the basis for grant of citizenships and covertly denying that there were any left out persons among the genuine Sikkimese. However, in response to Mrs. D.K. Bhandari's (MP) question on the citizenship issue in the Lok Sabha on July 25, 1985 the Union Minister, Mrs. Ramdulari Sinha, acknowledged the possibility of left out persons.[92] The Minister further clarified that "the Chief Minister of Sikkim (N.B.Bhandari) had recently made a proposal that a High Power Committee be appointed to go into the problem… The claims of stateless persons for citizenship are to be considered with due caution keeping in view the provision of the Citizenship Act, 1956"[93]

In mid-1986, the Prime Minister of India, Mr. Rajiv Gandhi, assured the Chief Minister, Mr. N.B.Bhandari, that the centre would examine and settle the citizenship issue. It was in this context a high level central team led by the Additional Secretary to the Union Home Ministry, I.P Gupta, visited the State in January, 1987. But the matter remained unresolved. As no decision regarding the issue could be reached, the ruling SSP in its resolution of May 24, 1988 rejected the decision of the central government to adopt Sikkim Subjects Regulation of 1961 as the basis for grant of citizenship to the Sikkimese.[94] The party pointed out that the Sikkim Subjects Regulation of 1961 (now repealed) was "anti-people and people of Sikkim had revolted against it. It ultimately led to the over-throw of the Chogyal".[95] The Chief Minister Bhandari further declared, "All the people of Sikkim be deemed to have become Indians from the day Sikkim merged with India or 1970 be taken as the cut off year for granting citizenship as passed by the Sikkim Legislative Assembly."[96]

Though it was difficult to substantiate Bhandari's claim that those who had been "left out" had also participated in the "Special Poll", but he was able to 'confuse or mislead', as alleged by the Congress (I) leaders, both the people and the central government. He even went to the extent of considering merger as 'illegal or unconstitutional' if the citizenship was not granted to the 'left out' persons. Such public utterances put the central government in a very awkward situation. If the central government fails to grant Indian citizenship to the 'left out' persons, who reportedly voted for the 1975 referendum, Bhandari could have termed the merger illegal and unconstitutional. On the other hand, if the centre officially recognizes that a section of the Sikkimese population were 'left out' from the Sikkim Subjects Register and grants them Indian citizenship, the merger once again would become illegal as a fairly large number of persons had participated in the 'referendum' who were not actually entitled to vote.[97]

The Sikkim Tribal Welfare Association (STWA) also demanded the Regulation of 1961 as the basis for the grant of citizenship. In its six-point memorandum submitted to the Governor, Shri Bhishma Narayan Singh, in October 1985, the STWA clarified "Ethnic representation and reservation of seats in the State Assembly envisages that this right will only be in respect of the ethnic communities of Sikkim. We now feel that all attempts are being made by interested groups and persons, much to the misfortune of the people of Sikkim as a whole, and particularly of the Bhutias-Lepchas, to induct and give citizenship status to a huge number of outsiders for inclusion of their names in the electoral roles, irrespective of the qualifying years of residence in Sikkim. This will undoubtedly create serious logistical problems and thus the very fabric of Sikkim's economic, social and political structures will be completely disarrayed and endangered the very existence of the genuine Sikkimese Indian citizens."[98] The memorandum went on stating that the names of foreign nationals, who had been included in the electoral roles, must be deleted. The identities of those with doubtful citizenship and those who were said to be stateless persons must be finalized before granting them rights of citizenship. The Association also contended that there should be no representation for such persons in the Assembly before finalizing their identity.[99]

In September 1988, a 14-member central team consisting of members of the Union Parliament and central government officials, headed by the then Maharastra Congress (I) M.P, Balasaheb Vikhe Patil, visited Sikkim to investigate into the issue and receive representations from the public. However, the time was too short for the central team to hear grievances from the entire cross sections of the people. Speaking on the occasion Mr. Patil, however, highlighted that "there have been a fifty per cent increase in the State's population during 1971 to 1981 (i.e. 2, 09,843 to 3, 16,385 persons) and hence the claim of citizenship must be substantiated by authentic documents and evidences."[100]

The Denzong Tribal Yargay Chogpa (DTYC), in its first ever State level Convention held in Gangtok in November 1988, adopted an eight-fold resolution basically aiming at safeguarding the interest of the tribals and spreading consciousness about their rights in Sikkim. On the issue of citizenship the resolution stated, "We cannot deny that names of a few genuine Sikkimese have been left out while granting citizenship. But unusual increase in population by one lakh within a short period of 10 years (1971-81) lends every reason to the Sikkimese people to become apprehensive. The Sikkim Subject Regulation 1961 should, therefore, be the basis for granting citizenship."[101]

Notwithstanding the stand taken by the Parliamentary team led by Mr. Patil, the Government of India finally decided to grant citizenship to the left out subjects of Sikkim. The Statutory Order No. 214 (E) was issued by the Home Ministry, dated 20 March, 1989, seeking to introduce amendment to the Sikkim Citizenship Order of 1975. It stated, "in exercise of the power conferred by section 7 of the Citizenship Act, 1955 (57 of 1955), the Central Government hereby makes the following order to amend the Sikkim (Citizenship) Order, 1975 namely;

a. This Order may be called the Sikkim (Citizenship) Amendment Order, 1989;
b. In the Sikkim (Citizenship) Order, 1975, to paragraph 2, the following proviso shall be inserted namely;

"Provided that any person whose names was eligible to be entered in the register maintained under the said regulation but was not so entered because of any genuine omission shall also be deemed to have become citizen of India on that day if so determined by the central government."[102]

Mr. Bhandari informed the Assembly that "the Government of India has already issued order granting citizenship to 40,083 persons out of 74,966 persons in the first lot vide MHA Order No. 26030/36/90-ICIof 7th August, 1990. Similar action for the balance persons is also expected to be finalized within the current month."[103] His statement was also corroborated by the Union Home

Minister for State, Subodh Kant Sahay, in the Lok Sabha in August 1990 stating that orders for declaring 40,083 'left out' persons in the State as Indian citizens had been given on August 7, 1990 and the centre was expected to issue another order in September 1990 for granting citizenship to another 35,000 persons in the State.[104] According to another report, a total of 94,000 persons applied for citizenship of which 75,000 persons were adjudged qualified for citizenship, 5,000 were under consideration and applications of 14,000 were rejected.[105]

There were mixed reactions among the people regarding the grant of citizenship. The opposition political parties and certain other social organizations were very much critical of the central and the state governments over the grant of citizenship to 80,000 left out persons. The Congress (I) party was suspicious of the process followed by the State government regarding the issue. Earlier, the party had urged the natural descendants of the subject holders not to fill up the citizenship forms and get themselves "cheated and exploited" by the ruling Sikkim Sangram Parishad Party. "The Sikkim Sangram Parishad government has successfully compelled a sizeable number of the genuine Indian citizens of the Sikkimese origin to declare themselves as stateless persons or no-citizens."[106] Mr. Bharat Basnet, President of the All Sikkim Youth and Contractors Association and the Sikkim People's Party, demanded withdrawal of the Center's decision regarding the grant of citizenship to some 80,000 persons.[107] The Rising Sun Party of R.C.Poudyal, though favoured the grant of citizenship to the left out persons, was critical of manipulation and indulgence in corrupt practices on the citizenship issue. A press statement issued by the General Secretary of the Party, Sonam Tshering, stated that the Party "strongly condemns the corruption indulged in by the Sikkim Sangram Parishad government on distributing more than four lakhs of so called citizenship forms completely misleading the public."[108] The Party also alleged that the ruling party even asked the Sikkim Subject Certificate holders to buy and fill up forms in respect of their children born after 1975. Later these people were asked not to fill up forms.[109] Y.N.Bhandari, the President of the Jana Mukti Morcha (JMM) party, also questioned the role of the Centre and State governments over the grant of citizenship. The party alleged both the governments for conspiring against the interest of the Sikkimese people and emphasized that citizenship should be given only to the genuine Sikkimese who were denied Subject hood during the Chogyal's rule.[110]

The Denzong People's Chogpa (DPC), a political organization primarily of the Bhutias, in a letter to the State's Chief Secretary, dated September 8, 1990 demanded publication of lists of applicants for citizenship in connection with Party's suspicion regarding inclusion of their names in the voters list without being declared as citizens of India. The letter stated, "we have come to learn that at least 90 per cent of applicants, who have filled up the (citizenship) forms, do not qualify to become Sikkim Subjects and thus the claim of their names being left out from the Sikkim Subjects Register cannot be justified on any ground. As Sikkim Subjects Certificate holders, we have every right to raise objections against those applicants. Unless these applicants can prove that they have basic qualifications to be Sikkim Subjects and they have been wrongly left out, they cannot get Indian citizenship."[111]

Apart from political parties, the social organizations, especially Tribal organizations representing the interests of Bhutias and Lepchas, were also vehemently critical of the decision of the government for refusing to recognize the importance of Subject Regulation of 1961. The Mayel Lyang Tribal Organization adopted a resolution demanding the Regulation of 1961 as the basis for the grant of citizenship to the left out persons.[112]

The Bhandari government never came out with clear picture and statistics as to whom Indian citizenship should be granted and to how many. The uncertainty prevailing over the cut-off year perhaps was the major contributing factor regarding gradual increase in the demand for citizenship firstly for 30,000 persons, then 54,000 in 1987-88, and 80,000 in 1989 and the cause of growing apprehension among the people. There was fear among the Sikkimese that a large number of people who were settled in Sikkim during 1970-80 would claim for being 'left out' persons and try to infringe upon the rights and interests of the Sikkimese besides diluting their distinct identity. In this connection J.N.Kazi writes, "It is an open secret, for instance, that from 1972-73, in fact prior to the merger, Kazi Lhendup Dorje's government encouraged the influx of outsiders, including people from Kalimpong, Darjeeling, West Bengal and Bihar, as well as rich businessmen and traders originally from Rajasthan."[113] He further added, "These people were either absorbed in the State administration or given economic assistance to settle in the State. The resultant phenomenal rise in Sikkim's population approximately from 2.10 lakhs in 1971 to 3.16 lakhs in 1981 accounts for the widespread fear and insecurity among the local people, including the Sikkimese Nepalis, who feel that the majority of those who entered Sikkim during the seventies will somehow manage to prove that they have been residents since 1975 or even before then and thus obtain the necessary legal status."[114]

The inclusion of eight other Bhutias namely the Tibetans, Tromopas, Dopthapas, Drukpas, Chumbipas, Sherpas, Yolmos and Kagateys, within the definition of the Sikkimese Bhutias by the Scheduled Tribes (Sikkim) order 1978 had been perceived as one such threat to the ethnic identity and political-economic security of the Bhutias whom the later considered not meriting inclusion. The grant of citizenship to some 80,000 left out persons, among which members of the above groups were also present in significant numbers, further created sense of insecurity among the Bhutias in particular and Lepcha tribes in general. It must be mentioned that under the same impression the Bhutias and Lepchas showed resentment at the decision of the Chogyal P.T. Namgyal to rehabilitate Tibetan refugees in Sikkim in the 1960s. Thus, by demanding the Subjects Regulation of 1961 as the basis for the grant of citizenship, the Mayel Lyang Tribal Organization was actually expressing desire for protection of their political-economic interest from further dilution and alienation of resources to others.

Besides the Bhutias and Lepchas, the Sikkimese Nepalis too were apprehensive about their future economic wellbeing mainly due to the fact that people from Darjeeling and plains were far more educated with fairly good knowledge of entrepreneurship. The Nepalis, whose reserved seats were converted into an open general seat in 1979 in which anybody who was a citizen as per the Sikkim Citizenship (Amendment) Order 1989 could contest election, were the major victim of this political-administrative arrangement.

The unprecedented growth of population through large scale influx of outsiders was viewed as endangering the distinct identity and economic security of the Sikkimese Nepalis.[115] At present, the Bhutias and Lepchas, for being minority and Scheduled Tribes, enjoy constitutional protection but whatever legal-political protections that Nepalis enjoyed before 1975 were obliterated making them completely vulnerable and rootless in their own homeland. The impact of the Citizenship Order was overwhelmingly reflected in the 1989 Assembly and Lok Sabha elections and despite apprehension the Sangram Parishad party led by Mr. Bhandari won all the 32 Assembly and the lone Lok Sabha seats.

After merger, there have been large scale development activities in Sikkim. The growth of economy, modernization, expansion of administrative structures and service sector opened up new frontiers of employment opportunities vis-à-vis influx of population from other parts of India. Since the Bhandari government was opposed to the Sikkim Subject Regulation of 1961 as the basis for grant of citizenship, there was apprehension among the people that the Regulation of 1961 would be obliterated and the emerging economic opportunities meant for them would be exploited by the outsiders. Thus, the primary reason behind the controversy over the citizenship issue was influx and apprehension over denial of opportunities to the Sikkimese. By introducing amendment to the Sikkim (Citizenship) Order, 1975, the government of India successfully managed to contain the anti-merger or anti-India elements in Sikkim and, at the same time, protected the political and economic interests of the Sikkimese by making the Sikkim Subject Regulation as the basis for citizenship and for public employment, including for pursuing certain other economic activities.[116]

The normal practice in India for fixing the cut off year regarding grant of citizenship has been either from the date of issuance of the Order or five years preceding the date of issuance of the Citizenship Order. In case of Sikkim the Sikkim Subject Regulation of 1961, which had been the subject of controversy and ethnic tension earlier, was adopted as the basis for grant of citizenship and became the source of contradiction. The social tension accentuated with the way the political parties used the issue for mobilizing voters for electoral gains and with the way socio-cultural organizations used it as a means for ventilating community's grievances and apprehensions.

Issue of seat reservation:

The system of reservation of seats in Sikkim was based on the pre-merger scheme provided under the Representation of Sikkim Subject Act, 1974 which created for an Assembly of 32 members of which 15 seats were reserved for Nepalis, 15 seats for the Bhutia-Lepcha communities, 1 for the Scheduled Castes and 1 for the Sangha (Monasteries). The basis of such reservation was the so-called "Parity Formula" of 1951 and its purpose was maintenance of power-equilibrium between Nepalis and Bhutia-Lepchas. As mentioned earlier (Ch.-IV), seat-reservation and parity formula constituted a major source of discontent among Nepalis of Sikkim who perceived the system as a means by which the majority Nepali were compelled to accept "parity" with minority Bhutia-Lepchas. The Nepali viewed the system as an instrument of Bhutia domination. After merger, the Representation of the People Act 1950 and 1951 of India were amended in 1976 in order to validate the Assembly elections held in 1974 on the basis of seat arrangement provided by the Representation of Sikkim Subject Act of 1974. The Representation of the People Act of India did not contain any provision for reservation of seats on the basis of racial-linguistic and religious considerations. The Act provided reservation only for Scheduled Castes and Scheduled Tribes. Hence, the amendment to the said Act was necessary.

In view of the first Assembly election after merger, the Janata government proposed for an amendment to the Representation of the People (Amendment) Act, 1950 and 1951 (Bill No. 79 of 1979). The Bill proposed to reserve 12 seats for the Bhutia-Lepchas, 2 for the Scheduled Castes, 1 for the Sangha and the remaining 17 as General/open seats. Besides, it proposed to extend political rights to the plainsmen who were till date denied right to vote in Sikkim. This obviously created resentment among the three communities, i.e. Bhutia-Lepcha and Nepalis, for the proposal had clear intention to do away with the Nepali seats on the one hand and reduction of the Bhutia-Lepcha seats to 12 from 15 seats reserved earlier on the other. The Bill was introduced in Parliament in May 1979.[117]

The Janata Party government in the State led by L.D.Kazi was criticized both within and outside the government for failing to take up the issue effectively with its central counterpart. Nanda Kumar Subede, MLA from the Bormoik Assembly constituency, even initiated a 'Call Attention motion' to bring the issue for discussion in the Assembly. N. B.Khatiwada criticized State government and its two representatives to the Union Parliament, S.K.Rai (Lok Sabha) and Pahalman Subba (Rajya Sabha), for not informing the Assembly about the details of the proposed amendment to the Representation of People Act of 1951 and demanded that a high power delegation be sent to Delhi immediately to apprise the Parliament on the actual state of the affairs.[118]

The abolition of the Nepali seats and grant of political rights to the plainsmen had been the two major political issues in 1979 Assembly election. Irrespective of party affiliation, the majority of the Nepali leaders were apprehensive about their political future in Sikkim. A section of ruling Janata party led by R. C. Poudyal called the proposal a 'Black Bill', which sought to abolish seats reserved erstwhile for the Sikkimese Nepalis. Through a signature campaign Poudyal mobilized a substantial number of M.L.As in his camp. A memorandum signed by 14 M.L.As and ruling party leaders was submitted to the Union Law Minister with a plea to reconsider the Bill.[119] Poudyal was removed from the Janata party for his anti-party activities during the middle of June 1979 but he along with B.B.Gurung, N.K.Subedi, Adhiklall Pradhan, continued to campaign against the 'injustice' inflicted upon the Nepalis. Poudyal said, "It was necessary to have reservation of seats for the Nepalis as they were likely to be reduced to minority in near future, unless some safeguards were immediately provided."[120] He continued, "In 1975, people of Sikkim had accepted Sikkim's merger with India subject to certain conditions. Out of these conditions, one was that only the people of Nepali, Lepcha and Bhutia origin of Sikkim would be able to contest elections to the State Assembly. This condition was also made a part of the Representation of the People Act by inserting a new provision in it in September, 1975."[121] Poudyal also refused the proposal of the Prime Minister Desai to have 60:40 ratio as formula for seat sharing between others (Nepali) and Scheduled Tribes (Bhutia-Lepcha) as unfair. He suggested that 40 per cent seats for the Scheduled Tribes should also include Scheduled Castes seats.[122] The main contention of most of the Nepali leaders was that the Bhutias and Lepchas did not constitute 40 per cent of the total population and, therefore, it was unconstitutional to allow 40 per cent representation to them.[123]

Poudyal circulated petitions among the members of the Union Parliament intending to draw their attention to the grievances of the Sikkimese people against the Bill No. 79, which according to him, was proposed in Parliament without the prior knowledge of the Sikkim Assembly and the State Cabinet.[124] He further stated that the Bill was in violation of the sacred commitments given to the people of Sikkim prior to the merger.[125]

Meanwhile, Morarji Desai resigned as a result of sudden political development at the center. It was said that Chaudhury Charan Singh, who succeeded Mr. Desai, was sympathetic towards the demands of the dissidents in Sikkim led by Mr. Poudyal. The Poudyal camp sent a telegram to the Prime Minister, Chaudhury Charan Singh, requesting him to correct "the constitutional distortions committed by the Kazi government in Sikkim."[126] The Prime Minister was also urged upon to undo the injustice committed on the Sikkimese through the Bill No. 79 introduced by the Morarji Desai government.[127]

The controversy pertaining seat reservation issue led to split in the ruling Janata Party in Sikkim and the Assembly was dissolved on 13th August 1979[128] by the Governor. Though Kazi maintained that dissolution was necessary, as the term of Assembly had expired, he, including the Governor, had no other option than what they did in view of the plan of the dissident to pass a proposal countermanding the merger of Sikkim with India in the forthcoming Assembly session.[129] The Chief Minister, L.D.Kazi, and his colleagues resigned on the 17th August[130] and on the 18th August the President rule was imposed.[131] However, the proclamation of the President rule in Sikkim could not be endorsed by the Lok Sabha for it too was dissolved following the resignation of the Charan Singh government.

The Election Commission postponed the date of Assembly election to 12th October 1979[132] so that the new government in the state could be formed before the expiry of the term of President's Rule. In the meanwhile, the President of India, Neelam Sanjiva Reddy, promulgated an Ordinance called the Representation of the People (Amendment) Ordinance, 1979[133] seeking to amend rules governing elections and schemes of reservation of seats in the State Assembly. The Presidential Ordinance also provided for a 32 member Legislative Assembly to be filled by persons chosen by direct election as per the following norms:

a. Twelve seats should be reserved for Sikkimese of Bhutia-Lepcha origin;
b. Two seats should be reserved for the Scheduled Castes of the State; and
c. One seat should be reserved for the Sangha.[134]

Further, regarding qualifications of the members of the Assembly, the Ordinance clarified that "notwithstanding anything in section 5, a person should not be qualified to be chosen to fill a seat in the Legislative Assembly of Sikkim unless:

a. In the case of seats reserved for Sikkimese of Bhutia-Lepcha origin, he should be a person either of Bhutia or

Lepcha origin and should be an elector for any Assembly constituency in the State other than the constituency reserved for the Sanghas;

b. In the case of seats reserved for Scheduled Castes, he should be a member of any of those castes in Sikkim and should be an elector for any assembly constituency in the State;
c. In the case of a seat reserved for the Sangha, he should be an elector for the Sangha constituency;
d. In the case of any other seats, he should be an elector for any Assembly constituency in the State".[135]

It must be noted here that the term 'Bhutia' was redefined in 1978 to include other sub-groups of the Bhutias viz. Chumbipa, Dopthapa, Kagatey, Sherpa, Tibetan, Tromopa, Yolmo and Drukpa and, therefore, these groups also became eligible to contest from the 12 seats reserved for the Bhutia-Lepcha community. A Bhutia dominated organization namely Sikkim Tribal Welfare Association expressed unhappiness over the reduction of seats from 15 to 12 and demanded increase in the number of reserved seats in view of expansion of the Bhutias. Thus, like the Nepalis who were denied reservation, the Bhutias and Lepchas too resented changes in the seat allotment and felt betrayed by New Delhi. It is said that a majority of Bhutias and Lepchas "saw in this changes a subtle and systematic move by New Delhi to erase the distinct identity of the Sikkimese."[136]

Historically, the Sikkimese Nepali had been representing the State Council since the days of the Chogyal Tashi Namgyal. In 1925, the Chogyal inducted three Nepali Councilors namely Ratna Bahadur Pradhan, Bal Krishna Pradhan and Hari Prasad Pradhan in the State Council. There were two Nepali representatives in the popular ministry formed in May 1949 - Reshmi Prasad Alley and Chandra Das Rai.

In 1951 a formula, called Parity formula, was evolved as a norm for sharing seats equally between Bhutia-Lepcha and Nepalis. Thus, in a 17 member State Council 6 seats were reserved for Nepalis and 6 for Bhutia-Lepcha community while the remaining

5 seats were nominated by the Chogyal. The breakup of seats was as follows:

Table No. 5.2: Community-wise Distribution of Seats, 1953.

Bhutia-Lepcha	6 seats
Nepali	6 seats
Nominated by the Chogyal	5 seats

Source: Sikkim Darbar Gazettee, Ex. Gazttee, dated 23.03.1953.

Apart from this, Mr. Kashi Raj Pradhan, belonging to Nepali community, was appointed as the member of a three-member Executive Council. Parity was maintained in the Executive Council irrespective of the number of the elective seats won by a party. Loyalty towards the Chogyal was, therefore, the norm of appointment.

In 1958 the composition of the State Council was once again reformulated vide the Royal Proclamation of March 1958. The new proclamation enhanced the council seats to 20 (Table No. 5.3) with 5 executive members. The demand of the Scheduled Caste League for a separate representation in the State Council was rejected.

Table No. 5.3: Community-wise Distribution of Seats, 1958.

Bhutia-Lepcha	6 seats
Nepali	6 seats
Sangha	1 seat
General	1 seat
Nominated by the Chogyal	6 seats

Source: Sikkim Darbar Gazette, vol. VII, No. 5, dated 17.03.1958

This Royal Proclamation also laid down a complicated mode of election in which the winning candidate of one community was required to obtain a minimum of 15 per cent votes of other community.[137]

The Government of India maintained that the new system of election was meant to facilitate the political integration of the Nepalis and the Bhutia-Lepcha communities[138] but, in reality, it created social division and strengthened ethnic consciousness among the two communities.

The Proclamation of 1958 was further altered in 1967 when the Sikkim Subjects Certificate was made a mandatory qualification both for candidates seeking election and the voters. The total strength of the members of the State Council was also increased to 24 with Tsongs having a separate seat reserved for them for the first time in the State Council. The rules pertaining voting and counting and qualifications for membership were retained as in 1958.

Table No. 5.4: Community-wise Distribution of Seats, 1967.

Bhutia-Lepcha	7 seats
Nepali	7 seats
Sikkim Scheduled Castes	1 seat
Tsongs (Limboos)	1 seat
General	1 seat
Sangha	1 seat
Nominated by the Chogyal	6 seats

Source: Sikkim Darbar Gazette, Ex. Gazette, dated 21.12.1966.

The Fourth Council election was held in April 1970 in two different dates.[139] The rules pertaining delimitation of constituencies, system of elections, qualifications for membership and voting system remained as in 1967.[140] The distribution of seats and method of election also remained unchanged in the Fifth State Council election held in the month of January, 1973. By winning 9 seats (7 B-L, 2 Nepali) the Sikkim National Party made inroads among the Nepali voters.

The next major development in the history of seat reservation was the signing of the Agreement of May 8, 1973 between the government of India, the Chogyal and the political parties of Sikkim. The Legislative Assembly was set up in place of the State Council with a total of 32 members. The parity formula was retained as the norm for seat sharing between Bhutia-

Lepcha and Nepali in the Assembly but the Tsong seat and provision of nominated members by the Chogyal were abolished. The election was conducted by the Election Commission of India for the first time.

Table No. 5.5: Community-wise Distribution of Seats, 1974.

Bhutia-Lepcha	15 seats
Nepali	15 seats
Sangha	1 seat
Scheduled Caste	1 seat

Source: Representative of Sikkim Subjects Act, February 1974.

After merger in 1975, the spirit of the historic 8th May Agreement of 1973 was retained as a part and parcel of Indian constitution. The Assembly which was constituted according to the provision of the Representation of Sikkim Subject Act, 1974 was continued as per the provision of article 371F (k) unless amended or repealed by a competent authority within two years of the accomplishment of the merger. Article 371F (f) exclusively authorized the Union Parliament of India to enact laws for ensuring proper representation of different sections of population in Sikkim for whom such rights had been existing historically. The ethnic Nepali community of Sikkim was one of three ethnic communities of Sikkim defined as "different sections" by article 371F (f), just as the Agreement of 1973 and Government of Sikkim Act, 1974 defined them as "various sections of the population." The Representation of the people Act, 1950 and 1951 were amended in 1976 to provide legal-constitutional backing to the 1974 elections and the nature of seat arrangements in the State Assembly.

In 1979 the Presidential Ordinance sought to readjust distribution of seats in the Assembly. The Ordinance abolished Nepali seats, reduced Bhutia-Lepcha seats to 12 from 15 seats and the plainsmen were given political rights for the first time. Both Nepalis and Bhutia-Lepcha communities criticized the Ordinance vehemently.

Table No. 5.6: Distribution of Seats in 1979/80

Bhutia – Lepcha	12
Scheduled Castes	2
Sangha	1
General	17
Total	32

Source: Representative of the People (Amendment) Act, 1980.

The Congress (I) party led by Mrs. Indira Gandhi formed the government at the center in January 1980. On February 2, 1980, Mr. P. Shiv Shankar, Union Minister for Law, Justice and Company Affairs, introduced the Representation of the People (Amendment) Bill, 1980 in the Lok Sabha seeking to replace the Representation of the People (Amendment) Ordinance, 1979. Participating in the discussion over the Bill, Mr. Ananda Pathak, M.P. from Darjeeling, opposed the Bill on the ground that the contents of the present Amendment Bill, 1980 and the Bill proposed earlier by the Janata Party Government on 18th May 1979 were same and identical.[141] He further said, "Immediately after the introduction of the Bill of 1979, there were widespread resentment, discontent, dissension and disharmony among the people. Even the Sikkim Legislative Assembly was not consulted, nor were the people taken into confidence… It was against the democratic tenets of the constitution, against the national urge and aspirations of the overwhelming majority of the people, against the provisions of the Representations of the People Act in as much as it took away the safeguard provided to the people of different ethnic groups in section 5 (a) and it was against the secular character of the Indian constitution."[142] Talking about the seat arrangement he said, "I am not against the reservation seats for the Scheduled Castes and Tribes but outright reservation of 12 seats for the Bhutias and Lepchas has created serious doubts and misgivings in the minds of the other section… (The) Kazis, landlords and other vested interests call themselves Tribal or Janajati whom the Bill has given an open cheque to perpetuate the minority rule of well-to-do people… Arithmetically also 12 seats represent 37 per cent of the population."[143] Considering the Sangha seat as against the secular character of the Indian constitution, he expressed concern that it might set up a dangerous precedent in the country."

He emphasized that the Bill in the present form was full of faults and should be reintroduced only after consulting all concerned including the Sikkim Legislative Assembly and parties in Parliament.[144] Pahalman Subba, the lone Rajya Sabha member from Sikkim, told the House that the government in the State was in favour of reservation of seats for the Nepalis.[145]

Table No. 5.7: Distribution of Seats proposed by Pahalman Subba

Bhutia-Lepcha	12 seats
Nepali	15 seats
Sangha	1 seat
Scheduled Caste	2 seats
General	2 seats

Source: Prajashakti, dated 23-29 August, 2000, p. 3.

The formula on distribution of seats proposed by the SSP candidate for Rajya Sabha, Mr. Pahalman Subba, is given in table No. 5.7. The notable feature of the above formula suggested by Mr. Subba was a deviation of the proposals submitted earlier by the party. In this regard the 'Parity' was not the governing principle for seat sharing between the two ethnic groups (Bhutia-Lepcha and Nepali) of Sikkim.

The Representation of the People (Amendment) Bill, 1980 was passed without reserving seats for the Sikkimese Nepalis. Replying to a question in the parliament, P. Shiv Shankar told the House that the said Bill had a very limited purpose, i.e., to preserve the validity of the elections that had taken place when the Ordinance was in force.[146] Regarding Sangha seat, minister said that though the provision was offensive under article 15 (2) of the constitution but, since article 371F was an overriding provision; the reservation of Sangha seat was constitutional and valid.[147] The minister added that the issue of reservation of seats for Nepalis might be taken up at a later stage.[148] The Minister also informed the Rajya Sabha on February 5, 1980 that there is something perhaps that will have to be considered in a wider perspective and it does not call for any consideration at this stage".[149] The Governor of Sikkim, B.B.Lal, while addressing the Legislative Assembly on 10th March 1980 also emphasized on the consideration of the genuine aspirations of the people at a later date. As I said, primarily we are intending to revalidate the elections that have taken place under the Ordinance".[150]

The above statements were indicative of the fact that though the Representation of the People (Amendment) Act, 1980 had a very limited purpose, i.e. to revalidate the election concluded according to the norms of the Presidential Ordinance of 1979, it had no immediate desire to restore seats for the Nepalis.

The 45th Amendment Bill, 1980 seeking to validate the Presidential Ordinance of 1979 was discussed in the Legislative Assembly of Sikkim on the 11th March 1980. It must be mentioned here that the Amendment Bill also sought to extend protection provided to the Scheduled Castes, Scheduled Tribes and Anglo-Indian Communities by another 10 years. Participating in the discussion B.B.Gurung emphasized on the need to implement uniform policy regarding the Scheduled Castes (SC) and Scheduled Tribes (ST) in all the 22 States of India and alleged that the distribution of seats for Scheduled Castes and Scheduled Tribes in the Assembly was not done in an adequate manner. Mr. Dorji Tshering Bhutia of Ranka (BL) Constituency demanded inclusion of Tsong (Limboo) community in the Scheduled Tribes list of Sikkim whereas Mr. P.L.Gurung stressed on the need to include only the genuine Sikkimese in the SC/ST list of Sikkim. He also demanded Sikkim to be declared as a Tribal State. N.B.Khatiwada of Sikkim Prajatantra Congress pointed out that the reservation of seats for the Scheduled Tribes of Sikkim was not done according to article 332 (3) of the Indian constitution. He further added that in Sikkim those who were forward in social, economic and educational fields had been included in the Scheduled

Tribes list and demanded a status of Tribal State for Sikkim.[151] The Amendment seeking to abolish reservation of seats for Nepalis, however, was passed in the Sikkim Legislative Assembly by those who themselves were advocating for reservation of seats for Nepalis. Surprisingly the discussion in the Assembly centered around the SC/ST issue rather than abolition / reduction of Nepalis / BL seats.

The Chief Minister Bhandari was confident over the leadership of Mrs. Indira Gandhi for it was she who was instrumental behind the continuation of the provision of reserved Nepali seats even after the merger. He was elated at her assurances that the matter of seat reservation was receiving her attention.[152] In July 1983, when Mrs. Gandhi visited Sikkim, Chief Minister Bhandari submitted a memorandum demanding restoration of seats for the Nepalis. A proposal to restore seats for the Nepalis, including the Tsong (Limboo) seat, was also unanimously approved in the Assembly in September 1983.[153] The copy of the proposal was sent to the then Minister of State for Home Affairs, Shri Nihar Ranjan Laskar also. On December 14, 1983 the Minister concerned informed the Lok Sabha saying "there have been proposals for reservation of seats in the Sikkim Legislative Assembly for Nepalis and Tsong communities of Sikkimese origin. A resolution for reservation of seats for different communities of Sikkimese origin including Tsong community in the State's Legislature has also been received in this regard."[154] It was stated that abolition of Nepali seats in the Assembly would dilute their political identity and would be detrimental to the interest of the Nepalis in view of the influx of people from other parts of the country. They believed that by all accounts the Nepalis of Sikkimese origin continued to be educationally, politically and economically backward. The distribution of seats in the Legislative Assembly of Sikkim, as proposed earlier and later to the Prime Minister, Rajiv Gandhi, by the Chief Minister Bhandari, was as follows:

Table No. 5.8: Distribution of Seats as suggested by N.B.Bhandari in 1987.

(1) Bhutia, Lepcha and Sherpa of Sikkimese origin including monasteries.	13 seats
(2) Nepalis of Sikkimese origin.	13 seats
(3) Scheduled Castes of Sikkim	2 seats
(4) Tsongs (Limboos) of Sikkim.	2 seats
(5) General	4 seats
Total number of seats.	34 seats.

Source: Three Basic Issues, Govt. of Sikkim Publications, 1987.

Another landmark in the history of seat reservation deserves special mention. R.C.Poudyal, the President of Sikkim Congress (R), filed a writ petition in the High Court of Delhi on September 18, 1979. On June 6, 1980 the said petition was withdrawn from Delhi High Court and was again filed before the Sikkim High Court and on July 30, 1982 the case was once again transferred to the Supreme Court of India. The Supreme Court fixed the hearing on February 2, 1984. It must be noted that the Supreme Court made all the 32 members of the Sikkim Legislative Assembly as respondents in the case and, thus, on behalf of the Sikkim government, Mr. Ranjit Singh Basnet, the Chief Liaison Officer of the Government of Sikkim at New Delhi, was nominated for attending the court and answering the queries. The nature of correspondences which took place between the Chief Minister Bhandari and Mr. Basnet were neither discussed in the Cabinet nor in the meetings of the M.L.As. The Union Government and Sikkim Tribal Welfare Association (STWA) were other two respondents in the case.

Poudyal's (including his brother Somnath Poudyal) main contention was that the reservation of seats in the Assembly for the Bhutia-Lepchas community and the Sangha were based on 'race' and 'religion' and were, therefore, illegal and unconstitutional. Subsequently, the petitioners demanded abolition of the lone Sangha seat and reduction of seats reserved for the Bhutia-Lepcha from 12 to around 6-7 seats in proportion to their population.[155] Besides, the petition also maintained that article 371F of the constitution was destructive of the basic structure of the constitution.[156]

The case was taken up by a five-member constitutional bench consisting of the Chief Justice, Y. B. Chandrachud, Justice P.N.Bhagwati, Justice M.P.Takar, Justice A.N.Sen and Justice D.P.Mandon. Advocate Siddarth Shankar Ray, the former Chief Minister of West Bengal and senior advocate of the Supreme Court, and advocate K.K. Venugopal represented the case on behalf of the petitioners. After hearing the points highlighted by the defense counsels, the constitutional bench was quite convinced that the matter was one of political than legal. Justice Bhagwati stated, "Article 371F(f) gives the Parliament the right to reserve seats for various sections of the people. Court cannot examine how many seats should be reserved for various communities. Only when it is totally unreliable can the court intervene, for example, if only one seat is kept for the Nepalis. Bhutias are a section, Lepchas are a section. We cannot go beyond legislative facts. We do not know the reason why Parliament reserved for them. We cannot examine whether they need reservation of seats or not."[157] Regarding Sangha seat, he remarked "it is a section of the people"[158] hinting that seats could be reserved for them as per provision laid down in article 371F(f) of the constitution. Eventually the constitutional bench told the petitioners to withdraw the case to which the latter pleaded for keeping the case pending.[159] After keeping the judgement pending for 14 years, the five-member constitutional bench of the Supreme Court by a majority of 3:2 announced its final verdict on February 10, 1993 upholding reservation of 12 B-L and one Sangha seat in the State Legislative Assembly.[160]

The judgment also upheld the validity of the 36th Constitutional (Amendment) Act, 1975, which inserted article 371F in the constitution of India to provide special status to Sikkim. Though representing minority view, the observation by the then Chief Justice of India, Justice L.M.Sharma, regarding seat reservation issue was worth mentioning. He observed that reservation of 12 seats for the Bhutia-Lepchas was disproportionate to the ratio of population of the Bhutia-Lepchas in the State. He further added, "The choice of the candidate and the right to stand as a candidate at the election are inherent in the principle of adult suffrage, i.e. one-man-one-vote. By telling the people that they have a choice to elect any of a selected group cannot be treated as a free choice of the candidate. This will only amount to services, too thinly veiled to conceal the reality of an oligarchy underneath......So far the Sangha seat is concerned even this transparent cloak has been shed off. It has to be appreciated that the very purpose of providing reservation in favour of a weaker class is to aid the elemental principle of democracy based on one-man-one-vote to succeed. The disproportionately excessive reservation creates a privileged class, not brought to the same plane with others but put on a high pedestal, causing unhealthy competition, creating hatred and distrust between classes and fostering divisive forces."[161]

As it stands today, the 19 seats (17 General and 2 Scheduled Caste seats), for all practical purposes, are Nepali seats. A certain section of the Nepalis belonging to Tamangs and Gurungs are Buddhists by religion and, therefore, the Sangha seat does not represent Bhutia-Lepchas alone though the election scenario till 2004 Assembly Election indicates domination of Bhutias in the seat. Moreover, excluding the three Bhutia-Lepcha constituencies namely Lachen-Mangshila, Dzongu and Kabi-Tingda in North Sikkim, the rest of the reserved Bhutia-Lepcha constituencies are having Nepali voters evenly distributed. These Nepali voters play a crucial role in determining the victory of Bhutia-Lepcha candidates from these reserved constituencies. Thus, even though seats are not reserved for the ethnic Nepalis in the Legislative Assembly of the State, the community is in fairly good position in the affair of the State.

Ever since the abolition of Nepali seats, the government of Sikkim had been, from time to time, making representations to the government of India seeking restoration of the same. The State Government was of the opinion that under article 371F (f) of the constitution Indian Parliament is competent to enact laws seeking to ensure proper representation in the Legislative Assembly of the State for different sections of the population, including Nepalis, for whom seats were reserved historically.

Sometime in 1995, the Government of Sikkim constituted a six-member Committee under the Chairmanship of the former Chief Secretary of Sikkim, K. A. Varadan, to consider the demands for (a) restoration of seats for Sikkimese of Nepali origin; (b) delimitation of constituencies; and (c) inclusion of Limboos and Tamangs in the list of Scheduled Tribes of the State. The other members of the Committee were B.R. Pradhan, Secretary, Department of Law, N.D.Chingapa, Chief Electoral Officer, G.K.Subba, Special Secretary for Home, G.S.Lama, Chief Engineer, Department of Rural Development, and Chandrakala Cintury, Secretary, Welfare Department.

The Committee observed that the rights of 'certain section' should be specially recognized, as done in the case of Bhutia-Lepcha, rather than clubbing a number of sections under the head 'Scheduled Tribes' or any other category. The Committee, in other words, recommended for reservation of seats separately for the Lepchas and Sherpas who were generally clubbed and shared seats with the Bhutias. The Committee after ensuring no dominant position to any community recommended for an increase of Assembly seats to 40 with the following distribution[162]:

Table No. 5.9: Seat distribution proposed by the Varadhan Committee Report.

Caste/Communities	Seats
Lepcha	6
Bhutia	6
Sherpa	1
Limboo (Tsong)	3
Tamang	2
Sangha	1
Nepalis	17
Scheduled Castes	2
General	2

Source: Varadhan Committee Report, Govt. of Sikkim, undated, P.8.

The Limboos and Tamangs were not separate category in the same way as Lepchas, Bhutias, Sherpas (they are Scheduled Tribes) or, for that matter, Sangha, but were sub-groups of a larger Nepali community and recommendation for seat reservation on ethnic - cultural ground was unconstitutional. Perhaps it was done in contemplation to recognition of the two as scheduled tribes. The recommendation of the Varadan Committee was, however, not implemented. The Bhutia organization, called Survival Sikkimese, criticized the report as an 'act purporting to exterminate the Sikkimese community by division'.[163] The organization also resented the idea of reserving seats for the Sherpas.[164]

The Organization of Sikkimese Unity, formed for the protection of rights and interests of the three ethnic communities of Sikkim[165] boycotted the Assembly and Parliamentary elections in October 1999 in support of restoration of the Bhutia-Lepcha and Nepali seats.[166] The organization also requested the political parties to introduce the seat reservation Bill in the Assembly and to pass it.[167] In August 2000, J.K. Bhandari, the Sikkim Sangram Parishad M.L.A. from Loosing Pacheykhani constituency, proposed a Bill in the Assembly (monsoon session) seeking to restore seats to its pre-merger position.[168] The Bill was, however, withdrawn in view of stiff opposition from the ruling Sikkim Democratic Front (SDF) party.[169] The Sikkimese Nepali Unity (SNU), an organization of the Sikkimese Nepalis, also condemned the issue of seat reservation as being totally 'irrelevant' and a 'non-issue'. According to the President of the organization, Pradeep Yonzon, the issue was "a psychological problem of the Sikkimese Nepalis. Technically, seat reservation of Nepalis means restoration to pre-merger position on Parity basis which is not only objectionable but also detrimental for the interest of the Nepalis."[170] The majority of the Sikkimese Nepalis believed that population should be the criteria for seat reservation and not the 'Parity' formula which the Organization of Sikkimese Unity led by J.N.Kazi had been insisting.

Far from being resolved, the issue of seat reservation embroiled into yet another controversy with the inclusion of the Limboos and the Tamangs in the Scheduled Tribes list in the year 2003. They were declared scheduled tribes without delimiting number of seats in favour of them in the State Assembly and were also not allowed to contest from the 12 reserved seats which were exclusively reserved for Bhutia-Lepcha. In the meanwhile, the Union Minister for Law, Arun Jaitley, also denied that reservation of seats for the newly included tribes before 2004 Assembly and Lok Sabha elections was possible.[171] The decision of the Union Cabinet to postpone delimitation process of Parliamentary and Assembly constituencies to till 2026 added further uncertainty over the question of seat reservation for the Limboos and Tamangs. The Sikkim Limboo and Tamang Joint Action Committee (SLTJAC), a Congress (I) sympathizer led by P.R.Subba, demanded reservation of seats in the Assembly without restructuring the existing Assembly constituencies.[172] The Gorkha Apex Committee (GAC), the Sikkim Sherpa Association (SSA) and the Communist Party of India (Marxist) also subscribed to this demand.[173] On the other hand, the Bhutia-Lepcha Apex Committee (SIBLAC) maintained that according to the Representation of the People (Amendment) Act, 1951 (as amended in 1980), the 12 seats reserved in the Assembly were Bhutia-Lepcha seats and they alone were eligible to contest election from those seats. The organization maintained that seats for the Limboo and Tamang tribal communities must be allocated from the 17 general seats. The SIBLAC was corroborating the view expressed by the Union Minister for Tribal Affairs, Joel Oram, in which he anticipated possible reduction of the Bhutia-Lepcha seats in the Assembly[174] in view of the inclusion of Limboo and Tamang in the Scheduled Tribe list of Sikkim.

The State Government, sensibly enough, sought legal advice from the country's renowned constitutional experts namely Soli Sorabji, the then Solicitor General, Government of India, K.K.Venugopal and F.S. Narimann.

The trio equivocally maintained that Limboo and Tamang communities could not have seats reserved in the State Assembly automatically by virtue of their being recognized as Scheduled Tribes of Sikkim. According to them the reservation of the Bhutia-Lepcha seats in the Legislative Assembly was due to the section 7 (1) of the Representation of the People Act, 1950 and so long as the section 7 (1) did not get amended, the inclusion of the newly notified Scheduled Tribes could have no impact on the B-L seats.[175] Article 371F (f) explicitly authorizes the Union Parliament, for the purpose of protecting the rights and interest of the different sections of the population of Sikkim, to make provisions for the number of seats in the Legislative Assembly of Sikkim which may be filled by candidates belonging to such sections and for the delimitation of the Assembly constituencies from which candidates belonging to such sections alone may stand for election.

In December 2005, the State Government vide notification No. 73/Home/2005 set up a commission for Review of Social and Environmental Sector Plans, Policies and Programmes (CRESP).[176] The eight member Commission headed by Prof. B.K.Roy Burman, an eminent social scientist, was to review the constitutional status of castes and communities of Sikkim in historical, cultural, ecological, political and economic contexts and make appropriate recommendations.

Among others the Commission was to consider (a) to recommend reservation of seats for Limboo and Tamang tribal communities in the State Legislative Assembly, (b) to recommend for enhancement in the total number of seats in the Legislative Assembly and (c) to recommend for protection of 12 seats reserved for the Bhutias and Lepchas in the Assembly.

Table No. 5.10 : Distribution of seats recommended by Burman Commission, 2008

Communities / Category	Number Seats to reserve
Bhutia – Lepcha	12
Schedule Tribes	20
Scheduled Castes	02
Sangha	02
General (Open)	04
Total	40

Source: Burman Commission Report, March 2008.

The Commission in its report submitted on March 31, 2008

recommended for (a) enhancement of Assembly seats to 40, (b) allocation of 20 seats for the Scheduled Tribes including Tamangs and Limboos and any other communities who would be notified as tribes in future, (c) continuation of 12 reserved seats for Bhutias and Lepchas, (d) 4 seats to General community, (e) Sangha seats to increase to 2 in view of growing monasteries and monks belonging to Gurung and Tamang Buddhist communities and 2 Scheduled Castes seat. (Table no. 5.10)

It is on the basis of special provision of 371 (F) and Burman Commission recommendation that the Chief Minister, P.K.Chamling, demanded for increasing the total number of seats of the State Assembly to 40.[177] Mr. Birbal Subba, the President of the Sikkim Limboo-Tamang Tribal Forum (formerly Sikkim Limboo Tamang Apex Committee for Tribal Status), once stated that the size of the population was the major discouraging factor behind Assembly seat enhancement initiative. The present delimitation itself was far short of the criteria laid down for the purpose.[178] Therefore, if seats for the Limboos and Tamangs were at all to be reserved in the Assembly, he reasoned, 'it must be reserved from within the existing 12 reserved seats'.[179] It is to be noted here that in the R.C.Poudyal vs. Sikkim Government, Justice Y.B. Chandrachud of the Supreme Court of India, had observed that "if Bhutia-Lepchas were Scheduled Tribes, then reservation for them was on a Scheduled Tribe basis and not on race as alleged by the petitioners."[180] It is a sticky question with both political and ethnic overtones.

The central government is constitutionally obliged to reserve seats for the newly recognized tribes of Sikkim but since the legal-constitutional provisions concerning seat allotment for different sections of Sikkimese population in the State Assembly are ambiguous and involve the interest of the Bhutia-Lepcha community, the issue of seat reservation for the Limboo and Tamang tribal communities is unlikely to be resolved very soon. In the meanwhile, the exchange of claims and counter claims between the two groups could not be in any way considered as healthy ethnic relationship.

State Policies and Tribal Communities of Sikkim:

The constitution of India, being consecrated by the ideals of equality and justice, seeks to abolish all forms of discriminations either against or in favour of an individual or group on grounds of religion, race, religion and place of birth. But considering the nature of the Indian society beset with diverse social structures, social belief and forms of social discriminations associated to it and educational and economic backwardness of the people, the logical application of ideals of justice and equality could not be possible. Hence, the framers of the constitution designed certain temporary affirmative measures for the advancement of those historically and traditionally relegated backward sections of the community. Indeed, the principle of democratic equality can work only if the nation as a whole is brought on the same footing as far as it is practicable. In India the majority of these culturally distinct and socially, economically and educationally backward sections of population is identified as the Scheduled Castes and Scheduled Tribes and is provided with certain special concessions in political, educational and economic fields, including in public appointments.

A significant development which came along the merger of Sikkim with India in 1975 was that the erstwhile ruling community of Sikkim, i.e., the Bhutias, became ordinary citizens of a large Indian nation. This they had been contemplating ever since the political process for establishing democratic government began in 1949. By the time the merger took place, the Chogyal had accomplished whatever was possible in his capacity as a ruler to safeguard the political and economic interests of the ruling community. The 36th Constitutional Amendment Act, 1975 made these measures a part and parcel of the Indian constitution.

However, in pursuance of the spirit of the Constitution of India, certain modifications in the existing rules governing the affairs of the minority community of Sikkim were felt necessary. Accordingly, the Chief Secretary of Sikkim, T.S.Gyaltshen,[181] requested the central counterpart to furnish details for the specification of the Scheduled Castes and Scheduled Tribes communities in Sikkim. The norms approved by the Government of India for specification of Scheduled Castes and Scheduled Tribes and communicated to the Chief Secretary, Government of Sikkim, was based on Lokur Committee Report of 1964, were as follows;

A. *Scheduled Castes:* Extreme social, educational and economic backwardness arising out of the traditional practice of untouchability;

B. *Scheduled Tribes:* Indications of primitive traits, distinctive culture, geographical isolation, shyness of contact with the community at large and backwardness.[182]

The letter further revealed that the Lhendup Kazi government had earlier proposed for Scheduled Tribe status for the Lepchas and Bhutias. The latter community was classified into three sub-groups: (i) Sikkimese Bhutia, (ii) Bhutias including Dopthapa, Tromopa, Chumbipa and Drukpa, and (iii) the Tibetans. The proposal of the State government seeking to recognize the three sections of the Bhutias as Scheduled Tribe, however, seemed to have created lot of confusion in Shastri Bhawan. Hence, a clarification was sought from the State government by the Ministry of the Home Affairs stating "it appears that there are no great cultural differences between the Sikkimese Bhutia and other sub-groups of Bhutia. It is also not clear whether inclusion of only these terms would cover all the sections of the Bhutias or some sections would be left out. Information available here also seems to show that the term "Tibetan" is used to denote those Bhutias who have been preserving their tradition of having migrated from Tibet. Altogether it might be best not to include the term "Tibetan". The Sikkim Government may consider whether it could be sufficient to mention only the generic term Bhutia in the Schedule to cover all the sub-groups including Tibetan."[183]

The central government also categorically wanted to know from the State government as to why Limboos (also called Tsongs) could not be included in the Scheduled Tribes list. Under para no. 5 the letter stated that "it would also appear that there is another primitive tribe namely the Limboos who have social affinity with the Lepchas and some of them are animists. The Limboos have been mentioned as autochthonous inhabitants of Sikkim and are sometimes considered as Limbuan (Limbuwan) Lepchas .... The status of the Limboos will have to be spelt out clearly and if necessary they may be grouped with Lepcha, and the entry could be "Lepcha Limboo".[184] The letter also highlighted the inability of the State government to include other tribal communities i.e., Gurung, Mangar, Tamang and Rai, and instructed the state government "to review the case of these communities and also other communities which may have been left out."[185]

The then Kazi government, however, did not pursue the matter seriously. However, when the Constitution (Sikkim) Scheduled Tribes Order, 1978 was promulgated, only the Lepchas and Bhutias, including Chumbipa, Dopthapa, Dukpa, Kagatey, Sherpa, Tibetan, Tromopa and Yolmo, were declared scheduled tribes of Sikkim.[186] The Order substantiated the fact that the government of the day agreed to include all sub-groups of Bhutia into a single generic term 'Bhutia'.[187] While other groups like Limboos, Tamangs, Gurungs, Rais, Mangars etc. were denied scheduled tribe status.

Logically, from ethnic-cultural point of view, the Sherpas, Kagatey and Yolmos should not have been included in the category of Bhutias though by tradition and religion they are mostly Buddhists. Bhutias in Sikkim refers to people who migrated to Sikkim from Tibet and Bhutan; and Bhutias include certain sub-groups like Chumbipas, Dopthapas, Tromopas from Tibet, Drukpas from Bhutan and also Tibetans who came later. But Sherpas and Yolmos are believed to be migrated from Nepal, while Kagatey stands for the occupational name of Yolmos. Besides, Sherpas and Yolmos are not recognized as Bhutia-Lepchas in the Revenue Order No. 1 of 1917.

Socially, various socio-cultural groups of the Nepalis community like the Rai, Limboo, Gurung, Tamang, Mangar and others (Bhujel, Sunuwar, Thami) should have been included in the Scheduled Tribes list of Sikkim in view of their distinct culture, language, religion and overall backwardness. Besides, the Ministry of Home Affairs, Government of India, had also expressed desire for their inclusion in the Scheduled Tribes list of Sikkim, and accordingly had instructed the state government to review the case of these 'Left out' communities.[188]

The policy of the Sikkim government on tribal affairs was not only ambiguous but also discriminatory. If the period of settlement had been the criteria for being included in the Scheduled Tribes, then the Limboos, Mangars, Gurungs, Rais and Tamangs should have been included. On the other hand, the Drukpas and Tibetans do not merit inclusion on this ground. On socio-economic grounds these communities were far more backward, downtrodden and alienated than the ruling Bhutias. And if religion was the criteria (for the Nepalis are basically Hindu and Scheduled Tribes are, at least officially, Buddhist), then at least Tamang and Gurungs community who are basically Buddhist should have been recognized as a scheduled tribe.

Mr. N.B.Bhandari, after coming to power in 1979 Assembly election, took up the issue with the central government. In 1981, he wrote to the then Prime Minister of India recommending inclusion of the Limboo community in the list of Scheduled Tribes of Sikkim.[189] In June 1987, he further wrote to the Central Government recommending inclusion of Limboos and Tamangs of Sikkim in the list of Scheduled Tribes.[190] The response of the central government, as always had been positive and expressed desire to conduct a meeting for comprehensive revision of the list of Scheduled Castes and Scheduled Tribes.[191] Accordingly, on July 31, 1987 the Secretary, Ministry of Welfare, Government of India, sent a telegram to the Secretary, SC/ST Welfare Department, Government of Sikkim, requesting him to present positively in the meeting of the Ministers organized on August 13, 1987 at Parliament House, New Delhi, to discuss on the issue of comprehensive revision of the lists of Scheduled Castes and Scheduled Tribes.[192]

As scheduled, the meeting was held under the chairmanship of the Union Minister, Shri Buta Singh. One of the agenda of the meeting was inclusion of Limboos and Tamangs in the list of Scheduled Tribes of Sikkim. Mr. Pasang Namgyal, Secretary, SC/ST & Welfare Deptt., Government of Sikkim, submitted a favourable report to the Committee of Ministers for SC/ST regarding inclusion of Limboo and Tamang in the Scheduled Tribes list. Later in his report, dated August 19, 1987, to Shri Sanchamana Limboo, Minister SC/ST & Welfare Deptt., Govt. of Sikkim, Mr. P. Namgyal noted that the "deliberation indicated sufficient recommendation in favour of the above two communities. It is further learnt that sitting of the group of Ministers was final scrutiny in the process of the comprehensive revision of the lists of Scheduled Castes and Scheduled Tribes".[193] However, by this time, the priorities of SSP government headed by Mr. Bhandari had been shifted to some other areas than inclusion of Limboos and Tamangs in the Scheduled Tribes list. Bhandari's view was that the issue of Tribal status of Limboo and Tamang communities could not be isolated from the issues of citizenship, seat reservation and recognition of Nepali language. His official note dated August 22, 1987 on the report presented by the Secretary, SC/ST and Welfare Department, stated 'we cannot separate the demands. We do not want divide and rule policy. All Sikkimese are one'.[194]

It substantiated the view that there had been a major shift in the priorities of the State government after June 1987. Mr. N. B. Bhandari who supported recognition of Limboos and Tamangs as Scheduled Tribes initially was now opposed to it. Bhandari Government was apprehensive of the fact that recognition of the Limboos and Tamangs as Scheduled Tribes might split the Nepali community[195] and weaken the demands for the grant of constitutional recognition to Nepali language, citizenship to 'left-out' Sikkimese and reservation of seats etc. which the State Government was pursuing vigorously.

Considering the then prevailing political development, it can be assumed that the pressure from the existing tribal community (Bhutia and Lepcha) and perhaps the publication of a book entitled "The Hidden Facts in Nepali Politics" by Gopal Gurung highlighting domination of the high caste Nepalis over the others, might have compelled Mr. Bhandari to take decision opposing inclusion of Limboo and Tamang communities in the Scheduled Tribes list.[196] The decision of the State Government was not only contradictory to the stand taken earlier but it also put the Central government in a dilemma. The Bhandari government's opposition to granting of Tribal status to Limboos and Tamangs became more evident when Mr. Bhandari sought explanations from two of his legislators (Mr. Sanchaman Limboo and Mr. Birbal Limboo) for participating in the delegation of Akhil Sikkim Kirat Limbu Chumlung which met the Prime Minister of India, P.V.Narashimha Rao, on June 14, 1990.[197] There was no doubt that Mr. Bhandari had reservation regarding inclusion of the Limboo and Tamang communities in the list of Scheduled Tribes of Sikkim.

The Sikkim Democratic Front (SDF) led by Mr. P.K.Chamling assumed power in 1994 and with it the tribal issue attained a new height and dimension. On the eve of Assembly elections the party promised to work for the protection of the rights and privileges of the Bhutia-Lepcha tribals together with recognition of five different socio-cultural groups – Limboos, Tamangs, Gurungs, Mangars and Rais – in the list of Scheduled Tribes of Sikkim. Interestingly, had there been a consensus-reached between the Central and State governments, these communities could have been declared Scheduled Tribes in 1994 itself.[198]

In June 1995 the Chief Minister, Shri P.K.Chamling, wrote to the Union Home Minister, Shri S.B.Chavan, for inclusion of the Limboo, Tamang and Gurung communities in the Scheduled Tribe list of Sikkim.[199] Later, some other communities namely Mangar, Rai, Sunuwar, Bhujel and Thami were also included in the proposed list of communities for the status of Scheduled Tribes and under his dynamic leadership efforts were made at all levels to have these communities recognized.[200] In December 2002, the Bill seeking to amend the Constitution (Sikkim) Scheduled Tribes Order, 1978 (Bill No. 62) was placed in the Union Parliament and the discussion on the Bill was held on December 19, 2002 in the Lok Sabha (December 18, 2002 in the Rajya Sabha). Mr. Chamling's presence in New Delhi since December 2, 2002 was immensely helpful in the smooth passage of the Bill (No. 62) on the scheduled dates. The Bill received Presidential assent on January 7, 2003.[201] The Limboos and Tamangs were notified as Scheduled Tribes while the other deserving communities like Gurung, Rai, Manger, etc. were denied the status once again.

The Sikkim Bhutia Lepcha Apex Committee (SIBLAC) in its first ever convention held on September 23, 2001 adopted a resolution demanding not to grant Scheduled Tribe status to the Limboos and Tamangs in the interest of the Bhutias and Lepchas.[202] The Committee believed that government's proposal to grant Scheduled Tribes status to them would have detrimental effect on the rights and privileges as well as identity of the Lepchas and Bhutias.[203] There were rumours about the fall of the Chamling Government. Even Mr. Chamling contemplated worst for his government, '"My government will go on December 19, 2002. Let it go if it has to but I'm not afraid. I will work for the Limboos and Tamangs".[204] But nothing unprecedented happened. In 2004 Assembly election Chamling returned to power with 31 seats though, according to a reliable source, majority of the Bhutia-Lepcha did not cast vote in favour of the Sikkim Democratic Front party led by Mr. Chamling.

A new dimension was added to the tribal issue after the inclusion of Limboos and Tamangs in the list of Scheduled Tribes of Sikkim. By virtue of being the Scheduled Tribes, they deserve reservation of seats in the State Assembly under article 332 (1) of the Indian constitution. It must be noted that as of now the State Assembly does not have provision for seat reservation for the tribals. Though the Bhutias and Lepchas were notified Scheduled Tribes in 1978, the 12 seats reserved in the State Assembly continued to be ethnic seats meant exclusively for the Bhutias and Lepchas. No change or amendment was thought necessary in the Representation of the People Act, 1950/51 (as amended in 1980), basically on the impression that the groups for whom seats were reserved on ethnic ground earlier were alone scheduled tribes too requiring no separate reservation.

The Sikkim Limboo Tamang Joint Action Committee,

P.R.Subba group and supported by the state unit of the Indian National Congress (I), submitted a proposal to the central government and the State Delimitation Commissions demanding special census of the two communities immediately to provide seat reservation or to reserve seats in the same way or method as was followed to reserve seats for the Scheduled Tribes earlier.[205] The Committee also demanded amendment to the Representation of the People Act, 1980 and expedite the process for seat reservation for the two tribal communities before the commencement of the Assembly election scheduled in 2004.[206] The Sikkim Limboo Tamang Joint Action Committee for Tribal Status (Birbal Subba group) also demanded for reservation of seats before the completion of the work by the Delimitation Commission 2002. Both the organizations also urged the visiting President of India, A.P.J. Abdul Kalam, to grant the political rights to the Limboo and Tamang tribal communities before the implementation of recommendation of the Delimitation Commission 2002.

The memorandum submitted by the Sikkim Limboo Tamang Joint Action Committee (SLTJAC) to the President Kalam read “”if the delimitation proposal in the present form is allowed to see passage, the Limboo and Tamang communities will be deprived of their political rights for another 25 years as the next delimitation exercise will be taken only after 25 years.”[207] They expressed resentment over the discriminatory treatment meted out to the communities by the state government earlier and now by the central government.

The Sikkim Bhutia Lepcha Apex Committee, on the other hand, made it clear that the 12 seats reserved in the Assembly were exclusively meant for the Bhutia-Lepcha community and any attempt to dilute the existing provision would be viewed as a threat to the rights of the minority Lepcha-Bhutia by the majority. Similar view was also expressed by Ven. Lama Chosphel Zotpa, Vice-Chairman of the National Commission for Scheduled Castes and Tribes, Government of India, in a letter entitled “Threat faced by Bhutia and Lepcha Tribes in Sikkim from Nepalis”, addressed to the Chief Secretary, Government of Sikkim.[208] The inclusion of the Limboo and Tamang communities in the Scheduled Tribes list also had its effect on the existing reservation policies of the state government in employment and higher professional educational institutions. Earlier, the Scheduled Tribes (Bhutia and Lepcha) enjoyed 23 per cent reservation.[209] In September 2003 the percentage of reservation for the Scheduled Tribes was increased to 33 per cent[210] including the share of the Limboo and Tamang tribal communities. Since then, the Bhutias had been expressing resentment over the possible domination of the Nepalis in the area monopolized exclusively by them earlier. Thus apart from the seat issue, the Bhutias and Lepchas also feared deprivation in terms of employment and resource distribution which the community now have to share with the Limboo and Tamang tribal communities.

In fact, as early as September 2001, the state government clarified that the seats reserved for the Bhutias and Lepchas would not be disturbed.[211] While alleging the Opposition parties and organizations for fomenting communalism on the issue, Mr. Chamling assured that "My job as the Chief Minister is to protect the people of Sikkim and the day I am not able to do so I will not only retire from politics but will excommunicate myself from Sikkim".[212] The issue being ethnically contentious, the government sought legal advice from the constitutional experts. The major points expressed by them (Shri K.K.Venugopal, Shri Soli Sorabji and Shri S.S. Nariman) were as follows;

a) Limboos and Tamangs could not claim any of the 12 seats reserved for the Bhutia-Lepcha in the State Assembly;
b) The total percentage of reservation to the Legislative Assembly could exceed 50 per cent without affecting the provision of article 14 of the constitution;
c) Article 332 would proporio vigour operate on the reservation of seats for the Limboos and Tamangs;
d) On the basis of available population data about 16 per cent of the 32 seats, i.e. at least 5 seats, could be reserved for the Limboos and Tamangs;
e) The State government would retain the right to make a

demand for readjustment of seats before 2006 provided that the Union Parliament deems it necessary to take decision in the matter.[213]

As a solution to the problem, in July 2003 the Chief Minister wrote to the Prime Minister, Mr. A.B.Bajpai, requesting him to increase the number of Assembly seats from existing 32 to 40 seats to enable a provision of reservation of seats for the two newly included tribal communities.[214] The discussion in the Rajya Sabha over the issue reaffirmed that the Chief Minister, P.K.Chamling proposed for reservation of seats for Limboo and Tamang tribal communities without affecting the reservation provided to the Bhutia-Lepcha community.[215]

The State government also requested for conducting a special census of the Limboo and Tamang tribal communities in order to fulfill the constitutional obligation mentioned under article 332 (1) and (3) of the constitution.[216] In response to the Chief Minister's letter to the Prime Minister written in December 2004[217] the Joint Secretary, Ministry of Home Affairs, informed about the examination of the matter by the Ministry in consultation with the Union Law Ministry and requested the State government to choose one of the three options short listed by the Ministry and communicate to it immediately.[218] The options were:

a) A Reservations to be carved out of the 17 unreserved Assembly seats arrangements in Sikkim on the basis of proportion of their population…without increasing the size of the State Legislature;
b) Strength of the State Legislature be increased to 40 and reservations be considered out of 25 seats (i.e. present 17 plus 8 additional seats) subject to the condition that in the event of any more communities being declared as Schedule Tribes in future they may also be accommodated within the overall size of 40 without having to request further increase in number of seats;
c) The size of the Legislative Assembly be increased to 60 to bring at par with other States and in conformity with article

> 171 (1) and reservation from Limboos and Tamangs be considered in proportion to their population out of the 45 seats (17 + 28) subject to the condition that in the event of any new communities being declared as Scheduled Tribes in future they will also be accommodated within the overall strength of 60 without having to ask for any further increase in the strength of the Assembly.[219]

In the meanwhile, the State Government set up a four member commission in February 2005 under the Chairmanship of Prof. A.C. Sinha, to prepare an ethnological account of Rai, Yakha, Sunwar, Mangar, Gurung, Bhujel and Jogi for the inclusion of these communities in the Scheduled Tribes list. The other members of the Commission were Prof. T.B.Subba (NEHU), Prof. S.R.Mandal (NBU) and Prof. G.P.Singh (Mizoram University). The Commission, in its report submitted in May 2005, presented a very impressive account of the ethno-genesis and diagnostic ethnic traits of the above communities.

The Report suggested that, firstly, if any community is to be considered for the status of Scheduled Tribes in future the entry "Kiratas" make the most suitable case as their constituents – Lepchas and Limboos – have been already accorded Scheduled Tribes status in Sikkim and West Bengal. Secondly, the next eligible communities as mentioned above are constituents of "Kiratas" and should be considered for the status of Scheduled Tribes under the same cognate term. Thirdly, the Commission was against the inclusion of 'Jogi' community in the ST list but in view of their socio-economic and cultural attributes the Commission located their best place in Other Backward Class.[220]

A high level delegation of the State government, including some senior bureaucrats and citizens, called upon the Prime Minister and the Home Minister among others in November 2005. It was learnt that, besides talks on Limboo and Tamang seats, discussion on inclusion of other communities like Gurung, Rai, Mangar, Thami and Bhujel for tribal status was also figured prominently in the meeting. But nothing substantive happened. The issue also did not come up in the Budget Session of the Lok Sabha in 2006. In the meanwhile, Shri H.R. Pradhan, President of the State Unit of the Bharatiya Janata Party (BJP), lodged a writ petition in the Supreme Court seeking clarification as to why the seats for the Limboos and Tamangs could not be reserved in the State Assembly. In its preliminary hearing, dated 20.03.2006, the Supreme Court issued show cause notices to both the Central and State Governments asking as to why the prayer of the President of the Sikkim Unit of the BJP, Shri H.R.Pradhan, should not be granted.[221] On behalf of Shri Pradhan, the former Union Minister, Shri Arun Jaitley, who was assisted by Advocate Ranjit Kumar, represented the case.

In view of the State government's recommendation for enhancement of Assembly seats to 40, the Ministry of Home Affairs, Government of India, asked the State Government for further clarification on two fronts – a) convincing justification as to why Assembly seats be enhanced to 40, and (b) whether the seats reserved for B-L should be correspondingly enhanced if the Assembly seats were raised to 40.[222] The second explanation has been sought in view of the memorandum submitted to the Welfare Ministry by the Sikkim Bhutia Lepcha Apex Committee (SIBLAC) demanding corresponding enhancement of B-L seats if the Assembly seats were raised to 40.[223] This demand for corresponding enhancement of B-L seat has further complicated the issue. It seems that there has been a general apprehension among the members of the Sikkim Bhutia Lepcha Apex Committee that if seats for the Limboo and Tamang are reserved outside the 17 open seats, the domination of the Nepalis over the affairs of the state will increase. In other words, the 12 Bhutia-Lepcha seats will no longer remain as decisive as it is at present in the making and unmaking of the government.

The Burman Commission Report which the State Cabinet approved in April 24, 2008 also recommended for continuation of 12 seats reserved for Bhutias and Lepchas. Apart from this the Commission also recommended for inclusion of all the Nepalis in the Scheduled Tribes list, allocation of 20 seats for the Scheduled Tribes including the Limboos and Tamangs and any other communities notified in future and Assembly seats to increase to

40. This report which was sent to the Central government in 2008 was seen as the kind of justification that the State Government was trying to provide in support of its claim for 40 Assembly seats. However, State Government was not in favour of corresponding enhancement of the Bhutia – Lepcha reserved seats possibly on the ground that enhancement would be highly disproportionate to population.

The problem with the tribal issue is that the Government has failed to introduce any reliable criterion or measure for determining 'tribe-ness' of a group. The question of determining communities as scheduled tribes has been addressed arbitrarily since the merger

Considering the socio-cultural and political peculiarities of the state of Sikkim, the government of India was rather lenient and accommodative in its dealing with Sikkim. After the merger article 371F, as a special provision, was incorporated in the constitution of India extending legal-constitutional sanctions to the laws and institutions prevailing just before the merger. These old laws had been designed to maintain politico-cultural hegemony of the ruling community and, therefore, were communally oriented and discriminatory in intention. Briefly speaking, most of these laws are in contradiction to the spirit of democratic and secular constitution of India. The continuation of these laws, particularly the Revenue Order No. 1 which prohibits alienation of Bhutia-Lepcha land to the Nepalis or other communities, Parity Formula as a governing norm for political representation and public appointment, pattern of seat reservation continue to maintain social division at the community level and very often the source of ethnic tension. For example, in 1989 when the Sikkim High Court judgement allowed L.D.Kazi, a Lepcha, to gift a piece of land located in the prime urban area to his foster son N.B.Khatiwada, a Nepali, tension grew between the Nepalis and Bhutias. The Bhutias feared that it would facilitate further alienation of Bhutia-Lepcha land and an appeal was lodged in the Supreme Court of India against the judgement of the Sikkim High Court. Nepalis, on the other, believed that the plot being in the urban area the jurisdiction of Revenue Order No. 1 do not apply. It was the opinion of the Sikkim High Court also. Though the Supreme Court too upheld the judgement of the Sikkim High Court in 2006, the affidavits submitted by both the parties in defense of the case became the source of ethnic tension between the two. The Revenue Order No. 1 is also the source of discontent between the Bhutia and Lepcha on the one hand and between the Bhutia and Other Bhutias on the other. Both the Lepchas and other Bhutias, particularly the Sherpas, are demanding modification in the said Order so that the Lepcha land could not be purchased by the Bhutias and other Bhutias (Sherpas) should be allowed to buy traditional Bhutia-Lepcha land respectively. The Revenue Order No. 1 in its present form is considered bias towards the affluent Bhutia community.

Apart from this, the new laws introduced after the merger of Sikkim with India in 1975 also have been the source of ethnic discontent. The promulgation of various laws like Sikkim Citizenship Order, 1975 legitimizing the controversial Sikkim Subject Regulation, 1961 as the cut off year, the Constitution (Sikkim) Scheduled Tribes Order, 1978 denying scheduled tribes status to many deserving cultural communities like Limboo, Tamang, Gurung, Rai, Mangar etc. and displeasing the 'Real Bhutias' by including 'Other Bhutias' within the definition of the Bhutia, Representation of the People (Amendment) Act, 1979-80 abolishing seats reserved for the Nepalis while maintaining reservation in favour of Bhutia-Lepcha ethnic community on communal and religious grounds besides reducing the Bhutia-Lepcha seats to 12 from 15 seats reserved erstwhile etc.

All these legislative actions are understood to be mostly against the interest of the Nepalis and whenever the protagonist of it tries to address the issue, one way or the other, the ethno-cultural differences gets sharpened besides strengthening of the community-oriented consciousness and mobilization. For instance, when R.C.Poudyal, the then President of Sikkim Congress (Revolutionary), sought legal remedy on the Nepali seat abolition issue, he was condemned for instigating or perpetuating communalism. Moreover, when the Nepali community rallied for equal treatment by exempting them from the Central Income Tax Act, 1961 (Bill No. 15 of 1994) along with other communities, it resulted in ethnic tension.

Sikkim is basically a traditional society. Political parties and other political organizations, like many other parts of India, therefore do not always represent ideological and policy divisions. Political parties, in such circumstances, are often organized on the basis of traditional bonds, networks and relations. The Sikkim National Party during the pre-merger period clearly demonstrated the creation of a modern political organization on the basis of traditional ethnic-cultural identities. This trend is continuing even after the merger primarily due to the prevalence of symbols of ethnic differences in legal and structural forms. The seats in the State Assembly is so precariously designed that traditional bonds and networks play pivotal role both in terms of electoral success and continuation in power. The political parties, while attempting to widen their support base, enter into some forms of alignment with various socio-cultural organizations and formulate policies favouring or denying a particular social group. Thus, Bhandari's pro-Bhutia-Lepcha and pro-upper caste politics alienated Other Backward Class (OBC) communities while Chamling's pro-OBC attitude and formulation of policies favouring inclusion of certain communities into the Scheduled Tribes status have created apprehension and alienation among the communities who were affected or felt affected by it.

FOOTNOTES AND REFERENCES

1. Article II, *Convention between Great Britain and China relating to Sikkim and Tibet, 1890.*
2. Sir Olaf Caroe, the Foreign Secretary in India during the viceroyalty of Linlithgow and Wavell, in a letter to Daily Telegraph of London, dated 19.12.1974, cited in P.R.Rao: *Sikkim – The Story of its Political Integration with India*, Cosmo Publications, New Delhi 1978, Pp. 69-70.
3. V.H.Ceolho: *Sikkim and Bhutan*, Vikas Publication, New Delhi, 1970/1971, P. 25.
4. Ibid, P. 26.
5. Text of the Indo-Sikkim Agreement of 1950.

6. Sikkim State Congress's petition to the Maharaja of Sikkim, dated 09.12.1947.
7. Proceedings of the Sikkim Legislative Assembly, October 1976, P. 43.
8. Sikkim Express, Vol. III, No. 107, dated 8.10.1979; N. Sengupta: *State Government and Politics in Sikkim*, Sterling Publication, New Delhi, 1985, P. 238-39.
9. B.S.Das: *The Sikkim Saga*, Vikash Publishing House Pvt. Ltd, New Delhi, 1983, P. 99.
10. Bhowmick & Dhamala: *"Land Reforms in Sikkim"*, in S.K.Chaube (Ed.) 'The Himalayas: Profiles of Modernization and Adaptation, Sterling Pub.,New Delhi, 1985, P.121.
11. *Narbahadur Khatiwada and Nine Others – Sikkim's Merger: A Brief Resume.*
12. Ibid
13. Ibid
14. N.Sengupta: *State Government and Politics in Sikkim*, Sterling Publishers Pvt. Ltd., New Delhi, 1985, P. 104.
15. Amrita Bazar Patrika, dated 9.9.1978.
16. Mohammed Hidayatullah: '*Opinion in the Matter of the Chogyal of Sikkim and the 35th Amendment of the Constitution of India'* cited in "Smash and Grab: Annexation of Sikkim" by S.K.Dattaray, Vikash Publication, New Delhi, 1984, Pp. 254-55.
17. Interview with the late K.C.Pradhan in his residence at Development Area. 2001.
18. Legislative Assembly Proceedings, Eighth Session, March 1978, Pp. 133-35.
19. The Representation of the People Act, 1950 as amended in 1976.
20. The Representation of the People Act, 1951 as amended in 1976.
21. The Nation, dated 30.09.1978.

22. *'Election in Sikkim'*, Broader News and Views, Vol. 1, Nos. 11 & 12, dated August-September, 1978, P. 15.
23. The Nation, dated 21.10.1978.
24. The Statesman, dated 15.10.1979.
25. Sikkim Government Gazette, Ex. Gazette, No. 80, dated 12.09.1979.
26. Sikkim Express, Vol. III, No. 105, dated 27.09.1979.
27. Interview with Shri R.C.Poudyal at his Ranipool house, 2001 and 2005.
28. The Nation, dated 9.7.1979.
29. Ibid.
30. Ibid.
31. Petition circulated by Shri R.C.Poudyal to the Members of Parliament, dated 31.07.1979.
32. Ibid.
33. Election Manifesto of Sikkim Congress (Revolutionary), dated 22.09.1979.
34. Election Manifesto of Sikkim Prajatantra Congress, 1979.
35. Sikkim Herald, Vol. 20, No. 89, dated 19.10.1979.
36. *'Wanted Politician Governor'* Sikkim Express, Vol. IV, No. 66, July 18, 1980.
37. Statesman, dated 31.08.1983.
38. The Opposition leaders in Rajya Sabha urged the President to admonish the Governor for having attended a meeting of the Congress (I) addressed by its President, Mrs. Indira Gandhi, in Sikkim.
39. T.R. Sharma: *Sikkim Hinja Dekhi Aaja Samma*, Ankur Prakashan, Gangtok, 1996. Pp. 277-78.
40. Late Chamla Tshering Bhutia in 'SMARIKA' published by Sikkim Sangram Parishad, 1992, P. 40.
41. Letter of the Chief Minister Bhandari to the Prime Minister Indira Gandhi, dt. 14/11/1981.
42. Election Manifesto of the Sikkim Sangram Parishad, Inkprint, Siliguri, 1984,-85.

43. Op.cit. No. 41.

44. Bhandari's noting on the Report of the Secretary, SC/ST Welfare Department, Government of Sikkim, dated 22.08.1987. Also refer letter of Shri Mata Prasad, Additional Secretary, Ministry of Welfare, Government of India, to Shri P.K.Pradhan, Chief Secretary, Government of Sikkim, D.O.No. 12016/17/810 SCD (R-CELL), dated 18.12.1991.

45. Interview with Shri Birbal Subba (Tamling), Ex. MLA and the signatory in the memorandum submitted to the President of India, dated 14.06.1990.

46. *'Limboo and Tamangs to be made Scheduled Tribes'*, Sikkim Observer, dated 08.10.1991.

47. *Sikkim Perspectives and Vision*, Government of Sikkim Publication in association with Indus Publishing Co., New Delhi, 2003, P 5.

48. *Footnote*: actually Non-Backward Classes but in the context of Sikkim it meant Newar, Bahun (Brahmin) and Chhetri.

49. J.N.Kazi: *Inside Sikkim-Against the Tide*, Hill Media Publication, Gangtok, Sikkim, 1993, P. 321.

50. Ibid, P. 30.

51. Memorandum submitted to the President of India, R. Venkataraman, by the Chief Minister of Sikkim, Shri N.B.Bhandari, dated 21.10.1991.

52. B.B.Basnet: *'Comment on Gopal Gurung's book "Hidden Facts in Nepalese Politics"*, Baba Offset Press, Tadong, Sikkim, 2004, P. 128.

53. *Footnote*: The President of India assented to the Bill on 31st August, 1992 and was published in the Government Gazette on 1st September, 1992.

54. Cited in Op cit. No. 39, P. 288.

55. Press release by Shri P. Thondup, Joint Secretary, Deptt. of Information and Public Relations, Government of Sikkim, dated the 29th March, 1994.

56. Ibid.

57. Abstract from the memorandum submitted by N.B.Bhandari, Chief Minister of Sikkim, signed by all the 31 member of the SSP to the

President of India, Shri S.D.Sharma, on 19.04.1994.

58. Legislative proceedings, Special Session, 17th March 1994, Sikkim Legislative Assembly Secretariat, Gangtok, Sikkim.
59. Ibid.
60. Op. cit. No. 47.
61. Ibid.
62. Ibid.
63. Ibid.
64. Prajatantra, dated 25.05.1994.
65. Times of India, dated 16.11.1994.
66. The Telegraph, dated 22.10.1994.
67. Op. cit. No. 47.
68. Sikkim Government Gazette, No. 60, dated 02.06, 1994.
67. Sikkim Government Gazette, No. 94, dated 11.04.2000.
68. *Footnote*: the expression 'Limboo' includes 'Tsong', 'Subba' & 'Yakthungba' and the expression 'Sunuwar' includes 'Koincha' & 'Mukhia'. Sikkim Government Gazette, No. 60, dated 02.06.1994).Sikkim Government Gazette, Extraordinary No. 307, dated 17.09.2003.
69. Memorandum of the State Government, dated 25.08.1995; Memorandum of the State Government, dated 19· 12. 1995 and others.
70. Sikkim Government Gazette, Extraordinary Gazette no. 308, dated 17/09/2003
71. Sikkim Government Gazette, Extraordinary Gazette no. 307, dated 17/09/2003.
69. Reference No. CON/CAB/55/2003, dated 16.09.2003.
70. Speech Delivered on 1st January 2000, Gangtok.
71. Sikkim Government Gazette, Extraordinary No. 11, dated 21. 06. 1975.
72. Notification LR. No. 12089/L & F 91950.
73. Noting of the Chief Minister Bhandari on the Report of the

Secretary, SC/ST and Welfare Department, Government of Sikkim, dated 19/08/1987.

74. Brass: *Ethnicity and Nationalism*, Sage Publication, New Delhi, 1991, Pp. 272-277)

75. Speech Delivered on 1st January, 2000, Gangtok.

76. Sikkim Government Gazette, Extraordinary No. 11, dated 21/06/1975.

77. Notification LR. No. 12089/L & F /91950.

78. Three Basic Issues, a government publication (undated).

79. Ibid.

80. Op. cit. No. 25.

81. Op. cit. No. 25.

81. Amrita Bazar Patrika, dated 25.11.1978.

82. Op. cit. No. 14, P. 171.

83. Ibid.

84. The Nation, Gangtok, dated 27.01.1979.

85. *'Election Scene in Sikkim'* by Santosh Nirash, Broader News and Views, Vol. II, NO. 6-7, April-May, 1979, P. 5.

86. Amrita Bazar Patrika, dated 05.09.1979.

87. Sikkim Express, Vol. VI, No. 21, July 9-15, 1981.

88. Op. cit. No. 78, P. 263.

89. Legislative Proceedings, Fourth Assembly, 17-18 January, 1990, SLAS, Gangtok, Pp. 155-56.

90. Legislative Proceedings, Third Assembly, Seventh & Eighth Session, 1987-88, SLAS, Gangtok, Pp 155-56.

91. J.N.Kazi: *Inside Sikkim- Against the Tide*, Hill Media Publication, Gangtok, 1993, P 264

92. Legislative Proceedings, Third Assembly, Fourth Session, 17-21 March, 1986, SLAS, P. 254.

93. Ibid. P. 254.

94. Resolution taken on the Fourth Annual Anniversary of Foundation of Sikkim Sangram Parishad, Gangtok, dated 24.05.1988.

95, Ibid.

96. Op. cit. No. 91, Pp. 269-70.

97. Ibid, P. 266.

98. Memorandum of the STWA to the Governor of Sikkim, Bhishma Narayan Singh, October 1985.

99. Ibid.

100. The Statesman, dated 02.10.1988.

101. Resolution of the Denzong Tribal Yargay Chogpa, Gangtok, November, 1988.

102. Sikkim Code, Vol. II, Part I, Deptt. of Law, Government of Sikkim Publication, Gangtok, P. 288.

103. Legislative Proceedings, Fourth Assembly, Monsoon Session, August 1990, SLAS, Gangtok.

104. Shillong Times, dated 26.08.1988; Times of India, dated 07.08.1990.

105. Op. cit No. 97, P. 277.

106. Press Statement issued by the State Pradesh Congress Committee (I), dated October 1989.

107. Election Manifesto of Sikkim People's Party, Lok Sabha Election, dated 20th May, 1991, pp. 7-8.

108. Op. cit. no. 105, P. 278.

109. Ibid, P. 278-79.

110. Memorandum submitted by Jana Mukti Morcha to the Governor of Sikkim, R.J.Tahliani in August 1990.

111. Letter of L.G.Rimpoche, President, Denzong People's Chogpa, to the Chief Secretary, K.C.Pradhan, Government of Sikkim, dated 08.09.1990.

112. Resolution of the Meeting of the Mayel Lyang Tribal Organization, dated 08.10.1989.

113. Op.cit. No. 109, P. 284.

114. Ibid, P. 284.

115. Interview with Bharat Basnet, President of the All Sikkim Youth

Contractors Association, dated 22.06.1998.

116. *Footnote*: The Sikkim (Citizenship) Amendment Order, 1989 did not obliterate the Sikkim Subject Regulation of 1961 as the basis for grant of Citizenship to the left-out persons. It simply facilitated entry of few more names in the Subject Regulation omitted genuinely earlier.
117. Amrita Bazar Patrika, dated 25.08.1979.
118. Ibid, dated 24.02.1979.
119. Broader New And Views, Vol. II, No. 8 & 9, June-July 1979, Pp. 14-15.
120. The Nation, dated 09.07.1979.
121. Ibid.
122. Broader New and Views, Vol. II, No. 6 & 7, April-May, 1979, P. 5.
123. The Nation, dated 06.01.1979.
124. Copy of the petition circulated by R.C.Poudyal to the members of the Parliament, dated 31.07.1979.
125. Ibid.
126. The Nation, dated 06.08.1979.
127. Ibid.
128. Amrita Bazar Patrika, dated 14.08.1979.
129. The Statesman, dated 19.08.1979.
130. The Statesman, dated 18.08.1979.
131. The Statesman, dated 19.08.1979.
132. Amrita Bazar Patrika, dated 02.09.1979.
133. Sikkim Government Gazette, No. 75, dated 07.09.1979.
134. Ibid.
135. Ibid.
136. Op. cit. No. 109, P. 229.
137. Sikkim Durbar Gazette, No. 2, dated 07.08.1956.
138. Op. cit. No. 3, P. 31.
139. Sikkim Durbar Gazette, Extraordinary Gazette, No. 15, dated 06.12.1969.
140. Sikkim Durbar Gazette, Extraordinary Gazette No. 19, dated 31/

12/1969.

141. Legislative Proceedings, Seventh Lok Sabha, Budget Session, February-March, 1980, P. 141.

142. Ibid, Pp. 139-40.

143. Ibid, Pp. 141-43.

144. Ibid, Pp. 145-46.

145. Ibid, Pp. 150-52.

146 Ibid, Pp. 147-48.

157. Ibid. Pp. 148.

158. Ibid, P. 148.

149. B.B.Gurung, *"Seat Reservation in Sikkim Assembly'* in Sikkim Express, Vol. XXVII, No. 23, Dated 23.05.2003 and No. 25, dated 26.05.2003.

150. Legislative Proceedings, Second Assembly, Second Budget Session, 10-11 March, 1980, SLAS, Gangtok.

151. Ibid.

152. Op. cit. No. 78

153. Legislative Proceedings, Second Assembly, Ninth Session, September 1983, Pp. 86-120.

154. Op. cit. No. 152.

155. Op. cit. No. 136.

156. Ibid, P.133.

157. Ibid, P.129.

158. Ibid, P.131.

159. Ibid, P. 132.

160. Ibid, P. 336.

161. AIR, September 1993, Pp. 1832 – 1836.

162. Varadhan Committee Report, Government of Sikkim, p. 7.

163. Survival Sikkimese: The Final Conclusion, Gangtok, December 1995, P. 7.

164. Ibid, P. 2.

165. 'Document' published in Sikkim Observer, Vol. XV, No.33, dated 21-27 October, 2000.

166. Weekend Review, Vol. 2, No. 10, dated September 3-9, 1999.

167. Sikkim Observer, Vol. XV, No. 33, dated 21-27 Oct., 2001.

168. Copy of the proposal published in Hamro Parajashakti, dated 2-8 August, 2000.

169. Op. cit. No. 167.

170. Ibid; Weekend Review, Vol. 2, No. 14, dated 20-26 October, 2000.

171. Letter of Arun Jaitley, Union Minister for Law, Government of India, to Anjan Upadhyay, Prsident of the CPI(M) State Unit, Sikkim, dated 23.12.2003.

172. NOW, Vol. 1, No. 2, dated 16-22 April, 2003.

173. '*Kranti'*, No. 1, published by Gorkha Apex Committee, 2003; NOW, vol. 1, No. 31, dated January 29-4 February, 2003.

174. NOW, Vol. 1, No. 34, dated 19-25 February, 2003.

175. Weekend Review, dated 21-27 February, 2003.

176. Sikkim Government Gazette, Extraordinary Gazette No. 440, December 2005.

177. NOW, Vol. 2, No. 3, dated 9-15 July, 2003.

178. Op. cit. No. 45.

179. Ibid.

180. Op. cit. No. 160, P. 126.

181. D.O. No. 18 (3)/Home/75, dated 19th April, 1976.

182. D.O.No. BC-12016/24/75-SCTV, dated 21.07.1976, Ministry of Home Affairs, Government of India, Shastri Bhawan, Room No. 604, A-Wing, New Delhi.

183. Ibid.

184. Ibid.

185. Ibid.

186. Sikkim Government Gazette, Ex. Gazette No. 93, dated 12.07.1978.

187. *Footnote*: B.B.Gurung, who was part of the L.D.Kazi government,

once stated that *"Kazi Saab told me that if the Sherpas had not been included in the list, then the B-Ls (Bhutia-Lepcha) would never have got the 12 seats that they enjoy today"*. NOW, Vol. 1, No. 34, dated 19-25 February, 2003.

188. Op. cit. No.183.

189. Copy of the letter of the Chief Minister, Shri N.B.Bhandari, to the Prime Minister of India, Morarji Desai, dated 14.11.1981.

190. D.O.No. 155/SC/ST WD, dated 02.06.1987.

191. D.O.No. 12016/28/87 – SCD (R. Cell), dated 22.07.1987.

192. Copy of the telegram sent to Shri Pasang Namgyal, Secretary, SC/ST Welfare Department, Government of Sikkim, by Shri S.S.Verma, Secretary, Ministry of Welfare, Government of India, D.O.No. 12016/28/87 – SCD (R. Cell), dated 31.07.1987.

193. Copy of the Report submitted by Passang Namgyal, Secretary, SC/ST Welfare Department, government of Sikkim, to Shri Sanchaman Limboo, Minister, SC/ST Welfare Department, Government of Sikkim, dated 19.08.1987.

194. Ibid with official noting of State's Chief Minister, N.B.Bhandari, on the Report submitted by Passang Namgyal, Secretary, SC/ST Welfare Department, Government of Sikkim.

195. Copy of the letter of Shri Mata Prasad, Additional Secretary, Ministry of Welfare, Government of India, to Shri P.K.Pradhan, Chief Secretary, Governmtn of Sikkim, D.O.No. 120616/17/810 SCD (R. Cell), dated 18.12.1991.

196. *Footnote*: The book *"Hidden Facts in Nepali Politics"* by Gopal Gurung talks about racial division and discrimination against the Mongoloid by the Aryan within the Nepali community in Nepal. The time of publication of the book (i.e. first print 1986 and second in 1988) and imposition of ban on its circulation in Sikkim had been crucial in this regard.

197. Copy of the letter of N.B.Bhandari, President, SSP, to B.B.Subba, Minister of Power, Gov ernment of Sikkim, Ref. No. 291/SSP/90-

91, dated 30.06.1990.

198. Copy of the letter of Ministry of Home Affairs, Government of India, D.O. No. 11012/1/87 – NE-111, dated 20.09.1994; Draft copy of the Scheduled Tribes Order (Amendment) Ordinance, 1994.

199. D.O.No. 26/CMS/95, dated 17.06.1995.

200, Memoranda of the Chief Minister Chamling to the concerned Ministry, Government of India dated 25th August, 1995; 19th December, 1995; 18th July,1997; 30th March, 1998; 10th November, 1999; 22nd April, 2000.

201. The Gazette of India, Ex. Gazette Part II, Section I, No. 10, New Delhi, dated 08.01.2003. Published for information by Home Department, Government of Sikkim vide Ref. No. 17/Home/2003, dated 05.04.2003.

202. Hamro Prajashakti, dated September 26 – 02 October, 2001.

203. Ibid.

204. Birbal Subba (Tamling), *'Sikkimay Limboo and Tamang Birodhi Narbahadur Bhandari ko Kalo Kartutharo'*,Tamling Family, He Gaon, West Sikkim, 2004, P. 33.

205. Memorandum of the Sikkim Limboo Tamang Joint Action Committee, dated 30.04.2003.

206. Ibid.

207. Sikkim Express, dated 27.09.2005.

208. Copy of the letter of L.B.Senate, Jt. Secretary, National Commission for SC/ST, Government of India, to the Chief Secretary, Government of Sikkim, No. 17/11/2003 (C-CELL), dated 15th October, 2003.

209. Sikkim Government Gazette, No. 130, dated 6th July, 1995.

210. Sikkim Government Gazette, No. 307, dated 17th September, 2003.

211. Hamro Prajashakti, dated 19-25 September, 2001.

212. NOW, dated 18-24 December, 2002.

213. Weekend Review, dated 25-27 February, 2004.

214. Weekend Review, dated 18-24 April, 2003; Also read memorandum submitted by Shri P.K.Chamling, Chief Minister of

Sikkim, to Shri A.B.Bajpai, Prime Minister of India, dated 23rd July, 2003.

215. *Footnote*: Answer given in the Rajya Sabha by the Minister for State for Law and Justice, Shri K. Venkatapathy, dated 14th March, 2005 to the unstarred question no. 1325 asked by Shri Pyarelal Khandelwal, Member of Rajya Sabha.

216. D.O.No. 405/CMS-2003, dated 05.05.2003.

217. D.O.No. 1021/CMO/SKM, dated 27.12.2004.

218. D.O.No. IV/11015/1/2005-CSR-11, dated 30.05.2005.

219. Sinha Committee Report, May 2005.

220. Op.cit. no. 219. Also read NOW, dated 22.10.2005.

221. NOW, Vol. 5, No. 7, dated 22.03.2006.

222. Letter of Shri A.K.Srivastava, the Joint Secretary, Ministry of Home Affairs, to Shri N.D.Chingapa, the Chief Secretary of Sikkim, dated 01.05.2006.

223. NOW, dated 09.05.2006; Hamro Prajashakti, dated 15.05.2006; Sikkim Express, dated 18.05.2006

6

Political and Ethnic Organizations: The Issue of Ethnic Identity

It is an acknowledged fact that political parties and organizations tend to be ethnically oriented in terms of their membership, goals and support base in societies where ethnic cleavages play a significant role in determining social relations. Political parties and organizations in their turn may enhance the possibilities of ethnic divisions and conflicts. In a parliamentary democracy or a democratic polity which is ethnically divided, chances of emergence of ethnic political parties and organizations are greater for the simple reason that democratic institutions allow and facilitate such ethnic mobilization in the form of a party or organization. On the other hand, ethnic groups also may find it convenient to organize themselves around political party or organization because it facilitates ethnic groups to permeate democratic institutions and thereby influence the decision-making process.

But interestingly, parties based on ethnic cleavages are in a sense incompatible or inconsistent with the image and meaning of a political party. Political parties as modern institution are expected to convert exclusive and segmental interest into public interest. The political party appeals to common interests or attempts to create a combination of interests. Harowitz remarks that the very concept of party is challenged by a political party, i.e. both ascriptive and exclusive.[1] In this sense ethnically based party or an ethnic party is a misnomer. Gabriel Almond points out that 'particularistic parties' like the ethnic party are more like pressure groups.[2] In India, however, exclusivist ethnically oriented parties like Akali Dal, Asom Ghana Parishad etc. are legally recognized as political parties. In Sikkim the social differences in ascriptive terms are manifested in the formation of political parties and social organization which emphasize exclusive ethnic goals. Often political party or organization uses a more general name to conceal its ethnic bias. In such cases the ethnic party concerned may try to project or define the particular ethnic interest in such a way that it becomes a general interest. For instance, the Sikkim National Party was essentially a party representing Bhutia-Lepcha interest but had used the nomenclature 'national' party. There was a deliberate attempt at identification of Sikkim's 'national interest' with the Bhutia-Lepcha interests. Similarly, the Sikkim State Congress though clearly representing interests of the Nepalis, masked its identity with a universal demand for 'democracy'. At another level, as Harowitz points out, that the influences of ethnic politics is not limited to ethnically based parties and organizations but even the non-ethnic parties are also compelled to fall in the line by supporting ethnic demands in order to ensuring electoral survival.[3] Hence, it is found that the political parties like Sikkim Sangram Parishad (SSP) and Sikkim Democratic Front (SDF) in Sikkim which otherwise focus on common issues and interests had also in the past raised and defended demands of a particular ethnic community with a view to mustering electoral support from that community – this section explores the relation between ethnically based political parties and organizations in the one hand and contours of ethnic politics on the other.

Political Organizations: Pre-merger era.

Before 1947 the political environment was basically unfavourable for formation of political organization though elements representing ruling elite like Kazis/landlords and Lamas representing monasteries, had maintained organization like Denzong Lhade Tsogpa, for their own parochial and vested interests. Thus, political parties as an institution based on democratic principle emerged only after 1947 in Sikkim. Darjeeling being politically advanced and ethno-geographically contiguous with Sikkim played a contributory role in the growth of political consciousness and formation of political organizations in Sikkim, particularly after the independence of India and introduction of parliamentary democracy.

As stated earlier, three social welfare organizations namely Praja Sudharak Samaj at Gangtok, the Rajya Praja Sammelan at Temi and the Praja Mandal at Chakhung were formed in 1947.[4] These social organizations also had certain political demands. On the 7th of December, 1947, Praja Sudharak Samaj called its first ever public meeting at Polo Ground (now Palzor Stadium) at Gangtok under the leadership of Tashi Tshering and C.D.Rai. The other two social organizations namely Praja Sammelan and Praja Mandal were also invited in the meeting. Mrs. Helen Lepcha, Gandhiji called her Sabitri Devi a veteran leader of Indian National Congress from Darjeeling, was specially invited to address the gathering. A pamphlet entitled "A Few Facts about Sikkim State" written by Tashi Tshering and translated into Nepali by C.D.Rai was distributed among the people. The pamphlet was an attempt to educate people with the nature of exploitation and atrocities perpetuated by the Kazis and Thikadars upon them. In the evening the leaders of all the three organizations met at the residence of Dimik Singh Lepcha and decided to form a strong political party by merging the three premier social organizations. The meeting was chaired by Dimik Singh Lepcha.

Sikkim State Congress (SSC): Beginning of political process:

It was in this tripartite meeting of the three premier organizations on December 7, 1947 at Gangtok that Sikkim State Congress (SSC) was born.[5] Tashi Tshering was elected as the President while Raghubir Singh Basnet became the Vice-President of the party. Bhim Bahadur Rai and Dimik Singh Lepcha became the Joint Secretaries and C.D.Rai, Prem Bahadur Basnet, Nagendra Singh Gurung, C.B.Rai, Brihaspati Prasai, Sonam Tshering, Martam Topden, Dathup Tshering, Chuk Tshering, Chedup Lepcha and

Ram Prasad were the members of the working committee. On December 9, 1947 a five-member delegation of the party met the Chogyal and submitted a memorandum consisting of three major demands: (i) immediate abolition of landlordism, (ii) installation of an interim government leading in due course to full-fledged democratic government and (iii) accession of Sikkim to India.[6] A copy of the article "A Few Facts about Sikkim State" was enclosed with the memorandum.

The Chogyal agreed to abolish Zamindari system in phased manner. He also agreed to induct three representatives of the party in the government as Secretaries. The State Congress in its meetings held on 2nd and 3rd of February, 1948, recommended Tashi Tshering, Sonam Tshering and Raghubir Singh Basnet as Party's representatives to the Chogyal's administration. Later Tashi Tshering was replaced with Captain Dimik Singh Lepcha.[7] The Chogyal appointed the trio as Secretaries to the government.[8] The activities of the three party nominees, however, appeared to be against the three basic demands of the party.[9] The State Congress in its meeting, dated 21st March, 1948, passed a resolution asking its nominees to resign, but they did not resign. In another meeting at Namchi, dated 22nd October, 1948, the party passed three resolutions namely removal of the three nominees from the party, merger of Sikkim with India and sending a two-member delegation to New Delhi to meet the Indian Prime Minister, Jawaharlal Nehru. Though Dimik Sing Lepcha apologized and joined the party again in March, 1949, the exit of Sonam Tshering from the Sikkim State Congress affected the party tremendously.

In November, 1948, Tashi Tshering and C.D.Rai met the Prime Minister of India and apprised him with Party's three basic demands. After returning from Delhi, the Party launched a "No-Rent Campaign" in February 1949 and some of its leaders were arrested. The Sikkim State Congress resorted to Satyagraha movement as the negotiation with the Chogyal for release of their leaders was failed. Thousands of party supporters participated in the movement and ultimately the Chogyal agreed to form a five-member Council of Ministers in May, 1949 along with assurances to abolish Zamindari system and differential rate of revenue.

In May 1949, a five-member 'popular ministry' was formed in which three members (Tashi Tshering and Dimik Singh Lepcha) were nominated by the Sikkim State Congress.[10] Tashi Tshering was appointed the Chief Minister by the Chogyal. The ministry, however, could not function owing to stiff contradiction prevailing between the supporters of the two rival parties regarding abolition of landlordism, and also due to the absence of rules delineating powers between the Chogyal and the Ministry.

In 1950, a friendship treaty between the Chogyal and the Government of India was signed in New Delhi but the demand of the Sikkim State Congress for merger was not materialized. With the signing of the Treaty of 1950, which declared Sikkim as a protectorate of India, the establishment of a democratic government became SSC's first priority.[11] It participated in the Panchayat election held in 1950 and also in the conference called upon by the Chogyal to decide on the issue of number and nature of representatives in the State Council of Sikkim in 1951. As mentioned earlier, contrary to the instruction of the party high command, the two SSC representatives signed on the "Parity Formula" which provided for equal number of seats for minority Bhutia-Lepcha and majority Nepali communities in the State Council of Sikkim. The parity formula was designed to check the domination of the Nepalis in the affairs of the State. The two representatives were removed from the Party. The party also demanded changes in the March 23, 1953 Proclamation which prescribed for two types of election rules – one for the Bhutia-Lepcha and another for the Nepali candidates. Though the party won all 6 Nepali seats in 1953 council election, all the leading Bhutia-Lepcha candidates contesting from SSC, including the party President Tashi Tshering and Kazi Lhendup Dorji, were defeated in the primary election itself due to the communal nature of the election rules. Tashi Tshering died shortly after his defeat in the 1953 Council election and Kazi Lhendup Dorji became the President of the Party. But, the growing intimacy between the

SSC councilor, Kashi Raj Pradhan, and the Chogyal intensified differences between the President Kazi and the Councilor, which necessitated Kazi to leave the Party sometime in 1957. Kashi Raj Pradhan became the President of the Party while Kazi Lhendup Dorji formed his own 'Swatantra Dal' party.

In view of the Second Council election in 1958, the State Congress demanded representative government with the Chogyal as constitutional head and abolition of communal pattern of election rules introduced in 1953.[12] The election rules were modified in 1958 but the essential motive, i.e. division of society on ethno-cultural and religious grounds, continued. The SSC won 8 seats including one Bhutia-Lepcha and 1 General seat. Despite clear majority, Kashi Raj Pradhan did not stake claim to form the government. Apparently, he seemed to have been satisfied with the way he and his nephew, Nahkul Pradhan, were appointed as Executive Councilor. He perhaps also did not like to antagonize the Dewan and the Chogyal by making such demands. Basnet writes that "the SSC under the Presidentship of Kashi Raj Pradhan had come to completely identify itself with the interest of the Maharaja (Chogyal).......though it continued to talk of democracy and responsible government and pass pious resolutions to that effect as a sop to the masses".[13] The Election Tribunal, formed by the Chogyal to investigate into the allegation of election malpractice, found the two SSC Councilors (Kashi Raj Pradhan and Nahkul Pradhan) guilty and 6 years ban from seeking election was imposed on them. They participated in the 'Joint Convention' organized by L.D.Kazi (Swatantra Dal), Sikkim National Party of Sonam Tshering faction, D.B.Tiwari (Praja Sammelan) and P.B.Khati (Scheduled Caste League) at Melli on the 24th of September, 1959. The Chogyal, however, reduced the sanction against the duo to 6 months with effect from the 15th of May, 1959 which made them eligible to contest the Council bye-election while Sonam Tshering, the Sikkim National Party councilor, was banned for 3 years who by this time had seized to enjoy the goodwill of the Chogyal. Interestingly, C.D.Rai, who was persuaded to resign from the post of Magistrate and projected as the official party candidate in the bye-election by none other than Kashi Raj Pradhan himself, was eventually denied party ticket. C.D. Rai, however, contested as an independent candidate and defeated Kashi Raj Pradhan by a huge margin.

It appeared that by the end of 1950s and early 1960s, the Sikkim State Congress had virtually become a family party in the hands of Kashi Raj Pradhan and his nephew, Nahkul Pradhan. The competition over party leadership led to desertion by those who founded the Party in 1947. Apart from this, the concerted effort displayed by the Chogyal and the Dewan, N.K.Rustomji, at the time of selection of members of the Executive Councilors also facilitated division and differences within the SSC leadership. For instance, when C.D.Rai was elected from the Namchi constituency in February 1960 bye-election, he was denied the Executive post whereas Nahkul Pradhan who retained his candidature from North-Central constituency was appointed as the Executive Councilor. As a consequence Sikkim National Party was born at Singtam on 8 May, 1960 by the SSC dissidents like C.D.Rai, Kazi Lhendup Dorji Khangsarpa and Sonam Tshering which, within a very short span of time, gained dominance over the SSC.

Sikkim National Party and Bhutia-Lepcha consolidation:

The growing popularity and organizational success of the Sikkim State Congress naturally created alarm among the ruling elite who, in order to counter the Sikkim State Congress politically, formed the Sikkim National Party, also called Chogyal's party, on the 30th April, 1948. Sonam Tshering, formerly the Sikkim State Congress's nominee to the Chogyal's government and was removed from the party for his anti-party activities, became the President of the party. L. B. Basnet observed, "The Sikkim National Party has sprung up with a curious programme which may be called the very antithesis of the policy of Sikkim State Congress."[14] This party soon became primarily the party of the Bhutia-Lepcha group.[15] The party adopted resolution showing inability to wipe out landlordism suddenly without giving rise to administrative difficulties and disruption.[16] The resolution also opposed accession of Sikkim with India on historical, social, cultural, linguistic, religious, ethnic and geographical grounds and called "democratic government in a small state like Sikkim is a farce".[17] By quoting Charles Bell, the party floated the concept of restoration of autonomous status of Sikkim of 1918.[18]

The two members of the Sikkim National Party, namely Kazi Dorji Dadul and R. P. Alley, were appointed in the Popular Ministry of May 1949[19] They, from the very beginning, were opposed to the demands of the Sikkim State Congress. The contradiction prevailing within the members of the Ministry led to dissolution of the same. The Panchayat election was held in December 1950 but the Sikkim National Party boycotted the election on the ground that the indigenous population, i.e. Bhutias and Lepchas, were not given adequate safeguards.[20] The contention of the National Party was that the Nepalis were later immigrants, while the Bhutias and Lepchas constituted the indigenous population.[21]

The National Party through its various pro-Bhutia-Lepcha propaganda campaigns succeeded in creating its own image as the nationalist party representing Bhutia and Lepcha communities and committed towards preservation of 'independence of Sikkim' and 'rule of the Chogyal' while the Sikkim State Congress was branded as the Nepali party and its sympathizers as anti-Sikkimese and supporters of the 'rule of the Dhotiwalas', i.e. Indians.[22] In fact, the National Party disliked the idea of introducing an alien system of Panchayati Raj at the cost of indigenous and age old institution of village administration, called Dzumsa. The Dzumsa system actually symbolized the cultural-political identity and domination of the Bhutias in rural administration but by introducing the Indian system of village administration, i.e. Panchayati Raj, it could have certainly diluted the Bhutia identity besides facilitating Nepalis to be in the helm of rural administration which the Bhutias always resented.[23] Basnet wrote that "in a country with low literacy and extreme all round backwardness, the combined forces of the National Party, the ruling house, the landlords and the Lamas succeeded"[24] in legitimizing an anti-national, anti-

Chogyal and anti-Bhutia-Lepcha image of the Sikkim State Congress and the Nepalis alike. However, in view of the demand for a representative government by the Sikkim State Congress, a Parity Formula was worked out in 1951 which arbitrarily clubbed the Bhutia-Lepcha communities into one and 6 seats were reserved for them in the 17-member State Council whereas Nepalis got 6 seats.[25] The provision of 5 nominated members by the Chogyal together with communal pattern of voting system introduced by the Proclamation of March 1953 was intended to perpetuate ethnic division and domination of the ruling elite in the legislative affairs of the State. The proposal of the Sikkim State Congress favouring one representation each from the three major communities of Sikkim was opposed by the Sikkim National Party.[26] The affect of the communal system of seat reservation and peculiar nature of voting was reflected in the 1953 Council election in which all the Bhutia-Lepcha candidates contesting from Sikkim State Congress, including Kazi Lhendup Dorji Khangsarpa and Tashi Tshering, were defeated in the preliminary election itself while all the Nepali candidates contesting from the Sikkim National Party suffered defeat at the final election. The defeat of the leading SSC members together with differences over the issue of 'Parity Formula' led to split in the Sikkim State Congress.

In view of the 1958 election, the State Council was enlarged while the communal and complicated system of election continued. The Sikkim National Party supported Chogyal's decision to create one 'Sangha' seat for the monasteries and one 'General' seat. The Sangha seat was yet another means to legitimize religious polarization between the Bhutia-Lepchas, who were Buddhist and Nepalis who were basically Hindus. The logic behind the creation of General seat was also ambiguous as it was not meant for the plainsmen community settled in Sikkim.

After the polls the candidature of Sonam Tshering (SNP) was challenged on the ground of adopting election malpractice. The Election Tribunal found him guilty of the charge and was deprived of his seat in the Council and disqualified for contesting Council Election for 6 years. Later, the ban was reduced to three years.

Sonam Tshering left the party after he was removed from party's Presidentship and formed a faction within the SNP. He nursed animosity with the Darbar for he believed that his disqualification for a period of three years was effectively to bar him from contesting the bye-election scheduled in February 1, 1960. Sonam Tshering along with other SSC dissidents like Chandra Das Rai and L.D.Kazi formed Sikkim National Congress in 1960.

Netuk Tshering, popularly called Netuk Lama, was given party ticket in the bye-election and was elected from the Gangtok constituency. Netuk Tshering was initiated in Lamaist tradition in his childhood (belonged to Teling Monastery located near Gyantse in Tibet) which made him loyal towards the Royal family and the community to which he belonged. He would ask belligerently "Is the map of Sikkim separate or is it shown just like one of your (Indian) states?"[27] He joined Sikkim National Party in 1948 when he realized that the SSC would press for merger of Sikkim with India. He observed, "We must remain Sikkimese. There can be no merger with India, Tibet, Nepal or Bhutan."[28] He accused the politicians for country's 'disintegration' and expressed confidence that "the Government of India will not lag behind in fulfilling the ambitions of our people in enabling us to enjoy the status like that of Nepal and Bhutan."[29] He also wanted Sikkim to issue its own passports, export abroad and receive aids directly from other countries.

However, Netuk Tshering (Lama) did not belong to Darbar's inner circle and the Kazis viewed his loyalty towards the Chogyal with considerable misgivings. This perhaps had incited Netuk Tshering (Lama) to demand for more powers to the People's representatives. Such a demand being unusual in the Sikkim National Party, it led to a split in SNP in 1969 – one led by Martan Topden and another group by Netuk Tshering (Lama). But, despite division within the party, it enjoyed patronage from the Darbar to which the Bhutia-Lepcha voters were completely loyal and emotionally attached. It won 7 seats of which 4 belonged to the Netuk Tshering (Lama) faction in 1970 Council Election. Netuk Tshering (Lama) was elected the leader of the SNP in Council in an attempt to bridge the differences. But, Netuk used this opportunity to renew his demand for devolution of more powers in the hands of the elected representatives. He also parlayed with Kazi Lhendup Dorji Khangsarpa with a view to forming a "democratic coalition" in the Council. The Chogyal, on the other, took this opportunity to alleviate Martam Topden as the leader of SNP in the Council and the Senior Executive Councilor replacing Netuk Tshering (Lama). As a result, the differences between the two SNP leaders continued.

In view of the political developments of the 1960's and early 1970's in favour of 'separate political identity of Sikkim', the SNP adopted more persuasive and an all-embracing approach. Martam Topden, old and sick, had retired from the leadership of the SNP leaving the command in the hands of a 66 year old Netuk Tshering (Lama). Under his leadership the nature of the party as an exclusive Bhutia-Lepcha party had been diluted to some extent. It had Nepali Councilors from the North, a Nepali General Secretary in Man Bahadur Basnet and a vice-President in Harka Bahadur Basnet. The Party's 1973 election manifesto promised to serve "the country, the King and the welfare of the Sikkimese masses" and announced that "the main objective of the party is to work for and to lead the country and her people towards prosperity and advancement commensurating the progress of the world under the able guidance of the Chogyal Chempo".[30] The strategy benefited the party immensely and in 1973 Council Election the party won 11 seats (Seven Bhutia-Lepcha, two Nepali seats), including the support that the Party enjoyed from the Sangha candidate (Panchen Lama) and the Scheduled Caste candidate (Purna Bahadur Khati).

Apparently, Netuk Tshering (Lama) believed in constitutional monarchy with people's representative exercising more powers and right of the majority party in the Council to form government in Sikkim. The Chogyal, however, was adamant to any drastic change and continued with the usual coalition of six-member Executive Council – 4 from the SNP, 1 Sikkim Janata Party (SJP) and 1 Sikkim National Congress. But, the allegation regarding rigging of election results in favour of the Sikkim National Party was followed by political turmoil which ultimately resulted in signing of the so-called Tripartite Agreement of the 8th May, 1973. The Agreement postulated the formation of a responsible government, wider legislative and executive powers for the elected representatives of the people, equitable representation to all sections of the people based on adult suffrage and one-man-one-vote principle, a Legislative Assembly to be elected for four years term and appointment of Election Commissioner by the Government of Sikkim to conduct and supervise the elections in Sikkim. The introduction of new election rules and reduction of Chogyal's powers in the affairs of the State had damaged the prospect of the party tremendously. In 1974 Assembly election it won only one seat out of a 32 elected seats.

The Independent Front and the Lepcha community:

In spite of being a ruling coalition of Sikkim, the Lepchas were subjected to discriminatory treatment of various kinds during the Bhutia rule. Their confinement in geographically isolated and infertile area of Dzongu, denial of modern education and separate political representation had profound effect on the socio-economic and political conditions of the Lepchas. Moved by the deteriorating socio-economic and political conditions of the Lepchas, Ruth Karthak (Lepcha), formed the Sikkim Independent Front party in 1966. In 1967 Council election the party fielded six candidates – one Nepali and five Lepchas – but all six nomination papers were rejected. According to L.B.Basnet the nomination papers were rejected on filmsy grounds.[31] On March 23, 1967, both Ms. Ruth Karthak Lepcha and her husband, A. Halim, were arrested under the Sikkim Security Act. Though, on January 3, 1968, Mr. Halim was deported, the same order could not be carried out against Mr. Ruth Lepcha for being a Sikkim Subject holder.[32] In the meanwhile, the Government Proclamation was issued declaring 'a Sikkimese woman marrying a non-Sikkimese shall automatically lose her Sikkim Subjecthood.' Under this provision Ruth Karthak Lepcha was stripped of all legal-political protection and was subsequently banished from Sikkim allegedly for fomenting communal hatred and instigating rebellion against the Chogyal and the Government.

Reportedly, she was alleged to have questioned the very foundation of the Bhutia rule in Sikkim that 'the present ruler of Sikkim is not its real ruler.... The Chogyal is a Bhutia, and the real rulers of Sikkim were Lepchas'.[33] It is said that Kazi Lhendup Dorji, who was then the President of the Lepcha Association of which Ms. Ruth Karthak Lepcha was the subscribing member, was reported to have maintained eloquent silence like leaders of other organizations. Her forceful deracination from the place of origin and the silence maintained by other Lepcha leaders was reflective of the political environment and deteriorating condition of the Lepchas under the Bhutia rules. It was the first recorded evidence of an attempt by the Lepchas to assert their separate identity, other than the combined B-L identity, and to present the grievances of the Lepcha community against the prevailing domination of Bhutia ruling elite.

Political Developments during the 1970s:

In October 1972 the Sikkim Janata Congress was formed by merging the Janata Party of L.B.Basnet (1969) and Sikkim State Congress of Nahkul Pradhan. The party accused the Darbar for the deteriorating condition of the Nepalis and demanded joint electorate system and abolition of the 'Parity' Formula.[34]

The 1973 election was followed by allegation of rigging. A minor political altercation between the candidates of Sikkim National Congress and the Sikkim National Party flared up into a communal tension between the Nepalis and Bhutias. A Joint Action Committee consisting of the members of the Sikkim Janata Congress and Sikkim National Congress was formed in March, 1973 and demanded abolition of 'parity' formula and communal voting system, full fledged democracy, a written constitution and fundamental rights, substitution of the discriminatory Sikkim Subjects Regulation of 1961, an advisory Council with people's representation etc.[35] The Joint Action Committee also alleged the Chogyal for arming the Tibetan refugees and using them against the people observing peaceful movement.[36] The Committee, in other words, was essentially demanding for representative government and abolition of preferential treatment or special privilege status for the ruling ethnic community.

On the 8th May, 1973, a so-called Tripartite Agreement was signed between the Chogyal, the Government of India and the two major political parties namely Sikkim National Congress and Sikkim Janata Congress. The Agreement promised for the establishment of a full responsible government, a democratic constitution, fundamental rights, the rule of law, an independent judiciary, greater legislative and executive power for the elected representatives of the people, adult franchise, equitable representation to all sections of the people and one man one vote principle of voting.[37] The election to a 32 member Legislative Assembly was held in April, 1974. The Sikkim Congress, formed after merging the Sikkim Janata Congress and Sikkim National Congress, swept the poll by winning 31 seats, including the Sangha seat. The National Party won only one seat. On 10 May, 1974, the Chogyal inaugurated the newly constituted Sikkim Legislative Assembly but formation of Ministry was delayed till July due to contradiction prevailing between the Chogyal and the Assembly over the passage of the Government of Sikkim Bill, 1974. The Chogyal, however, assented to the Bill on the 4th of July, 1974, in anticipation to New Delhi's unsupportive gesture. On 23 July, 1974, a five member Sikkim Congress Ministry led by Kazi Lhendup Dorji Khangsarpa was installed. Care was taken to maintain ethnic balance in the Ministry (i.e. 2 Lepchas, 2 Nepalis and 1 Bhutia).

Political Parties: Post – merger era:

Soon after the merger of Sikkim with India, the Sikkim Congress, as a part of political strategy, merged with the Indian National Congress. Later, the lone member of the National Party in the Assembly too joined the Congress Party and with it the State Assembly was virtually left with no opposition. But dissension within the party persisted.

Till 1977, the Chief Minister Kazi Lhendup Dorji maintained a complete grip over the party. In February 1977, N.B.Khatiwada, the youth Congress leader, along with three other M.L.As deserted

L.D.Kazi and formed a state unit of the Congress for Democracy formed by Jagjivan Ram.[38] Khatiwada criticized the Chief Minister Kazi for depending completely on the "imported bureaucrats" who, according to Khatiwada, "knew nothing of Sikkim and felt nothing for Sikkim".[39] By emphasizing the need for maintaining Sikkim's distinct character and needs, Mr. Khatiwada sown the seeds of regional politics in Sikkim after the merger. When the Janata Party came to power at the centre, Kazi along with 26 M.L.As merged with the Janata Party. Kazi was criticized by the opposition as the 'man of mergers'.[40]

It was during this period series of agitations and public demonstrations took place all over Sikkim in protest against the performances of the government and merger with India. As an alternative to Kazi's party, N.B.Bhandari formed Sikkim Janata Party, a regional political organization, on 22 March, 1977.[41] Later, he changed its name to Sikkim Janata Parishad. After realizing no immediate political benefit, Khatiwada too changed the name of his party as the Sikkim Prajatantra Congress and joined hands with anti-merger forces. He demanded restoration of Sikkim to pre-1974 status. He and three other M.L.As of the party (Hemlata Chettri, Kushu Das and Chattur Singh Rai) also submitted a memorandum to the Prime Minister, Morarji Desai, stating "neither the Kazi nor the Sikkim Congress nor we as leaders had the mandate of the people to seek for the merger of Sikkim with India".[42] During the period (post 1977) a number of leaders like K.C.Pradhan, B.B.Gurung, the merger veterans, began to question the merger. Their main allegation was that the government of India headed by the Indian National Congress was violating the conditions of merger of Sikkim with India.[43]

There were disappointments and apprehensions among the people. The Kazi government failed to provide a better administration in Sikkim. The prices of essential commodities continued to rise, influx of outsiders could not be checked, the land reforms could not be implemented, agriculture sector remained neglected, corruption continued unabated and the gap between the rich and the poor was ever widening. It was said that the economic opportunities had remained confined to the privileged few. As a result anti-merger and anti-Indian feeling prevailed over the hearts and minds of people. The political parties, which were founded virtually to oppose the Chogyal and his administration, were devoid of long-term objectives and foresightedness and hence fallen prey to factional politics, which further weakened the prospects for political stability.

Regional Political Parties and Sikkimese Identity:

The ethnic mobility process and political organizations very often behave in symbiotic relationship. In a parliamentary democratic system where election becomes sole means to legitimate power, political parties find ethnic group as prospective source for fulfillment of their articulated objective. On the other hand, the ethnic groups also use political organizations as a platform for articulating community's demands and grievances. Since ethnic demands or questions generally include issues of protection and preservation of 'one' against the 'other', the regional parties, by virtue of their homogeneous nature and local outlook, naturally become favourites of ethnic organizations in comparison to the national parties.

The bitter experiences of the people of Sikkim with the national parties, especially with the Indian National Congress and the Janata Party in the post-1975 era, also seemed to be significant behind the emergence and support of the people towards the regional parties in Sikkim. The regional parties are in absolute control of the State's political machinery ever since the merger. Though their party constitutions do not highlight or proclaim preferences to any particular community or ethnic group but in practice, particularly through election manifestoes, they pursue policies highlighting issues of regional and ethnic importance, including allocation of party tickets considering the electoral strength of candidate's community in the constituency. In a constituency of hardly eight thousand voters at the maximum such alignments and strategies play decisive roles in the election. The regional political parties depend on local-parochial pattern of mobilization and once such mobilization is legitimized and become accepted, it contributes towards further escalation of mobilization on the basis of even more parochial identities. As a natural consequence, the communities are further divided into smaller group and ethnic communities, who so far considered as part of a relatively larger community, asserting their separate cultural identity. A brief excursion on these regional political parties, especially those having some degree of permanence, is, therefore, essential.

Sikkim Prajatantra Congress (SPC):

N.B.Khatiwada, owing to growing differences with Kazi Lhendup Dorji, left Indian National Congress in February 1977 and formed the state unit of the Congress for Democracy (CFD) under the tutelage of Jagjivan Ram. Later, it was renamed as Sikkim Prajatantra Congress. The party criticized the Kazi government for failing to implement land reform laws, for facilitating and increasing the number of the Indian servicemen to work in various government departments on deputation, for failing to check influx of Indian plainsmen, for failing to abolish parity system and Revenue Order No. 1. The party also demanded recognition of Nepali language as state language and its inclusion in the 8th Schedule of the Indian constitution.

He also questioned the legal basis of the merger and demanded referendum to ascertain the wishes of the people of Sikkim regarding merger.[44] Considering the merger as illegal, he stated, "All our questions with regard to the Bill were harshly brushed aside by the Chief Executive, B.S.Das, inside the Assembly, and by the Political Officer, K.S.Bajpai, and his senior staff members, outside the House. We were threatened to support the Bill or else face the consequences....There was a spontaneous demonstration by about ten thousand people of Gangtok, including government employees, objecting the passage of the Bill. The members of the Assembly and the leaders along with Kazi were virtually confined and kept hidden by the CRP...The proceedings of the Assembly were over in less than a record time of 15 minutes, which gives an indication as to the indecent haste with which the

Assembly was forced to pass the government of Sikkim Act in a midnight session of the Assembly. The Act was in English and about 20 members, including the Chief Minister Kazi, were not at all conversant with the language."[45] He and three other M.L.As of his Sikkim Prajatantra Congress (Hemlata Chettri, Kushu Das and Chattur Singh Rai) also submitted a memorandum to the Prime Minister, Morarji Desai, which stated, "neither the Kazi nor the Sikkim Congress nor we as leaders had the mandate of the people to seek for the merger of Sikkim with India, or to change the political status, or to perpetuate the kind of constitutional relationship with India into which we find our self today. Their mandate was for establishment of a full-fledged democracy on the basis of one-man-one-vote and a written constitution, whereby the Sikkimese people can enjoy basic human rights. All these promises to our innocent masses have been thrown to the wind and people have been sadly deceived and we deprived of our country".[46] He demanded restoration of Sikkim to the status of pre-1974 period and associated merger with loss of identity of the Sikkimese.

In 1979 Assembly election the Party demanded inclusion of Nepalis left out of the electoral rolls, restoration of Nepali seats in the State Assembly, maximum representation of the Sikkimese in the State administration and promotion of the interest of the Indian Nepalis settled in Sikkim after the merger.[47] The party also vehemently criticized the grant of political rights to the plainsmen, i.e. to contest and cast votes, in the Assembly election and did not give ticket to the plainsmen.

There was an anti-incumbency wave against the Kazi government in 1979, but SPC could not reap the best out of the situation as the other two parties (Sikkim Janata Parishad and Sikkim Congress Revolutionary) carried out relentless propaganda campaign against N.B.Khatiwada branding him as the right hand man of Kazi Lhendup Dorje in disguise. It managed to win only three seats in the 1979 election. In 1985 Assembly election the party did not win a single seat and with it the party gradually disappeared from the public eye. N.B.Khatiwada later became a sympathizer of the Indian National Congress (I) and even contested unsuccessfully in 1995 Lok Sabha election from the Darjeeling constituency as a Congress (I) candidate. In 2002, he was appointed as the Deputy Advocate General of the Government of Sikkim but resigned in 2004 amidst political pressure owing to his involvement with an ethnic organization, called Gorkha Apex Committee. In 2005, he, along with G.M.Rai and C.D.Rai, founded a new regional political party, called Sikkim Gorkha Prajatantrik Party.

Sikkim Janata Parishad (SJP):

The Sikkim Janata Party, formed by N.B.Bhandari on 22 March, 1977 at Gangtok,[48] was renamed as Sikkim Janata Parishad after the ruling Congress (I) party headed by Kazi Lhendup Dorji joined the Janata Party which came to power at the centre following the 1977 Lok Sabha election.

In 1979 Assembly election the party took up the issues of citizenship and reservation of seats for the Nepalis. Mr. Bhandari contended that a good number of genuine Sikkimese subjects were left out of the electoral rolls. He also alleged that the 1974 electoral rolls were full of discrepancies as because names of many persons who were neither Indian citizens nor Sikkim Subjects were included in the voters' list.[49] The party also accused the Kazi government for selling Sikkim to the 'Dhotiwalas', raised issues like abolition of the Tsong and Nepali seats in the State Assembly, protection of the rights of the Sikkimese by implementing 'Sons of the Soil' policy. The other notable slogans raised by the party in 1979 election were 'Sikkim for the Sikkimese', 'Bring back Sikkim', 'Ushering in Democracy', 'Destroy Communalism' and 'Discontinue Divisive Policy' etc. The party also assured self-respect and self-dignity to the people, if voted to power.[50] Regarding the issue of reservation of Nepali seat in the State Assembly, the party emphasized on the continuation of the formula as agreed upon in the Tripartite Agreement of 1973. The Party expressed fear that "the people from the plains would gradually oust them from all positions of importance."[51] Further, the party was also critical of the Kazi government for importing bureaucrats from Delhi on deputation and demanded dissolution of the Ministry for the sake of free and fair election.

The SJP won 16 seats in 1979 Assembly election and formed government with the support of the Sangha candidate (Gyaltsen Gomchen Rimpochey) and Chamla Tshering, a Sikkim Congress (Revolutionary) candidate who after the election defected to SJP. Bhandari's anti-merger stand and demand for reservation of seats for the Tsongs and Nepalis in the Assembly received overwhelming support both from the tribals, including the members of the defunct Sikkim National Party, and the Nepalis. The Party also won the lone Lok Sabha seat in 1980 but lost Khandong (SC) and Chakung Assembly seats in the bye-election held alongside the Lok Sabha election. In 1981 it enbloc joined the Congress Party (I). Thus, by merger Bhandari became the second Congress (I) Chief Minister, after Kazi Lhendup Dorje Khangsarpa.

Sikkim Congress (Revolutionary):

The introduction of the Representation of the People (Amendment) Bill in May 1979 in the parliament occasioned a rift within the ruling Janata Party in Sikkim. The Bill proposed to reserve 12 seats for the Bhutia-Lepcha, one for the Sangha, two for the Scheduled Castes and 17 as General seats. The Bill had no provision for reservation of seats for the Nepalis. Within the ruling Janata Party, R.C.Poudyal and his group opposed the 'Black Bill', as they preferred to call it. The general perception among the Nepalis, both leaders and layman alike, was that the government of India had discriminated against the Nepalis while the 25 percent Lepchas and Bhutias were provided with 40 percent seats in the Assembly.

Poudyal sent a memorandum signed by 14 ruling party leaders and M.L.As to the Union Minister for Law requesting him to reconsider the 'Bill'.[52] The Janata Party leadership at the centre condemned anti-party activities of Mr. Poudyal and was expelled from the party in the middle of June, 1979.[53]

On 8 July, the dissidents, including R.C.Poudyal, B.B.Gurung, N.K.Subedi, Adhiklall Pradhan and others, organized a public meeting at Gangtok. They expressed apprehension that if adequate steps were not taken immediately the Nepalis could be reduced to a minority. [54] Poudyal also circulated a petition among the members of the Union Parliament highlighting grievances of the Nepalis over the Bill No. 79.[55] In the meanwhile, Charan Singh replaced Morarji Desai as the Prime Minister of India. The dissident group requested the new Prime Minister to undo "the constitutional distortion committed by the L.D.Kazi government in Sikkim."[56] In the first week of September 1979, R.C.Poudyal declared the formation of a new party, called Sikkim Congress (Revolutionary), in a party convention at Jorethang.[57] The Party maintained that it would work for the abolition of Bill No. 79 or Black Bill, grant of citizenship to all the people living in Sikkim till 1970, to work for the recognition and inclusion of the Nepali language in the 8th schedule of the Constitution.[58]

The Sikkim Congress (Revolutionary) won 11 out of 31 contested seats and became the second largest party in 1979 Assembly election. R.C.Poudyal, however, did not contest the election in protest against the Bill No. 79 or Black Bill. In November 1984 the Sikkim Congress (Revolutionary) merged with the Congress (I) party and Poudyal became the President of the state unit of the Congress (I). The party was clearly appealing to and articulating the interest of the Nepali community. This was an instance of the process of gradual ethnicization of politics in Sikkim.

Sikkim Sangram Parishad (SSP):

Mr. N. B. Bhandari was dismissed from the post of the Chief Minister of Sikkim in May 1984 by the then Governor of Sikkim, H.J.Taleyarkhan, supposedly for ceasing to enjoy his pleasure. Bhandari left Congress (I) party in disgust along with his majority of legislators. He formed a new regional party, called Sikkim Sangram Parishad (SSP), at New Delhi on 23 May, 1984. It is said that the basic difference between Mr. Bhandari and the Governor Taleyarkhan revolved around the issue of Sikkim Subject. The Sikkim Subject certificate was/is the basis for public appointments in Sikkim. The Governor was of the impression that after the merger everyone living in Sikkim was an Indian national and, therefore, eligible for public appointments.[59]

In 1984, the B.B.Gurung government instituted C.B.I. enquiry against Mr. Bhandari on alleged charges of corruption in water supply scheme and import of cement. Bhandari during those days was reported "to have agreed to the merger with Indian National Congress (I) on the condition that the corruption charges filed against him by the Central Investigation Bureau were withdrawn".[60] It was also reported that he had requested the central government to withdraw the corruption charges against him should the merger of SSP with Congress (I) takes place.[61]

The SSP made a come back after winning the lone Lok Sabha seat in December 1984. The manifesto of the Party pledged to work for democracy, protection and preservation of the interests and rights of the Sikkimese, fostering communal harmony, national integration, secularism and development of Sikkim.[62] The SSP also secured majority in the State Assembly elections in 1985 and Bhandari became the Chief Minister of Sikkim for the second time. In 1985 Assembly election the Sikkim Sangram Parishad contested on the basis of five cardinal issues namely;

a) To maintain parity and restore seats reserved erstwhile for Sikkimese Nepalis;
b) To grant citizenship for people rendered stateless in Sikkim and to fix the cut off year at 1970;
c) To implement 'son of the soil' policy regarding all government jobs and trade licenses for maintaining Sikkimese identity;
d) To work for the constitutional recognition of the Nepali language under Eighth scheduled of the constitution; and
e) To demand for more financial and political freedom for the states of the Indian Union.[63]

It is to be noted that Mr. Bhandari condemned his opponents namely L.D.Kazi, B.B.Gurung, R.C.Poudyal etc., as architects of the merger and 'Desh Bechuwas' (sellers of the country) or 32 thieves. Thus, by raising the issue of Sikkim's merger with India, the SSP under Bhandari's leadership popularized the notion of Sikkimese identity as distinct from the Indian identity. It may be considered as a systematic exploitation of identity issue for political gains though he was not specifically using ideas of Nepali identity or Bhutia identity. Since then the Sikkimese view Indian identity as different from the Sikkimese identity.

In January 7, 1987 the Sikkim Government withdrew the consent given to the CBI for investigation of offences against Mr. Bhandari.[64] This notification put legislative restriction on the investigation process initiated against him by the Central Bureau of Investigation. However, in 1993, the Supreme Court reinforced the jurisdiction of the Central Bureau of Investigation in Sikkim and N.B.Bhandari was again charged in three cases - two cases for accumulating assets disproportionate to his known sources of income and another regarding abuse of power.[65] In 1987, as against central government's proposal, the Bhandari government declined to recommend for inclusion of the Limboos, Tamangs and Gurungs in the Scheduled Tribes list, most likely, not to offend the Bhutia-Lepcha tribal community of Sikkim. The decision favouring the Bhutia-Lepcha tribal community together with the grant of citizenship to about 80,000 left out Sikkimese in March 1989 had won him landslide victory in the November 1989 Assembly election. His party won all 32 Assembly seats and a lone Lok Sabha seat.

The National Front government under V.P.Singh (Janata Dal leader) assumed power at the centre in 1989. It sought to implement Mandal Commission recommendation regarding Other Backward Classes which was kept in abeyance since 1980. In compliance with the central directives the government of Sikkim prepared a list of OBC by introducing suitable adjustment in the list prepared earlier in 1980 by the Rajya Sabha member, Pahalman Subba. But the National Front government led by Janata Dal leader V.P.Singh was dissolved and fresh parliamentary election was held in 1991. The Congress party, which returned to power at the centre after 1991 Lok Sabha election, also went ahead with the Mandal Commission recommendation. Mr. Bhandari, however, was not interested in implementing Mandal Commission Report on the impression that such action might create division within the Nepali community.[66] The decision created a rift within the ruling Sikkim Sangram Parishad particularly between the OBC leaders and, the so-called, NBC (actually Non-Backward Classes but in Sikkim it represented the upper caste Nepalis like Newar, Bahun and Chhetri). Mr. P.K. Chamling, belonging to the OBC community, was expelled from the ministry on 16 July, 1992 as a consequence of the growing differences within the ruling party.[67] Even though the Nepali language was accorded recognition in the Eighth Scheduled of the constitution in August, 1992, it became a bone of contention within the Nepali community owing to the growing tension between the OBC and NBC. It must be noted here that the groups falling within the OBC communities belonged to the mongoloid stock and are linguistically different from that of the NBC Nepalis of Aryan stock. The OBC group perceived that the Nepali language grew to maturity at the cost of their own languages. A festoon at Damthang in 1993 which read "Bhasa Hoina, Bhat Deo" (Do not give language, give rice) indicated the general resentment of the OBC community over the language issue. Besides the OBC, the tribal group also alleged Mr. Bhandari for working in the interest of his own castes (i.e. NBC). Kunzang Dorjee, the Chief General Secretary of the Denzong Tribal Yargay Chogpa (DTYC), while commenting on the demands of the State government such as recognition of Nepali language, reservation of seats for the Nepalis and grant of citizenship to stateless persons, accused the Chief Minister Bhandari for encouraging "his own people - the Nepali Bahun and Chettri - to settle in Sikkim. The demands if met would virtually eliminate the Bhutia-Lepcha from Sikkim.[68]

The nature of politics during the rule of Mr. Bhandari and his SSP party can also be assessed with respect to the controversy surrounding the extension of the Income Tax Act, 1961 in 1993-94. In 1993, the central government proposed for extension of the Central Income Tax Act, 1961 to Sikkim. In a letter, dated 21.07.1993, Bhandari requested the Union Finance Minister to exclude the tribals (i.e. Bhutias and Lepchas) from the ambit of the said Act. The proposal was certainly an attempt to win support of the Bhutia-Lepcha communities in view of the growing differences between Mr. Bhandari and Mr. P.K.Chamling. Such a move, however, was bitterly criticized by the Sikkim People's Forum, a Nepali dominated ad-hoc body formed in March 1994, for being anti-Nepali and for favouring the Bhutia-Lepcha communities. The Union Finance Minister, Dr. Manmohan Singh, eventually withdrew the Finance Bill, 1994 (No. 15 of 1994) for further examination, but the way the Bhandari government treated the issue, created ethnic tension between the two major communities. The immediate fall out of this incident was that all the Bhutia-Lepcha MLAs withdrew their support and the Bhandari government was defeated in the no-confidence motion held on 17 May 1994 in the Assembly. The SSP also lost the November 1994 Assembly election which symbolized the end of the SSP domination in Sikkim's politics. It won 10 seats in 1994, 7 seats in 1999 and mere 1 seat (Sangha) in 2004 Assembly elections.

In 2000, Mr. Bhandari, through his M.L.A, Mr. J.K.Bhandari, proposed a Bill in the Assembly seeking to restore Nepali seats on the basis of 'Parity formula', but was forced to withdraw it in view of stiff opposition from the members of the Nepali Ekta Sangathan, an organization of the Nepalis. It was a tactical move by Mr. Bhandari to win the confidence of the tribals and other former SSP leaders who had joined the Congress (I) party, known as tribal party, before switching his own loyalty to the latter. Bhandari eventually merged the SSP party with the Indian National Congress (I) after having his post as the President of the Sikkim Pradesh Congress Committee (I) was confirmed by the Congress high command.[69] Though the event was described by SSP vice-President, Biraj Adhikari, as a 'practical necessity'[70] the tribal leaders, including his own former SSP colleagues who were already in the Congress (I), left the party. He contested 2004 Assembly election under the Congress (I) flag but lost all but one Sangha seat.

N.B.Bhandari and the SSP as a regional political organization did not initially emphasize community identity for political mobilization or during electoral campaigns. It came to power with the slogan of Sikkimese identity, but later was caught in the coils of identity politics. On the one hand the SSP wanted to maintain unity within the Nepali community and refused to implement the directives of the Mandal Commission recommendation and on the other hand the party attempted to win over the Bhutia-Lepcha communities by denying Scheduled Tribes status to certain deserving Nepali castes/community, by proposing special tax provisions for them and by demanding restoration of parity formula. Such proposals only helped to aggravate divisions between the two major communities (Bhutia-Lepcha and Nepalis) and between the OBC and NBC groups within the Nepali community. On the whole the politics was ethnicised.

Sikkim Democratic Front (SDF):

The two former Chief Ministers, Kazi Lhendup Dorji Khangsarpa and B.B.Gurung, described the political condition during the 80's and early 90's as one of "dictatorship of the worst type".[71] After 1989 Bhandari showed no appetite for criticisms. The opposition party leaders and print media were among his primary targets. P.K.Chamling, who began his political career as the sympathizer of the Sikkim Sangram Parishad and won Assembly elections from Damthang constituency consecutively in 1985 and 1989 with 95 per cent votes, was not always supportive of the vindictive policy unleashed by his political mentor Bhandari. His differences, however, became quite noticeable on the issue of rejection of central proposal for inclusion of the Limboo and Tamang in the scheduled tribes list in 1987.[72] Later, on many pertinent issues like imposition of legal sanctions on Christianity, rejection of the Mandal Commission Recommendation, extension of Central Income Tax Act, 1961 etc., Mr. Chamling performed the role of an opposition within the ruling party. Considering his views and actions as anti-party activities, Mr. Chamling was removed from the ruling SSP Ministry on 16 June, 1992[73]

After his expulsion from the SSP, Mr. Chamling formed Sikkim Democratic Front Party on 4 March, 1993 at Namchi.[74] P.T.Luksom, G.M.Gurung, I.B. Gurung, Vinod Pradhan, D.B.

Basnet, G.M.Rai, P.R. Sherpa, D.B.Thapa, A.B.Bhutia, Aita Singh Baraily, Chandra Khaling, Mohan Dungmati, Ashok Gurung, Girish Chandra Rai, Bhoj Raj Rai, Sonam Gyaltsen, C.B.Karki, Vinod Rai, Nahkul Rai, I.B.Rai, S.S.Bokim, Passang Lepcha, R.M.Rai, P.S. Tamang, J.B. Subba, J.B.Rai, to name a few, were other important office bearer of the party.[75] The party initially did not have its branch office in the North district. The list of the office bearer indicated domination of other backward classes yet it had other priorities in the formative stage like restoration and strengthening of democratic values, correction of anti-people and anti-poor policies of the SSP government etc.[76]

Following the clashes between the supporters of the SSP and SDF on 18 June 1993 at Namchi, some SDF activists were arrested on 19 June (Binod Pradhan, Hissey Lachungpa, Bhojraj Rai, Anil Lachungpa) but Mr. Chamling escaped to Gangtok. The SDF party was declared as terrorist party and an arrest warrant under National Security Act (NASA) was issued against Mr. Chamling which forced him to remain underground for some time. The vice-President of the SDF party, Mr. P.T. Luksom, criticized the imposition of the Act "to malign and arrest our party workers under the shadow of National Security Act to foil our party activities."[77] By this time the clashes of the two parties had become or at least viewed by many as the clashes between the higher caste Nepalis (Aryan) represented by N.B.Bhandari and the lower caste (Mongoloid/ OBC) led by P.K.Chamling. For example, during the 1993 agitation an innominate but highly provocative poster was seen in West Sikkim targeting the higher caste Nepalis and the Bhutia-Lepcha alike. The text metaphorically read, "Bahun Lai Kashi (Brahmin to go to Kashi), Chhetri Lai Fashi (Chhetri to hang), Bhutia-Lepcha Jata Tatai Tashi" (Bhutia-Lepcha may stick anywhere). It was difficult to quantify the impact of the poster propaganda but considering the course of political development and social stratification prevailing in Nepali community of Sikkim then, one could figure out that there were indications of division within the Nepali community on ethnic or racial lineage. During the period Mr. Chamling, however, continued to issue leaflets focusing on the issues of restoration of the Nepali seats in the Assembly, enhancement of Bhutia-Lepcha seats, tribal status for Limboos and Tamangs of Sikkim, Other Backward Caste status for Chhetri, Bahun, Newar, Jogi, etc.[78]

Chamling returned to Sikkim on 22 September, 1993 when the SSP government was under tremendous political pressure on the issue of extension of the Central Income Tax Act, 1961 to Sikkim. Through the press release, dated 14 March, 1994, the SDF criticized the divisive policy of the Bhandari government and supported the demand of the Sikkim Peoples Forum.[79] The SDF party declared a three-day strike in support of the demand of the Sikkim Peoples Forum and was an absolute success. The issue brought unity among the Nepalis but the Bhutia-Lepcha community who alone wanted exemption from the income tax Act became apprehensive. On 4 May, 1994, Dr. Manmohan Singh, the Union Finance Minister, withdrew the finance Bill for de novo examination. The Bhutia-Lepcha reacted accusing Bhandari for deception and Sikkim Peoples Forum for inhibiting smooth passage of the Bill in the Lok Sabha. The acrimony was followed by exchange of derogatory and extremely provocative ethnic remarks against each other instigating ethnic violence.[80]

On 7 May, 1994, the Bhutia-Lepcha took out a protest rally in Gangtok. On 12 May, 1994, the Governor addressed the representatives of both the Forum and Scheduled Tribes and appealed to maintain ethnic harmony.[81] On May 17, 1994 all the tribal leaders voted in favour of the no-confidence motion and Bhandari was ousted from power. The speech given by Late Chamla Tshering Bhutia, known as Bhandari's trusted lieutenant but instrumental in anti-Bhandari campaign in 1994, on that day embodied the crux of the grievances that the community had been cherishing since the merger. He said, "What was Sikkim? It was a country ruled by a king. It was the country of the Bhutias and Lepchas. Ok! We lost our country. We were compelled to accept it. We lost our king (Chogyal) and became a State of India. Ok! We accepted the State also. But we heard that the Chief Minister would be from the Bhutia-Lepcha community only. After

L.D.Kazi, N.B. Bhandari became the Chief Minister of Sikkim and with it the Bhutia-Lepcha also lost the post of the Chief Minister".[82] P.K.Chamling also accused Bhandari for promoting ethnic division through his divisive policies.[83] During those days, both the groups approached Chamling to form the government under his leadership, which he declined.[84] The developments during 1993-94, i.e. prior to SDF's electoral success, actually reflected the gradual deterioration of ethnic harmony and a sharp rise in ethnicity oriented political mobilization. It was a clear fall out on the part of the SSP politics which had been pursuing sectarian/communal politics to remain in power.

The election to the Fifth Assembly was held on 16 November, 1994. The SDF contested in all the 32 seats. It had as many as 13 OBC and 4 General candidates out of which 11 OBC and 1 General candidate won election. It is said that the Backward class community overwhelmingly voted in favour of the SDF party. It had 19 seats in a 32 member Legislative Assembly after the election. Mr. Chamling himself got elected from the traditional Damthang constituency for the third time. On 12 December, 1994 the SDF government was formed with 13-member Council of Ministers.

It was observed that alignment and mobilization of racial or ethnic categories had been significant in 1994 Assembly elections. For instance, it was reported that a member of the higher caste Nepali and a staunch supporter of the SDF party was approached by his relatives to support the SSP saying 'Time has come to see not the party but Jati (Caste/community)'.[85] Commenting on the 1994 Assembly election Marcus Dam wrote, "Political alignment in Sikkim is mostly short lived. But with various divisions cutting deeper and deeper into a socially heterogeneous society the trend is unlikely to change. This electoral politics has only quickened the process of the integration of the Tribals with some Other Backward Class groups".[86] Another instance of alignment at racial level was resignation by many high caste Nepalis like Nandu Thapa, Jagat Bandhu Pradhan, Madan Chettri, including M.M.Rasaily and Bhutia-Lepcha leaders from the SDF party on 21 October 1994. In a joint statement they accused P.K.Chamling of favouring the Nepalis of mongoloid stock and of failing to give proper representation to the Nepali Bahun (Brahmin), Chhetri, Bhutia, Lepcha etc.[87] Besides allegations, the issues and demands raised by the SDF party in 1994 elections clearly indicate that the party was primarily banking on the lower-caste/OBC votes of the Nepalis who formed about 50 percent of the population of the State.

In the Budget session, the Governor of the State, Shri P.Shiva Shankar, who was responsible for abolition of the Nepali seats in 1980, highlighted the priorities of the SDF government as;

a) To demand for restoration of reserved seats for the Nepalis of Sikkimese origin abolished by the constitutional Amendment Act, 1980;
b) To work for the inclusion of Limboo, Tamang and Gurung in the list of Scheduled Tribes;
c) To include Newar, Bahun, Chhetri, Jogi etc. in the list of Other Backward Classes;
d) To persuade the Central government to withdraw its decision to extend Central Income Tax Act, 1961 from Sikkim and to recognize the State Tax Manual currently in vogue.[88]

As promised in the election manifesto, the languages spoken by Newar, Gurung, Tamang, Rai, Mangar, Sherpa and Sunuwar were recognized as the State languages[89] including the teaching facilities of these languages in schools. The Mandal Commission Recommendation was implemented and Bhujel, Gurung, Limboo, Rai, Mangar, Sunuwar, Tamang, Thami, Jogi and Dewan were included in the OBC list.[90] In 1997 the Panchayat election was held for the first time in party basis and 33 percent seats were reserved for the women candidates. The party won about 80 per cent of the total Panchayat seats. The party also won the 1998 Lok Sabha election with absolute majority.

In January 7, 2003 the Limboos and Tamangs were accorded the status of the Scheduled Tribes of Sikkim.[91] In September 2003 Bhujel, Dewan, Gurung, Jogi, Rai, Mangar, Sunuwar, Thami were upgraded as the Most Backward Communities (MBC) and Bahun, Chhetri, Newar and Sanyasi were included in the State's list of Other Backward Classes.[92] Accordingly, the reservation policy regarding jobs and higher studies outside the State was revised in September 2003 as 33 % for ST, 6 % SC, 21 % for MBC, 14 % for OBC and 5 % for children of other business community and government servants.[93] The reservation for the Scheduled Tribes was inclusive of the Limboo and Tamang scheduled tribes until a fresh notification was issued in this regard.

The issues of inclusion of the Limboos and Tamangs in the ST list and Bahun, Chhetri, Newar and Sanyasi in the state list of OBC played an instrumental role in the landslide victory of the SDF party in 2004 Assembly election. Many ethnic/social organizations expressed their tacit support in favour of the SDF Party. But according to the former Minister and a supporter of the SDF party commented that the majority of Bhutia-Lepcha communities did not vote in favour of the SDF. The reason was obvious that they were not happy with the inclusion of the Limboos and Tamangs in the Scheduled Tribes list of Sikkim.

The Local Protection Act was implemented in 1994. Under the provision of the Act the Sikkim Subject Certificate/Identification Certificate/Residential Certificate was made mandatory for pursuing economic activities in Sikkim.[94] The practice of leasing out trade licenses by the local to the non-local was forbidden. The implementation of the Local Protection Act created resentment among the non-Sikkimese business community in the State. A notable businessman of Gangtok reacted by saying "if the government introduces new measures to put economic pressure on non-Sikkimese living in the state there will be revolution here".[95] Later, certain concessions were assured to those non-Sikkimese Indians and Non Residential Indians wanting to invest or do business in Sikkim.

After coming to power in 1994 Mr. Chamling re-commissioned the Rathang Cho Hydel Project. The Project was originally started in 1977 by the then Kazi government. In fact, the site of the Project falls on one of the sacred places of Sikkim. Every year in the month of February the lamas of Tashiding monastery perform 'Bumchu' festival for which the water of the river Rathong Chu is used for all ceremonial activities. A large number of Lepcha and Bhutia associations like Denzong Lhomen Chodru, Rong Arat Sa Tarzum, Sikkim Tribal Women Association, Sikkim Tribal Welfare Association, Denzong Lhodey Chokpa as well as environmental organization like 'Concerned Citizens of Sikkim' protested against the reconstruction of the Hydel Project on the ground that it would destroy the sanctity of the sacred place and cultural heritage of Sikkim. The government, in an attempt to accommodate the religious feeling of the Sikkimese, finally abandoned the project in 1997.

The SDF government was equally concerned about the social and religious aspirations of the people of Sikkim. The Lepcha community had been recognized as 'primitive' (indigenous) tribe of Sikkim. Cultural cum research centers for the Limboos and Lepchas were established at Hee Bormoik (West Sikkim) and Dzongu (North Sikkim) respectively. A statue of a Limboo spiritual leader 'Siri Junga' and a 'Manghim' (place of worship) at Hee Bormoik and a 108 feet statue of Guru Rimpochey (Padma Sambhava) at Samdruptse (South Sikkim) were also established. As a part of the emotional integration of Sikkimese in the Indian mainstream, the ruling SDF party had been instrumental behind the appointment of Sikkimese in the dignified constitutional posts like Indian ambassador to Mongolia (Karma Topden in 2000), Advocate General (Sonam Wangdi), Additional Advocate General (N.B.Khatiwada) etc. Parity in terms of representation and ministerial berth was maintained between the Bhutia and Lepcha, and for the first time a Lepcha candidate was elected to the Rajya Sabha of India.

In 2009 Assembly and Lok Sabha election the SDF won all the 32 Assembly seats and the lone Lok Sabha seat despite the fact that about fifty percent of its candidates were contesting for the first time. This landslide victory of the SDF may be attributed to the ideological shift from the parochial caste / identity politics of earlier days to the politics of 'performance'. "Vote for performance" was its avowed slogan in this election. People were euphoric about the way that the party had created employment and economic opportunities through its holistic development initiatives and self-employment schemes. The immediate causes of the success, however, could be credited to the exemption granted to the Sikkimese from the central income tax in 2008 and the failure of the opposition parties to work jointly.

During the last fifteen years of its consecutive rule under the leadership of Mr. P.K. Chamling, the SDF party seems to have to a large extent substituted parochial aspiration with the politics of performance and economic opportunities. In the last one decade of the SDF rule there has been no ethnic disturbance in Sikkim which in itself is the most remarkable achievement of the party.

Sikkim Ekta Manch (SEM):

The Sikkim Ekta Manch, popularly called Third Force, was established on August 27, 1997 at Singtam.[96] L.P.Tiwari, Biraj Adhikari (the SDF dissident) and Sonam Dorjee were founder members of the party.[97] The primary objective of the party, called 'Mool Mantra', was to preserve the 'communal harmony' and strengthen the unity and solidarity among various sections of the Nepalis.[98] One of the party's leaflets wrote, "...before 1973 we were Sikkimese but later we became Bhutia, Lepcha and Nepalis. Alongside the division our rights as Sikkimese were lost and robbed. Today the division is not limited to Bhutia, Lepcha and Nepali alone but the Nepali itself is divided into OBC, NBC and Scheduled Castes. Today Sikkim is divided into fragments and some vested politicians are enjoying the fruits of division in order to grasp political power...The Sikkim Ekta Manch is formed with a clear objective to protect and preserve the rights of Sikkimese and maintain ethnic harmony among them which has eroded due to the faulty policies of both the Bhandari and Chamling governments."[99]

Apart from this, the party also demanded protection and faithful implementation of the rights of the Sikkimese enshrined under article 371F of the constitution, to enact Local Protection Act, to initiate dialogue with the central government for the restoration of Nepali seats in the Legislative Assembly, to work for the inclusion of

Limboo, Tamang and Gurung in the Scheduled Tribes list, to maintain ethnic balance at the time of formation of government, to ensure protection of old business and other communities in Sikkim, to include all the sub-groups of the Nepalis in the OBC list and to ensure unity and solidarity among them, to appoint qualified ethnic Sikkimese in the highest administrative, police and forest services in order to prevent the outsiders in such posts etc.[100]

The party opposed SDF government's decision to hold Panchayat election on party basis and lodged a legal complaint in the Sikkim High Court challenging the decision. The court, however, reserved the verdict in favour of the government. The party boycotted the Panchayat election in 1997 but supported independent candidates.

The party also boycotted February 1998 Lok Sabha election but supported the Congress (I) candidate, Sanchaman Limboo, under the impression that lone Lok Sabha member of a regional party would be ineffective without the support of the national party at the centre, secondly, the understanding reached among the opposition parties of Sikkim to project only one candidate for the Lok Sabha election and, thirdly, the political understanding with the Congress (I) party on issues like (a) exemption of the Sikkimese from the purview of the Income Tax Act, 1961, (b) Restoration of the Nepali seats in the Assembly, (c) enactment of Local Protection Act, (d) inclusion of left out communities in the list of Other Backward Classes, (e) inclusion of Limboo, Tamang and Gurung in the list of Scheduled Tribes without harming the interest of the Bhutias and Lepchas etc.[101] However, due to growing intra-party differences the party could not function properly and fell apart soon.

Sikkim Gorkha Democratic/Prajatantrik Party (SGDP/SGPP):

The Sikkim Gorkha Democratic Party was formed at Singtam in April 1, 2004 under the leadership of G.M.Rai and N.B.Khatiwada.[102] G.M.Rai was the founder member and vice-President of the SDF party while N.B.Khatiwada was the Deputy Advocate General of Sikkim before resigning from the post.

The party believed that there exist certain incongruities in old Sikkimese laws and systems which required immediate rectification. The party alleged the ruling SDF party for failing to do so.[103]

The major demands of the Sikkim Gorkha Democratic/ Prajatantrtik Party as highlighted in the manifesto for May 2004 Assembly and Lok Sabha election were;

a) To change the Revenue Order No. 1 to make it applicable for the protection of the Nepalis land also;
b) To work for reservation of seats in the Legislative Assembly on the basis of population;
c) To identify the "creamy layer" from among the Scheduled Tribes population in the interest of those who need them most;
d) The party supports creation of a separate state of Gorkhaland but discourages any attempt to merge Darjeeling with Sikkim.[104]

Influx was not a major problem for the party as they were basically engaged as construction workers in various projects undertaken by the National Hydro Electric Power Corporation (NHPC), construction and repairing of roads, carrying of loads, hair cutting saloons, cobbler, washing clothes etc, which, according to the party, do not generally fall in Sikkimese list of job priorities. The party also believed that if there would be no outsiders the developmental works would not complete in time.[105]

In May 2004 election Mr. G.M.Rai contested as an independent candidate (as the party was not registered) from the Central Pandam Assembly constituency but was defeated. It shows that political parties generally rely on ethnic issues for electoral gain but ethnic political parties are seldom benefited in term of seats. In 2005 the party was renamed as Sikkim Gorkha Prajatantrik Party. The party criticized the Draft proposal of the Delimitation Commission, 2002 for failing to represent all the section of the Sikkimese population for there had been 4 representations from 20 per cent population and 1 from the 80 per cent population of Sikkim.[106] Taking Rakdong-Tintek and Central Pandam constituencies as examples he alleged that the constituencies were the non-backward caste (NBC) concentrated areas but by declaring them as BL and SC constituencies respectively the Commission had victimized the NBC communities. He also criticized the decision of the Commission to convert Gangtok and Singtam as BL and SC constituencies instead of considering them as General constituencies.[107]

The formation of the ethnic party like SGDP was suggestive of growing apprehension among the Nepalis. It expressed concern over continuation of certain old laws which discriminated Nepali from other two communities of Sikkim. The party demanded population as the basis for representation in the Assembly, reservation of seats for the Limboos and Tamangs in the Assembly within the 12 seats reserved for the Bhutia-Lepcha community. The party believed that certain existing political or legislative arrangements provide extra privilege to the Bhutia-Lepcha community and justified modification in view of present requirement and constitutional obligations.

The issues which the party had raised were of contemporary in nature. The party emphasized on the need for modification of certain old laws which favoured differential treatment of communities on ethnic/communal grounds. The continuation of such laws no chase also viewed as a major contributing factor in the continuation of ethnic tension or apprehension among communities. But the way the party raised issues and mobilized supporters had, directly or indirectly, accentuated ethnic differences and division in the society.

Denzong People's Chogpa (DPC):

The party was formed in 1989 in Gangtok in the eve of the Fourth Assembly and Ninth Lok Sabha elections scheduled in November 1989. Its primary objective was to protect and safeguard the interest of the tribals of genuine Bhutias and Lepchas of Sikkim.

The party demanded Sikkim Subject Certificate as an eligibility for candidates in the election. In its letter to the Chief Electoral

Officer of Sikkim, dated 3 November 1989, the working President of the party wrote, "In the first democratic elections held in Sikkim in 1974, all candidates were required, without exception, to attach copies of their Sikkim Subjects Certificate as an essential criterion or eligibility. These laws were never amended and rightly so. I, therefore, request you to ensure that every candidate attach a copy of his or her Sikkim Subjects Certificate and prove their basic eligibility to contest elections in Sikkim giving due cognizance to special character and history of the State".[108]

The party also demanded for release of the list of 'stateless persons' and expressed concerns over influx through the process of grant of citizenship to 'stateless persons' in Sikkim. The letter added "The State Government has noted that 54,000 people of Sikkim do not have Indian Citizenship and their cases are under process. It must be ensured that these people do not participate in the elections until their status is first made clear".[109] The copies of the letter were sent to the Chief Election Commissioner, New Delhi, Secretary, Ministry of Home Affairs, New Delhi and the Returning Officers of all the four districts of Sikkim. The party also lodged a writ petition in the High Court of Sikkim.

In another letter, dated September 1990, the President Lachen Gomchen Rimpochey also reiterated "Unless these applicants can prove that they have basic qualifications to be Sikkim Subjects and they have been wrongly left out, they cannot get Indian Citizenship".[110] The DPC, as a party of the tribals, was also closely involved in the famous seat reservation case of 1979. The general secretary, Tashi W. Fonpo, also alleged that ruling SSP party was having secret parleys with R.C.Poudyal to get a verdict against the tribals[111] which, however, was proved wrong as the Supreme Court reserved the decision in favour of the Bhutia Lepcha community in February 1993. The party was also actively involved in the anti-Bhandari campaign in 1994 and was one of the members of the Joint Action Committee formed under the leadership of Kazi Lhendup Dorje Khangsarpa in June 24, 1993 to oppose repressive and dictatorial rule of the Sangram Parishad government.[112]

Sikkim Rastriya Morcha (SRM):

It was established in May 1997 by M.M.Rasaily.[113] The other notable members of the party were P.B.Yata, R. Moktan, Madan Kumar Chhetri and Loden Tshering Bhutia etc. In a pamphlet entitled 'An Appeal to the Sikkimese', the party highlighted the following objectives, called Foundation Stones, namely:

1. The reservation of seats in the Sikkim Assembly for three communities - Bhutia, Lepchas and Nepalis as agreed on 8th May 1973 agreement;
2. Issuance of Sikkim Subject Certificate only for genuine Sikkimese left out earlier and subsequent grant of Indian Citizenship to them;
3. Removal of derogatory remark of "immigrant" leveled against the Sikkimese Bhutia and Nepalis;
4. To declare Sikkim as a Tribal state to resolve the OBC and NBC contradiction;
5. Delimitation of constituencies on the basis of present population of Sikkim and subsequent increase of one seat each in the Rajya Sabha and Lok Sabha;
6. Prohibition on the entry of unauthorized person from nearby state and eviction of those who have entered already;
7. Construction of statues of the Chogyal Tashi Namgyal and Palden Thendup Namgyal as a mark of respect and unity of the Sikkimese;
8. Declaration of Basant Kumar Chhetri as the martyr of Sikkim who died defending the Palace Gate on 9th April, 1975;
9. Immediate end to the policy of dividing Nepalis into castes and sub-castes;
10. To oppose any demand/effort for merger of Sikkim with Darjeeling;
11. To oppose ill treatment meted out to the Newar, Bahun and Chhetri (NBC) and develop Sikkimese identity rather than OBC or NBC;
12. Restoration and preservation of rights and privileges of

Sikkimese as envisaged in article 371F of the Indian Constitution;

13. Appointment of Sikkimese in the highest administrative posts like IAS, IPS, IFS (Forest) etc;[114]

In 1997, the party opposed the decision of the ruling party to hold Panchayat election on party basis and also submitted a memorandum to the State's Governor, Chaudhury Randhir Singh.[115]

In 1998, R.Moktan and P.B.Yata resigned from the party owing to differences with the party President, M.M.Rasaily, regarding latter's unilateral decision to support the Congress (I) candidate in the Lok Sabha election and failure to secure registration for the party even after one year of its formation.[116] The resignation of the two most outstanding office bearer and think tank of the party virtually proved to be an irreparable loss for the growth of the party. The party, by and large, emphasized on the need for upholding the Sikkimese identity but had no rural support.

Sikkim Nebhola National Liberation Front (SNNLF):

The party was founded in 1997 by the former Deputy Chief Minister, P.T.Luksom. The word 'NEBHOLA', like the one existed once in Darjeeling, stands for the three indigenous communities of Sikkim - Nepali, Bhutia and Lepcha. Its primary objective was to ensure unity and harmony among the three ethnic communities of Sikkim by restoring seats for the Nepalis, Tsongs and the Bhutia-Lepcha to its pre-merger status.[117] Besides seat reservation, the major demands of the party included return of Chumbi valley to Sikkim by China, opposition to extension of the Central Income Tax Act, 1961 and Central Employment (Compulsory Notification of Vacancies) Act, 1959 to Sikkim, inclusion of Gurung, Mangar and Sunuwar (Mukhia) in the Scheduled Tribes list of Sikkim, appointment of the Sikkimese in the Central government departments etc. The demands of the party were common to that of other political parties with an exception of return of Chumbi Valley to Sikkim. Moreover, Party's demand for restoration of seats to its pre-merger status ran counter to the demands of the other Nepali organizations to reserve seats on the basis of population.

In 1998, the Party contested the Lok Sabha election but was unsuccessful. In 2004 Assembly and Lok Sabha elections, it forged an alliance with Sikkim Himali Rajya Parishad Party (SHRPP) of Dr. A.D.Subba, called Sikkim Democratic Alliance. The alliance fielded 28 candidates but none of them were returned.[118]

Sikkim National Liberation Front (SNLF):

After resigning from the Sikkim National Party in 1998, R.Moktan and P.B.Yata formed the 'Sikkim National Liberation Front' in January 9, 1998.[119] The bulletin no. 5 issued by the party highlighted its 13-point objectives as follows;

1. To review merger issue if article 371F is not implemented in 'letter and spirit';
2. To demand seat reservation for Sikkimese as per the Tripartite Agreement of the 8th May 1973, Sikkim Bill 1974 and article 371F of the Indian Constitution;
3. To demand Indian Citizenship under clause 7 of the Indian Citizenship Act, 1955;
4. To declare Sikkim as Tribal State;
5. To increase seats in the State Assembly, in the Lok Sabha and Rajya Sabha;
6. To evict persons of foreign nationals and to stop influx in the state;
7. To install statues of the late Chogyal, Sir Tashi Namgyal at Kurseong and that of Palden Thendup Namgyal at Gangtok in honour of ushering democracy in Sikkim;
8. To declare Basant Kumar Chhetri, who died guarding the palace on 9 April 1975, as the first martyr of Sikkim;
9. To work for the unity of the three ethnic communities of Sikkim viz. Nepali, Bhutia and Lepcha;
10. To restore Darjeeling to Sikkim if the demand for a separate State of Gorkhaland is not achieved;
11. To provide equal justice to all the electors of Sikkim;
12. To oppose extension of any central laws, regulations and

rules that may harm the identity and interests of the Sikkimese; and

13. To demand for the restoration of the rights of the Sikkimese people existed prior to 26th April, 1977.[120]

According to the Party any law promulgated after 26 April, 1977 in relation to Sikkim should be done away with because they contravene constitutional provision envisaged under article 371F (l). The relevant provision clearly stated that no such order shall be made after the expiry of two years from the appointed day i.e. 26 April 1975.[121]

The party also criticized the policy of the SDF government to undertake survey of Sikkim Subject holders. The party expressed concern over the deteriorating social and political condition in the state due to the ruling party's faulty policies segregating 'outsider' and 'insider'. Its demand for merger of Darjeeling with Sikkim and poster campaign in 2005 created political tension in the State followed by escalation of anti-Darjeeling sentiments, particularly among the Nepalis of Sikkim.

From the survey of the political parties it became quite reveling that politics in Sikkim is a play ground of the regional parties with one party emerging as most dominating political party. The Sikkim Janata Parishad and later Sikkim Sangram Parishad led by Mr. N.B.Bhandari had been a dominant party till 1994. It relied basically on issues of Sikkimese identity as distinct from the national identity and ingenious manipulation of emotal elements concerning ethnic groups for its political success. The Sikkim Democratic Front which has been a dominant party since 1994 also has a history of articulating and aggregating ascriptive elements whether inclusion of Limboo and Tamang communities in the ST list or implementation of Mandal Commission or issues of general interest like protection of rights and privileges of Sikkimese or exemption of Sikkimese from the central income tax laws etc., for political success. Another noticeable feature of politics in Sikkim is that overnight emergence of political parties during election time with all types of community oriented appeals and promises together with magical disappearance of the same after the election. They, including the major opposition parties, generally do not win seats or even if they win one or two seats often fall prey to politics of patronization making mockery of democratic tradition. There exist some ethnic parties like sikkim Gorkha Prajatantrik Party (GPP) Denzong People's Chogpa but they are not electorally successful parties. Similarly, parties with limited or very weak support base suffer from frequent intra-party squabbles and factionalism.

Ethnic Social Organizations of Sikkim:

In a multi-ethnic society, the community relationship often exhibit in dominant-dependent scenario. The sense of being dependent also breeds a feeling, real or imaginative, of marginalization or alienation among minority groups and stimulates strength for resistance and asserts distinct identity challenging the process of assimilation under a dominant discourse. It reflects or produces deep emotional feelings,[122] exhibits wider political ramification based on the ideas of freedom, pride, equality and justice, and emphasizes need for preserving symbols of primordiality. This also creates an atmosphere in which the government policies or that of a dominant group, which might affect their cultural identity, is viewed with apprehension; it unites them to act against such policy or development. Hence, the formation of organizations and their style of functioning reflect group's desire for identity in the changing political scenario. They articulate political demands and very often act as pressure groups intending to influence or alter political decisions in favour of the concerned group/groups.

In view of the introduction of modern democratic institution and a liberal secular constitution in the post-merger Sikkim, the rules governing the affairs of Sikkim were adapted to suit various political and administrative challenges. But along with these structural changes, the level of anxiety and apprehension among the various communities also increased considering the nature of functioning of a democratic government and the question of resource distribution. The Nepalis, though benefited both in political and economic fronts, were apprehensive in view of influx of the outsiders and abolition of the Nepali seats in the Assembly in 1979 together with the extension of voting rights to the plainsmen. The Bhutias, on the other, suffered from loss of political and economic domination in the society.

The political-administrative arrangement, which reduced the size of the B-L seats in the Assembly in 1979 even though the definition 'Bhutia' was expanded to include eight other Bhutias, the inclusion of the Limboo and Tamang communities in the Scheduled Tribes list in 2003, further aroused a sense of insecurity among them. In view of the introduction of a new formula of seat reservation, the Bhutia-Lepcha were afraid of being dominated by the Nepalis while the Nepalis were apprehensive of losing control over state power. The Nepalis and Bhutias were educationally forward and thus dominated economic and political power, including the bureaucracy. Their strong presence in the decision-making and implementing institutions often resulted in the exploitation of the benefits by the two communities, while the Lepchas, by virtue of socio-economic and educational backwardness, were denied the fruits of economic and political opportunities and felt discriminated. The feeling of deprivation among the Lepchas led to strengthening of ethnic consciousness and articulation of community oriented demands by forming organization. Similarly, on the issue of Mandal Commission recommendation, the Nepalis were divided along racial line – the Aryans and Mongoloid. Like the Lepchas, the mongoloid groups within the larger Nepali community too were educationally and economically backward groups and were deprived of economic and political opportunities. The inter-community resentments and feeling of deprivation and domination naturally culminated in the form of formation of socio-cultural organizations with a view to maintaining separate identity and claiming larger share of the resources. It is in this context the formation of various socio-cultural organizations is studied and explained.

Sikkim Tribal Welfare Association (STWA):

The Sikkim Tribal Welfare Association was formed in December 24, 1978 at Gangtok. Officially, it was an organization of the Bhutia,

Lepcha and Sherpa tribal communities of Sikkim. Some of the aims and objectives of the organization were as follows;

1. To effectively and efficiently establish a healthy and strong organization of the Bhutias, Lepchas and Sherpas of Sikkim;
2. To promote educational, cultural and economic advancement of the Scheduled Tribes mainly Bhutias, Lepchas and Sherpas of Sikkim;
3. To protect and work for the furtherance of the rights and privileges of the Scheduled Tribes of Sikkim;
4. To create, foster and promote the spirit of fellow feelings, service, solidarity, cooperation and mutual help with members of the Nepali community and the plainsmen;
5. To inculcate a sense of loyalty among the Scheduled Tribes of Sikkim and also to subscribe allegiance, faith, confidence and cooperation to the government of India.[123]

Its primary intention was to function as pressure group in the interest of the tribal communities, including the Sherpas. It demanded for creation of a Standing Committee for reviewing legislations which had or seemed to have adversely affected the social, economic, cultural and religious interests of the tribals in Sikkim.[124] It was an apolitical association though some of its members were also involved in political activities, including contesting elections.

In 1979, the Association emphasized on the need for evolving a suitable substitution to the 'Parity Formula' for full protection of the interest of the Bhutias and Lepchas, fresh delimitation of the Bhutia-Lepcha (B-L) constituencies, the continuation of the Revenue Order No. 1 of 1917 or substitution of it by enacting 'Special Tribal Land Alienation Act'.[125] Under the chairmanship of P.O.Pazo, a Joint Action Committee (JAC) of all the tribal organizations of Sikkim was formed in 1985 to press for genuine demands and issues concerning the tribals of Sikkim.[126]

In October 1985, the Association submitted a six-point memorandum to the State's Governor, Shri Bhishma Narayan Singh, demanding restoration of 16 seats (including 1 Sangha seat) in the

Assembly for the Bhutia-Lepcha, delimitation of Assembly constituencies to ensure genuine tribal representation in the Assembly, grant of citizenship to the 'stateless persons' on the basis of the Sikkim Subjects Regulation, extension of inner line permit system to check influx of outsiders, protection and safeguards of the rights and interest of the tribals on the basis of article 371F of the constitution and deletion of the names of foreign nationals included in the electoral rolls.[127] The memorandum further expressed concern over the gradual destruction and disintegration of the distinct socio-cultural identity of the Bhutia-Lepcha people after 1975 and also demanded for a fresh delimitation of the Assembly constituencies in order to ensure a genuine representation of the tribals in the Assembly. [128]

The reasons behind the demand for fresh delimitation of Tribal constituencies can be found in the demographic composition of these constituencies. The ethnic community-wise voters' strength of 12 (BL) reserved and Gangtok (General) constituencies during last three Assembly elections (1994-2004) are provided below for reference.

Table No. 6.1: Community–wise voters in B-L reserved & Gangtok General Constituencies.

	1994			1999			2004		
Constituencies *	B-L	Nep.	Oth.	B-L	Nep.	Oth.	B-L	Nep.	Oth.
Tashiding	1574	3201	26	1776	3891	20	1864	4431	61
Rinchenpong	1708	4179	18	2063	5217	45	2164	5718	59
Ralong	1827	2776	110	2273	3512	05	2435	3849	100
Pathing	2571	4490	23	3227	5269	54	3267	5420	102
Dzongu	3203	955	xx	3940	1479	37	4281	1587	34
Lachen-Mangshila	3968	1111	270	5352	1676	266	5523	1811	341
Kabi-Tingda	3452	947	130	3956	1300	76	4527	1498	90
Rakdong Tintek	1749	4298	50	1950	4999	137	2026	5329	125
Martam	1972	4115	86	2406	5864	115	3596	6390	228
Rumtek	1925	4870	497	2596	7243	710	3104	9077	1147
Assam Lingzey	2289	5933	397	2696	4615	149	3409	5515	187
Ranka	1982	4870	497	2764	5712	117	3307	7367	282
Gangtok (General)	2212	3163	2641	3561	6193	3218	3567	6096	3824

Source: Calculated from the voters list published by Chief Electoral Officer, Sikkim.

* The Delimitation Commission 2002 has changed the nature of constituencies in 2005. (See Appendix)

The above table clearly shows that the Bhutia-Lepcha candidates in these B-L constituencies have to depend on other communities for election excluding the three constituencies namely Dzongu, Lachen-Mangshila and Kabi-Tingda where the Bhutia-Lepcha voters are in majority.

During the SSP rule, the Sikkim Tribal Welfare Association had virtually lost its autonomous status. The Association, however, regained some of its lost autonomy with the coming of the SDF party in power in 1994. In 1995-96 the Association was instrumental in having the ongoing Rathong Chu Hydel Project discontinued.

It installed the statue of Thekong Tek and Khye Bhumsa, called 'Statue of Unity', near Thakurbari, Gangtok, and constructed a conference hall, called B-L House, at Tibet Road, Gangtok. The Association was also active in setting up of the Tribal Development Corporation and Tribal Development Finance Corporation in Sikkim.[129]

In March 2001, the Association submitted a memorandum to the Prime Minister, A.B. Bajpayee, expressing its concern over the "sustained attempts being made to erode the special rights and safeguards in the land of their origin" and demanded "protection under the provision enshrined in article 371F of the Indian constitution, creation of a permanent Standing Committee of the tribals in the Assembly with sufficient power to carryout scrutiny of all legislations pertaining social, economical, cultural and religious interest of the tribals in the State, distribution of excess land taken over from the tribals under land ceiling programme among the tribals only, exemption of the tribals from the jurisdiction of land ceiling law and allocation of sufficient number of seats in the State Assembly."[130]

In January 2003, the Association took certain resolution at the BL House, Gangtok, in view of the inclusion of Limboo and Tamang in the Scheduled Tribes list. The Association emphasized on the protection of the Bhutia-Lepcha interests and extension of the existing reservation in the Panchayats also. It also demanded for inclusion of Bhutia-Lepcha representatives in the delimitation process and revelation of the stand of the government in matters relating to political, social and economic rights and privileges of the Bhutias and Lepchas.[131]

The Bhutia-Lepcha communities are the most privileged and protected communities in Sikkim. But despite being so, the Association fears that uncontrolled influx of Nepalis had been posing a threat to their culture and existence. This is an exclusive attitude on the part of the STWA with tendency to create ethnic disharmony. In fact, the feeling of being affected or overtaken by another cultural group actually intensifies efforts for protection and preservation. The history of Sikkim is conspicuous of the fact that despite conscious and deliberate attempts, both political and cultural, in the past, the Limboos and Lepchas have been successful to protect their cultural identity. And as regards to the fear of alienation of land from Bhutia-Lepcha to the Nepalis, the Revenue Order No. 1 of 1917, which prohibits alienation of Bhutia-Lepcha lands to others, including other tribals, is still in vogue. The Sherpas, for whom the Association claims to work for, are denied protection under this provision.

The main lacuna of the Association is factionalism besides being unnecessarily too assertive and apprehensive. The tribal Lepchas alleged that the Bhutias have cornered the lion share of the privileges meant for the Tribals. The Lepcha Youth Association also demanded for a legal prohibition on the sale/purchase of their land by the Bhutias and 50 per cent reservation in employment and the Assembly seats reserved for the B-L in Sikkim. Similarly, the demand for removal of the Sherpas from the list of Bhutias regularly featured in most of the resolutions of the B-L conferences/conventions since 1994 and to counter the allegation, the Sherpas too had formed separate association and demanded for separate reservation of seats in the Assembly from within the 12 seats reserved for the B-L and expansion of the Revenue Order No. 1 to include the Sherpas as the third beneficiaries of the provision. Obviously, the contradictions prevailing within the member communities have shaken the very foundation of the Association for which it was formed in 1978.

Lepcha Associations:

Through the legend of 'Blood Brotherhood' the Lepchas in Sikkim are considered as close kins of the Bhutias and are referred in combined term 'B-L'. The Lepchas who are described as mild, honest and culturally rich community have been subjected to discriminatory treatment and enormous suffering in the past. At present, majority of educated Lepchas emphasized on the need for maintaining a separate identity other than the 'B-L' combined identity.

After the beginning of the democratic movement in the late 1940s Lepchas too began to assert their claims organizationally. In 1966, Ruth Karthak (Lepcha) founded Sikkim Independent Front party which served as a platform for articulation and aggregation of the socio-economic and political interests of the Lepcha community. The party fielded five candidates, one Nepali and four Lepcha, in the 1967 Council election but their nomination papers were rejected. Ms. Karthak too was removed from Sikkim allegedly for challenging legitimacy of the Bhutia rule in the land of the Lepchas.

Thus, it was only after the agitation of 1973 that some Lepcha elders namely Nayan Tshering Lepcha, Rinzing Topden Lepcha, D.C.Luksom, Shypzong Lepcha, Adar Singh Lepcha, Nim Tshering Lepcha, Loder Singh Lepcha and Tasha Tengay Lepcha secretly conducted a meeting in the house of Shri A.D.Rai at Sichey in the month of May 1973. The meeting was chaired by the late Nayan Tshering Lepcha. It was in this meeting the first ever apolitical organization of the ethnic Lepchas, called Rong Seyzum, was born. The present day two Lepcha organizations, formed sometime in 1996, namely 'Renjyong Mutanchi Rong Ong Seyzum' (Sikkim Lepcha Youth Association) and Renjyong Mutanchi Rong Tarzum (Sikkim Lepcha Association) owe their origin to this premier Lepcha organization. In contrast to these two organizations, the Mayel Aahit Mutanchi Tarzum (Sikkim Original Lepcha Association), established in March 2004, is of recent origin. The resolution of the Mayel Aahit Mutanchi Tarzum emphasized preservation and promotion of the Lepcha language and culture, opposition to the construction of Teesta Stages III and IV Hydel projects at Dzongu, opposition to the delimitation process of the Dzongu constituency and safeguarding various interests of the Lepchas of Sikkim[132] Despite organizational variations, they share common objective, i.e. to fight against injustice of all kinds perpetrated against the Lepcha community and to protect the socio-economic, cultural and political rights guaranteed to them by the constitution of India.

In September 20, 1996, a high level delegation of both the Ong Seyzum and Tarzum consisting of Sonam Dupden Lepcha (President, Renjyong Mutanchi Rong Tarzum), P.T.Luksom (Deputy Chief Minister), Ram Lepcha (MLA), Sonam Chhyoda Lepcha, (MLA), Menlom Lepcha (MLA) and Dorji Tshering Lepcha (MLA) met the Chief Minister, Shri P.K.Chamling, at his Mintogang residence and submitted a list of grievances which included:

1. Political, social and economic insecurity and backwardness compared to other communities of the State;
2. Deprivation of the Lepchas from the welfare activities of the government, including in higher studies, engineering and medical courses;
3. Alienation of the Lepchas from their ancestral land; and
4. Discrimination in employment opportunities.[133]

In 1996 the Sikkim Lepcha Youth Association presented a charter of four point demands namely:

1. Separate delimitation of Assembly constituency for the Lepchas and 50 per cent reservation out of the 12 seats reserved for the B-L in Assembly;
2. 50 per cent reservation from the seats reserved for the Scheduled Tribes in higher studies and services managed by the State Public Service Commission;
3. To prohibit sale of Lepcha land to other communities, including the Bhutias;

4. To provide proper compensation either in cash or land and judicious rehabilitation of the Lepchas who have been displaced or whose lands have been used for various purposes by the government or non-governmental organizations.[134]

The Association also asked for justification as to why the lands belonging to the Lepcha alone were being targeted for several governmental and non-government projects and proposals, including the proposal of National Hydel Project Corporation in the protected area of Dzongu.[135]

In another state level meeting, held on 26th October 1997, the Sikkim Lepcha Youth Association reiterated the above demands in addition to two other demands such as (i) to protect the cultural heritage and language of the Lepcha community and (ii) to declare the death of Changzod Bholek as the "Martyr Day" in Sikkim.[136] Changzod Bholek was the Lepcha Prime Minister of Sikkim reportedly murdered at the instance of the Chogyal Tsugphod Namgyal (1785-1865). The Association's main apprehension underlying the demands was that though the Lepchas had been invariably recognized as autochthones of Sikkim, the use of hybrid term such as "BL" had undermined their separate identity as Lepchas and this had in many ways also justified their discrimination and domination by the Bhutias. Chie Nakane also wrote that the Bhutias enjoyed somewhat superior social status over the Lepchas and that social difference was overwhelmingly thicker among the peasants than professionals.[137] Considering the importance of protecting the Lepcha identity, the Renjyong Mutanchi Rong Ong Seyzum (Sikkim Lepcha Youth Association) along with other sister organizations, initiated a state level awareness campaign appealing its members to write 'Lepcha' title and not to use any sub-title.[138]

In September 1999, an organization of the Bhutias and Lepchas, called Sikkim Bhutia Lepcha Apex Committee (SIBLAC), was formed in Gangtok. Unlike in the past, the Lepcha organizations made it clear that their support to the SIBLAC was for mutual benefit and not at the cost of their own disadvantage. They wanted protection of their identity and rights within the organization and submitted a two-point demand to the SIBLAC for consideration namely;

1. To reserve 50 per cent seats from the 12 seats reserved for the Bhutia-Lepcha in the Assembly, i.e. implementation of 'Parity' between the two; and
2. Amendment of the Revenue Order No. 1 of 1917 prohibiting the sale of land belonging to the Lepchas to other communities, including the Bhutias.[139]

The SIBLAC refused to concede to their demands on the ground that such decision might create division within the B-L community.[140] Eventually the Lepcha organization withdrew its representatives from the SIBLAC and subsequently issued notifications to Shri Nima Lepcha and other members deputed to the above organization informing the decision of the organziation.[141] The All Sikkim Lepcha Joint Action Committee (ASLJAC) also told the SIBLAC to delete the letter "L", meaning the Lepcha, from the organization's name.[142]

At the outset, it is important to know as to why the Lepchas have been demanding for 50 per cent reservation and prohibition on the sale of land to the Bhutias. As tribals both the Bhutias and Lepchas are the common beneficiaries of the welfare measures of the government, but the statistics suggest that the Bhutias have been largely benefited by the welfare scheme than the Lepchas. According to the Lepcha Associations this became possible because of the ingenuity of keeping the "ruling class" (i.e. Bhutia) with the "subjects", (i.e. Lepchas) under the same footing.[143] The Associations have pointed out the disparity between the Bhutias and Lepchas in matters of employment and political representation also.

According to the information collected from the Bureau of Economics and Statistics, Government of Sikkim, out of the total of 1341 posts in various government departments in 1998 there were 397 Bhutias and 61 Lepchas. Out of a total of 84 IAS, IPS and IFS (Forest) officers in 1998, there was no Lepcha representation in these three elite services whereas there were 13 IAS, 4 IPS and 6 IFS from the Bhutia community. In 2002 there was one Lepcha IAS officer compared to 11 of the Bhutias.[144] This proportion in three elite services continued in 2004-05 also.[145]

Apart from service sectors, the disparity between the two communities also exists in political representation where parity was supposed to be maintained. From 1975 to till the Seventh Assembly Election in 2004 about 60 Bhutia compared to 31 of the Lepchas have found place in the Legislative Assembly of Sikkim.[146] This was despite the presence of parity as governing formula between the two. The parity between the two was restored in the Seventh Assembly Election 2004, including in the allocation of ministerial berth. Substantial changes in other areas too have been initiated – Mr. P.T.Luksom was appointed Deputy Chief Minister of Sikkim in 1994, Tendong Lho-Rum Faat, an important Lepcha festival celebrated in honour of the Mount Tendong, was declared a gazetted holiday since 1997, Lepcha language was given enough leverage, Mr. S.W.Tenzing became the first ever Lepcha Chief Secretary of the State, Lepcha traditional house at Namprikdang in Dzongu, a Lepcha museum and "Stairway to Heaven" at Daramden were constructed, Lepcha language was recommended for recognition in the Eighth Schedule of the Indian constitution, the tribe was recognized as the premier tribe of Sikkim and election of a Lepcha Candidate to the Rajya Sabha in 2006.

Yet there are other issues of land reforms, decline in the number of Lepcha population and delimitation of Assembly constituencies which concern the Association very much. The distribution of land among the tribals is very much skewed and reflects traditional pattern of land holdings. Similarly, the Lepchas feared that the Dzongu Assembly constituency, the Lepcha protected area, would be done away with as the Dzongu population fall short of the stipulation of the Delimitation Act, 2002 regarding reserved constituency. According to the Delimitation Act 2002, a reserved constituency should have 15,000 populations whereas it is 12,000 for open constituencies. Earlier the State government maintained that there would be no change in the 12 Lepcha-Bhutia constituencies though rotation system was considered useful. The representatives of the State in the Central Delimitation Commission were instructed to present suggestions while keeping in mind the peculiarities of the State of Sikkim. The report of the National Delimitation Commission published in September 2006 seemed to have satisfied the concerned raised by the community.

The new generation Lepchas are not only educated but also conscious of their separate identity. They articulate their grievances independently and want sincere implementation of governing formula of parity in every conceivable field including protection of their land from the Bhutias.

Sikkim Bhutia-Lepcha Apex Committee (SIBLAC):

The apex body of the 12 registered Bhutia-Lepcha organizations, called "Sikkim Bhutia-Lepcha Apex Committee" (SIBLAC), was formed in September 1999 at Gangtok.[147] Mr. Tashi Fempo, former General Secretary of Denzong Yargay Chogpa (DYC), and Mr. Nima Lepcha, former President of Nepali, Bhutia and Lepcha Unity Organization (NEBHULA), were elected as ad-hoc conveners of the Committee.[148] The primary objective of the Committee was to work for the restoration of political rights of the Bhutias and Lepchas as guaranteed by the Tripartite Agreement of the 8th May 1973, to demand for the amendment to the Constitution (Sikkim) Scheduled Tribe Order, 1978 for restoration of the original definition of the 'Bhutias' as laid down in the Revenue Order No. 1 of 1917.[149] The Apex Committee expressed no objection against inclusion of the Chumbipas (the people of Chumbi Valley) with the Bhutias, but for other seven Bhutias (Dopthapa, Tromopa, Sherpa, Yolmo, Tibetan, Kagatey, Drukpa) the Committee demanded for preparation of a separate list of tribals.

In view of the Sixth Assembly and Thirteenth Lok Sabha elections, to be held in October 3, 1999,[150] the Committee adopted a four-point resolution on 12 September 1999 at the B-L House declaring;

1. To boycott the ensuing Assembly and Lok Sabha elections;
2. To observe hunger strike on 2nd October (Mahatma Gandhi's Birthday);

3. To appeal the Bhutia-Lepcha candidates to withdraw their nominations in support of the boycott call; and
4. To demand for restoration of their political rights as per the provisions of the Tripartite Agreement of 8th May 1973 and Article 371F of the Indian Constitution.[151]

The Committee boycotted the election in protest against fielding of the Sherpa candidates from the reserved B-L seats by both the major regional parties, i.e. SSP and SDF. The Committee argued that the Revenue Order No. 1 of 1917 neither recognize the Sherpas as Bhutias and nor were allowed to purchase the Bhutia-Lepcha land in Sikkim.[152] In a memorandum submitted to the Governor, Chaudhury Randhir Singh, the Committee expressed ignorance about the provisions of Scheduled Tribes when the Bhutias and Lepchas were included in the Scheduled Tribes list in 1978. Further, the Committee alleged that the inclusion of alien tribes in Bhutia was intended to destroy Revenue Order No. 1 of 1917 and to pave the way for dispossession and displacement of the indigenous Bhutia-Lepcha people.[153] The memorandum demanded amendment to the Representation of Peoples (Amendment) Act, 1980 (No. 8 of 1980) as at the time of amendment in 1980 there were no one to represent the interest of the Bhutia-Lepcha people and were also not given opportunity to be heard.[154]

It must be noted that in 1994 Assembly Election two Sherpa candidates, one each from the SSP and SDF, contested from the Rakdong-Tintek (BL) reserved constituency. Shri Mingma Tshering Sherpa of Sikkim Sangram Parishad won the election with over 51 per cent votes. The Committee vehemently resented this new political alignment and termed it as the political conspiracy of the regional political parties. The Committee contended that they being the descendents of Khye Bhumsa should alone enjoy the claim over the seats reserved for the Bhutias in the State Assembly.

The Denzong Sherpa Association, on the other hand, claimed that the Sherpas, as being Bhutias, were not only eligible to contest from the Rakdong-Tintek constituency but also from all the 13 reserved seats including the Sangha constituency.[155] Rakdong-Tintek constituency was the high caste Nepali dominated constituency and as such the sitting MLA of the SSP, Shri Mingma Tshering Sherpa, won election with 51.53 per cent votes [156] The Committee's call for boycott of election and withdrawal of nominations by the Bhutia-Lepcha candidates proved ineffective because as many as 42 B-L candidates, both official and independents, contested the election and about 81.71 per cent voters, including the Bhutia-Lepcha voters, exercised the franchise.[157] Only Shri Tseten Lepcha, a Congress (I) candidate from Lachen-Mangshila withdrew nomination in support of the boycott call of the SIBLAC.[158] In 2004 Assembly election also Shri Mingma Tshering Sherpa, now a Sikkim Democratic Front candidate, defeated the Congress (I) candidate and the President of the SIBLAC, Shri Tseten Tashi Bhutia, by a margin of 2655 votes.[159] Reacting to fielding of a Sherpa candidate in B-L seats, the Apex Committee expressed fear that "if the present trend of fielding non-Bhutia Lepcha candidates from the reserved constituencies continued, then the inclusion of more communities in the list will wipe out all the rights we have".[160]

In May 2000, the Apex Committee again submitted a memorandum to the Chief Minister, Shri P.K.Chamling, reiterating its earlier demands.[161] The Committee also adopted a resolution in June 11, 2000 to urge all the 12 Bhutia-Lepcha M.L.As in the Assembly for passing a resolution in the ensuing budget session scheduled to begin from June 19, 2000 in this regard.[162] In spite of assurances of support, the Bhutia-Lepcha M.L.As of both the ruling and opposition parties failed to come up with the resolution mainly due to the differences existing between Lepcha and Bhutia members of the Assembly and Apex Committee. The Lepcha organizations on the other contended that unless their own demands were fulfilled, they would not support the issues raised by the SIBLAC.[163] As stated earlier, the Lepcha organizations wanted 50 per cent reservation both in terms of seats in the Assembly and in quota for higher education and employment besides legal prohibition in the sale of Lepcha land to others, including the

Bhutias.[164] Though the Apex Committee assured the Lepcha Association for taking up the issues after the demands of the SIBLAC were resolved, the Lepchas, who had suffered immensely in the past, were skeptical at the assurances and were reluctant to succumb to pressure of all kinds. The SIBLAC was allegedly held responsible for distributing spate of ethnically provocative and malicious pamphlets circulated throughout the State though the SIBLAC convener refuted the allegation in strong terms.[165]

The government appointed an Advisory Committee under the chairmanship of the Tourism Minister, Shri K.T.Gyaltsen, in July 2000 to look into the grievances or issues raised by the SIBLAC.[166] The Chief Minister also assured the members of the SIBLAC that he would take full responsibility for protecting and preserving the rights and interests of the Bhutias and Lepchas of Sikkim.[167] Shri P.K.Chamling told the members of the Committee that "people should understand that Limboos and Tamangs are not same as Bhutias and Lepchas and we have no intention of having it so".[168] In fact the SIBLAC was worried by the statement of the Union Minister for Tribal Affairs, Joel Oram, that "2001 census figure would be the base for delimitation and could cause a reduction in the seats reserved for the Bhutias-Lepchas in the State".[169]

In April 2003 the Committee met the Prime Minister of India, Shri Atal Bihari Bajpayee, at Gangtok, and submitted memorandum demanding "preservation of the distinct identity and restoration of political rights of the B-L community" and also for setting up "a high-level Expert Committee of the Union Government to examine the situation and to take bold remedial measures at an early date".[170] Regarding the allegation for fomenting ethnic tension the Committee clarified saying "we have not talked about any party; neither have we circulated pamphlets against anyone. We are looking for our survival under the facts of history and Acts of parliament. But everything has limits and after September, we will be forced to opt for 'Delhi Chalo'".[171]

In the last week of September 2003, a high level delegation of the SIBLAC, led by its two conveners Mr. Tseten Tashi Bhutia and Mr. Nima Lepcha, left for New Delhi with three-point agenda such as sit-in demonstration accompanied by a protest rally, meeting the central leadership on Nathula impasse and garnering support in favour of their four-point demands namely;

1. Restoration of the original definition of the Bhutia by 'emptying the eight bracketed communities from the term';
2. Safeguarding the political rights of the Bhutias-Lepchas by amending the Representation of People (Amendment) Act, 1980;
3. Delimitation of Assembly constituencies in order to ensure genuine B-L representation in the State; and
4. Opposition to reopening of trade route with China over Nathula till adequate safeguards of the B-L were not guaranteed in Sikkim.[172]

The Committee's action was criticized by the government and other tribal organizations of Sikkim. In a public meeting at Pakyaong, Shri Chamling warned SIBLAC members for "playing a dangerous game by by-passing the State government. If something goes wrong now (including the issue raised by the SIBLAC) then we should not be held responsible".[173] The Minister for Health and Family Welfare, Shri D.D.Bhutia, also criticized the SIBLAC leadership as "people who were confused about their real identity and, in turn, confusing the people".[174] The most scathing criticism against the SIBLAC, however, came from its own constituent partner. The press release of the Renjyong Mutanchi Rong Tarzum (Sikkim Lepcha Association) stated "we have long withdrawn from the organization (SIBLAC) and they should delete the word 'L' (meaning Lepcha) from SIBLAC...The Lepcha community does not have any representative in the SIBLAC. Thus the trade issue raised by the SIBLAC in New Delhi has no sanction of the Lepcha community of Sikkim. In fact, the Lepcha community of Sikkim has never thought of coming out on the street to raise such international issues and few Lepchas who participated in the rally had gone on their own for their self-interest and were not authorized by the organization. Lepchas have their own problems which are being taken up by the Lepcha Association of Sikkim."[175] The All Sikkim Lepcha Joint Action Committee also alleged violation of the provisions of the 8th May Agreement in favour of the Bhutias both in terms of political representation and service sectors.[176]

The SIBLAC was also criticized by the Sikkim Sherpa Association. The community after all was the main target of the former organization. In a letter written to the Prime Minister, Shri Atal Bihari Vajpayee, the Sherpa Association clarified that the "Sherpas had been accepted as Bhutias as far back as 1891 when the first ever census was conducted in Sikkim….If any amendment is required to the Constitution (Sikkim) Scheduled Tribes Order, 1978 the Parliament must under article 342 (2) exclude the king (Chogyal), his kin and kith and the Kazis from the list of the Scheduled Tribes of Sikkim".[177] The letter further stated that as there could be no two classes of Scheduled Tribes, the newly recognized tribes (Limboos and Tamangs) should be allowed to contest from the 12 seats reserved for the BL in the State.[178] Regarding the Sangha seat, the Association said that it "was incorporated in 1957 to make Sikkim a theocratic, autocratic, feudal State and should be done away with".[179] Referring to the issue of 'influx' and BL becoming minority in Sikkim, the Sherpa Association contended, "Influx has taken place within Bhutia ranks. While Lepchas outnumbered Bhutias in 1891, today there are more Bhutias than Lepchas in Sikkim."[180] The letter went on adding, "the SIBLAC representatives in Delhi constituted mostly of Tibetans and monks residing in Delhi who were made to wear Lepcha dresses and presented as Lepchas from Sikkim. We understand that there were no Lepchas representing the SIBLAC in the delegation and demonstration organized by the SIBLAC".[181]

Ever since the 'Delhi Chalo' campaign, the activities of the SIBLAC had grown in volumes. The incidents of defacement of the statue of Bhanu Bhakta and confusion over its reconstruction at Geyzing and construction of Mandir in the vicinity of the lake Khecheopalri triggered off tension between the supporters of the SIBLAC and the Gorkha Apex Committee (GAC). The incident of omission of 'BL' suffix from the voters' identity cards of the BL reserved constituencies also created some confusion which was later corrected by the State Election Commission.[182] Facts apart, it was interpreted as part of the Nepali conspiracy to convert the BL seats into tribal seats. In view of the Central government proposal for reservation of seats for the Limboos and Tamangs in the State Assembly and subsequent proposal for enhancement of Assembly seats to 40, the SIBLAC has demanded for corresponding enhancement of the Bhutia-Lepcha seats as well.

In the eve of the 2004 Assembly and Lok Sabha elections, Mr. Tashi Tshering Bhutia resigned from the Committee's Convener post to contest election as Congress (I) candidate from Pathing (BL) reserved constituency. The effect of the SIBLAC's assertive campaign on ethnic relations could be judged from the pattern of votes cast in the Pathing Assembly constituency. It was found that the number of votes polled by Shri Tashi Tshering Bhutia was almost same as that of the total number of Bhutia voters in the constituency. The Lepchas organizations had always viewed the SIBLAC as the Bhutia organization and severed the relationship. The activities of the SIBLAC had given way to emergence of ethnic organization like Gorkha Apex Committee in 2003. The contradiction between the two over the issue of defacement of the statue of Bhanu Bhakta and controversy over the construction of Mandir at Khecheopalri lake had almost resulted in communal ryot at Gayzing in West Sikkim. The circulation of pamphlet targeting particular community further deteriorated ethnic harmony in Sikkim. But for all apparent reasons, all such events and activities had political overtones orchestrated in view of 2004 Assembly election.

Survival Sikkimese:

It was established in 1995 at Gangtok by some anonymous individuals reportedly belonging to the Bhutia community. The aims and objectives of the organization were to provide identity, entity and security for the Sikkimese.[183] The organization claimed that "those who established the political entity of Deyjong (Sikkim) under the leadership of Ghe-Bumsa and Thekong Tek and those who defended

Deyjong down the ages against countless invasions of aliens – the Bhutanese from the east, the Mongols and Tibetans from the North, the Gorkhas from the west and the British India from the south" were Sikkimese.[184] In other words, for the organization the Bhutia-Lepcha alone were Sikkimese and others were neo-colonialist. In December 1995 the organization issued a document containing 40 different ways by way of which the Bhutia-Lepcha, in their opinion, were exterminated and urged to fight for the survival of their progenies. The main grievances of the organization were;

1. The extermination of Sikkimese began in all conceivable way immediately after Sikkim was merged with India;
2. The Scheduled Tribe Order of 1978 was genocidal and violated the definition of Bhutia as laid down in the Revenue Order No. 1. It was intended to erase the entity and identity of the Sikkimese community as a people native to the soils of Sikkim.
3. The continuation of Revenue Order No. 1 was not out of love but a section of the neo-colonialists considered that important for maintaining distinct character of Sikkim and draw more funds while another section wanted for its abolition.
4. The majority of the Sikkimese parents and children couldn't speak Sikkimese language…they speak broken Nepali making themselves a people without entity and identity….
5. The Representation of People's Act, 1950 and 1951 was amended to cut down our (B-L) representation in the Legislative Assembly of Sikkim. The 1994 election to the Assembly returned two Sherpas from the B-L reserved constituencies, it was expected that in the coming elections the Sherpas would be elected from all the B-L reserved seats including Sangha…
6. The names of places were named after the neo-colonialist (i.e. other than B-L) and not in the name of a single Sikkimese…

7. Sikkim would be renamed Indrakil and the history would be rewritten... At present B-L position was same as that of the Palestinians. We were dispossessed and being displaced....
8. The post-merger political system in Sikkim was biased against them.
9. The execution of the giant 1000 MW Teesta Project at Dzongu, the last exclusive preserve of the Lepcha brethren... would result in a colony of fifty thousand people from outside.
10. More than 90 per cent of the Chortens and Stupas (symbols of Buddhist culture) of Sikkim were obliterated out during the past 20 years and were replaced with milestones. Buddhist sacred places and caves were desecrated and usurped by people of other faiths in alarming degrees.[185]

Besides, the Survival Sikkimese alleged that the Bhutia-Lepcha community was discriminated as second class people in government appointments, allotment in M.B.B.S quota, engineering and other scholarships for higher studies, public distribution system, diversion of tribal funds for non-tribal people, political representation in the Lok Sabha etc.[186]

The first-ever conference of the organization was held on the 13th and 14th of April 1996 at B-L house, Gangtok. The objective of the conference was to identify measures for the protection of the B-L identity in Sikkim, to correct the wrongs committed by the former Bhutia elders and leaders and to chart out a list of grievances in order to ensure survival of the B-L community in their own terms.[187] It asked the members attending the conference 'not to succumb to threat of any kind or pressure'. The conference, presided over by Shri D.G.Shanderpa, had the following list of agenda:

1. To urge the government to constitute a high power Parliamentary Committee to review the political situation of Sikkim for reassessment of the survivability of the B-L community vis-à-vis the following;

a) To restore the entity of the Sikkimese tribe called "Bhutia" as identified by the Revenue Order No. 1 of 1917;

b) To restore the representation of the B-L community in the Legislative Assembly of Sikkim as provided under the Article 371F of the constitution of India;

c) To give representation to the B-L community in both the Houses of Parliament by special provision;

d) To delimit the B-L population of the State into as many electoral colleges as the B-L constituencies of the Legislative Assembly or to restore the Rustomji pattern of voting which existed before the election of 1974, on the basis of the proclamation of 16th March 1958 as a counterpoise to the deluge of voters holding multi-domiciles and multi-citizenships;

2. To urge the government to issue Indian Citizenship (Sikkim) Certificate in replacement of the old Subject Certificates on the basis of the Settlement Record of 1952 to safeguard the interest of the old Sikkim Subjects against the deluge of neo-colonialists;
3. To urge the government to stop acquisition of B-L lands by the State for public purposes and the excess lands of the B-L community if found any may be acquired by the Union Government for constitution of a land bank for rehabilitation of the destitute members of the community. It is anticipated that around eighty percent of the BLs would be landless in another twenty to thirty years;
4. To urge the government to exempt the BL land owners from the provision of the Land Tenancy Act;
5. To urge the government to revise the electoral roll of the Sangha constituency in conformity with the section 25A of the Representation of the People Act, 1950 and to consider at least 'Omzed' by rank eligible to contest election from the Sangha Constituency for ensuring genuine representation.[188]

Apart from these, the pamphlet also demanded for grant of survival allowances @ Rs. 15,000/- per family per month, 50 per cent reservation in employment in central and state government departments and Panchayat elections, promotion of Bhutia –Lepcha candidates in state services through a restricted competitive examinations and exemption of B-L contractors and suppliers from payment of earnest money in tenders for contract works. [189].

Sikkim has a tradition of protecting traditional land and land rights of the Bhutias and Lepchas. The 1991 survey report stated that about 42 per cent marginal tribal farmers possess 7 per cent of the total cultivable land; the semi-medium (20.5 %) and medium farmers (14.9 %) possess about 22.0 per cent and 23.5 per cent area of cultivable land respectively. However, the large farmers (possessing above 10 hectares) who constituted about 5 per cent (4.9 %) hold over 28 per cent (28.1 %) of land.[190] Thus it is a clear case of traditional pattern of land holding in Sikkim and, by and large, ineffectiveness of the land reform measures initiated from time to time. About 84.35 per cent of the Scheduled Tribes populations live in their own houses of different structures like 37.08 per cent in Katcha, 25.25 per cent in Pucca and 37.67 per cent in Semi-Pucca houses.[191] Similarly, among the three ethnic communities of Sikkim, the percentage of the Bhutias in the elite services, such as IAS, IPS and IFS (Forest), and in the Assembly has been dominant. According to the preliminary analysis of the economic survey carried out by the State government in 2005, the Bhutias have been found to be economically in a better position among the three ethnic communities of Sikkim. Hence, the claims of the organization do not corroborate with the ground realities.

The Survival Sikkimese wanted exclusion of the Sherpas from the Bhutia fold claiming that they were Nepalis and should not be allowed to contest from the seats reserved for the Bhutia-Lepcha community. They held the Nepalis responsible for the political transformation in Sikkim. J.N.Kazi's view reflects the general perception of the Bhutias when he writes, "If it was not for the large Nepalis population in Sikkim, the former Kingdom's merger with India may either have delayed or not have taken place at all".[192] The Bhutias, being the erstwhile ruling community, never seemed to have lost site of the fact that the resources, including the post of the Chief Minister of the State, belonged to the Bhutias alone. The aspersion and provocative statement targeting a particular community naturally created an anti-Nepali outburst and surge in ethnic tension from time to time. Late Kashi Raj Pradhan had very aptly portrayed the relationship between the three communities as "the Bhutias (Kazis) are in authority, the Lepchas are in minority and the Nepalis are in majority". [193]

Sikkim Sherpa Association (SSA):

The Sikkim Sherpa Association was formed in 1984 (registration no 179, 1984) at Gangtok. Its main objectives were to promote and protect their language and literature, socio-cultural interest and also to work in the field of economic and political development of the community. In 1978 the community was included in the Bhutia groups and declared Scheduled Tribes of Sikkim. The Sherpas who were legally eligible to contest election from the 12 reserved seats in the Assembly after the enactment of the Representation of People (Amendment) Act, 1980, were, however, denied representation.

In 1994, the Sikkim Sangram Parishad (SSP) floated two Sherpa candidates from the Bhutia-Lepcha reserved constituencies – Phurba Sherpa from Rinchenpong and Mingma Sherpa from the Rakdong Tintek Assembly constituencies. Though only one of the two Sherpa candidates, i.e. Mingma Sherpa, was elected, it created lot of resentment among the Bhutias. The Survival Sikkimese and later the Sikkim Bhutia Lepcha Apex Committee (SIBLAC) condemned the policy of the SSP and demanded restoration of the original definition of the Bhutias as enshrined in the Revenue Order No. 1 of 1917.[194] These organizations argued that the 12 seats reserved in the State Assembly were exclusively meant for the original Bhutia-Lepcha community alone and the Sherpas, including eight other Bhutia sub-groups, were not eligible to contest elections from the above 12 reserved seats.

The Sikkim Sherpa Association on the other had been contending that the Sherpas of Sikkim had been traditionally recognized as the Bhutias of Sikkim. Quoting from Risley's Gazetteer of Sukhim, the Association contested that Sikkim's Sherpas were Buddhist and accepted as Sherpa Bhutia in Sikkim as far back as in the census of 1891.[195] The Association was also critical of the "use and throw" treatment meted out to the community by various organizations, both political and otherwise. In the first ever press conference held on 5th February 2004, the President of the Association, Phurba Sherpa, clarified that the Sherpas was included in the definition of 'Bhutia' in 1978 because that suited the political requirement of the timc to inflate the Bhutia population figures and not because there was any lobbying by the Sherpas for such recognition. He further stated, "inclusion of Sherpas as Bhutias was obviously motivated with the intention to acquire more seats for the Bhutia-Lepcha (BL) segment. They succeeded and after having secured 12 seats, they want to evict us from the Bhutia bracket, after 26 years. This is a sleazy move and very demeaning towards the Sherpas."[196] The important demands of the Sikkim Sherpa Association are:

a) To accord rightful place in Revenue Order No. 1 enabling them to purchase Bhutia-Lepcha land;

b) To reserve 4 seats (in proportion to population) from within the 12 seats reserved for the Bhutia-Lepcha in the State Assembly;

c) To exclude the 'creamy layers', i.e. the kin and kith of the Chogyal and the Kazis, from the list of the Scheduled Tribes according to article 342 (2) of the Indian Constitution;

d) To do away with the Sangha seat incorporated in 1957 to make Sikkim a theocratic, autocratic and feudal State; and

e) Reservation of seats for the protection of rights and interest of different sections of the population of Sikkim in proportion to their population.[197]

In the context of Sikkim, the identity of the Sherpa community is not clear. They have been included in the Bhutia group in 1978 which is recognized as the Scheduled Tribes of Sikkim but considering certain other legal-political provisions presently prevailing in Sikkim, the community is often subjected to denial of benefits. For instance, they cannot buy Bhutia-Lepcha lands and do not have separate seat reserved in the State Legislature. Thus, with the gradual advancement in the field of education, they have become more assertive and more vocal about their rights and interests.

Sikkim Limboo-Tamang Joint Action Committee (SLTJAC): Sikkim Limboo Tamang Tribal Forum (SLTTF)

The Sikkim Limboo-Tamang Joint Action Committee (SLTJAC) was formed in 2003 with an objective to work for the reservation of seats for the Limboo-Tamang tribal communities. It is to be noted that, unlike the normal practice, the two communities were recognized as scheduled tribes in January 2003 though without specifying the number of seats to be reserved for them in the legislative Assembly of Sikkim.

According to the Representation of the Peoples (Amendment) Act, 1950/51, as amended in 1980, 12 seats are reserved for the Bhutia-Lepcha, 2 for the Scheduled Castes, 1 for the Sangha and remaining 17 as general seats in a 32 member State Assembly. Thus, as of now, no seat is reserved exclusively for the Scheduled Tribes community in the State Assembly and so far section 7(1A) of the Representation of the People (Amendment) Act, 1950 is not amended, the Limboo and Tamang tribal community cannot have seats in the Assembly. The communities became disillusioned further when all cases of delimitation of parliamentary and assembly constituencies were postponed till 2026 and subsequent statement of the central government denying any possibility for creation of tribal seats in the State Assembly before the 2004 Lok Sabha and Assembly elections.[198]

The Sikkim Limboo Tamang Joint Action Committee (P.R.Subba group) demanded reservation of seats for the two communities in the Assembly without restructuring the Assembly constituencies.[199] The Committee also submitted a memorandum to the central government and the State Delimitation Commission demanding special census of the two communities and allocation of seat for the Limboo and Tamang tribal communities in the same way or method as was followed while reserving seats for the Scheduled Tribes earlier.[200] The Committee demanded amendment to the Representation of People (Amendment) Act, 1950, as amended in 1980, and to take necessary step required for expediting the process for seat reservation before the commencement of the Assembly election scheduled in 2004.[201] The State government also requested the Prime Minister, A.B.Bajpai, for conducting special census of the Limboos and Tamangs in order to fulfill the constitutional obligation mentioned under article 332 (1) and (3) of the constitution of India.[202]

The SLTJAC also submitted a memorandum to the visiting President of India, A.P.J. Abdul Kalam, at Raj Bhawan, Gangtok, stating "if the delimitation proposal in its present form is allowed to pass, the Limboo and Tamang communities will be deprived of their political rights for another 25 years as the next delimitation will take place only after 25 years".[203]

The Sikkim Limboo Tamang Tribal Forum (SLTTF) led by Birbal Limboo (Tamling) also expressed resentment over the discriminatory treatment meted out to the Limboo and Tamang tribal communities by the government of India. He noted:

1. The Limboo and Tamang communities became Scheduled Tribes vide Scheduled Castes and Scheduled Tribes Orders (Amendment) Act, 2002, but they have been denied political rights guaranteed by the constitution for the Scheduled Tribes.
2. The census of India has not recognized Limboo and Tamang as Scheduled Tribes. The last census was conducted in 2001 when the two communities were not recognized as Scheduled Tribes. Hence, a special census must be carried out to determine the population of the two tribal communities of Sikkim.

3. The 12 seats reserved in the State Assembly are Bhutia-Lepcha seats and, therefore, even if the special census is carried out, Limboo and Tamang tribal communities cannot compete from the 12 reserved seats.
4. Only in the 22nd State of India, i.e. Sikkim, that tribals are classified into two groups – one with political rights and another without political rights. How did it happen? Why did it happen?

Mr. Limboo also observed that if the parliament makes rules enhancing the Assembly seats to 40, the State government will have no other option than to allocate seats to them politically. Considering the existing population of the communities in Sikkim, he justified reservation of at least five seats in the Assembly. He also met the President of India and requested for grant of political rights to the Limboo and Tamang tribal communities before the implementation of the delimitation proposals. [204]

The issue had been the breeding ground for speculation of all kinds and at all levels. The senior politicians warned the government to handle the case with utmost care while the Sikkim Bhutia Lepcha Apex Committee (SIBLAC) expressed fear over possible dilution of their political rights in Sikkim. The SIBLAC distributed pamphlets in Nepali warning that the Bhutia-Lepcha seats were in danger.[205] The SIBLAC justified its concern by quoting the statement issued by the Union Minister for Tribal Affairs, Joel Oram, in which the latter stated that the ongoing delimitation process in the State would cut down the Bhutia-Lepcha reserved seats from its present strength. The Vice-Chairman of the National Commission for Scheduled Caste and Scheduled Tribes, Ven. Lama Chosphel Zotpa, also expressed concerns over the constant threat faced by the Bhutia and Lepcha tribes in Sikkim in relation to the inclusion of Limboo and Tamang communities in the Scheduled Tribes list of Sikkim.[206]

The Representation of the People's Act, 1950/51, as amended in 1980, has been explicit regarding seat reservation in the Legislative Assembly of Sikkim. In clause 7(1A), sub-section (a) it is stated that twelve seats shall be reserved for Sikkimese of Bhutia-Lepcha origin.[207] Further, the subsequent rules outlining the qualifications for membership of the Legislative Assembly clearly stated that notwithstanding anything in Section 5, a person should not be qualified to be chosen to fill a seat in the Legislative Assembly of Sikkim unless: (a) in the case of seat reserved for Sikkimese of Bhutia-Lepcha origin, he was a person either of Bhutia or Lepcha origin and was an elector for any Assembly constituency in the State other than the constituency reserved for the Sanghas.[208] But it must be, however, noted that the 'other Bhutias' who have been declared Scheduled Tribes by expanding the definition of the term 'Bhutia' in 1978 vide Constitution (Sikkim) Scheduled Tribes Order, 1978, have been considered eligible to contest election from the 12 reserved seats by the Representation of the People (Amendment) Act, 1980. Thus, the prevailing legal-constitutional provisions regarding seat reservation is not only ambiguous but also a source of resentment and apprehension between the Bhutia-Lepcha and Nepali tribal communities of Sikkim. The circulation of provocative pamphlets together with the statements by the Union Minister for Tribal Welfare and the Vice-Chairman of the National Commission for Scheduled Castes and Scheduled Tribes further aggravated ethnic tension. Considering the sensitive nature of the issue, the State government sought legal advice from the constitutional experts of India.

The Attorney General of the Government of India, Soli Sorabji, in his letter to the State Government clarified that Limboo and Tamang communities do not get seats reserved for them in the State Assembly automatically by virtue of their getting notified as Scheduled Tribes. "The reservation of seats in the Legislative Assembly is by virtue of Section 7 (1) of the Representation of the People's Act, 1950. So long as this section stands and is not amended, the inclusion of the newly notified Scheduled Tribes can have no impact on the number of seats reserved in the Sikkim Legislative Assembly".[209] He added further that in view of the non-obstante clause of Article 371F, the reservation in case of Legislative Assembly of Sikkim would not be limited either by an interpretation of the Supreme Court or by any other provisions of the constitution itself, i.e. provision of the Article 332 (3) which mandated that the 'number of seats to be reserved shall bear, as nearly as may be, the same proportion to the total number of seats in the Assembly as the population of the Scheduled Tribes in the State bear to the total population of the State".[210] It must be noted here that the Supreme Court also held similar opinion in Ram Chandra Poudyal Vs. Government of Sikkim in 1994. Other two constitutional experts namely K.K. Venugopal and F.S.Nariman also shared the view of the Attorney General of India. They observed that the reservation of seats was a political issue, which could be effected by bringing in suitable proposal for the amendment of section 7 (1) of the Representation of the People's Act, 1950 in the parliament of the country.

Under article 371F(f), the union parliament is authorized to make provisions for reservation of number of seats in the Legislative Assembly for protecting the rights and interest of the 'different sections' of the Sikkimese population, including delimitation of the Assembly constituencies from which candidates belonging to such section alone may stand for election. In other words, the State government can demand for readjustment in the Assembly seats with the Union Government irrespective of limitation imposed by various interpretations of the Supreme Court or by any other provisions of the constitution itself. Hence, the union cabinet; decision taken in 2002 to postpone delimitation of constituencies to till 2026 may not be applied in Sikkim. Thus the Chief Minister Chamling demanded for increasing the total number of the Assembly seats to 40 to enable seat reservation for the two newly recognized tribal communities.[211] The Chairman of the National Delimitation Commission, Justice Kuldeep Singh, also wanted reservation of seats for the Limboos and Tamangs through constitutional amendment.[212].

The Union Home Ministry, government of India, in its letter dated 30.05.2005,[213] addressed to the Chief Secretary, Government of Sikkim, expressed desire to settle the issue and, in all likelihood, by raising the total number of Assembly seats to 40. A 35-member delegation, led by State's Chief Minister, Shri P.K.Chamling, met the Prime Minister, Dr. Manmohan Singh, on 3 December 2005 and submitted a ten-point memorandum requesting the Prime Minister to reserve seats for the Limboos and Tamangs under article 332 (1) of the constitution without disturbing the seats reserved the Bhutias and Lepchas.[214] This position of the government was further confirmed by Shri D.D.Bhutia, Minister of Urban Development and Housing, Government of Sikkim, while speaking on the "Kranti Dewas" of the ruling SDF Party on 22 June, 2006. Being the member of the Bhutia community, his statement was significant in view of the apprehension expressed by the Sikkim Bhutia Lepcha Apex Committee (SIBLAC) regarding seat reservation.

For the last three years the issue of reservation of seats for the Limboo and Tamang tribal communities remained undecided. The SIBLAC apprehend domination of the Nepalis in the Assembly if seats were raised to 40 in order to accommodate seats for the Limboo-Tamang tribal communities. Hence, they also demanded for corresponding enhancement of the Bhutia-Lepcha seats should the Assembly seats were raised to 40. Apart from the opposition from the rival organizations, the political affiliation of the two Limboo-Tamang organizations has been the major setback in the fulfillment of the demands. However, the Chief Minister Chamling has been very optimistic on this issue and has also asked the State Census department to enumerate Limboo and Tamang tribal communities separately in the 2011 census for which the process has been begun since April 1, 2010.

Sikkim Nepali Unity (SNU):

The Sikkim Nepali Unity was established on 20 January, 1997 at Namchi. Initially it was consisted of a ten-member organizing committee headed by Shri Pradeep Yonzon.[215] The principles and objectives of the organization were:

1. Sikkim Nepali Unity stands for the unity of Nepalis community. It takes up issues for the safeguard of the rights and privileges of the community including Rai, Limboo,

Tamang, Gurung, Mangar, Sunwar, Chhetri, Bahun, Newar, Kami, Damai, Majhi, Sarki, Sherpa, Jogi, Sanyasi, Bhujel etc;

2. The organization will always endeavour to uplift Sikkim Nepalis socially, economically, culturally and politically, and liberate them from exploitation by manipulators.
3. The national pride of the Sikkimese Nepali will be restored to its proper place. Cultures of all these castes (?) will be developed as they form the unified culture called the Nepali culture;
4. The organization believes that Nepalis are the first class subjects of Sikkim. The Nepalis have become full-fledged citizens of India following the merger of Sikkim with India and as such nobody can question the allegiance to the constitution of India;
5. The organization believes in the protection and safeguard of benefit and rights of other communities who are living in Sikkim for several generations;
6. The organization also believes in mutual cooperation amongst all the communities of Sikkim and mutual respects for each other's tradition, culture, social customs and religion;
7. The organization believes in the protection and safeguard of the rights of all the minority communities.[216]

The larger Nepalis community, in fact, has been a conglomeration of various sub-cultural groups speaking different languages/ dialects and pursuing, more or less, distinct cultural habits and religious aspirations. However, the Nepali language, which is the major language among these sub-cultural groups, has been the major unifying factor among the Nepalis. The constitutional recognition of the language in August 1992 further strengthened the unity, identity and dignity of the Nepalis living in various parts of India, including the Sikkimese Nepali.

However, division within the Sikkimese Nepali mostly in the line of race (Mongoloid vs. Aryans) or the shape of the nose, i.e.

thepche (flat) or Chuche (pointed) had been the primary concern for the Association. The Association considered certain factors responsible behind the resurgence of racial sentiments within the Sikkimese Nepalis namely the divisive policies of the SSP government, emergence of OBC politics and publication of materials alleging exploitation of the mongoloid Nepalis by the Aryan Hindus. Apart from these, the racial consciousness also developed as a consequence of the negative campaigns against the Sikkimese Nepalis often branding them as 'coolies', 'immigrants', 'foreigners' in Sikkim. Hence, the rationale behind the formation of the Sikkim Nepali Unity was essentially to emphasize unity among various sections of the Nepalis, to protect political identity and gather strength to fight against the anti-Nepali forces of various kinds.

The majority of the Nepalis believe restoration of the seats in the State Legislative Assembly is important as the symbol of protection, identity and unity of the community in Sikkim. The Sikkimese Nepali Unity, however, considered the demand for restoration of seats for the Nepalis as 'irrelevant and a non-issue' on the ground that the "demand for restoration of seats for the Nepalis, at this juncture, would technically mean (i) Restoration of pre-merger status of Sikkim and (ii) Restoration of 'Parity' formula as a basis of seat sharing. Both these options are highly detrimental to the overall interest of the Sikkimese Nepalis."[217] The Sikkim Nepali Unity though believed in protection and promotion of the rights and distinct identity of the Sikkimese Nepalis but it was critical of the traditional view that the above objectives could be achieved only by restoring seats according to obsolete scheme of parity. For the organization a united and vibrant Nepali community under the roof of one strong and all embracing organization was far more pragmatic option than being nostalgic to discriminatory scheme of seat reservation of the older days. Later, Shri Pradeep Yonzon joined the Bharatiya Gorkha Parisang and with it the influence of the Sikkim Nepali Unity also gradually disappeared.

Sikkimay Nepali Ekta Sangathan (SNES):

This organization was formed in June 2000 in Gangtok by the former Chief Secretary of Sikkim, Shri P.K.Pradhan. Its primary objectives were to maintain communal harmony in the State and to promote mutual trust, confidence and faith among the different communities of Sikkim. Initially, the organization kept its profile low and agenda undisclosed. But soon it became a household name when it campaigned against the proposal for seat reservation for Nepalis according to the age old Parity Formula.[218] In fact, the SSP MLA, J.K.Bhandari, on June 23, 2000 initiated a proposal in the Budget session of the State Assembly for restoration of the Nepali seats on the principle of Parity Formula of 1974 and removal of eight other Bhutias, included by the Constitution (Sikkim) Scheduled Tribes Order, 1978, from the list of the real Bhutias.[219] It was a tactical move of the leader of the opposition party, Shri N.B. Bhandari, to corner the Chamling government.

The Sikkimmay Nepali Ekta Sangathan vehemently criticized the proposal and appealed for its withdrawal.[220] The Sangathan also wrote to Shri N.B.Bhandari, the leader of the Opposition in the Assembly, Smt. Kalawati Subba, the Speaker of the Assembly, and Shri P.K.Chamling, the Chief Minister of the State, to condemn and disallow such a sensitive and outrageous proposal to be tabled in the Assembly.[221] In the letter written to the Opposition leader, Shri Bhandari, Sangathan stated, "The harmony, unity and peace is the tradition of Sikkimese society and is evident from her history. In 1973 the subjects of the Chogyal protested against the discriminatory Parity Formula and failure of the ruler to provide justice ultimately paved the way for democracy in Sikkim. In accordance with the norms laid down under article 371F the Sikkimese are living in complete peace and amity for the last 25 years. But besides knowing this fact your proposal for restoration of pre-merger Parity Formula regarding seat reservation, we feel, will be most damaging and unfortunate for the unity of the Sikkimese.

"The Parity Formula of the pre-merger era was unjust and discriminatory against the Nepalis and ….. In order to maintain unity and mutual understanding among the Sikkimese and to preserve existing ethnic harmony, we expect you to act as a responsible representative and request you to withdraw the proposal from the Assembly".[222]

The Sangathan was successful in having the proposal withdrawn. The ruling SDF party also abandoned its initial desire to have discussion on the proposal. It wanted the issue to be dealt by an All Party Advisory Committee for its amicable resolution.[223]

The Sangathan also criticized the irresponsible remarks made by the two members of the parliament about the Sikkimese Nepalis. The Parliamentary Committee on Internal Security and Economic Development led by the Rajya Sabha member, Shri Anandi Sahu, visited Sikkim in October 2000. On 10 October the visiting members met the Sikkimese delegation, consisted of Shri Tashi Topden, Secretary to Power Department, Shri R.S. Sharma, Secretary to Department of Personnel, and Shri L.S. Amarnathan, Superintendent of Police, in the Conference hall of the Power Secretariat.[224] Reportedly the two members from visiting team, Shri Rajkumar Bancha of Arunachal Pradesh and Shri Jayanta Rangpi from Assam, raised the issue of presence of plenty of Nepali immigrants in Sikkim and inadequate safeguards provided to the indigenous people in contrast to the agreement signed between the governments of India and Sikkim.[225]

The report further said that the power secretary had endorsed the incorrect opinion expressed by the visiting parliamentarians while the secretary, D.O.P, raised objection to the aspersion cast on the Nepalis by the duo. The Sikkimmay Nepali Ekta Sangathan demanded public apology from the duo and appropriate action against the power secretary, Shri Tashi Topden, for violation of Service Conduct Rules.[226] The Sangathan also held the visiting parliamentarians responsible for inciting communal hatred in the State in the same way as they might be doing in their own States.[227] The Sangathan wrote, "When tolerance surpasses its limit, a revolution will born. Nepalis have been humiliated for long and would accept it no more. We will sacrifice our life for the sake of the protection of the Nepali identity, the noblest among all human sacrifices."[228] This was perhaps the strongest condemnation made by any Nepali organization in the past 25 years. The Sangathan made it clear that it would be unacceptable for the Sikkimese Nepali to live in a situation conditioned by others but wanted to live a dignified life in their own terms.

Gorkha Apex Committee (GAC):

The enactment of the Scheduled Castes and Scheduled Tribes Orders (Amendment) Act, 2002 and constitution of a five-member State Delimitation Commission as mandated by the Delimitation Act, 2002 necessitated formulation of corresponding changes in the existing political-administrative setup. This was followed by an atmosphere of political uncertainty, intimidation and allegation pertaining modalities to be adopted for seat reservation. It was in this background the Gorkha Apex Committee (GAC) was formed in May 2003 at Singtam under the leadership of Shri G.M.Rai, one of the founder members of the Sikkim Democratic Front (SDF) Party.[229] It was a non-political organization of the Sikkimese Nepalis (Gorkhas) intended to work for the fulfillment of the following objectives;

1. To bring awareness among the different sections of the Gorkha community, emphasize on the need to live in peace and harmony, duly recognize the democratic values of equality – social, cultural, economic - to safeguard the sovereignty and integrity of India;
2. To safeguard the rights and liberties of the different sections of the Gorkha community and to move the appropriate forums for seeking redressal, if necessary;
3. To initiate, assist and promote schemes and programmes for the upliftment of the different sections of the Gorkha community.[230]

The Committee organized its first ever conference on 4 May 2003 at Marwari Dharamsala, Singtam, to discuss on issues concerning the contemporary socio-political development in Sikkim. Seven different issues constituted the agenda of the meeting for intellectual analysis and suggestions namely;

1. The delimitation of constituency is postponed but not cancelled in which 13 seats are reserved for the Scheduled Tribes, including Sangha, and 2 for the Scheduled Castes

in Sikkim Assembly. Thus out of a total of 32 seats 13 are reserved but not in the name of the Scheduled Tribes. With the inclusion of the Limboos and Tamangs the reservation may shoot up to more than 50 per cent from the existing 47 per cent. Therefore, the remaining 65 per cent population, besides being in majority, might become minority and would be unconstitutional and undemocratic. The Apex Committee considers the issue as one of serious and expects intellectual discussion for arriving at conclusion;

2. What is secret behind the application of 371F for the Bhutia-Lepcha people and article 332 for the Scheduled Castes in the 22nd State of the world's largest democratic country like India? Similarly, the seats in the Assembly for the Scheduled Castes are reserved on the basis of population but the same criterion is overlooked or overruled in case of the B-L seats. This is yet another area where a thorough investigation by experts is essential;

3. Article 332 of the Indian constitution provides for reservation of seats in proportion, nearly or so, to population. This provision is violated in Sikkim when 13 out of 32 seats were reserved for the B-L population. This conference, therefore, shall have to decide whether violation of important articles of the constitution which is the source of rights, is in the interest or against the interest of the country or state;

4. Should the existing members of the royal family, Kazis and their kin and kith as retired administrators and the present administrators be allowed to enjoy the facilities meant for the backward people or would they come under the definition of Scheduled Tribes? This issue needs to be discussed;

5. Is it democratic to provide 41 per cent political rights to 25 per cent of the people? Is it communal or anti-government or society or unconstitutional if the Committee considers this undemocratic? We want discussion on this issue;

6. Though Sangha seat is a violation of the spirit of the Indian

constitution, Sikkimese Nepali did not question on the historical importance of monasteries but how far the representatives representing the Sangha constituency can be politically justified or does it represent the true spirit of the monastery? We sincerely want this important issue to be discussed;

7. Finally, we want to discuss on the rationale behind the foundation of the Committee including the issues raised by it in today's context.[231]

The conference was chaired by Shri P.K.Pradhan, the former Chief Secretary and the President of the Sikkimmay Nepali Ekta Sangathan, and presided over by Shri C.D.Rai, the veteran politician and editor of the local weekly 'The Gangtok Times'.

The Gorkha Apex Committee demanded for reservation of seven seats for the Limboos and Tamangs from the 13 seats reserved for the Bhutia-Lepcha community and conversion of B-L seats into Scheduled Tribes seats[232] The Committee supported the All Sikkim Lepcha Joint Action Committee's demand for 50 per cent reservation in the 12 B-L reserved seats and amendment to Revenue Order No. 1 seeking to prohibit the Bhutias from buying Lepcha lands.[233] Further, the Committee also demanded prohibition of alienation of the Nepalis land to the Bhutia-Lepcha.[234]

The Gorkha Apex Committee was in favour of representation and reservation according to article 332 of the constitution of India and in pursuance of the spirit of democracy.[235] The Committee was also critical of article 371F for justifying abolition of seats reserved erstwhile for the Nepalis and Tsongs (Limboos) communities and for continuing undemocratic principle of 'one man two votes' by reserving 41 per cent seats for 20 (?) per cent population where as 80 per cent population were left with only 59 per cent seats.[236]

The Committee strongly condemned the use of the term 'coolies' against the Nepalis in the "Sikkim – Land of Mystique", a travel magazine, published in 2003-04 by the department of Tourism, government of Sikkim. It was also critical of the acts blemishing the statue of Bhanu Bhakta and attempts to secure stay order seeking to prohibit reinstallation of the statue at Geyzing, controversy regarding construction of a temple in the vicinity of Khecheopalri lake and demonstration by the members of the SIBLAC in New Delhi, circulation of inflammatory articles targeting particular ethnic community etc.

The stand taken by the GAC obviously created ethnic tension in Sikkim. Considering the deteriorating condition of communal harmony, Shri G.M.Rai was expelled from the primary membership of the Sikkim Democratic Front party on 31 March 2004. A day before his expulsion he converted the organization into a political organization, called Sikkim Gorkha Democratic Party.[237] Shri G.M. Rai contested the 7th Assembly election as an independent candidate from the Central Pandam constituency but was defeated by the Sikkim Democratic Front party candidate, Shri Somnath Poudyal, the brother of Shri R.C.Poudyal. In 2005 the party was renamed as Sikkim Gorkha Prajatantrik Party.

Akhil Sikkim Kirat Limbu Chumlung:

This organization was formed on 23 May 1973 at Tharpu in West Sikkim. Its first general meeting was held at Soreng bazar in West Sikkim on 19 July, 1973 under the chairmanship of Shri H.D. Chong. The organization stood for keeping a separate identity for the Limboo community other than Nepali and a resolution declaring Limboos as one of the indigenous tribes of Sikkim was passed in this meeting.[238] The organization also supported the demand for declaration of Sikkim as the tribal state.[239]

Its first major activity was that of submission of a memorandum to the Prime Minister of India on 14 June 1990 demanding inclusion of the Limbo community of Sikkim in the Scheduled Tribes list of the State.[240] The memorandum also highlighted community's apprehension about loosing the purity of their language and culture, and loss of identity.[241] The memorandum was signed by 34 important members of the Chumlung, including Shri Sanchaman Limboo, former Chief Minister of Sikkim, and Shri Birbal Limboo (Tamling), former Minister for Power and presently Chairman of the Sikkim

Limboo Tamang Joint Action Committee for Tribal Status (now Sikkim Limboo Tamang Tribal Forum). Mr. N.B.Bhandari served them show cause notices for violation of party discipline. In fact in view of three basic issues namely reservation of seats, citizenship for the left-out Sikkimese and inclusion of Nepali language in Eighth Schedule, Mr. Bhandari, who supported the issue of the inclusion of the Limboos in the Scheduled Tribes in 1981, declined to recommend for the same in 1987 perhaps due to fear of division in the society[242] Shri K.B.Subba, the General Secretary of the Chumlung, issued a press release demanding resignation of Bhandari for having retracted from his earlier stand to help the Limboo for tribal status.[243] In another press release he reiterated organization's demand for the restoration of the Limbu seat in the Assembly and recognition of the community as the scheduled tribes of Sikkim.[244]

The Sikkim Democratic Front party, which came to power in 1994 after a brief period of political instability, was sympathetic towards the demands of the Limboo organization. In a memorandum addressed to the Prime Minister of India, P.V.Narasimha Rao, Shri Chamling demanded for the Scheduled Tribe status for the Limboos, recognition of Limboo language in the Eighth Schedule of the Constitution, restoration of seats in the State Assembly and setting up of a language development fund in the State for the development of various languages, including the Limboo language.[245] In January 2003 the community was recognized as one of the Scheduled Tribes of Sikkim[246] At present the organization has confined its activities in the development of the Limbo language and culture rather than in political affairs of the state.

In a traditional society founded on kinship and community bonds and networks, it is not unusual that political parties and other organizations derive their strength and sustenance from such networks and bonds. As a consequence of such connections between political organizations and communal and affective ties, ethno-cultural or racial-linguistic elements obviously will influence the pattern of political mobilization as well as political decision making but, at the same time, the political parties (not necessarily the social organizations) are also committed to the legal constitutional process which in India prohibits any discrimination on grounds of race, caste, community, religion, sex etc. Moreover, India is a multi-cultural, multi-lingual, multi-religious country in which political parties are expected to contribute to the multi-cultural society. In case of Sikkim, the political parties from the very inception of party politics are operating as representatives of not citizens but communities. For example, the Sikkim National Party represented the Bhutia-Lepcha interests while the Sikkim State Congress, directly or indirectly, emphasized the Nepali interests. Even after the merger and installation of the parliamentary democratic framework various political parties often resorted to the practice of raising ethnically sensitive issues for the purpose of electoral gains rather than focusing on policies of development programmes. As such identity based politics in fact increased social tensions and divisions. It is interesting to note that none of the major regional parties of Sikkim like the Sikkim Congress (Revolutionary), or the Sikkim Sangram Parishad or the Sikkim Democratic Front in their party constitutions or proclaimed policies exhibit any preference for any particular community or ethnic group. But in practice they pursue such policies which contribute to further ethnic divisions in the society.

Such ethnic orientation of major regional parties has its consequences on future political development in the State. Ethnic mobilization and ethnic demands have some kind of spiraling or multiplier effect. For example, initially there were few ethnic organizations but the number has increased as smaller communities which were so far regarded as a part of a relatively larger community began to assert their separate cultural identity through separate organization or party.

FOOTNOTES AND REFERENCES

1. Harowitz: *Ethnic Groups in Conflict*, Berkeley, Univesity of California Press, 1985, P. 296.
2. Gabriel A. Almond: '*Introduction: A Functional Approach to Comparative Politic's*, in Gabriel A. Almond and James S. Coleman (Eds.) *The Politics of the Developing Areas*, Princeton, Princeton University Press, 1960, P. 44.)

3. Op. cit. No. 1
4. L.B.Basnet: Sikkim: *A Short Political History*, S.Chand & Co., New Delhi, 1974.
5. Namgyal Tshering: '*Sikkim' in Aajako Sikkim*, No. 4, September 1978, P. 2
6. Sikkim State Congress' *Petition to the Maharaja of Sikkim*, dated 09.12.1947.
7. Kashi Raj Pradhan: *Sikkim State Congress and the Communal Problems*, a Pamphlet.
8. *Sikkim: A Concise Chronicle*, published by the Government of Sikkim, 1
9. Interview with Mr. C.D. Rai, dated the 17th September, 2006).
10. Letter of the Maharajkumar of Sikkim to the President, Sikkim State Congress, dated 08.05. 1949.
11. Resolution adopted in the Fourth Annual Session of Sikkim State Congress, 1950.
12. B.B Gurung: '*Sikkim Ma Chunao*' in Kanchenjonga, Vol. 2, No. 4, dated 25.12.1958.
13. Op. cit. No. 4, P. 111.
14. Ibid, P. 85.
15. V.H.Coelho: *Sikkim & Bhutan,* Vikas Publication, New Delhi, 1971, P. 27.
16. Resolution of the Sikkim National Party, dated 30.04.1948.
17. Ibid.
18. Ibid.
19. Op. cit. No. 10.
20. Op. cit. No. 8.
21. Op. cit. No. 11, P. 98.
22. Tashi Tshering: *Sikkim At the Crossroad*, a Pamphlet.
23. Dzumsa is a traditional institution of rural/village governance. The institution of has been recognized as the lowest tier of the Panchayati Raj institution since 1982 and the 73rd Amendment Act, 1992 has maintained its constitutional status. At present the institution exist in two villages of Lachen and Lachung in North Sikkim.

24. Op. cit. No. 21, P. 48.
25. Proclamation of H.H. the Maharaja of Sikkim, dated 23.03.1953.
26. Op. cit. No.7
27. S. Datta-Ray: *Smash and Grab – Annexation of Sikkim*, Vikas Publication, New Delhi, 1984, P. 159.
28. Ibid, P. 159.
29. Ibid, P. 167.
30. Ibid, P. 159.
31. Op. cit. No. 24, P. 148.
32. Footnote: Till then marriage was not the criterion for loosing Sikkim Subject as per the Sikkim Subjects Regulation, 1961, as amended in 1962. Interestingly, even the present form of the Sikkim Subjects Regulation does not provide a clear idea as to when marriage as one of the criteria for losing subject hood was incorporated.
33. Op. cit. No. 31.
34. Bulletin No. 1, issued by K.C.Pradhan and S.K.Rai of the Sikkim Janata Congress.
35. P.R.Rao: *Sikkim-The Story of its Integration with India*, Cosmo Publication, New Delhi, 1978, P. 19. ; Op. cit. No. 33.
36. Letter of the Joint Action Committee addressed to the Prime Minister of India, New Delhi, dated 04.04.1973.
37. Text of the Tripartite Agreement of 8th May 1973.
38. N.Sengupta: *State Government and Politics in Sikkim*, Sterling Publishers Pvt. Ltd., New Delhi, 1985, P. 166.
39. Ibid, P. 167.
40. B.S.Das: *The Sikkim Saga*, Vikash Publication, New Delhi, 1983, P. 105.
41. The Statesman, dated 11.05.1977.
42. Sikkim Observer, Vol. XV, No. 34, dated 06.10.2000, P. 2.
43. Ibid, P. 2 : Weekend Review, Vol. 1, No. 5, July 30-05 August, 1999, Pp. 1-2.
44. Op. cit. No. 39, P. 169.
45. *'Narbahadur Khatiwada and Nine Others: Sikkim's merger – A Brief Resume'*, cited in Datta Ray's 'Smash and Grab –

Annexation of Sikkim, Vikash Publication, New Delhi, 1984, Pp. 219-20.

46. Op. cit. No. 42, P. 2.
47. Election Manifesto of the Sikkim Prajatantra Congress, 1979.
48. Op. cit. No. 59.
49. The Nation, dated 27.01.1979.
50. Election Manifesto of the Sikkim Janata Parishad, Himalayan Observer Press, Kalimpong, 1979.
51. The Statesman, dated 15.10.1979.
52. Memorandum submitted by R.C.Poudyal and Others to the Union Law Minister, Government of India, as published in the Broader News and Views, Vol. II, No. 8 & 9, June-July, 1979, Pp. 14-15.
53. The Nation, dated 25.06.1979.
54. The Nation, dated 09.07.1979.
55. Petition circulated by R.C.Poudyal among the Members of the Parliament, dated 31.07.1979.
56. The Nation, dated 06.08.1979.
57. Denzong Mail, Vol. I, No. 2, dated 05.09.1979, Gangtok.
58. Election Manifesto of Sikkim Congress (Revolutionary) Party, 1979.
59. T.R.Sharma: *Sikkim Hinja Dekhi Aaja Samma*, Ankur Prakashan, Gangtok, 1996, Pp 277-78 : Chamla. Tshering Bhutia: "*Hamro Aastha – Sikkim Sangram Parishad*" in SMARIKA published by Sikkim Sangram Parishad in commemoration of the Party's Ninth Foundation Day, 1992, Gangtok.
60. The Telegraph, dated 02.04.1985.
61. The Telegraph, dated 18.04.1985.
62. Election Manifesto of Sikkim Sangram Parishad, 1984, Inkprint, Siliguri.
63. Election Manifesto of Sikkim Sangram Parishad, 1985,
64. Sikkim Government Gazette, dated 07.01.1987.
65. Now, Vol. 2, No. 19, dated 5-11 November 2003.
66. *Sikkim: Perspectives and Vision*, IPR, Government of Sikkim Publications in association with Indus Publishing Co., New Delhi, 2003, P. 453 : Op. cit. No. 77, P. 282.

67. Ibid.
68. Times of India, dated 04.12.1988.
69. Weekend Review, dated 13-19 August, 2003.
70. Ibid.
71. Memorandum submitted to the Prime Minister, Shri P.V.Narasimha Rao, by L.D.Kazi and B.B.Gurung in December 1992.
72. Op. cit. No. 66, P. 5.
73. Ibid, P. 6.
74. Sikkim Telegraph, Vol. 3, No. 17, dated 7-13 March, 1993.
75. Ibid.
76. Constitution of the Sikkim Democratic Front Party, March 1993 : Party Literature, Part-I, Study and Research Wing, Sikkim Democratic Front Party.
77. Sikkim Telegraph, Vol. 3, No. 34, dated 13-19 August, 1993.
78. Sikkim Telegraph, Vol. 3, No. 36, dated 25-31 August, 1993.
79. Press Release of the Sikkim Democratic Front Party, dated 14th March 1994.
80. Legislative Proceedings, Emergency Session, SLAS, Gangtok,17th May 1994.
81. Op. cit. No. 59, P. 308.
82. Op. cit. No. 80
83. *'Twenty-five Years of Statehood'*, Published by IPR, Government of Sikkim, 2000, P.35.
84. Op. cit. No. 72, P. 12.
85. Times of India, dated 16.11.1994.
86. Marcus Dam: *'Caste May Draw New Lines of Battle in Sikkim'* in the Statesman, dated 15.11.1994.
87. The Telegraph, dated 22.10.1994.
88. Legislative Proceedings, Financial Session, 23rd March 1995, SLAS, Gangtok.
89. Sikkim Official Language (Amendment) Act, 1995 & 1996.
90. Sikkim Government Gazette, Extraordinary No. 60, dated 02.06.1995; Sikkim Government Gazette, Extraordinary No. 94, dated 11.04.2001.

91. The Gazette of India, Extraordinary, Part II, No. 10, New Delhi, dated 08.01.2003.
92. Sikkim Government Gazette, Extraordinary No. 308, dated 09/17.09.2003.
93. Notification No. CON/CAB/55/2003, dated 16.09.2003.
94. The Statesman, dated 27.06.1996.
95. Ibid.
96. Gangtok Times, Vol. 1, No. 52, August 30-05 September 1997.
97. Ibid.
98. Ibid.
99. *'Chamling Ko Jhoto Prachar Dekhi Janata Hoshiyar'*, Publicity Wing, Sikkim Ekta Manch, Divert Art Press, Calcutta.
100. Party Programme of the Sikkim Ekta Manch, Amit Offset Printer, Siliguri.
101. *'Sikkim Ekta Manch Ley Kina M.P.Chunaoma Congress Ummedwar Sanchaman Limboo Lai Samarthan Gardacha'*, Published by Sikkim Ekta Manch, Gangtok.
102. Weekend Review, Vol. 2, No. 44, dated 3-9 April 2004.
103. Ibid.
104. Weekend Review, Vol. 2, No. 43, dated March 27-01 April, 2004.
105. Op. cit. No.103.
106. Hamro Prajashakti, dated 11/5/2005.
107. Sikkim Express, dated 12/9/2005.
108. Letter of the Working President of Denzong Peoples Chogpa to the Chief Electoral Officer, Sikkim State, dated 03.11.1989.
109. Ibid.
110. Letter of Lachen Gomchen Rimpochey, President of Denzong Peoples Chogpa, to K.C.Pradhan, the Chief Secretary, Government of Sikkim, dated 08.09.1990.
111. The Statesman, dated 16.01.1991.
112. Sikkim Telegraph, Vol. 5, No. 29, dated June 30-06 July, 1993.
113. Bulletin of Sikkim National Front Party, Vol. 1, No. 1, Central Committee, Gangtok, June 1997.
114. Ibid.
115. Ibid.

116. Gangtok Times, Vol. 2, No. 1, dated 6-12 September 1997.
117. Weekend Review, Vol. 2, No. 32, dated February 23-01 March, 2001; Now, Vol. 1, No. 42, dated 16-22 April 2003.
118 The Six Realms, Vol. 2, No. 21, dated 19-25 April 2004.
119. Sunchari Samachar, dated 17.01.1998.
120. Bulletin No. 5, Sikkim National Liberation Front; Sikkim Observer, Vol. 16, No. 1, dated 13-19 January 2001; Weekend Review, Vol. 2, No. 38, dated 06-12 April 2001.
121. '*The Constitution of India'*, Published by Ministry of Law, Justice and Company Affairs, Legislative Department, Government of India, New Delhi, 1981.
122. Jordan Gleen and Chris Weeden: *Cultural Politics*, Blackwell Publishers, Oxford, 1995.
123. The Constitution of the Sikkim Tribal Welfare Association, 1978.
124. Representation of the Sikkim Tribal Welfare Association to the Prime Minister dated 08.04. 1979.
125. Ibid.
126. J.N.Kazi: *Inside Sikkim – Against the Tide*, Hill Media Publication, Gangtok, 1993, P. 164.
127. Memorandum of the Sikkim Tribal Welfare Association to the Governor of the State, B.N.Singh, dated October 1985.
128. Ibid.
129. Sikkim Observer, vol. 8, No. 37, 29th June 1996.
130. Sikkim Express, Vol. 25, No. 13, dated 24-30 March, 2001.
131. Resolution of the Sikkim Tribal Welfare Association, B-L House, Gangtok, dated 30.01.2003.
132. Resolution of the meeting of the Mayel Aahit Mutanchi Tarzum held on 16th & 19th March 2004.
133. Gangtok Times, Vol. 3, No. 38, September 28-04 October 1996; Gangtok Weekly Journal, Vol. 1, No. 32, September 28, 1996.
134. An Appeal for Justice and Rights, Bulletin No. 3, Sikkim Lepcha Youth Association, undated.Op. cit. No. 237.
135. Ibid.
136. Sunchari Samachar, dated 20.02.1999.
137. Chie Nakane: *"A Plural Society in Sikkim – A Study of the*

interrelationship of Lepchas, Bhutias and Nepalese", in C.Von Furrer Haimendorf (Ed.) 'Caste and Kin in Nepal, China and Ceylon, Sterling Publication, New Delhi, 1966, Pp. 243-49.

138. Weekend Review, Vol. 2, No. 35, dated 06-12 March, 2002.
139. Op. cit. No. 153; Now, Vol. 2, No. 15, dated 01-14 October, 2003.
140. Weekend Review, Vol. 2, No. 7, dated June 27-03 July, 2003.
141. Gangtok Times, Vol. 7, No. 21, dated May 26-01 June, 2003.
142. Weekend Review, Vol. 2, No. 22, dated 17-23 April, 2003.
143. Now, Vol. 2, No. 14, dated 24-30 September, 2003.
144. Sikkim: A Statistical Profile – 2002, Published by Directorate of Economics, Statistics, Monitoring and Evaluation, Government of Sikkim Gangtok, 2002.
145. Sikkim: A Statistical Profile – 2004-2005, Published by Director of Economics, Statistics, Monitoring and Evaluation, Govt. of Sikkim, Gangtok, 2005.
146. Information collected from various publications made by the office of the Chief Electoral Officer, Sikkim State and IPR, Government of Sikkim, Gangtok.
147. Weekend Review, Vol. 1, No. 12, dated 17-23 September, 1999.
148. The Statesman, dated 15.09.1999.
149. Op. cit. No. 147.
150. Report on General Election to Lok Sabha and Assembly, 1999, the Chief Electoral Officer, Sikkim State.
151. Op. cit. No. 148.
152. Op. cit. No. 149.
153. Memorandum submitted to the Governor, Chaudhury Randhir Singh, by Sikkim Bhutia Lepcha Apex Committee, dated 12.09.1999.
154. Ibid.
155. Op. cit. No. 152.
156. Op. cit. No. 150.
157. Ibid.
158. Weekend Review, Vol. 1, No. 13, dated 24-30 September 1999.
159. The Six Realms, Vol. 1, No. 24, dated 17-23 may, 2004.

160. Op. cit. No. 156.
161. Memorandum of the SIBLAC to the Chief Minister, Shri P.K.Chamling, dated 14.05.2000.
162. Resolution of the SIBLAC, dated 11.06.2000, B – L House, Gangtok.
163. Hamro Prajashakti, Vol. 1, No. 4, dated 21-27 June 2000.
164. Op. cit. No. 139.
165. Hamro Prajashakti, Vol. 1, No. 5, dated June 28-04 July, 2000.
166. Sikkim Observer, Vol. XV, No. 33, dated 21-27 October, 2000.
167. Hamro Prajashakti, Vol. 2, No. 15, dated 19-25 September, 2001.
168. Now, Vol. 1, No. 14, dated 04-10 September, 2002.
169. Ibid.
170. Memorandum submitted to the Prime Minister, A.B.Bajpaee, by the SIBLAC on 11.04.2003, Gangtok.
171. Weekend Review, Vol. 2, No. 17, dated 05-11 September, 2003.
172. Now, Vol. 2, No. 15, dt. 07 – 14 Oct, 2003.
173. Now, Vol. 2, No. 17, dated 22-28 October, 2003.
174. Ibid.
175. Press Release of the Renjyong Mutanchi Rong Tarzum, dated 06.10.2003.
176. Press Conference of the All Sikkim Lepcha Joint Action Committee, dated 09.10.2003, Gangtok.
177 Letter submitted to the Prime Minister, A.B. Bajpayee, by the Sikkim Sherpa Association, dated 23.10.2003.
178. Ibid.
179 Ibid.
180. Ibid.
181. Ibid.
182. Now, Vol. 2, No. 22, dated November 26-02 December, 2003.
183. Survival Sikkimese: *The Final Conclusion*, Gangtok, December 1995.
184. Ibid.
185. Ibid.

186. Ibid.
187. A Pamphlet of the Survival Sikkimese, Gangtok, dated 13-14 April, 1996.
188. Ibid.
189. Ibid.
190. State Report on Agricultural Census – 1990-91; Bureau of Economics and Statistics, Government of Sikkim; Sikkim Human Development Report-2001, by M.P.Lama, Government of Sikkim Publications.
191. Op. cit. No. 144.
192. Op. cit No. 126, P. 322.
193. Gangtok Times, dated April 20-02 May, 2004.
194. Op. cit. No. 183; NOW, Oct. 29 – 04 Nov., 2003 & Feb. 11 – 17, 2004.
195. Association's letter to the Prime Minister of India Shri A. B. Bajpai, dat. 23/10/2003.
196. NOW, dt. February 11 – 17, 2004.
197. Op. cit. No. 194.
198. Copy of Jaitley's letter released by the CPI (M) State Unit on December 23, 2003.
199. Now, Vol. 1, No. 42, dated 16-22 April, 2003.
200. Memorandum of the Sikkim Limboo Tamang Joint Action Committee, dated 30.04.2003.
201. Ibid.
202. D.O. No. 405 /CMS – 2003, dated 05.05.2003.
203. Sikkim Express, dated 27.09.2005.
204. Memorandum of Sikkim Limboo Tamang Joint Action Committee for Tribal Forum, dated 22.09.2005.
205. Now, Vol. 1, No. 31, dated January 29-04 February, 2003.

206. Letter of the Joint Secretary, Shri L.B.Sinate, National Commission for Scheduled Caste and Scheduled Tribes, Government of India, New Delhi, to the Chief Secretary, Government of Sikkim, Gangtok, No. 17/11/2003-C Cell, dated 15.10.2003.

207. The Representation of the People Act, 1950, Jain Book Agency, Commercial Law Publishers (India) Pvt. Ltd, Deli, 2004.

208. The Representation of the People Act, 1951 (Inserted by Act 8 of 1980 w.e.f. 01.09.1979), Jain Book Agency, Commercial Law Publishers (India) Pvt. Ltd., New Delhi, 2004.

209. Letter of Soli Sorabji, the Attorney General of India, to the Government of Sikkim, dated 15.02. 2003.

210. Ibid.

211. Memorandum submitted to the Prime Minister of India, A.B.Vajpayee, by the Chief Minister of Sikkim, P.K.Chamling, dated 23.07.2003.

212. Letter of Shri C.R.Brahman, Secretary National Delimitation Commission, to the Secretary, Ministry of Law, Justice and Company Affairs, Government of India, dated 11.06.2003.

213. D.O.No. IV/11015/1/2005 – CSR-11, dated 30.05.2005.

214. Hamro Prajashakti, Vol. 6, No. 257, dated 05.12.2005; Now, Vol. 4, No. 95, dated 28.11.2005; Sikkim Express, Vol. XXIX, No. 282, dated 09.12.2005.

215. Leaflet published by the Sikkim Nepali Unity, undated.

216. Ibid. Also read Gangtok Times, Vol. 1, No. 22, dated 01-07 February 1997.

217. Weekend Review, Vol. 2, No. 16, dated 3-9 November 2000.

218. Op. cit. No. 163.

219. 'Yug Chetna', Vol. 1, No. 1, published by Sikkimmay Nepali Ekta Sangathan, dated 21.06.2000.

220. *'Yug Chetna'*, Vol. 1, No. 2, Published by the Sangathan, dated 22.06.2000.
221. Ibid, P. 2 – 4.
222. Ibid.
223. Weekend Review, Vol.2, No. 4, dated 04-10 August 2000.
224. Hamro Prajashakti, Vol. 1, No. 17, dated 08-14 October 2000.
225. Ibid.
226. Hamro Prajashakti, Vol. 1, No. 18, dated 25-31 October 2000.
227. Weekend Review, Vol. 2, No. 15, dated October 27-02 November, 2000.
228. Op. cit. No. 209.
229. Press Release by Shri G.M.Rai, President of G.A.C.
230. Memorandum and Constitution of the Gorkha Apex Committee.
231. Copy of the Programme of the Convention, Published by Gorkha Apex Committee, dated 04.05.2003.
232. Memorandum submitted to the Chief Minister, P.K.Chamling, by the Gorkha Apex Committee, dated 29.08.2003.
233. *Kranti*, Vol. 1, No. 1, 2003, GAC, Tadong, Gangtok.
234. Now, Vol. 2, No. 21, dated 19-25 November, 2003.
235. Op cit. No. 233, P. 5.
236. Ibid, P. 5.
237. Hamro Prajashakti, Vol. 5, No. 28, dated 01.04.2004.
238. Iman Singh Chemzong: Kirat Sahitya Ko Itihas, Terethum, published by Manishankar Sering Limbu, 1973, Pp. 34-40.
239. Op cit. No. 192, P. 331.
240. Memorandum submitted to the Prime Minister of India, P.V.Narasimha Rao, by the Akhil Sikkim Kirat Limbu Chumlung, dated 14.06.1990.
241. Ibid.

242. Note written by N.B.Bhandari, former Chief Minister, on the Report submitted by the Secretary SC/ST Welfare Department, Government of Sikkim, dated 19.08.1987.

243. Sikkim Observer, dated 08.11.1990.

244. Sikkim Observer, dated 29.02.1991.

245. Memorandum submitted by the Chief Minister, Shri P.K.Chamling, to the Prime Minister of India, Shri P.V.Narasimha Rao, dated 25.08.1995.

246. The Scheduled Castes and Scheduled Tribes Orders (Amendment) Act, 2002, No. 10 of 2003.

7

Conclusion: Nature of Ethnic Politics in Sikkim

Ethnic cultural politics as a social phenomenon involves the issues of a particular variant of collective consciousness and collective identity in which members of a group irrespective of their social positions are viewed as a cohesive formation without any class barriers. Ethnic cultural consciousness and political mobilization on the basis of such consciousness, as indicated in Chapter I, has been explained by social scientists generally from two broad perspectives. The first one like Glazer and Moynihan, C. Greetz and others emphasizes that ethnicity is a natural social phenomenon. In any given society social exchanges and communication are based on and within a cultural framework. This social phenomenon is simply reflected in politics. Political articulation, communication as well as decision-making occur under the shadow of ethnic consideration.

The other perspective is generally known as instrumentalist view point which perceives ethnicity as a political resource employed by groups, classes, elites and others. From this viewpoint ethnic politics involves manipulation of cultural sentiments and affective ties to achieve certain tangible goals. Instrumentalist perspective argues that competition for resources between two distinct cultural groups actually give birth to ethnic political mobilization. The deprived group often resort to cultural sentiments and mobilize people to gain a share of resources;

contrarily, the privileged also may fall back upon culture for the protection of their status and resources. It is also argued that often the elites of a community or the middle classes belonging to a particular ethnicity manipulate ethnic sentiment to realize their own objectives. The political-economic analysis of ethnicity addresses the question from a class perspective in which the whole concept of wounded attachments and unity of a cultural group is the construction of a particular dominant class which reinforces its privileged positions with reference to ethnic solidarity.

In such analyses, however, political structures and institutions are presented as passive recipient of pressures emanating from socio-economic structures and formation. The role of the state, political parties and other political organizations in containing or aggravating ethnic consciousness is seldom recognized. In the history of Sikkim, however, it is apparent that ethnic division among various communities actually was a consequence of specific laws and state policies which discriminated against particular communities; and therefore ultimately produced separateness and mistrust in the minds of members of different communities.

The attempt of the state to exclude certain groups from the process of governance and from resources on the basis of ethnic criteria can create a political system founded upon ethnic considerations. Sometimes State may glorify or promote a particular culture or language, generally that of a dominant group, as national culture or national language. Thus, the ethnic relationship in a multicultural society expresses in terms of apprehension over such cultural or linguistic imposition or show inability to cope with the idea of cultural or linguistic uniformity or homogeneity. It intensifies demands for official status and activities for protection and promotion become resonant. This exactly happened in Sikkim under the Bhutia monarchy and the process continued partly even under parliamentary form of government after merger of Sikkim with India. Similarly, political parties and other political organizations also like the state have determinate relations with increase or decrease of ethnic consciousness. The political parties may try to promote a secular consciousness. On the other hand, parties may pick up ethnic cultural differences as a natural choice for political mobilizations by falling back upon social bonds, traditional social structures and community sentiments. Through ethnic identity political parties may discover civic kinship and try to appeal to electorate in ethnic terms. In case of Sikkim also it is evident that the activities of political parties and other organizations often have aggravated ethnic tensions as a result of articulation of exclusive community demands and slogans.

An examination of the government policies and decisions during pre-merger era in Sikkim reflect ample indications that they were designed to favour politically dominant ethnic community in all conceivable fields. For instance, the notification of 1897 (renamed later as Revenue Order No. 1 in 1917) prohibited Nepalis from buying Bhutia-Lepcha land while the same rule favours the Bhutias to have an access over the Lepcha land. Further, Nepali settlement and carrying on any business by Nepali subjects beyond the river Dikchu in north Sikkim was prohibited. This rule was extended for an indefinite period in 1956.

Two separate rate of revenue for the Bhutia-Lepchas and Nepalis for the same amount and quality of land, the Parity formula equating the minority Bhutia-Lepcha with the majority Nepalis, communal pattern of voting system denying adequate representation to the Nepalis in the legislative and executive organs of the government are instances of differential treatment meted out to the Nepalis during the pre-merger Sikkim. Such governmental policies discriminating against the Nepalis based on race/cultural identity naturally created a sense of alienation among the latter.

The Chogyal government justified differential treatment on the ground that the Nepalis were migrants and it was legitimate to protect and promote the cause and interest of the Bhutias-Lepchas who were considered indigenous populations of Sikkim, though many tribes which pass by the name Nepali today were present in Sikkim long before the establishment of the Bhutia rule in Sikkim. Thus, what occurred in Sikkim was a state sponsored rewriting of history which transformed some indigenous inhabitants into migrants. Apart from this, by highlighting politically intended notions like 'blood brotherhood' or 'Lho-Mon-Tsong-Sum' either by including or excluding communities arbitrarily in the official discourses further strengthened the feeling of alienation or separateness among those who have been sometimes excluded or included in the official notion of indigenous people, completely disregarding historical facts of being very much indigenous.

More importantly, the monarchy in Sikkim and Bhutia elites of royal court defined the Sikkimese nation in terms of Bhutia-Lepcha culture and Buddhism which effectively excluded the Hindu Nepalis. In this context it may be stated that the ethnic segregation may also take place in response to the way State involves in the process of constructing a particular culture as a national culture or national identity. The establishment of the Namgyal dynasty in 1642 has facilitated construction of a distinct Sikkimese identity based on the cultural aspirations of the ruling community.

The religion of the ruling community, i.e. Tibetanised Buddhism, became the State religion and monasteries and other ritualistic activities as symbols of Sikkimese identity. This happened despite the fact that Sikkim was a multi-cultural and multi-religious society. Interestingly, entry into some of these monasteries was forbidden to other Sikkimese, including the Lepchas. During the pre-merger era the Lepchas and Nepalis found difficulties in adapting to the Tibetanised version of national culture. In the post-merger period attempts to unify cultural aspirations of three ethnic communities of Sikkim have been made, though symbols of Bhutia culture, however, remained dominant as in the earlier days, including representation in the political institution.

The merger of Sikkim with India in 1975 and introduction of parliamentary democracy generated expectation that ethnic/communal discrimination and politics based on ethno-cultural identity would gradually make way for equitable society and secular political mobilization. But, unlike the expectation the government of India decided to continue with the provisions which existed in Sikkim before the merger. In other words, the State rules which discriminated the Nepalis on racial/cultural/religious grounds such as Revenue Order No. 1, settlement laws, communal voting and representation system etc. were provided constitutional sanctions (Article 371F) under the parliamentary-democratic and secular constitution of India.

Thus, when political mobilization took place, ethno-cultural demands continue to dominate political scenes in Sikkim and the governing rules and policies of the succeeding government (India) continue to reflect ethnic-cultural identity as a basis for political-administrative arrangement and distribution of resources. For example, introduction of Sikkim (citizenship) Order, 1975 with controversial Sikkim Subject Regulation of 1961 as the basis for grant of Indian citizenship to the Sikkimese despite the representation of the Nepalis for consideration of 1970 as the cut off year and amendment to the Representation of the People Act, 1950 and 1951 (as amended in 1976) which legitimizes 100 per cent seat reservation in the Assembly on communal and religious grounds. The constitutional arrangement of 1975, which was expected to assuage ethnic differences, was also directly or indirectly responsible for sustaining ethnic differences and, in some cases, aggravating it further.

How various government policies contribute to the continuation of ethnic division can be understood from yet another example. The central government had asked the state government to recommend names of communities for the preparation of Scheduled Tribes list for Sikkim as early as 1976. But, contrary to the desire of the Central government to include various tribal groups of Sikkim namely Bhutia, Lepcha, Limboo, Tamang, Gurung, Mangar, Rai etc. in the scheduled tribes list, the State government recommended for inclusion of only the Lepchas and Bhutias, the latter being the ruling and economically dominant community, in the list. The policy of the State government denying scheduled tribe status to some deserving communities in favour of certain other communities naturally created a feeling of alienation and discrimination among the communities who were denied Scheduled Tribe status.

The issue of scheduled tribe is just not an issue of affirmative action in favour of socially backward community but it also involves larger economic and political benefits. Thus, as the demand for scheduled tribe status grew along community line the level of apprehension among various communities also increased. In 1978, the Bhutias resented to the idea of inclusion of eight other communities in the Bhutia fold while in 2003 Limboo and Tamang scheduled tribe communities resented to the government policy which denied them any claim to seats reserved for tribals in the State Legislative Assembly. Such seats remain the exclusive privilege of Bhutia and Lepchas. Why do most modern states either select certain categories of the population for favoured or protected treatment or establish rules that distribute inequalities in life impartially, or randomly? According to Brass, they do so for variety of reasons such as; (a) the state may be controlled by a class or ethnic group or some combination of classes and/or ethnic groups, whose members the state chooses to favour; or (b) the dominant group may seek support among certain categories in the population and may adopt an 'equalitarian' policy for that purpose; or (c) the state may choose a particular equalitarian strategy for its own administrative convenience.

It is assumed that the State, through such 'equalizing' policies as 'affirmative action' and 'protective discrimination', actually creates or precipitates the formation of new identities among various categories of persons, but, such policies, however, do not necessarily precipitate organization among all relevant categories. The ethnic mobilization actually takes place when the Government/ State tends to work or shape policies on the advice of the leaders and elites within an ethnic group with which it enters into collaboration or understanding for the transmission of government patronage. Sometimes a particular leadership within a group may even gain control over an entire area of government policy and the institutions associated with it and use them as a means of consolidating the leadership of their own community.

Though it cannot be claimed that the State always and inevitably takes a stand on the side of one group or another in conflict situations but, on the contrary, it happens very often. Sometimes, the State may also choose to remain neutral but neutral policy often means, in effect, support for the status-quo, i.e. a refusal to rectify an existing imbalance between groups. The domination of regional parties in State politics and ethnic issues which almost all political parties raise and promise to fulfill during elections also exacerbate ethnic politics in Sikkim.

The role of the state policies in containing or accentuating ethnic politics is also clear in the sphere of language, i.e. in the area of recognition of a particular language as official language by the state. It is generally recognized that language is another symbol of contradiction and ethnic division. The group demanding 'a rightful place' to its language very often means recognition as 'official language'. In other words, it means recognition or glorification of people speaking that language and a legitimate claim to greater respect or worth in the society than others. On the contrary, for others it may mean demeaning to work or communicate in the language which is not their own. In the context of Sikkim, a three-language formula was adopted in 1977 as a reconciliatory effort to pacify community resentments. In 1984, Limboo language too was included in the official list of State languages. However, since the Nepalis are in majority in the State, Nepali language automatically became the lingua-franca of the State. As the social recognition affects group's self-esteem, it also encourages opposition. In 1994, a Bhutia organization, Survival Sikkimese' asked its members to speak in Bhutia language while various sub-cultural groups of Nepalis like Gurungs, Tamangs, Rais, Sunuwars, Sherpas, Mangars also demanded for official recognition of their languages/ dialects.

The protagonist of the dominant language often draw attention towards inadequacy of these languages in terms of their simplicity, shallow literary tradition, under-developed grammar and vocabulary, paucity of textbooks in concerned languages, unsuitability of the languages for use in technical field, and their general inferiority as compared to the dominant language. (For instance, the Limboo representatives who went to meet Mr. N.B.Bhandari, the then Chief Minister of Sikkim, in relation to recognition of the Limboo language were asked to supply information regarding the number of Limboo language graduates.) Sometimes, the inadequacy of the language or need for improvement are generally measured by comparing it with European languages, particularly the English language.

The most common statement or argument among the Nepalis during 1995-96 (when six other languages spoken by various sub-cultural groups of Nepalis were granted official status) was that whether these languages could adequately cope with advanced teaching. Their competitiveness was measured in terms of inability of even the Nepali language to compete with increasing domination of the English language and globalization.

The State, however, has the power to rectify the inadequacy or deficiency. As such politics can be used not only to confirm group status but to enhance it also. (In 1985, Mr. Bhandari demanded recognition of the Nepali language in the Eighth Schedule of the Indian constitution. In 1994-95, Mr. Chamling demanded the same status for the Bhutia, Lepcha and Limboo languages.) Hence, it is not necessarily the presence of ethno-cultural symbols which ethnicised a polity but the way the government looks at the issue and formulates policies often evoke community resentments and precipitate ethnic consciousness.

Political parties and other organizations like the state are also important determinants of ethnic political mobilizations. In the context of Sikkim it is found that the parties and organizations can be classified into three categories. First, parties with a general name and secular goals but use ethnic terminology, attachments and demands for electoral and other political purposes. The Sikkim National Party and Sikkim State Congress under the monarchy fall into this category. Sikkim Sangram Parishad and Sikkim Democratic Front may also be included in this segment. Secondly, parties with distinct ethnic regional bias but maintain some degree of restraint like the Sikkim Congress (Revolutionary). In the third category falls aggressive parties and organizations which often indulge in hate campaigns. These are small calvinist groups but electorally are not very successful. Such parties and groups, therefore, function more or less like a pressure group. The Sikkim National Party during the pre-merger days openly advocated in favour of the monarchy and interests of the B-L category, particularly the Bhutias. The campaigns of the National Party definitely created a gulf between the Nepalis in the one hand and Bhutia-Lepchas in the other.

The election campaigns of Sikkim Congress (Revolutionary) and the Sikkim Gorkha Prajatantrik Party favouring the interests of the concerned community also contributed towards the escalation of ethnic tensions in recent times. On the other hand Sikkim Sangram Parishad's call for Sikkimese identity transcending Nepali, Bhutia and Lepcha identity definitely helped in reducing ethnic tension among various communities though for a short period of time. In comparison, the present ruling SDF party, though had clear ethnic bias in the beginning, has been, to a large extent, successful assuaging ethnic tension through carefully orchestrated policies of accommodation of ascriptive interests with that of economic opulence. This also substantiates the fact that campaigns by political parties may generate a particular type of consciousness which may either contain or accentuate ethnic tensions.

All these state policies, activities of political organizations and ideas propagated by rulers and political leaders have contributed to the development of a particular type of community perception about itself and about other communities. It is necessary to throw light on perception of respective communities in this context. The Bhutias believed that the signing of blood brotherhood pact with the Lepchas and establishment of their rule in Sikkim was historically destined and prophesized according to their intricate Lamaist tradition. By virtue of the 'pact' the Bhutias became the legitimate ruler of Sikkim and protection of the Lepchas was considered their solemn pledge. The relationship between a 'protector' (Bhutia) and a 'protected' (Lepcha) through some mystical ordain was established and considered a just relationship between the two. The use of the hybrid term 'Bhutia-Lepcha' or simply 'BL' stand for this relationship. At some point of time, there had been attempt to include the Tsongs (Limboos), another tribe of Sikkim, as members of the same BL family through the concept of Lho-Mon-Tsong-Sum.

The Bhutias did not merit Nepalis suitable for inclusion in the definition of the Sikkimese. For the Buddhist theocratic and hereditary rulers, Nepalis were basically migrants from Nepal, Hindus by religion, troublesome as neighbours, Nepali by speakers and coolies by profession. This perception of the Bhutias was perhaps shaped by their long association with the Gorkhas which was marked by internecine wars, including circumstances leading to transfer of capital from Rabdentse in the West to Tumlung in the north by the Seventh Chogyal, Tsugphud Namgyal, in 1814. The use of racial or religious rhetoric against the Nepalis was part of the political strategy which the Bhutia ruling elite perfected to counter the numerical strength of the Nepalis in view of their demand for democratization of political institution particularly during the later half of 1940s.

This perception finds a special mention in J. N. Kazi view when he writes, "If it was not for the large Nepali population in Sikkim, the former kingdom's merger with India may either have delayed or not have taken place at all". Besides merger, the Bhutias also hold Nepalis responsible for the abolition of the symbols of Sikkimese identity, i.e. the institution of the Chogyal, and denial of the post of the Chief Minister of the State. The Bhutias believe that the post of the Chief Minister of the State should have been reserved for the Bhutias and Lepchas.

The contemporary educated Lepchas do not consider Bhutias as one of them or believe in combined 'B-L' identity. But, in practice, they view it as symbol of dependant-dominant relationship prevailing arbitrarily between the two ever since the foundation of the Bhutia rule in Sikkim. Past evidences show that the Lepchas did very often deny that the Bhutia ruler was their king or Sikkim as their kingdom. At present, majority of educated Lepchas feel that the Bhutias have denied them distinct position in the society and cornered the benefits meant for them as scheduled Tribes. They want protection of their land from the Bhutias and equal representation with that of the Bhutias in all respects. The Lepchas are separate community and want to be identified as Lepchas and certainly not as B-L.

Nepalis had been subject to discrimination of various kinds during the theocratic monarchical regime of the Namgyal dynasty. When the political development began in the late 1940s it was natural for the majority Nepalis to demand for democratic government as a means for eliminating discrimination and making them accessible to decision making organs of the State and resources of other kinds. The reservation of seats in the political institution and recognition of certain old laws of Sikkim after the merger are viewed as a distinct political/legal identity of the people of Sikkim. But the denial of this legal/political identity for the Nepalis (i.e. abolition of Nepali seats in 1979/80) and continuation of the old Sikkimese laws which discriminated the Nepalis in the past, in fact, constitute major cause of concern and apprehension for the Sikkimese Nepalis. This along with influx from other parts of India has further aroused the level of concern for the Nepalis in Sikkim.

Nepalis are also apprehensive to the way government policies have been formulated, by and large, undermining the interest of the Sikkimese Nepalis. For instance, 41 per cent of seats are reserved for the 25 per cent Bhutia-Lepcha (actually dominated by the Bhutias) population whereas 75 per cent people are left with 59 per cent seats in the Assembly, denial of tribal status to various tribes/castes of the Nepali community in 1976/1978, denial of seats in the State Assembly for the tribes (Limboos and Tamangs) of the Nepali community, different benchmarks for the reservation of seats for the Scheduled castes (Nepali) and Scheduled tribes (BL) of Sikkim etc.

The perception of different communities about others also created divergent views about Sikkimese identity and the place of the community in Sikkimese society. Because of divergent perception, different ethnic groups approached the issue of Sikkimese identity from different angles. Sikkim evolved into a monarchical form of government with Lamaist Buddhism as its national identity subduing other lesser cultural or religious identities. The official Sikkimese identity, based on the historical-cultural aspiration of the politically dominant Bhutia community began to confront serious challenges particularly after the formation of political parties and other socio-cultural organizations in the late 1940s. Consequently revision or reinvention of the 'Sikkimese identity' was felt necessary. The new definition attempted to rope together the mongoloid tribal communities of the Nepalis with the ruling community suggesting that they shared common place of origin, i.e. the Tibetan Plateau, and a common religion, i.e. Buddhism. Needless to say, this 'Tibeto-Burman' identity, which became so popular during the 1960s and excluded the Nepalis of Aryan stock and the Indians alike, was politically motivated. In 1961 the parameters of Sikkimese identity was expanded to include all those persons whose names were included in the Register of Sikkim Subjects.

Political parties and cultural organizations also have presented the concept of Sikkimese national identity in different ways. For Mr. N.B.Bhandari, former Chief Minister and now the President of the State unit of the Congress (I), the Sikkimese identity has been associated with the issue of 'De-merger' of Sikkim or with reference to the Chogyal's Sikkim. Similarly, for Mr. B.B.Gurung, former Chief Minister of the State and now the political advisor to the present Chief Minister, and many others viewed Sikkimese identity with reference to the continuation of the institution of the Chogyal should Sikkim was denied free access to run the affairs of the State. On the other hand, for the cultural organization like 'Survival Sikkimese' the Sikkimese identity was very much related with the concept of exclusion of the Nepalis and 'other Bhutias'. For the SDF Sikkimese identity is inclusive in the sense that it not only represents political/cultural elements of the major communities but also include aspirations of little cultural variants found within the larger Nepali or Bhutia communities.

In the above instances Sikkimese identity has been referred in terms of specific community or cultural identity of a particular community or communities. Such notion of identity along with its agenda for exclusion or inclusion has produced a chain reaction in the form of emergence of several other cultural organizations emphasizing community interests and identity. Thus the exclusionist view of the Sikkimese identity and the feeling of being excluded may have given way for proliferation of ethnic identity and consciousness and emergence of ethnic organizations demanding community identity and a boundary of their own. For instance, the Renjyong Mutanchi Rong Ong Seyzum (Sikkim Lepcha Youth Association) demands for separate identity for the Lepcha community outside the common reference of 'BL' and protection of their interest from the Bhutias. The Limboo organization, called Akhil Sikkim Kirat Limboo Chumlung, also claims that Limboos are not Nepalis; the Bhutia organizations like Survival Sikkimese and SIBLAC demand for exclusion of 'other Bhutias' from the present definition of the Bhutias; the Sikkim Sherpa Association demands for exclusion of kin and kith of royal family and the Kazis from the status of the Scheduled Tribes of Sikkim etc. Similarly, various groups within the Nepali community demand for self identity different from the Aryan identity. Sometimes, the identity question involves 'Sikkimese' as against the 'Plainsmen'.

Therefore 'politically defined' Sikkimese identity is not always clear and often re-demarcated. It is because of this flexibility, the Sikkimese identity often gets interwoven with the community identity. In brief, it gives an opportunity for manipulation of ethnic/ identity issues at the political level. Therefore, the political parties operating in Sikkim are also seemed to have fallen upon such ethnic demands and generally rely on ethnic demands and alignment for electoral success. The political parties are also often referred to with the community or group name, though they deny for being so. For example, the Congress Party (I) is known as Tribal party (earlier the 'Dhoti party' considering the central leadership), the Sikkim Sangram Parishad party was known as Upper caste party and the Sikkim Democratic Front party is associated with the Other Backward Caste/community.

Social beings have multiple layers of identities. They may be Hindus or Muslims, male or female, labourer or merchants, teachers or lawyers and so on. Among this plethora of identities, a particular identity in a specific context becomes prominent. With reference to Sikkim, ethnic issues often overshadow political issues or in certain cases ethnic issues are even presented as general political issues.

It seems attitude of members of government, state policies, activities of political parties etc. significantly contribute to development and consolidation of ethnic consciousness and politics. State and political parties create an atmosphere in which ethnic segregation and alienation occur. Such alienation tends to develop a particular perception about other communities and about identity itself. Such developments strengthen ethnic cultural politics. It appears that ethnic consciousness and mobilization in Sikkim has evolved in close relations with state policies and party politics. It definitely establishes a close relation between the two in which politics shapes the process of definition and development of ethnic identity. In this sense ethnic consciousness is conditional and can be contained through political actions.

Bibliography

Aitchison, C.U. 1909/1983. *A Collection of Treaties, Engagements and Sanads Relating to India and Neighbouring Countries* (Revised upto 1929), Vol. 12,New Delhi: Mittal Publications.

Anderson, Benedict.1991. *Imagined Communities - Reflection of the Origin and Spread of Nationalism*, London: Verso.

Bali, Yogendra. 2003. *Pawan Chamling – Daring To Be Different*, Gangtok: IPR in association with Har Anand Publications.

Barnett, M.R. 1976. *The Politics of Cultural Nationalism in South Asia*, Princeton N.J: Princeton University Press.

Barth, Fredric. 1969. *Ethnic Groups and Boundaries*: Boston: Little Brown & Co.

Barua, Indira, Sengupta. 2002. *Ethnic Groups, Cultural Continuities and Social Change in North East India*, New Delhi: Mittal Publications.

Basnet, B.B. 2004. *Comment on Gopal Gurung's Book ' Hidden Facts in Nepalese Politics' Besides some interesting and peculiar aspects of Nepali Society*, Gangtok: Baba Offset Press.

Basnet, L.B. 1984.Sikkim*: A Short political History*: New Delhi: S.Chand and Co.

Basu, D.D. 1977. *Commentary on the Constitution of India*, 5th Edition, Vol. 6, New Delhi: Prentice Hall.

_____ 1978. *Introduction to the Constitution of India*, New Delhi: Prentice Hall.

Basu, SaJal.1992. *Regional Movements.*

Bates, Robert H. 1974. *Ethnic Competition and Modernization in Contemporary Africa*: Comparative Political Studies, Vol. VI, Jan.

Bayley, B.H.V. 1838. *Dorje – Ling*, Calcutta: Bengal Military Orphan Press.

Bhadra, R.K. & Mandal, S.R. (Ed.). *Stratification, Hierarchy and Ethnicity in North-East India*:

Bhanja, Dr. K.C. 1948. *Mystic Tibet and the Himalaya*: Calcutta: Modern India Press.

Bhattacharya, P.K. 1984.*Aspect of Cultural History of Sikkim:* New Delhi: Bagchi and Company.

Brass, Paul R.1991.*Ethnicity and Nationalism*: *Theory and Comparison*, New Delhi: Sage Publications.

_____ 1982. '*Pluralism, Regionalism and Decentralizing Tendencies in Contemporary Indian Politics'*, in Wilson, A.J. & Dalton, Dennis (Eds.) 'The States of South Asia: Problems of National Integration, London: C.Hurst publication.

Campbell, C.A. 1845. *The Darjeeling Guide Including a Description of the Country and its Climate, Soil and Production*, Calcutta: Samuel Smith & Company.

Caplan, Lionel. 1970. *Land and Soil Change in East Nepal – A Study of Hindu Tribal Relations*, London: Routledge and Kegan Paul Ltd.

Chakrabarti, R. & Ghosh, A. 1991. *Ethnonationalism: Indian Experience*, Calcutta: Chatterjee Publications.

Chandra, Kanchan. 2004. *Why Ethnic parties Succeed?* United Kingdom: Cambridge University Press.

Chaube, S.K. 1973/1999. *Hill Politics in Northeast India*, Patna: Orient Longman Limited.

Chemzong, I.S. 1967. *History and Culture of Kirat People*, Part I, Kathmandu: Pushpa Ratna Sagar Publication.

Chemzong, I.S. 1973. *Kirat Sahitya Ko Itihas*, Terethum: Published by Manishankar Sering Limboo.

Chopra, P.N. 1979. *Sikkim*, New Delhi, S.Chand & Co.

Coelho, V.H. 1983. *Sikkim & Bhutan*, New Delhi:Vikash Publications.

Connor, Walker.1994. *Ethno-Nationalism*: *The Quest for Understanding*:

Cornell, S & Hertman, D. 1996. *Ethnicity and Race: Making Identities in a Changing World,* New Delhi: Sage Publications.

Dahal, D. 1984. *Sikkim Ko Rajnaitik Itehas*, Gangtok: Subba Publications.

Dalton, T. Edward. 1872. *Descriptive Ethnology of Bengal*, Calcutta: Office of the Superintendent of Government Press.

Das, B.S.1983. *Sikkim Saga*, New Delhi: Vikash Publications.

Das, K.K & Banerjee, S.K. 1962. *The Lepchas of the Darjeeling District*, Calcutta:

Dasgupta, Manas. 1992. *Sikkim–Problems and Prospects of Development*, New Delhi: Indus Publications.

Datta Ray, S.K.1984. *Smash and Grab: Annexation of Sikkim*, New Delhi: Vikash Publications.

Datta, Amal. 1991. *Sikkim Since Independence*, New Delhi: Mittal Publications.

Deepak, Subhas: 2004: *Sikkim Study Series, Language and Literature, Volume V*, Gangtok: IPR publications.

Desai, Mamta. 1988. *Economic System and Ethnic Constellation of Sikkim*, Calcutta: Best Books publications.

Despres, L.A. (Ed.). 1975. *Ethnicity and Resource Competition in Plural societies*, Hague: Mouton publications.

Devalle, Susana.1992. *Discourses of Ethnicity- Culture and Protest in Jharkhand*: New Delhi: Sage Publications.

Dhamala, Ranju (Ed.). 1993. *Problems and Strategies of Development in the Eastern Himalayas*, New Delhi, Gyan Publishing House.

Durkheim, Emile.1947. *The Elementary Forms of the Religious Life*, Glencoe, IL: The Free Press.

Edgar, J.Ware. 2005. *Report on a visit to Sikkim and the Tibetan Frontier*, Varanasi: Pilgrims Publishing.

Esman, Milton J. (Ed.). 1977. *Ethnic Conflict in the Western World*, London: Cornell University Press.

Fonning, A.R. 1987. *Lepcha My Vanishing Tribe*, Kalimpong, Chyu-Pandi-Farm.

Gans, Hebert J. 1974. *Symbolic Ethnicity: The Features of Ethnic Groups and Cultures in America*, in 'On the Making of Americans: Essays in honour of David Riesman', Philadelphia: University of Pennsylvania Press.

Geertz, Clifford.1963. *The Integrative Revolution*, in self edited "Old Societies and New States", New York: Free Press.

Glazer & Moynihan. 1970. *Beyond the Melting Pot*, Massachusetts: MIT Press.

_____ 1975. *Ethnic Theory and Practice*, Massachuset: Howard University Press.

Gopal, Gaunley.1988. *Ek Vyakti – Anek Vyaktitwa*, Banaras.

Gorer, Geoffrey.1996. *The Lepchas of Sikkim*, New Delhi, Gyan Publishing House.

Goyal, Narendra. 1966. *Political History of Himalayan States – Tibet, Nepal, Bhutan, Sikkim and Nagaland since 1947*, New Delhi.

Grover, B.S.K.1974. *Sikkim and Bhutan: Storm and Consolidation*, New Delhi: Jain Brothers.

Gupta, Dipankar. 1997. *The Context of Ethnicity*, OUP, Delhi.

Gurung, Gopal.1985. *Nepali Rajnitima Adhekha Sachai*, Kathmandu, self-published.

Gurung, M.M & Lama, R.P. 2004. *Sikkim Study Series – Culture (Part I)*, Gangtok, IPR Publications.

Gurung, Parlhad. 1997. *Tamu – Umai*, a book on Gurung's KHEMA script, Kurseong: Chandratula Publications.

Hall, F.S (Ed.). 1981. *The Himalayan Aspects of Change*, Delhi: Oxford University Press.

Haimendorf, C.Von(ed). 1966. *Caste and Kin in Nepal, India and Ceylon*, Bombay: Asia Publication House.

Hardin, Russell. 1995. *One For All: The Logic of Group Conflict*, Princeton, New Jersey: Princeton University Press.

Harowitz, D.L.1985. *Ethnic Groups in Conflict*, Berkeley: University of California Press.

Harowitz, D.L.1975. *"Ethnic Identity"* in Glazer and Moynihan (Ed) 'Ethnic Theory and Practice', Massachuset: Howard University Press.

Hechter, Michael.1975. *Internal Colonialism*, Berkeley: University of California Press.

Hermanns, M. 1954. *The Indo – Tibetans and Mongoloid Problem in the Southern Himalaya and North-Eastern India*, Bombay, Published by K.L.Fernandes.

Hooker, J.D. 1969 (Reprinted). *Himalayan Journal (Vol. I & II)*, New Delhi: Today and Tomorrow.

Hutchinson, J & Smith, A.D (Ed.). 1996. *Ethnicity*, Oxford, OUP.

Jha, Dr. P.K.1985. *History of Sikkim (1817-1904)*, Calcutta: OPS.

Jha & Mishra. 1984. *Sikkim – Government and Politics*, New Delhi, ESS.

Karan, P.P & Jenkins, W.M. 1963. *The Himalayan Kingdoms – Bhutan, Sikkim and Nepal*, Princeton,:D.Von Nostrand.

Kazi, J.N. 1993. *Inside Sikkim; Against the Tide*, Gangtok: Hill Media Publication.

Kohn, Hans. 1965. *Nationalism: Its Meaning and History*, Princeton.

Kothari, Rajni. 1989. *Rethinking Development – In search of Humane Alternatives*, Delhi: Ajanta Publications.

Kotturan, George. 1983. *The Himalayan Gateway – History and Culture of Sikkim*, New Delhi: Sterling Publication.

Lahiri, A & others. 2001. *Sikkim: The Peoples' Vision*, Gangtok IPR Publications.

Lall, J.S. (Ed.). 1981. *The Himalaya – Aspects of Change*, Delhi, OUP.

Lama, M.P. 1994. *Sikkim: Society, Polity, Economy, Environment*, New Delhi: Indus Publications.

Lama, M.P. 2001. *Sikkim Human Development Report-2001*, New Delhi: Social Science Press.

Lamb, A. 1960. *Britain and Chinese Central Asia – The Road to Lhasa 1767 to 1905*, London.

Limboo, Birbal (Tamling).2004. *Teyongsi Sirijonga Sambadit Satya Kathaharo*, Hee Gaon, Sikkim, Tamling Publications.

_____ 2004. *Sikkimmay Limboo Ra Tamang Birodhi Narbahadur Bhandariko Kalo Kartutharo*, He Gaon, West Sikkim: Self publication.

Macaulay, C. 1885/1977/2005. *Report of a Mission to Sikkim and the Tibetan Frontier – 1884*, Rachna Publications, Gangtok.

Mainwaring, G.B. 1898. *Dictionary of the Lepcha Language,* Berlin,: Unger Brothers.

Markhan, C.R (Ed).1971. *Narratives of the Mission of George Boghle to Tibet and of the Journey of Thomas Manning to Lhasa*, New Delhi: Manjushri..

Mero Sapanako Sikkim. 2002. Vol. I & II, Gangtok: Information and Public Relations Department.

Moktan, R. 2004. *Sikkim – Darjeeling: Compendium of Documents*, Kalimpong: Sumaralaya.

Morris, C.J. 1938. *Living with the Lepchas – A Book About the Sikkim Himalayas*, London: William Heinemann.

Morris, John. 1985. *The Gorkhas – An Ethnology*, New Delhi: B.R.Publications.

Nag, Sajal. 1990. *Roots of Ethnic Conflict: Nationality Question in North-East India*, New Delhi: Manohar Publication.

Namgyal, T. & Dolma, Y. 1908. *History of Sikkim (Manuscript)*.

Phadnis, Urmila. 1990. *Ethnicity and Nation Building in South Asia*, New Delhi.

Pinn, Fred. 1986. *The Road of Destiny – Darjeeling Letters 1839*, Calcutta: Oxford University Press.

Pradhan, D. P. 1997. *Pakim Ka Taksari: Chandrabir Pradhan Ko Bansawali*, Tadong: published by Dr. Sunder Kumar Pradhan.

Pradhan, Kumar.1991. *People and Society – The Gorkha Conquests*, Calcutta: OUP.

Pradhan, B. P. 1993. *Sikkimma Swargiya Laximidas Pradhanko Yogdan*, Gangtok: Sikkim Bolcha Prakashan.

Prapannacharya, Swami. 1981. *Vedma Ke Chha,* Pryag: Chirinjivi Dharma Prakashan.

Raha, M.K. 1987. *The Himalayan Heritage*, Delhi: Gyan Publishing House.

Rai, Gambhir Arya. 1980. *Hindu Dharma – Kirant Jati Ra Eshai Mat*, Kalimpong.

Rai, S.K. (Sampang). 2005. *Kirat Khambu Rais of Sikkim and Eastern Himalayas*, Gangtok: Shivika Enterprise publications.

Rao, P.R. 1978. *Sikkim: The Story of its Integration with India*, New Delhi: Cosmo Publications.

_____ 1972. *India and Sikkim (1840-1970)*, New Delhi, Sterling Publications.

Risley, H.H. 1981(Reprinted). *The Tribes and Castes of Bengal*, Vol. 11, Calcutta: Firma KLM Publications.

Roosens, Eugen E. 1989. *Creating Ethnicity- The Process of Ethnogenesis*, Frontiers of Anthropology, vol.V, California: Saga Publications.

Ross, R & Vos, George D (Ed.). 1975. *Ethnic Identity – Cultural Communities and Change*, Polo Alto: Mayfield Publishing Co.

Ross, R & Vos, George De (Ed.). 1995. *Ethnic Identity-Creation, Conflict and Accommodation* (3rd Edition), United Kingdom: Sage Publication.

Rothschild, Joseph. 1981. *Ethno-Politics: A Conceptual Analysis*, New York: Columbia University Press.

Roy, Sunil C. 1980. *States of Our Union – Sikkim*, Government of India: Ministry of Information & Broadcasting publications.

Richard, Temple. 1887/1977. *Hyderabad, Kashmir, Sikkim and Nepal – A Historical and Political Record*, New Delhi: Cosmo Publication.

Rustomji, N.K. 1971. *Enchanted Frontiers –Sikkim, Bhutan and India's North Eastern Borderlands*, London, OUP.

Rustomji, N.K. 1987. *Sikkim – A Himalayan Tragedy*, Ahmedabad: Allied Publications.

Schermenhorn, R.A.1978. *Ethnic Plurality in India.*

Shah, Ghanshyam. 1984. *Economic Differentiation and Tri al Identity*, Delhi: Ajanta Publications.

Sharma, B.D. 1978. *Tribal Development: The Concept and the Frame*, New Delhi: Prachi Prakashan.

Sharma, Rajesh. 1983. *The Images of Sikkim – The Land, People and Culture*, Gangtok: Regium Publications.

Sharma, Santiraj. 2000 (Reprinted). *Khas Kirat Sanskriti: Gorkha Sanskriti Ko Shrot*, Siliguri: Ajako Sahitya Prakashan.

Sharma, S.K. & Sharma, Usha. (Ed.). 1998. *History, Geography and Travels of Sikkim and Bhutan*, New Delhi: Anmol Publications Pvt. Ltd.

Sharma, S.K. & Sharma, Usha. (Ed.). 1998. *Documents on Sikkim and Bhutan*, New Delhi, Anmol Publications Pvt. Ltd.

Sharma, T. 1996. *Sikkim Hinja Dekhi Aaja Samma,* Gangtok, Ankura Publications.

Shrestha, S.K.1992. *Limbuwan Ko Aitihasik Adhyayan*, Dhankutta.

Sengupta, N. 1985. *State Government and Politics in Sikkim,* New Delhi: Sterling Publication.

Shipmo, Ugen.1971/2000. *Rong Aring Lhaptyol (A Lepcha Self-Taught)-Preface*, Gangtok: Dorjee Wangdi Kunchudyangmu publications.

Siiger, H. 1967. *The Lepchas: Culture and Religion of A Himalayan People*, Part-I, Copenhagen: National Museum of Denmark.

Sikkim – A Concise Chronicle. 1962. Gangtok, Government of Sikkim Publications

Sikkim Coronation. 1966. Gangtok: Government of Sikkim Publication.

Sikkim: Perspective and Vision. 2003. Department of Information and Public Relations, Gangtok, in association with Indus Publishing Company, New Delhi.

Sikkim Study Series. 2004. Vol. III & IV, Gangtok: IPR.

Singh, O.P. 1985. *Strategic Sikkim*, Delhi, B.R. Publications.

Singh, K.S.(Ed): 1993: *People of India - Sikkim*, Calcutta: Anthropological survey of India.

Singh, K.S. 1989. (Ed.). *Jawaharlal Nehru: Tribes and Tribal Policy*, Calcutta, Anthropological Survey of India.

_____ 1990. *Ethnicity, Identity and Development*, New Delhi: Manohar Publications.

Sinha, A.C. 1975. *Politics of Sikkim - A Sociological Study*, Haryana: Thompson Press.

Sinha, A.C. & Subba, T.B. (Ed) 2003. *The Nepalis in Northeast India: A Community in Search of Identity*, New Delhi: Indus Publishing Company.

Sinha, A.C. & Surjit. (Ed.) 1987. *Tribal Politics and State System in Pre-Colonial Eastern & North-Eastern India*, Calcutta: Centre for Studies in Social Sciences.

Smith, A D. 1972. *Theories of Nationalism*, New York: Harper & Row.

_____ 1981. *The Ethnic Revival*, Cambridge: Cambridge University Press.

Smith & Hutchinson (Ed.). 1996. *Ethnicity*: Oxford University Press.

Stock, C.D. Beauvoir. 1975. *Sikkim: Customs and Folklore*, Delhi: Cosmo Publications.

Subba, J.R.1999. *The Limboos of the Eastern Himalayas with Special Reference to Sikkim*, Gangtok, Sikkim Yakthung Mundhum Saplopa.

Subba, Mr.& Mrs. J.R.1994. *Cries Unheard*, Gangtok, Akhil Kirat Limboo Chumlung Association publication.

Subba, Pahalman. 1999.*Sikkim – Who Ruined It?* New Delhi: Print Shoppe.

Subba, T.B. 1989. *Dynamics of Hill Society*, New Delhi: Mittal Publications.

_____ 1990.*Politics of Culture: A Study of Three Kirata Communities in the Eastern Himalayas*, Chennai: Orient Longman Ltd.

_____ 1990. *Flight and Adaptation: Tibetan Refugees in the Darjeeling – Sikkim Himalaya*, Dharamsala: Library of Tibetan Works and Archives.

Sukla, Satyandra R. 1976. *Sikkim – The Story of Integration*, New Delhi: S.Chand and Company.

Tamsang, K.P. 1983. *The Unknown and Untold Reality about the Lepchas*, Kalimpong: Mani Printing Press.

Temple, Richard. 1887/1977. *Hyderabad, Kashmir, Sikkim and Nepal – A Hisorical and Political Record*, New Delhi: Cosmo Publication.

The New Encyclopedia Britannica. 1974/2003, Vol. 21, 15th Edition, Chicago.

Tshering, N. & Takchungdarpo, P.R. 2000. *The Bhutia-English Dictionary*, Gangtok: Kwality Stores.

Waddell, L.A. 1899/1998. *Among The Himalayas*, Delhi: Pilgrim Book.

Wangyal, S.B. 2002. *Sikkim and Darjeeling: Division and Deception*, Phuentsholing, Bhutan: KMT Press.

Weiner, Myron. 1978. *Sons of the Soil: Migration and Ethnic Conflict in India*, Delhi: Oxford University Press.

White, J.C. 1909/1999. *Sikkim and Bhutan – Twenty-one Years on the North Eastern Frontier 1887-1908*, Delhi: Low Price Publications.

Yasin, M. & Dasgupta, S. 2003. *Indian Politics: Protests and Movements*, New Delhi: Anmol Publications.

GAZETTEER AND CENSUS

Census of India (West Bengal and Sikkim), 1961, Vol. XVI, Part I-A.

Census of India - 1971, 1981, 1991.

Census of India: Sikkim District Handbook, 1981, Directorate of Census Operation, Sikkim.

Census of India (Sikkim), 2001.

Das, A.J. 1947. *Bengal District Gazetteer – Darjeeling*: Calcutta.

O'Malley, L.S.S. 1907/1985.*Bengal District Gazetteer – Darjeeling*, New Delhi: Logos Press.

Risley, H.H. 1894/1995. *The Gazetteer of Sikhim*, Low Price Publication: Delhi.

INDEX